Miss America By Day

Lessons Learned From Ultimate Betrayals and Unconditional Love

Marilyn Van Derbur

OAK HILL RIDGE PRESS

DENVER, COLORADO

WWW.MISSAMERICABYDAY.COM

www.MissAmericaByDay.com

ISBN 978-1-935689-51-5

Digital to Print Conversion by Wise Media Group

www.WiseMediaGroup.com

Dedication

Above all else, this book is a love story and is dedicated to my husband of 39 years, Larry Atler. Like champagne being poured into the top glass of a pyramid of glasses on New Year's Eve, his love has spilled over and filled all my empty places. Larry is my knight in shining armor, my dearest friend, the love of my life, my hero, the finest human being I will ever know.

Our daughter, Jennifer Atler, has taught me so much about who I am. An inexhaustible source of wisdom, compassion and unconditional love, she is, and has always been, the joy of our lives. It is my ultimate privilege to be her mother.

D.D. Harvey's love, commitment and insights saved my life.

Dedication

Table of Contents

Introduction

Tikkun.

One word that describes why I have written this book.

There is a belief in one of the mystical traditions that each individual has his or her own unique "tikkun" (tee-koon) or purpose, a mission that belongs to no other.

I had always wondered why I won Miss America. Not only did I not seek the title, I was petrified at the thought and tried to decline the nomination. For years, I wondered why I chose motivational speaking in front of 200 to 10,000 people at least three times a week when any size audience terrorized me. Why?

I didn't even "get it" when a newspaper reporter took my story of incest to the front pages of our Denver papers. Only when I saw my picture on the front cover of *People* magazine did I realize that this is the mission I had been given…a mission that belongs to no other. It doesn't mean there aren't other people doing amazing work in addressing the epidemic of childhood sexual abuse, helping survivors on their journey from victim to survivor, learning how to support a loved one or learning specific ways to keep children safe. It only means that mine is a unique mission.

I could never have imagined that, by using my story as the scaffolding, it would be my mission to educate judges, doctors, nurses, lawyers, teachers, therapists and especially, parents. The titles of "Miss America" and "Outstanding Woman Speaker in America" gave me entreé into being the keynote speaker for audiences as diverse as the National Association of Juvenile and Family Court Judges, the Colorado Judges Association, The Department of the Army International Health Care Providers Conference, Massachusetts Medical Society, Dallas Junior League, the Crystal Cathedral Women's Conference, and Children's Advocacy Center fundraisers.

When I addressed 250 doctors at the Mayo Clinic, I realized that information gleaned from my agonizing recovery process had a purpose. What did unrelenting, excruciating low back pain or blood red eyes have to do with sexual abuse? As I began addressing medical conferences, doctors and nurses began to better understand the connection between childhood sexual abuse and adult physical pain and disease. After hearing my message, physicians asked me to produce videos to help educate health care providers. These two videos are now being shown nationwide.

After my keynote address to the National Association of Juvenile and Family Court Judges, I produced a video, "Once Can Hurt a Lifetime," which educates teenagers about the long-term impact of violating a younger or less powerful child. This video is being viewed by teenage camp counselors, baby-sitters, Boy Scout leaders and juvenile offenders. Parents are also showing it to their teenagers, as an introduction to important family conversations.

Each year, as I addressed parents, teachers, judges, clergy and, of course, survivors, I delved more deeply into cutting edge research and gained more knowledge of survivors' experiences, shared in the 8,000 personal letters that I have received and answered. Even more personal contact came as thousands of men and women waited as long as two hours to speak with me after my presentations. I have been in personal contact with more adults, sexually violated as children, than anyone else in America. Each day, I learned more about common, adverse long-term effects of childhood sexual abuse, family support or non-support, and the effectiveness of different therapies.

When I was asked to write a book eleven years ago, after my story of incest first became public, I declined because I knew it would be a book about me. I knew if I ever wanted to write a book, I would want it to be about you, the reader. Now is the right time to share what I have learned.

I had never considered telling my story in more intimate or personal detail until I began addressing professional audiences. I knew that I would have to share personal stories to help them better understand the family dynamics that can occur, even in a seemingly "perfect family." For the first time, I felt compelled to be more specific about what my father actually did to me. It's too easy to casually dismiss trauma when vanilla words like "molest" and "abuse" are used. We cannot change what we do not understand.

I knew I was on the right path when I asked a casual acquaintance, a woman who has had no first hand experience with sexual abuse of any kind, to read part of this book. She wrote, "When the text arrived, I decided to sit down and read for an hour and then do errands. I never did the errands nor did I put the text down until I had finished every word. Then I went to the phone and called my daughter (who is in college) to ask her questions I had never before thought to ask. When

8

my two teenagers came home from school, we had one of the most important conversations we have ever had. Thank you for educating me about the necessity of having conversations with my children on subjects that would never have occurred to me."

One of my goals is that, no matter what your age or stage in life, whether you are a survivor of sexual abuse or one who has been spared, you will be compelled to ask a friend or family member, "Did you know…" "May I ask you a question?" "Have you ever thought about…?" And, hopefully, you will take action, such as writing a letter to a television reporter or newspaper editor similar to ones I have suggested. It is my fervent hope, that as I write about my story, you will be thinking about your life, family and friends, and that, ultimately, this book will have been more about you than about me.

Because this is my "tikkun."

Why?

An acquaintance, with obvious disapproval, asked, "Why would you choose to disclose the most intimate details of your life?"

I would rather face hundreds who condemn me than even one child or adult who, when I say, "I'm so very, very sorry for your pain," responds, "But you never tried to help."

Chapter 1 – Blessed by Being Born Into a Perfect Family

My father was my role model and I adored him. He was successful, handsome, intelligent, articulate, charitable, charming and gracious. He was reverential when he was in the beauty of the mountains, rode a horse as well as John Wayne and loved dogs. As a child and young adult he was everything to me. I wanted to please him and make him proud of me.

His given name was Francis, but everyone called him, "Van." He was a Renaissance man. He played the piano by ear, soulful music, the kind you would hear in a piano bar at 2 a.m., the kind of music Frank Sinatra sang. He would recite poetry from memory for hours. I listened to him recite poetry so often that I can recite it from memory, too.

He bought a mortuary business from my mother's father and built it into the largest mortuary chain between Missouri and California. My father's office was large and elegant. He had an immense desk, a huge, dark leather reclining chair, two different telephones (one was private and no one answered it but him), a white baby grand piano, a white sofa and beautifully upholstered formal chairs. After I was named Miss America, a large color portrait of me, in an elegant white frame with a spotlight, hung above the sofa.

My father wanted to buy an entire mountain that all of Denver could see when looking to the west. When he did, he built a mausoleum and a mountain home on it. The entire family and many other people attended the dedication. Standing outside among the Colorado pine trees, he recalled a conversation he had with his father about his plans for the mountain, "My dad said, 'I want to be buried there and I want you to put up a huge light so that your mother can look out of her bedroom window at night and see where I am.'" My father continued, "…and so we buried my dad here on the mountain. I installed a huge light but there were so many lights on surrounding mountains, my mother could not distinguish one from another. So, I put up larger and larger lights until, finally, I installed this 400-foot illuminated cross so that my mother could see exactly where her beloved husband was buried." The way my father told this story there wasn't a dry eye in the crowd.

To say my father was a highly recognized and esteemed member of the community would not be an overstatement. After he died, his obituary was on the front page of the newspaper. He did a weekly radio and television show for several years that featured his inspirational readings. Accompanying him on the organ was Mildred, his executive vice president from the mortuary.

My parents met while at the University of Denver, when they were cast in leading roles in the annual college play. His interest in the theater never waned. Once a year, he had the lead in our very popular and well attended civic theater. Later in life, he became the president of the Denver Center for the Performing Arts.

My father was extremely active in his college fraternity, Kappa Sigma. While in his 50's, he became the national president and then, a few years later, he was elected president of the National Inter-fraternity Council—which meant he was president of all the college fraternities in America.

He was also very supportive of the Boy Scouts of America and gave them so much money that the Denver headquarters was named, "The Francis S. Van Derbur Boy Scout Building." He also became a 33rd degree Mason. He had been a member of the board of trustees of the University of Denver and Colorado Women's College and Chairman of the board of trustees of Wallace Village for Handicapped Children.

My mother was a beautiful woman from a wealthy, well-known and highly regarded Denver family. She grew up on a large estate with life-sized white Roman statues, and fountains and gardens which were so extensive that a gardener lived on the premises. My grandparents traveled around the world five times by ocean liner (there were no airplanes to jet them from Paris to Nairobi). Their home was vast and fascinating, filled with artifacts from many countries.

I can't remember anyone who didn't adore my mother, whom everyone called by her nickname, "Bootsie." She was charming and had a wonderful sense of humor. Perhaps her best quality was her positive "today is a beautiful day" attitude. In fact, Mother was always happy. I have very few memories of her crying. She didn't even cry when my father died.

She was active in civic theater and participated in P.E.O. (a Masonic organization). She would spend hours memorizing long "readings," and then recite them at P.E.O. meetings. She was superb.

I am the youngest of four daughters. We are all two years apart.

Although my sisters and I were born during the Great Depression, I would never have known it. When I was born, my family lived in a huge old home. It was the only house on the block. There was a circular driveway, large carriage house, tennis court, and the biggest children's playhouse I had ever seen. Just before going to the hospital to give birth to me, my mother hired a 16-year-old girl, Norma, for full time help. She was hired to care for my older sisters, ages two, four, and six, and me. Norma had her own room and bath on the second floor where our family also lived. Ruth and Virginia, the two women who cooked and cleaned, lived in the carriage house. Another woman came one day a week to do the laundry. We also had a gardener.

My mother and father shared the largest bedroom. My eldest sister, Gwen, and I each had our own bedroom. My two middle sisters shared a room. They were very close and always played together. I don't remember Gwen very well as a young child, because she was six years older.

Gwen was elected Queen of Aspenskol—a ski festival in Aspen. She was elected national sweetheart of Kappa Sigma fraternity and at the University of Colorado, she was the only woman elected to the 13-member student Board of Governors. She graduated from the College of Law of the University of Denver and established a successful law practice out of state. It was very unusual for a woman to be an attorney at that time. My other two sisters are equally accomplished and outstanding. Gwen has encouraged me to include her in my story; my two middle sisters have asked that I not, a request they have every right to make and I always wish to respect.

Mother was very religious. She read the Bible every night. Many nights, the last thing I would see before going down the hallway to my bedroom, was Mother on her knees, next to her bed, with her hands clasped, praying like a small cherubic child.

We were required to accompany Mother to church every Sunday. (My father never attended.) But if anyone asked my mother what the sermon was about, she would never be able to answer the question. I began to understand that we went to church so that everyone could see what a perfect family my mother had.

I disliked church. The minister always droned on about what thou should and should not do. I didn't like bowing my head and praying to "Our Father…" It would be many years before I understood why I didn't want another father—certainly not a more powerful one.

My father believed he owned my mother and his four daughters. We were his property and he could do anything he wanted with us. He believed and lived it so strongly that we believed it too. To my knowledge, my father never hit my mother. There was no need. He dominated her totally; she would do exactly as she was told. It was common to hear my father say, "God damn it, Bootsie, shut up." Or "You lose so many opportunities to be quiet."

I can never remember my mother saying, "Don't speak to me that way," or "I will not allow you to treat me with disrespect." He treated her any way he wanted and she took it. She didn't cry, act hurt or get angry. It was as if she believed that he did own her and that he had the right to do whatever he wanted.

When we went out for dinner, none of us was allowed to speak to a waiter, not even to order. We were to tell my father what we wanted and *he* would place the order. One night, after dinner at the famous Chasen's restaurant in Beverly Hills, Mother asked my father if she could please tell the waiter how wonderful the dinner was and what superb service he had given us. She didn't just want to tell him, she wanted to express herself. The answer was always the same, "No."

Mother never spoke up about anything that bothered her, with the exception of my father's driving, which terrified her. He would commonly drive 70 or 80 miles an hour and in the 1940's and 1950's, most roads were narrow and there were no freeways. Time after time, my mother would say, "Please, Van, please don't drive so fast. Please slow down." In response to her pleas, he would drive even faster.

Once, when she was fervently pleading with him to slow down, my father sped up as fast as the car would go and said, "Hey, kids, who wants to let Bootsie out of the car? If she doesn't like the way I'm driving, let's vote on who wants to let her out." Then he called out each one of our names to see if we agreed with him, and one by one, each one of my sisters and I said, "Okay." We were too frightened to cross him. When my father terrified my mother by driving so fast, why didn't she say, "Just *stop the car*." Perhaps she was too frightened to exert her own will or, more probably, he controlled her completely.

Mother told me that my father said to her, shortly after they were married, that if she were ever sick or handicapped, he would not care for her. When she was in her 70's, she had to have an operation on her arm. She didn't tell anyone about it, except my father. After she checked herself into the hospital, she went to the gift shop and ordered

16

flowers to be delivered to her room so she could tell the nurses that my father had sent them to her.

My father often said these exact words: "I don't need anyone. I don't need you. I don't need Bootsie," and then, as if to be sure I understood what he was saying, he would say it one more time, "I don't need anybody." Recently, I was told by a woman who had worked in our home that my father often said to Mother, "If you don't like it here, leave."

Every summer, for six weeks, my mother, my three sisters and I would go to Black Lake, a mountain retreat my father owned. My father didn't go. He hired "Pop" Clark to saddle the horses each morning and take us on all day rides. He was a tall, gangly, wonderful old man. My memories of our days of riding are vivid and happy. A cook, Mrs. Bridwell, prepared all our meals. She also helped us make moss gardens and showed us how to place dainty mountain flowers between pieces of wax paper and then carefully place them in books to press them. I remember as if it were yesterday being in the kitchen with Mrs. Bridwell.

I search for any memory of time spent with my mother. She didn't ride horses or hike. She didn't cook, read or knit. There was no phone or television. We were miles away from anyone else. It must have been desperately lonely for her.

After the six weeks in the mountains, my father would drive us to California for six weeks on the beach. My father rented the same house in Laguna Beach each summer. After driving us there, he would stay a day or two and then fly home.

While driving to Laguna Beach the summer after my 5th grade year, I wanted to send my friends something. My resources were limited but, while in Las Vegas, we stopped at the biggest 5 and 10 cent store I had ever seen. There were rows and rows of trinkets. What did I choose from those hundreds of cheap items? Post cards? Rings like you would find in Cracker Jack boxes? No, I chose little bright colored panties—about 8" by 5"— made out of cheap rayon with "Don't get caught with your pants down," printed on them. I shudder at the memory. I had no understanding of why I made that selection, nor did I question it. Neither did anyone in my family.

As a child, I had a facial tic. I would squeeze my eyes together as tightly as they would go and then even more tightly. Again and again. I did this so often, Mother would make me leave the beach and take a nap at the house. She seemed to think it had something to do with being tired. So, I would go back and read comic books. I was never able to fall asleep during the day. My mother didn't see what was going on around her. When I squeezed my eyes shut, I didn't want to see either.

My father had a very strong work ethic. We were never *given* money. As early as age five, an allowance had to be earned by doing "jobs" in addition to the chores we did daily. Each day, we would write down the things we had done without being asked. At the end of the week, we would put our "initiative slips" on my father's bed and when he came home, he would give us an allowance based on what we had done. While in Laguna, I collected and redeemed enough glass pop bottles to buy ice cream bars when the ice cream truck came to the beach each afternoon. We were given lessons in anything we chose, and fine educations, but we were never given spending money. That money had to be earned. I started work when I was nine, earning a minimal wage, filing eight hours a day on weekends at my father's business. When I was thirteen, I worked from 10 a.m. to 10 p.m. on Sunday as a receptionist at the mortuary. Many times I would be the only (live) person in the building. I would continue working at the mortuary until I left for college.

In order to see my father at his office in the mortuary, everyone, including my mother, my sisters and I, had to ask the telephone operator in the back office to call him and announce us. We would then climb a winding staircase, stop at a tall white door, and push a buzzer. He would then push a button next to his desk, which would unlock the door. It was unusually high security at a time when most people didn't even lock the exterior doors to their homes. To his left was a short, narrow hallway that led to Mildred's office where a full-length oil portrait of my father hung. Her office was also locked to outsiders. However, there were no doors or locks between their two offices.

My father was never home for dinner, except for occasions such as Thanksgiving and Christmas. Every night, from before I was born until a year or two before my father's death at age 76, he went out to dinner with Mildred. And not secretly. They walked into the finest restaurants in Denver. My father would come home around 9 or 10 p.m. I never once heard my mother say, "If you won't come home and have dinner with your family, then don't come home." Or "I will not tolerate your being with Mildred every night for dinner." "Where were you?" could *never* be asked of my father. "Where did you have dinner tonight?" was a forbidden question. "What did you *eat* for dinner?" was not asked. I can never remember hearing my parents argue nor can I recall them having any meaningful discussion. I'm sure the reason they didn't argue is because my mother would just accept whatever he said or did.

I remember once when my mother asked my father to allow her brother to take his dog, a well-trained, constant companion, to Black Lake, the mountain home her family had owned.

"Please, Van. He won't go without his dog."

"No. And that's the end of it."

My father loathed my mother's family. After he purchased the mortuary business and Black Lake, he felt no obligation to make them welcome.

My mother had several stories about our childhood that she enjoyed telling. One of them occurred when my sister, Gwen, was ten. She had misbehaved. My father began beating her, as always, in front of us. Finally my mother cried out, "Van you're going to kill her." I'm sure, as a four-year-old, I believed my mother—that he was going to kill her. I'm also sure that we were all terrified by that scene. That my mother enjoyed telling that story still perplexes and hurts me.

There was another often-repeated story. When Mother was in her late 70's, she chose to write it, in the Grandmother's Memories book I had given her. This is a book in which the grandmother fills out beautiful pages of memories and answers questions such as "Where did you meet your husband?" and "What is a humorous memory about your child's early years?" My mother wrote: "I still smile when I think about the flashlight experience." I had heard Mother tell the story often. "Marilyn was four years old and the other girls were six, eight and ten. Van left a new flashlight in the room where the four of them were playing. When he came back, the flashlight had been completely taken apart. He demanded to know who had done it. When no one would admit to it, he grabbed each of the girls by the hair and began knocking their heads together, cracking them together, two by two, until one of the girls cried out, 'I did it Daddy.' When Van left the room, she said, 'I didn't do it but I knew he wouldn't stop hitting us until one of us admitted to it. Marilyn did it.'" I had done it. I was four years old…and curious…and terrified.

Mother immediately told my father. He hit me and then told each of my three sisters that they, too, should hit me. Then he took everyone out for ice cream, leaving me alone in the car as an additional punishment. I don't remember my father hitting me or saying, "Marilyn can't have an ice cream cone." My only memory is of sitting in the back seat of the car, alone, while everyone went into the creamery. This is my first memory. And it is also my first memory of having *feelings*. I was a bad girl. Guilty. Punished. No empathy from anyone. Isolated. Alone.

It makes me sad every time I recall how my mother could have remembered and repeatedly recounted that event as humorous. I search my mind for a way to even begin to comprehend how my mother could stand there while my father terrorized us. How could she not have stood between her husband and her children and said, "If you want to hit them, you're going to have to go through me." Then again, I cannot remember any experience where my mother comforted, much less attempted to protect me.

My father controlled me by terror. I was five years old when he held me over the second floor banister by my ankles. All that was between me and the bottom of the long winding staircase were my father's hands. He did not do this in fun; my father never played with us. He did it to show his power. We were reminded of that power every time we looked at the top of a door frame. There was a stick above every door.

Just as my father owned us, he also owned his employees. He owned his executives' homes. They rented from him. He owned their cars. They either leased from him or he provided the cars as a part of their employment. He even controlled where his employees vacationed. Each key employee was allowed to invite twelve guests to Black Lake for several days and nights where they would be welcomed by a couple preparing fabulous food. There were seven boats and incredible fishing in a privately stocked lake. Horses to ride. Nights by the fire. No charge. He was shrewd in his ability to maintain control and loyalty at the same time.

After my father died, one of his top employees called Gwen, the executor of his estate, and said, "Your father gave me my home in his will." My sister had to say words he found impossible to hear, "I'm so sorry but he didn't leave you anything." The executive continued, "but

I rented my home from him for years. I went to him years ago and told him I would like to purchase the home, instead of renting. Van said, 'I've left it to you in my will.'" Gwen had to repeat, "I'm so very sorry but there is no mention of you or the home in the will."

There was another employee, whom I'll call "John," who was perhaps my father's most loyal employee. He did everything for my father. John would come to our home in the middle of the night if there were a problem with anything in the house. For decades he was like his personal assistant…available day and night.

After my father died, John called Gwen with a similar story. "Van always told me he had provided for me, in his will, for the rest of my life. He didn't show me any formal agreement but he assured me that he had." "John, I'm sorry but you are not even mentioned in his will. He didn't leave you anything." Gwen later told me it was as if John hadn't even heard what she had said. He continued, "Van told me so many times that he would take care of me for the rest of my life." Gwen told me he called her at least once a month for over a year to say, "Did you find the papers yet that stipulated what Van left for me?" There were no such papers.

My father's animals were also his property. He always had chow dogs. I especially remember Ching. He was my father's dog during most of my childhood and teen years. Once, when he was a puppy, he disobeyed my father. My father grabbed him, stormed to the back door, opened the screen and threw him, like a football, over the back picket fence. After the puppy landed and rolled over and over, he cowered and cried. No one disobeyed my father.

My father demonstrated the same kind of ownership with his horses. When I was a teenager, his new, feisty quarter horse began trying to buck my father off his back. My father, with spurs digging into his horse's flesh, kicked him into a gallop and ran him straight up the mountain, to total exhaustion. The horse was soaked with sweat; white lather poured off him. He almost ran the horse to death.

My father was the master. You did it his way, always.

The Van Derbur family. I am on the
far left. Gwen is on the far right.

Gwen and I are together on the left.
My father and David Chasen, owner
of the famous Chasen's resteraunt,
are kneeling in front of Bob Hope, who
is dressed in a costume for a movie.

My father was national president
of his fraternity, Kappa Sigma.
Gwen is on the far left;
I am wearing the corsage.

Chapter 2 – The Night Child

Note: The first few pages of this chapter are difficult for some to read. So many people said my father "molested" me. It is important to face the stark facts of what he did. If it is overwhelming to you, skip to the paragraph "As a child I would usually fall asleep from exhaustion" on page 27.

My room was right above the garage door. I would go to bed around eight or nine and wait…and wait…and wait. Would it be tonight? I would lie, frozen in my bed, unable to move, just waiting.

I would feel adrenalin rush through my body when I heard my father's car pull into the alley and then into the driveway. It was the same kind of feeling I would have if I were walking home alone down a dark, deserted street, knowing a man was following my every move. The garage door would go up and my anxiety would become instantly overwhelming. Terror was my nightly blanket, whether he came or not. Many times he wouldn't come to my room until close to midnight. Sometimes he wouldn't come at all. The waiting, however, was every night.

My father always wore a white terry cloth robe and gray felt slippers. I would listen so hard, I could actually feel my ears listening—like megaphones reaching out to catch the slightest sound. Many times I wouldn't hear his felt slippers on the linoleum steps leading to my room but I would always hear the slow, almost silent turning of the knob on my bedroom door and then the scuff, scuff to my bed. I always pretended to be asleep. For 13 years, I pretended not to know what he was doing.

The second I felt his hands on my body, I would tighten every muscle as tightly as I could, like a starfish does if you turn it over and touch it with a stick. The starfish instantly, violently, contracts every part of its being in an effort to protect itself.

I would shut my eyes, squish them closed until they hurt from squeezing them so hard. I wouldn't open them again until he left. He usually stayed at least an hour. Many nights he stayed longer.

He pried me open night after night, lacerating my mind, my body and my soul. Like a delicate piece of crystal smashed into concrete, my father took my belief system, my sense of self, my very soul and shattered it into shards.

Because I had no way to escape and no one to turn to, I dissociated, or, in my words, I "split my mind." This is the deal I believe I made as a little girl. I (whom I call the "day child") said to the part of me that was being penetrated again and again (whom I call the "night child"), "You stay here in the bedroom and take all the feelings and pain, all of the humiliation and degradation, and I will go out and 'be somebody.' After I'm safe and successful, I will come back for you. I promise." And so, the deal was struck. In order to survive, my mind created another separate self to stay and endure the invasions of my body. I need to be clear: I have no memory of that "conversation," nor did I use the term "night child" until, in my adult life, I was forced to confront my past. But there is no doubt in my mind this split occurred because I had no way out.

The night child tried everything to keep my father out. During the winter, I opened both windows as widely as they would go. My room would be freezing cold. It never stopped him. As children, we took the train to go skiing every Saturday. There was a sign on the train that said "Please go 'way and let me sleep." I took the sign and hung it on my doorknob. It didn't stop him. I didn't bathe for days. I was smelly and yucky. I wore panties and pajamas. It didn't stop him. As a teenager, I would wear a Kotex on nights when I didn't even have my period. It didn't stop him. (Gwen told me some years ago that he kept a calendar of our periods.)

Sometimes I would lie on my stomach, tighten my legs and my buttocks, and bring my arms up across my breasts, tightly against my sides. He would slowly begin to rub my back gently, rhythmically and then slowly he would begin to force his hands between my upper arms and my body. Forcefully. Powerfully. Until his hands were fondling my newly forming breasts. His hands were hot and his fingers pulsated. He breathed quickly and heavily, lost in an almost sexual frenzy. It was about control and winning. I would fight with every ounce of my being to not feel anything he was doing. My mantra was "shut down." Shut all feelings down. Every time my father said, "Just let go. Just go with it," I would tighten my body and then I would tighten it more. To "let go" was to feel. He was determined to bring my body to orgasm.(It's so difficult for me to write that sentence.)

Each night I would fight valiantly. I would bury, in the deepest part of my being, the memories and the *feelings* of the nights when my body responded and he won. Most nights he did not win. The nights I won, he would finally leave, having brought my body to a sexual arousal no child's body could accommodate. I would be left in a heightened sexual state, with feelings I had no way to resolve. I would be left with a body on fire—a body that could find no resolution—no peace. Every pore, every muscle, every cell of my being had fought from opposite ends…it feels good…I *hate* the feelings. The overwhelming sexual energy, with no release, would be locked in my body for decades. Feelings, buried, do not die. The feelings I was forced to bury deep within my being, would *torment* my body for decades.

Whether I was awake with an intense alertness, or awakened by his hands touching me, my body was as electrified as if a huge, growling bear were standing over my bed just ready to pounce on me. Just the waiting brought on feelings of inexpressible dread, of the need to be hyper-alert, ready for battle, ready for the bear, the warriors with huge knives, my father. It didn't matter which showed up; the feelings were the same.

I know I willed my breasts to stop growing. I was so humiliated and shamed, I didn't want breasts. I had gotten pretty good at cutting off my lower body. Do anything with it you want, I'm not there. It was more difficult to cut myself off from my breasts.

One night, as a young child, when my father laid on me and forced his tongue into my mouth, I was revolted and completely disarmed. I couldn't believe what he was doing. His tongue was wiggly and wet with spit. I couldn't imagine anyone in the world had ever done that to another person. I thought I would die from smothering—not just from his forceful invasion of my mouth but because it involved my face. I had always tried to "go away in my mind" as my father entered my body but when he assaulted my face, for some reason, that allowed him entrée into my "self" and I was unable to escape in my mind. Of all the things my father did to me, this was one the most difficult for me to cope with. The revulsion was overwhelming.

As a child, I would usually fall asleep from exhaustion. As a teen, falling asleep would become more difficult. Eventually, I lost my ability to "fall asleep." How I ever went to school the next day is something I cannot fathom. I have few memories of school life before age ten. In fact, I only have one memory of school from kindergarten through fourth grade. I am sitting on a dirt playground playing marbles. I can't remember any kids sitting with me, or anything about the game. All I remember is one incredibly beautiful light blue marble that was mine. It was the exact color of my father's eyes.

I do know that, in the morning, I was the happy, sparkly, respected, disciplined, highly moral young girl. That was real to me, the day child. The happy child was real. My mind had found a way to take the memories and feelings of terror, humiliation, rage, helplessness and hopelessness and compartmentalize them into a different part of my brain, body and soul. The only way I could survive facing another night was to not remember what had happened. How could I get through a day at school playing with my friends, answering the questions the teacher asked, riding my bike home—how could I survive a daily routine if I *remembered* what awaited me at night? If my father came into my room one night a week for 13 years, that's 676 nights. How could I remember, especially knowing there was no escape and *no one* to turn to for help?

What made it even worse is that someone *did* know. When I was five, I was given a huge doll for Christmas. I sat her in a small rocking chair, in front of my large bedroom window. After my father left, I would open my eyes and stare at the silhouette of the doll, sitting motionless in the rocking chair. She had seen everything. She knew…and I hated her for knowing.

Many people are inclined to believe that children born into the same family are brought up in the same environment. Wrong. Gwen was the first-born. My mother was most eager for her first child. My parents had not planned on having four children. I was one of those "accidents." There can be a huge difference being the first-born and the last-born. Just my father's nicknames for us told volumes: Gwen was "The Countess"; I was "Squirt".

When I was seven, Gwen was thirteen and ready to enter 9th grade as an honor student. Unexpectedly (at least to me), she was sent to a boarding school in Kansas City. It was as if she suddenly disappeared. Who had ever heard of a boarding school? At that time and in our community no one I knew ever went to a boarding school…other than Gwen.

All I knew is that she had been rebellious and defiant. I learned, as a very small child, if you defy, you get beaten and sent away. I saw no possible escape. I believe that is why, as a five-year-old, my mind could find only one way to survive—split. Repress completely all memories of the night. I found a way to never let my mind, during the day, know what had happened because to know that it would happen again and again and again was just too unbearable.

After Gwen was sent away, I was left alone with my disconnected mother and my nighttime father because my two very lucky middle sisters shared a room.

One of the most devastating results of sexual abuse is that the secret is so shaming, you tell no one. *No one.* That cut me off from any relationship, any sharing or deep friendship with my mother or my sisters. One of my saddest memories is putting money under one of my sister's pillows so she would come to my room and thank me. I was obviously starved for attention and friendship. As children, we were punished much more harshly if we "told" on another sister than if we were the one who did the reported bad deed. There was no worse sin than telling on one another.

In 5th grade, George Linger would walk me home from school, carrying my books. We would play "horse" (a basketball game) in the backyard and I would win as often as he did. One afternoon, we went in the back door to get something to drink. George opened the door that led from the kitchen up the dark, steep staircase to the landing that led to my room. He told me he wanted to see my room. It was a simple, casual statement. I remember the feelings I had as he said those words. I went crazy inside. I cried out, "No!" He thought I was playing and playfully, in return, he grabbed for the door. As he turned the knob, I leapt at him and physically pulled him away. He quickly realized this wasn't a game. I was frantic. I would *never* allow anyone to go into my bedroom. I had no conscious knowledge why, but years later I would learn that was where the night child lived and no one could ever see her. To see her would be to know the truth.

Without realizing it, I fought to keep my two worlds separated. Without ever knowing why, I made sure, whenever possible, that nothing passed between the compartmentalization I had created between the day child and the night child.

But the invasions of the night were beginning to take a toll on my daytime body as early as elementary school. During 5th grade, while trying to be accepted at a new school, the gym teacher embarrassed me in front of the class. She had asked us to lean over and touch our toes. My body had become so tight and stiff that I couldn't even come close.

I couldn't even reach to the middle of my calves. She singled me out and said that I should be able to. She asked me to bend over again and then she began pushing on my back, trying to force my fingers down to my toes. It was impossible for me to do. My body had already tightened and become rigid.

By middle school, I had developed sciatica pain that ran down my right leg. Although tightening every muscle of my body never kept my father out, I was left with a body that I learned to tighten so well, my muscles still *feel*, to this day, as if they are contracted in the fetal position.

As I lay in the fetal position each night, bending my arms and legs, pulling them up and into my body, I would also tighten my buttocks. If I could just pull it tighter, nothing could get in. Tighter. Tighter. I would try to keep everything in. Even waste products. As a result, chronic constipation has plagued my body since childhood. I could never allow my body to "let go" because that would mean to submit, to feel, to respond, to lose, to be wholly and reprehensibly bad.

Some nights are as crystal clear as if they were last night. One night is, perhaps, my most vivid memory. I was ten or eleven, asleep in my bed. My father had come into my room that night later than usual…around midnight. I was awakened, as always, by feeling his hands on my skin. He had been in my room for at least thirty minutes when we both heard footsteps. We hadn't heard my mother on the carpet walking down the long hallway but the second she stepped on the top linoleum step, we heard the click of her shoe. She always dressed elegantly for bed, in a light pink or blue negligee and mules (dressy slippers with leather heels).

Click. She was on the first step. Then, slowly, very slowly, click, down to the second step. Then even more slowly we heard the third click as she stepped down the third step. My door was less than six feet away. *Finally! My mother was coming. Finally it would be over.*At the sound of the first click, my father had frozen. I had frozen. We remained motionless at the second click and the third. It was a dramatic moment in time when each of us knew what the other was thinking. It seemed like minutes, but I'm sure it was only seconds. Then we heard another click, but she wasn't coming to save me, she was going back up the steps. She knew.

There was never any doubt in my mind, after that night, that she knew. She walked away from me, back into her perfect world—a

30

world in which she was admired, respected and charming. I knew she would never come back and for the hundreds and hundreds of nights to come she never did, and yet I still called her "Mother." Until she died, at age 88, I called her "Mother."

My need to excel, win and be perfect began to surface during elementary school. Although my memories of 5th and 6th grade are few, I can still see (and feel) Mrs. Lucas asking me to walk to the front of the class and play a piano piece. There was a large piano in our homeroom class. It was the beginning of my "performing." I dreaded performing. I hated it. I had incredible angst worrying about it.

I began competing in sports in junior high school. My friend Robin McDougal and I did every sport together. We swam in AAU meets, competed in city golf tournaments, galloped horses across meadows and raced on junior high, high school, and college ski teams. Our idea of a perfect ski day was to take the lift to the very top and then will ourselves to ski straight down without stopping. Our legs would burn, our skis would chatter and we loved every run. No stopping for lunch, just skiing until the lifts closed for the day.

At our junior high graduation, I was the only student selected to perform. I played a very difficult piano piece, *Finlandia,* by Sibelius, from memory. My thoughts were always the same: "What if I forget a note?" "What if my fingers won't go as fast as they have to for the complex notes and chords?" I had intense anxiety from the minute I was asked until the graduation was over. I never missed a note and no one ever knew my inner terror. I looked confident and composed. I taught myself at an early age to "act as if it's true." I would visualize myself performing successfully—walking to the piano, sitting down, playing with confidence and authority…and it worked.

Little did I know that, in just a few months, I would meet a man who would change my life forever. As clearly as if he had swum out to rescue me from a strong rip tide that was pulling me out to sea, D.D. Harvey would save my life. When D.D. moved to Denver and became the youth minister of Montview Presbyterian Church, I was 15. My older sisters, 19 and 21, were away at college. That left Mother, my 17-year-old sister and me to attend his first service.

He vividly remembers that first Sunday. He recalls seeing us seated right in front, but what intrigued him, was what my mother said to him as they left the sanctuary. She told him that her husband didn't go to church with her but that she "had 23 years of a perfect marriage." He remembers that comment as an odd thing for her to say, but I was accustomed to hearing it because it was her mantra until the day she died…changing only the number of years.

D.D. was different from any minister I had ever heard of. He drove a sports car, was married to a former Hollywood "starlet," and would soon be named one of the Ten Outstanding Young Men in America by the National Junior Chamber of Commerce (a young man's service organization). It would be an honor justly deserved.

I was enthralled by him. He was passionate—on fire—with issues that touched our lives. He was twice my age, but he knew how to relate to teenagers. He began his Bible study class every Friday morning at 6:30 a.m. The day I turned sixteen and could drive, I began attending. Many years later, he told me he could not figure out why I came every week. Most of the eight or ten teens who came were very religious or, far more commonly, troubled. I didn't fit either category.

One Friday morning, he looked out the window to see the city of Denver buried in snow. He knew no one would even try to come to the meeting, but since he lived next door to the church, he decided to trudge over. Just as he was unlocking the door, I pulled up in my red convertible, searching for a place to park between snow banks. Years later, he would remember that morning and it would become a piece to a puzzle it would take him years to solve. If I had gone to him because I was depressed or unpopular, it would have been a much easier puzzle, but he and I both believed I had no problems. I was the happiest teenager in the world. I had been born into a beautiful family who "had it all."

I met Larry Atler the same year I met D.D. I had graduated from junior high and was entering a large high school (almost 2,000 students). I wasn't just shy, I was walking anxiety. But I always appeared confident and self-assured. Within weeks, I was elected sophomore representative to student council. The meetings were held on the fourth floor. When I walked in and sat down, I saw him standing at the front of the room, laughing and talking with other seniors. I had always pictured myself falling in love with a tall, blonde, Swede sort of a boy. Larry had dark hair, brown eyes and an olive complexion. My heart raced when I watched him. I believe in love at first sight, because it happened to me.

Even though I was only 15, I had always had boys who wanted to walk me home or go swimming or skiing with me. I had never met a boy who wouldn't ask me to a movie or for a Coke after school if I as much as glanced his way. Until Larry. He was a senior, dating a senior, Donanne. She couldn't have been more different from me. She was very feminine, almost fragile. Beautiful. Porcelain skin. Brown hair. Non-athletic. I, on the other hand, was always ready to strap on skis (that's what we did in the days before safety bindings) and race down the mountain or go off a regulation ski jump (I really did that—once!). I could ride a horse as wild as you could find. I was a tomboy with long blond, perfectly combed hair.

I quickly figured out Larry's class schedule and would run madly down a hallway and up a back staircase so that I could casually stroll by him and say "hi," only to run madly down another staircase and down another hallway to avoid not being late for my next class. He was always friendly but he paid no special attention to me, until December. One afternoon the student council members stayed after school to decorate the front hall for Christmas. As we were busy working, Larry came over to me and said, "Would you like to go to the drugstore with me to get some wire?" I had never heard such beautiful words. We drove in his car with the top down—even though it was winter. Soon after, he asked me out for a Friday night date.

On that first date, as we were walking to his car, he said, "Your name, Marilyn, doesn't fit you. Okay if I tell you what name I'd like to call you after our date tonight?" Our first date was magical. A friend of Larry's was having a dance in her basement. There were about 15 couples. Everyone there was a senior but me. When Larry took me in his arms, I never wanted him to let me go. I would *never* have kissed any boy on a first date. Or the second date. Or the ninth date. Maybe the tenth. But never in front of anyone. Because respect was more important to me than anything else in my life. I had a perfect reputation, and would never have done anything to impair that. We all knew the girls who did not have good reputations.

But as we danced, nothing mattered except him. I remember looking up at him and he kissed me, ever so gently. Right there on the dance floor. For those who say a 15- or 16-year-old knows only puppy love, I disagree. I had fallen deeply in love with Larry. When he walked me to my door, he said, "I will call you Lynn." (To this day, Larry, his family and our closest friends call me Lynn. My family, old friends and business contacts call me Marilyn.)

After that, I became his Friday night date, but Donanne was still his

Saturday night date. One spring weekend, I had a date with another senior and we went to the mountains for a steak fry. Larry was there with Donanne. He had sprained his ankle and she was caring for him. I couldn't imagine why I wasn't the one to be with him, but by summer, I was his only date.

Right from the start, Larry was different from the other boys I knew. Typically, whenever I skied or swam with a boy, it would *always* be competitive. Because I was good, other boys had to prove they could beat me. Even if we just seemed to be skiing together, one of us would take off at the top and not stop—going faster than we should—knowing it was a race.

Larry had never skied, surfed or ridden a horse, but he could play tennis better than I. One summer night, we went to a lighted court and began hitting the ball back and forth. Tennis certainly wasn't my best sport but I was hitting it as hard as I could. I naturally expected him to hit it back harder and try to place it where I couldn't return it.

However, when I hit the tennis ball back to Larry, he said, "Good shot. I'm going to hit you a few balls; bring your racket head through a little faster and follow through more." He began hitting balls right to me. It was an experience I had never had before. He didn't want to beat me. He wanted to help me be better. Always. No matter what we were doing. When we began skiing together, he would always suggest I go first so he could be sure I was okay. It would never occur to him to try to beat me. It was always foremost in his mind to be sure I was safe. It wouldn't be long before we would realize how much I had to be first and in control.

During our first summer together, he worked on construction. I remember sitting in our living room, alone, after dinner, listening to Nat King Cole sing "Blue Gardenia" or "Too Young," just waiting and waiting for Larry to call. It was a nightly ritual.

There was an amusement park in Denver, Elitch Gardens, that had a huge dance floor and big name bands. Larry took me dancing there often. I fit perfectly in his arms. He was a fantastic dancer. I was stiff but I did okay unless he wanted to jitterbug or do any dance step where we were not together. I was far too shy and uncomfortable in my body to do something apart from him.

I loved the roller coaster, especially sitting in the front seat. Whatever the scariest ride was—that's what I wanted to do. He didn't share my enthusiasm *at all* but he would go with me. Other nights we would row a boat on the lake in City Park, take a long walk or get a Dairy Queen (or two). But the part of the night we both waited for was being in his car, parked, kissing. We had such a passion for one another. But he would never try to take it any further than kissing. I had long blond hair, worn in a pageboy. When I would go home, one side of my hair would be wet and straight from his holding and kissing me.

At 11:55 p.m., we knew it was time. I always had to be in by midnight. Not 12:01. Not 12:04. Midnight. Sharp. My father was never home for dinner but he was usually home by 9:30 or 10:00. And he would wait for his daughter(s) to come home. Every boy who ever dated a Van Derbur girl knew the rule.

How the day child and the night child remained starkly separated still astonishes me. I remember kissing Larry good night at the door with all the feelings of a young girl in love. But what did I, a teenager with strong morals, have to do to walk through the front door, up the long, winding staircase, down the long hallway to my room, only to be violated minutes or hours later in ways that were unspeakable— literally. I marvel at the mental gymnastics that allowed me to survive.

I can only remember one time when an experience broke through this perfect, happy teenager belief system I had. I had been pledged to the most popular high school sorority. It was large—maybe 60 girls— and it was the club every girl wanted to be invited to join. I was asked as a sophomore. There was an initiation. I had no idea what to expect. I was brought, alone, into a dark basement. While the 60 girls sat and watched, a spotlight was shown into my face. The light was so intense, I couldn't see them. I was to answer questions. The first question was: "What is digitational intercourse?" I felt extreme anxiety well up into every part of my body. I couldn't think. I couldn't breathe. I felt my heart pounding. My head dropped. I couldn't move. "What is digitational intercourse?" a girl asked again. There was no possible way I could even begin to answer that question. My mind had completely shut down. I just knew I had to get out of there.

"Okay then—what is osculation?" I could feel my body being overwhelmed with extreme emotion. I tried so hard to hold myself together. So hard. But I couldn't. All of a sudden I burst into loud, heaving, convulsive sobs. I had lost control completely. Someone took me to another room where I sobbed to exhaustion. Later I was told that digitational intercourse is holding hands and osculation is kissing.

I had no idea what made me cry. I had no conscious memories of my nights. The night was buried so deep. Only something as confrontational and humiliating as this initiation could even begin to puncture the wall I had built around my secret.

If someone had been looking for clues, my reaction to this situation would have been a clue. But no one was looking. Most of the time I was the epitome of what a high school sophomore should be.

It had taken me until late spring to "hook" Larry, but once I did, the hook was set for life. In future years, his love would be tested. And tested. And tested.

Although Larry was my focus during my sophomore year in high school, when he left for college in the fall, my entire focus was on excellence.

The Dean of Women called me into her office to tell me that I had been one of two girls selected to go to Girls State. It was an incredible experience. Two girls from every high school in Colorado met together on a college campus for one week, to learn about our state government. While there, each delegate voted for two girls to go to Girls Nation. I was selected. That August, I flew to Washington, D.C. where we stayed at American University. One of my clearest memories was of the heat. I didn't believe it was possible to be as hot and sticky as it was there, especially with no air conditioning. It is also the first time I remember being unable to fall asleep. Lying awake all night, listening. I was aware of every noise, from the ambient room sound to someone opening her door down the hall.

One of the highlights of the week was going to the White House to meet President Eisenhower in the Rose Garden. My picture was in the paper and when I returned to Denver I was expected to speak to groups of women's organizations about my experiences. This began a pattern I established in high school of winning positions that would require me to perform or speak in public. Just the *thought* of doing a public performance brought feelings of extreme terror, almost incapacitating terror. I don't use those words cavalierly. I would feel a heavy weight on my chest, my breathing would become shallow and fast, and overpowering dread would invade every day of my life, even if the event were six weeks or six months in the future. My need to win and my need to be a positive role model were more powerful than the angst

I lived with as I constantly reached for positive acknowledgments.

When Mrs. Kreiner, the speech teacher, asked me to be Mary in the Christmas Pageant, I was fairly comfortable because I didn't have many lines. However, later that year when she asked me to play the lead in the senior class play, I felt great tension begin building. The night of the play, my father was the male lead in the same exact play, in our civic theater, literally across the street from our high school. Because his opening curtain was an hour later than ours, he was able to see the first thirty minutes of my performance. I so wanted him to see me play my part to perfection.

As a senior, I was elected May Queen. All I had to do was smile. I had wanted to be voted "Best All Around Girl." I wanted to be respected for who I was, not honored for what I looked like. When I didn't win "Best...," I was devastated. I'm not sure it was a conscious thought but somewhere deep inside me, I knew I had to win respect— big time. It would be a motivation that would rule my life.

I remember very little of what life was like at home during the day. I didn't play or spend time talking with my sisters or mother. My father was rarely home during the day or evening. One of the reasons I became an accomplished student, pianist, skier, golfer, horseback rider, and swimmer is because practicing gave me something to do as I developed a lifetime habit of staying busy, very busy.

If I had not met Larry as a young teenager, I do not believe I would have survived the long-term effects of 13 years of incest. He was the first person I had ever felt close to. I believe that falling in love with Larry when I was 15 was what allowed me to *ever* have a loving relationship. He had also tapped into another part of me. I tended to be aloof. Stiff. He found me cute and clever and funny. I laughed a lot but no one ever found me cute. I began using different voices to make him laugh. He relished my antics, which only encouraged me. We were very playful with one another. (We still are.)

He graduated from high school at the end of my sophomore year. He attended Indiana University as a freshman and then transferred to Washington and Lee University for his final three years. I couldn't imagine life without Larry. I drove to the train station, alone, to see him off to Indiana. His parents were there, of course. I felt very uncomfortable—not because of anything they did or said. They were always very welcoming. I was just so in love with Larry and I wanted my "goodbye" to be private. I stood off to the side. He came to me immediately and we stood behind a very large post. His kissed me. Several times. He then kissed his parents and boarded the train. We wrote to one another every single day. Long distance calls were uncommon in the '50s, so we rarely spoke on the phone.

Dating, while a boyfriend was away, was very common, unless you were "pinned" and no one my age (that I knew, anyway) was pinned. I had no interest in dating but when, in the fall, the vice president of our class asked me to the junior prom, I wasn't fast enough to think of a reason why I couldn't go! It was *months* away.

The Friday before the Saturday night prom, the headlines of our Denver paper read, "THREE EAST DENVER BOYS ROB STORE." The article went on to say that these three boys were from "very fine families" and they were students at my school, East High. Students were looking up and down the absentee list trying to figure out who these three boys were. For teens that we knew, robbing a store was unheard of.

The second I arrived home from school, the phone rang. It was D.D. He told me that John (not his real name), my date for the prom the next night, was one of the three. He had spent the day with him at the police station. John had admitted everything and was going to be out on bail. D.D. wanted to give a sermon on how John (who was a member of our church), had let his family and community down and how we, as a community, had let him down. John agreed to be there on one condition—that I sit with him. Just the two of us together in the front row. I had never even had a *date* with him. I told D.D. that I would, of course, be there and then I added, "But I'd better talk with my parents."

I told my mother about the request. I could tell she really did *not* want me to do it. About seven hundred people attended Sunday services and I knew she was concerned about how it would look.

Shortly after my father came home that night, my mother sent me to discuss it with him. Whenever there was to be a discussion, it would always be in his room, with him in bed, covered with a sheet and a thin green blanket. He would have nothing on. During these years, I had no conscious memories of what went on in my bedroom at night but I remember all too well how unbelievably uncomfortable I was trying to have a conversation with him while he was in bed.

I explained the situation to him. He responded with one question,

"What would you like to do?"

"I'd like to be there for him."

"Then that's what you should do."

This may seem like an insignificant experience but it illustrates how little connection I had with my mother. The only person who, on rare occasions, "heard me" as I grew from a teenager into an adult, was my father.

D.D. never talked about some far off "Heavenly Father." He always talked about our lives—our values and commitments—what decisions we were making. His entire sermon was on John and the community. D.D. was a brilliant speaker and communicator.

John was sent to jail for many months. I would visit him often. I had so much compassion for him and for what he had done to his life. It would be one of many times I would reach out to someone so alone in the world. I wrote Larry about John, the sermon and going to see John in jail. He was always supportive of my decisions.

I was constantly bringing people to D.D. who were troubled. D.D. would be in his office and his office door was always open. If you wanted to talk, he had the time. He never talked about the weather or attendance the prior Sunday. He always went right for it—whatever "it" might have been. He was intensely involved in so many teens' lives.

Since I didn't need any help or counseling, we just talked. I found myself finding reasons to see him often. Looking back, I know there were two central reasons why I kept bringing teens with problems to D.D. The first is, I believe I knew subconsciously that I had found a safe man who might one day reach into the depths of my soul and find my secret. The second reason is a red flag when looking at common characteristics of children who have been sexually violated. I was compulsive about helping those "less fortunate." It went far beyond being kind and thoughtful.

For instance, as soon as I turned sixteen and could drive, I began making a simple dinner and driving it way across town to Ben's house. Ben was well into his 80's and he had absolutely no one in his life—but me. I can't remember how I met him but I would cook for him and visit him frequently. Because his voice trembled, he was difficult to understand and he would never go out to dinner because he dropped and dribbled his food. One day when I arrived, I found the huge valentine I had sent him hanging on his wall. He had taken a nail and just pounded it in.

Similarly, I visited a young boy, Bob, at a hospital as often as three afternoons a week. He was severely physically handicapped and delightful company. When I would arrive around 5 p.m., he would be in his wheelchair waiting for me at the elevator. Every day that I didn't go, I would see him in my mind, waiting for me at the elevator.

When I was in college, I saw a blind boy who seemed lost, trying to find his way to class. I asked him if I might walk with him. He began waiting for me every day. And almost every day I would walk with him.

There were many other "needy" people I was attentive to, but I was overly committed to them and avoiding normal friendships; that is not natural for a teenage girl who is also very involved in all school activities. I genuinely cared about disadvantaged people but it was obsessive behavior and I always chose people who were completely isolated and alone.

My junior and senior years of high school are a blur. Without Larry there and without the close friendships that my hidden shame denied me, I stayed very, very busy with school, outside activities and taking care of isolated, lonely people.

When Larry left for college, my last sister also left for college. I was now alone, the last daughter. Home alone with my mother and my father, for two more excruciating years.

I have very few memories of my mother and me those last two years. I'm sure the reason is because we had no connection with one another. One memory was her afternoon ritual after I came home from school. She almost always took a nap. I remember her filling a little blue bowl with some kind of solution. I'm not sure what witch hazel is but that's what comes to mind. She would soak cotton pads in the liquid and then put them on her eye lids. She would then rest for at least an hour. It didn't strike me as unusual then but it certainly does now—that she always waited to take her nap until after I came home from school. Since my father was never home for dinner and there was no television in homes yet, we obviously sat alone together every night for dinner. I don't remember her cooking. Who did the dishes? Did she? Did I? What did we talk about? Did I go to my room right after dinner to study? I don't remember.

During my junior year of high school, my father allowed me to bring my horse down from the mountains and board her about 30 minutes away. One day my mother came out to pick me up. When we got home, she said, casually, as I walked into the house, "Oh, there's a package from Larry." *A package from Larry.* I felt a rush of excitement. A package! From Larry! I dashed into the kitchen and tore the box open. It was an adorable stuffed dog with a Washington & Lee emblem on its ears. I started crying I was so happy with the gift.

It is a simple example of how little my mother knew me. *Anyone* would have known that I would have literally jumped for joy if I had been told, at the stable, that I had a present waiting from Larry. Nothing else would matter. The first thing I did *every* day after school was look for my letter from him—then sit down and write to him. That she would forget to even mention a gift from Larry was unfathomable. How could she not have hidden the box in the trunk and then said the *second* I saw her, "There is a surprise for you!"

"What, Mother?" (We were only allowed to call her "Mother.")

"Guess?"

When she told me, I would have hugged her from the sheer joy of it. She would have stood there while I opened it and we would have ooed and aahhed together. That is the uniqueness of a mother-daughter relationship. Sharing the joy and sometimes the sorrow. But that was never our relationship.

Larry and I would count the days until summer, until we could be together again. It was a major focus of our energies—the upcoming summer. When Larry arrived home in June, I sat by the phone, waiting, waiting, waiting for him to call. He came over immediately. It was as if we had never been apart. But I had to tell him something. I wasn't sure how to tell him so I just said it straight out: "I'm going to Europe this summer with a teacher and other students. I'll be gone most of the summer." He just stared at me. He could not believe what I was saying. Why on earth would I go away when all we wanted was to be together?

I would find an excuse to go away every summer. I couldn't leave high school but I could find ways to never sleep in my room again during the summers. When I went to college, I would go to summer school at the University of Colorado, and, another summer, at the

University of Wisconsin. I was always an A student. I always carried the maximum hours. There was never a need for me to go to school in the summer.

Larry knew I loved him. He never doubted that. It was incomprehensible to him why I would keep going away. I had no explanation because I didn't understand it either.

The only other person who found my leaving Larry astonishing was D.D. He told me, years later, he would think about it and think about it. "Why is she leaving? Why is she leaving Larry when she is so in love with him?" *My repressed memories and feelings were beginning to run my life.*

During my senior year in high school, *Seventeen Magazine* had chosen Denver as a city in which to hold a contest—to choose a "Miss Young America of Denver." It was sponsored by the Junior Chamber of Commerce and *Seventeen Magazine*. It was a citywide contest in which anyone in Denver could vote. The magazine would then do a major feature story on the teen winner.

I don't remember who submitted my name but I won. The night of my high school graduation, immediately after my speech and the acceptance of my diploma, Mother, the editor, a top photographer, the president of the Junior Chamber, "Bill Collier," and I drove to our mountain lodge to take pictures the next morning.

It was after 11 p.m. when we left Denver. I was exhausted. Mother suggested I sit in the back with Mr. Collier and try to rest. As we started the two-hour drive, he suggested I lie down and put my head on his lap and try to go to sleep. I remember resting deeply and then feeling his legs suddenly lift my head up, as his arms slid under my head and he drew me up. It happened so fast. I had no idea what he was doing. He quickly leaned down and kissed me. Really kissed me, sticking his tongue deep into my mouth. I was completely stunned. I didn't know what to do. Cry out? Yell, "Stop the car?" This was the day child he was kissing. It was the first of many betrayals I would endure by men in positions of trust, especially during my early 20's.

An East High School graduation was always well-attended by as many as 3,000 people. I was chosen to give the commencement address. The night of the graduation, I knew I was going to faint, throw up, or both. I was terrified. Just before we were to walk on stage, I turned to Mrs. Kreiner and said, "I don't think I can do this."

She responded, in her flamboyant, eccentric way, "You will be *fabulous* tonight!" And with that, the graduation exercises began.

It was during that year that I began to notice the physical feeling of wanting to throw up and it became progressively more persistent. I was in college before I was diagnosed with ulcers.

I looked like I had close friends. I looked like I belonged. I'm sure no one even noticed that, my senior year, I took a sack lunch into Mr. Weimar's class and had lunch with him every day. He was my history teacher. He sat at his desk and I sat in the last chair in the last row. I can never remember "hanging out" or going to the movies with girl friends. Not even one time.

There aren't too many things I long for, but when I hear someone tell me they cannot wait to go to their reunion to see their friends again, I am reminded that I never had a circle of friends. I have never gone to my high school, sorority or college reunions. I always made a few lasting friendships that were rock solid, but when a group of girls got together during lunch or late at night to share secrets or talk about boys, I would never be there. Never.

During my freshman year of college, I came home for Christmas. One night will always remain deeply etched into my memory. It was about 10 p.m. My father was lying in his bed. My mother was three floors below in the basement wrapping presents. I went in to kiss him goodnight. I leaned over to kiss him on the cheek and I smelled liquor. Although my father drank socially (my mother never drank alcohol), it was unusual to smell such a strong scent of liquor.

As I leaned over, he forcefully pulled me down to him. I was stunned. My hands went spontaneously to his shoulders to push away from him. My push was an angry don't-even-think-about-it push. A defiant, powerful statement of *never* think of doing *that* again. I walked out of there in disbelief. His pull-down had been very sexual. I couldn't believe what had happened. I guess I just found a way to dismiss it by how much he had had to drink.

Never has there been a clearer example of the day child and the night child. If he had come into my room that night, the night child *would not have believed* she was able to protect herself. As I would have to be reminded time and again during my recovery work, like Pavlov's dogs, I had been conditioned since age five. The hundreds and hundreds of times he pried me open, were always in my room and always late at night. The night child, in her bed, could not stop my father. The nighttime pattern never varied, except that one night in his room when I was the day child-college student, who could protect herself.

I also remember what my father said to me the last night I was home—before the first time I went to college. I remember every word exactly as he said it, "If you get into trouble, you come to me because I'm the only person you know who can keep his mouth shut. I'm the only person you can trust." I did not respond. I always pretended to be asleep. In future years, I *would* come to him in times of incredible distress because he *was* the only one I had to turn to. He was a sugar pill laced with arsenic.

Like red dye poured into a can of white paint, incest would color every aspect of my life.

I appear to be three or four years old.
I was five when my father started
coming into my bedroom.

The four Van Derbur daughters.
We are all two years apart.
Gwen, the eldest, is on the far right.
I am the youngest, in the center.

Until I was in my late forties,
I fervently believed this child should
have been able to stop my father.

Chapter 3 – College Life and Miss America

There was never a question about where I would go to college. My three older sisters had all gone to the University of Colorado. I would go there as well. I loved it. I quickly became extremely active. Although I had no understanding of it at the time, that was my *survival mechanism*, staying so busy there was no time to have unthinkable memories surface.

I had barely settled into the freshman dorm when I read in the daily paper that the music school was having tryouts for The Modern Choir. It did *not* go on to say that only music majors should audition and that it was their small, elite traveling choir or that freshman *never* auditioned. Sometimes ignorance *is* bliss!

Did I have the courage to try out? I tried out for everything. It never mattered how scared I was. I always did it anyway. If I had understood where the fear was coming from or *why I was continuously choosing* to walk into what felt like terror, my entire life would have been different. It would be years before I would have this insight.

Just as I entered the Dean of the Music School's office, my books dropped heavily to the floor. They had slipped. I was so embarrassed. Dean Imig said, "Are you angry or determined?" I had a one word response, "Determined."

His next question was: "Do you have perfect pitch?" Perfect pitch? What in the world was that? I had no idea what it *was* much less if I had it!

I just smiled. "I don't know."

"Are you a music major?"

"No."

"Are you taking *any* courses in the music school?"

"No."

"Are you a soprano?" "Alto?" He named several other categories for me to choose from. I said, "Sometimes when I'm in the dorm bathroom, I sing so low, girls think there is a man in the bathroom." I smiled and concluded: "I have a very low voice." He asked me to sing some notes and then said, "Welcome to The Modern Choir."

The Modern Choir rehearsed every day at 4 p.m. There were no excuses. Two students to a part. The Dean would play one note on the piano and all the music majors could then figure out exactly what their harmony notes were. All of them except me. How would I have any idea what my starting note was? Ah, Peg, my partner in the low notes. She would always "hmmmmm," loudly humming the first note into my ear. Then I was fine. I could read music.

Being a part of The Modern Choir was as close as I ever came to feeling a part of a group, feeling as if I really belonged. It was all business at rehearsal but I became friends with Dave Grusin who went on to become a major Hollywood composer/musician and Gene Johnson who became a funny, clever, singer-piano-player entertainer. We would ski together every weekend. There was no romance or sharing of our lives. Just fun and fast skiing.

When we prepared for our first out of state concert, Dean Imig said, "Marilyn, I would like you to sing this one line solo." I hadn't heard him correctly, had I? Sing a line by myself? Absolutely impossible. No way could I do that. Shyness wouldn't even *touch* how I felt. I was even embarrassed that he had singled me out to talk to. I said, "I'd rather not. " He said, "This is the line. You'll do fine." And that was the end of it…for him. The terror of even thinking about singing a line by myself became overwhelming. It wasn't that I didn't have a good enough voice—I did. It was that I was just too shy. (Today I would ask if I could sing the entire song—alone!) I sang that line at every concert—and I remember right *now* the feelings I had each and every time I did.

Sorority life also became an important part of my college experience. Most of the girls in the dorm went through "rush week," hoping a sorority would ask them to join. One girl had told me that she had purchased all new clothes. She wanted to join a sorority more than anything she had ever wanted in her entire life. When the bids came back (when sororities invited you) she did not receive one bid to join. She was devastated.

My father had been the president of all college men's fraternities in America and now I was questioning the value of sororities when I saw the heartache the fraternal system could cause. I had the best possible experience with rush week but I still question the system. Whether or not one young woman has a positive experience doesn't negate the

50

extreme trauma another young woman can experience when she is completely rejected, when she sits home alone in her dorm room while all the other freshman trot off happily to their new sororities. I wondered if all of us shouldn't be thinking about what medical students are taught, probably the first day…"First, do no harm."

I had been interested in Pi Beta Phi. I was thrilled to accept their offer. Near the end of my freshman year, one of the most popular Pi Phis, Georgie Palmer, asked me if I would be her roommate when I moved into the huge, gorgeous Pi Phi house. It was extremely unusual for a senior to request a sophomore roommate. I couldn't believe she was asking *me*—that out of all the girls who would want to room with her, she would choose me. Although I won many awards, I never felt anyone wanted to be with *me* as a one-on-one friend. As insignificant as it might seem, it was a major life event for me.

I looked like I fit into college life, but I didn't. I never drank beer or went to "Friday afternoon club." If fraternities were having a "mixer" party, I passed. I never "hung out" with my sorority sisters. I was a loner, but I was very good at disguising it by constantly being busy and involved in so many college activities.

Sometime during my freshman year, I went home and found that Mother had put mail in my room. Later she asked, "Wasn't that an exciting invitation?"

"What invitation?"

"To be a debutante. Denver has never had a Debutante Ball before. You are being asked to be in the first group of debutantes ever. They are only asking 12 girls."

"Oh, yeah, I saw that. I threw it away."

"You *threw it away?*"

"Yes." I always wanted to be a boy. At least I could be a "tomboy." I certainly never wanted to be a debutante.

Later that night, after my father had come home, my mother said, "Your father would like to talk to you."

"Your mother tells me you have been asked to be a debutante."

"Yes. I threw the invitation away."

"I think you should do this…for your mother. I really think you should do this." What he was saying was, "Do it."

"Okay."

Weeks later, we flew to New York City. I don't remember why we went but while we were there, we shopped for my deb dress. We found the most beautiful long, white formal I had ever seen. It would be my deb dress and later the dress I would wear at The Miss America Pageant in Atlantic City.

At the Ball, our fathers would escort us and two additional escorts followed as we were introduced to "society." The men wore black tuxedos; the college debutantes wore white evening gowns.

Of course, Larry would be one of my escorts. After I mentioned that to my mother, my father asked to speak with me again. I don't remember what words he used. I only remember leaving the conversation knowing that Larry was not an acceptable escort. He was Jewish. I would need two caucasian white, Anglo Saxon Protestants. Lyle Taylor and John Hodgson. Tall, blonde, blue eyed. There aren't many things I *could* have done differently in my life but I could have and should have done that one differently. I will always feel ashamed of myself because I didn't take a stand.

It would be a score I would settle 33 years later when our daughter, Jennifer, received her invitation to be a debutante. When I saw the envelope, I knew exactly what invitation was inside. I said, "I'm going to ask you to consider being a debutante. I've told you how ashamed I still am about not standing up to my father and having your dad be my escort. Seeing your dad walk down those steps with you would finally make it right. Would you consider doing it?" She smiled and said, "Of course I'll do it."

Watching them walk down the steps at our elegant Brown Palace Hotel settled my personal score. To top it off, it was a happy, memorable event!

Sometime during my freshman year, Gary, a junior who played on the football team, asked me out. I was deeply in love with Larry, but for reasons I didn't understand, I was starting to distance myself from him.

I think it would be accurate to say that there wasn't one person, including Gary's friends, who felt Gary and I were suited for one another. I could not explain to others, as I cannot explain now, what drew me to him. We were an incongruous couple. At best. It wasn't that he was a "bad guy" or that I was. We were just very wrong for one another. My father loathed him. If Gary walked into a room, my father would walk out. That was unusual because my father wasn't involved in my life, but he always made it clear what his feelings were about Gary. It is too simple to say that I was "acting out" against my father by continuing to date him but I know it was a factor. *Unless and until I could understand the deep underlying issues that were driving my life, I would continue to act in ways I could not understand.*

During my Miss America year, Peg, my chaperone would always say, "I could always tell who was calling. If you were crying, it was Gary. If you were laughing, it was Larry." I'm not sure anyone has ever given a more apt description of the two very different relationships I had.

The spring of my sophomore year, I ran for office. There were 13 members of a Board of Governors for the University. They were almost always 13 males. Rarely did a girl run. It meant debating with another candidate (a fraternity boy) in front of every sorority and fraternity house on campus. It meant sitting in front of 60 or 70 Sigma Nu's or Phi Delt's and answering individual questions about what I would do as a student governor. How could I have allowed myself to be in such a terrifying position? But I did and I won. All my life I compulsively put myself in those positions. Needing to win; needing to be a role model. I would be in my 40's before I would have any understanding that I was *choosing* to live in the terror that seeking to win and then winning would put me in. *I couldn't change what I didn't understand.*

I didn't know there was a name for what I lived with. I didn't know there was a name for terror, a feeling I would have to die, fear so extreme it was difficult to breathe, adrenaline pumping hard and fast, an inability to even think. I was in my late 40's, when, watching a television talk show, I saw a list of what comprises a "panic attack." Bingo! It has a name. "Panic attack." I believe I willed myself to function as I kept putting myself in positions where I would be forced to do things that would create acute anxiety. My subconscious would continue to drive me until I made the connection between self-disdain and the need to prove my self-worth. That is such a simple sentence. For too many, it is our life-long challenge.

During my sophomore year, I was also elected to Mortar Board (an honorary society, largely determined by grades), and song leader of the Pi Phis. I would take on these responsibilities when I returned for my junior year. But all of that would pale before something else I would win. Something I didn't even choose to go after. Attendance at weekly sorority meetings was required. One of the very few reasons you could excuse yourself from a meeting was if you had a long distance phone call. I was called out of the meeting to take a long distance call. It was Larry, calling from Washington and Lee. I was so excited to talk to him. After a lengthy conversation, I stepped out of the small phone room just as the 80 Pi Phi's were leaving the meeting, most of them rushing out for "coffee dates."

Two of the last girls out said, as they were rushing by me, "Oh, Marilyn, you're our nomination for Miss University of Colorado." I was barely able to integrate the words before I called to them… "Wait. Stop. What does that mean?" They were somewhat annoyed that I was delaying their dates but they came back. "It means you're our nomination for Miss University of Colorado! Every sorority, fraternity and dorm must submit a nomination. Congratulations!"

"But," I asked quickly, "What do I have to do?"

"Oh, you just have to appear in an evening gown." I could tell by the way they looked at each other when they said that, that there was more.

"And?"

"Well, you do have to do a talent number."

"*Talent*?" I was stunned. "What in the world would I do for talent?"

They shrugged and one of them said, "Oh, you'll think of something."

The other girl then dropped her eyes and tried to be casual about her next comment. "There is one more thing…" She knew me well enough to know how I was going to react to the last requirement. "You have to appear in a swimsuit."

I was beyond shy. I *never* showered with other girls in the shower room. I could never let anyone see my body. I was fine with a swimming suit at swim meets but on a runway? Never. And they knew that. "*I could never do that!*" I left no doubt in their minds that this was a "*never.*"

"You don't have to do it in front of an audience. They have group judging backstage before the Pageant begins. You just have to wear a swimsuit in front of six or seven people. C'mon, it's not a big deal."

I said, "No. I decline."

"You can't decline. The application has to be in by morning and we will be fined if we don't turn one in. The meeting is over. There is no way to vote again on someone else. C'mon, be a good sport."

There was nothing about this competition that appealed to me, but it became my new mission. I had played the piano well, even as a child, but I hadn't practiced in years. Trying to resurrect a piece as difficult as the one I played at my junior high school graduation would be impossible on such short notice. I could never play well enough to be the best pianist and no matter what I competed in, I needed to be the best.

I decided to play the organ. I knew how to play an organ and it sounded flashier and more difficult than it was. I asked the music department if I could schedule time to practice the organ because the competition was only two or three weeks away. I'm not sure when I found out this was the local pageant for the Miss America Pageant but it wouldn't have mattered as I had developed an ability to focus my attention like a laser beam. This skill had been honed by the night child. I could only concentrate on the challenge directly in front of me. I was so overwhelmed with anxiety and panic at the thought of competing at the University, I couldn't even *think* about what winning might mean…and I didn't really focus on winning.

I know that sounds incongruous with what I have said about the need to win, but I was so possessed by dread at the thought of wearing a swimsuit in front of seven people and playing the organ in front of an audience, that all of my available resources were consumed. It was unthinkable to have sheets of music in front of me where I could easily read the music. When playing from memory, if one finger forgot where to go, it was over. I couldn't improvise or "see" the music in my head. I would have to stand up like a six-year-old and say, "I forgot my piece." That was the terror that haunted me every single day and night.

The night of the Pageant, I told my family and my sorority sisters that if *one of them* showed up, I would walk off the stage. I also told Gary not to come. I didn't want anyone there that I knew. They knew I was serious and no one came. I was grateful for that.

I had more competition, by far, at the University of Colorado than I had at the state competition. Each sorority, fraternity and dorm sent their best candidates. Strikingly beautiful co-eds. Wonderful singers, dancers and pianists. I was the only organist (as I thought I would be) and therefore, the best.

I won. I, the quintessential tomboy, had won. It was late spring of my sophomore year. That night was the first time I had to face the fact that I had won the local pageant for the Miss America Pageant and that I was automatically entered in the Miss Colorado Pageant, held in July. Not again. How could I do that again? Only this time, the swimsuit competition would be in front of the entire audience. I would walk a runway. It was truly an overwhelming thought.

Even though I would urge people I knew to *not attend*, no one knew my feelings. I was presenting myself as smart and wholesome. Not beautiful, but attractive. Most importantly, I was a young woman of high morals and character. Respected. I didn't smoke. Or drink. Or sleep with boys. It would take years before I would understand that every time I stood up to perform or accept an honor, part of me was silently screaming, "If you really knew who I am, you would see how bad and ugly I am. I am not this person you are looking at. This is all show, I'm a fake." Trying to reconcile those screaming subconscious thoughts with the honors I was winning, was the fight of my life.

While preparing for the Miss Colorado Pageant, I was unable to focus on anything other than practicing the organ and visualizing myself walking down the runway in a swimsuit. I would have to visualize and visualize—see myself walking with pride, with dignity, in order to be able to get through it. Act as if it were true. I was the poster girl for knowing how to do that.

I don't remember too much about the Pageant except that when I went out to play my piece on the organ, the organ didn't work. Trying to stay composed and dignified was a challenge, but I think it was one of the reasons I won. Who knows how I won? I've always known that different judges would have chosen a different contestant.

The thought of competing in Atlantic City put me into extreme anxiety, although no one saw it. I always appeared in control; this-is-easy, no problem. The stress just continued to build like a pressure cooker.

As part of my Miss Colorado winnings, I had won sessions at a "charm school." I couldn't imagine anything worse, but I was required to go. The woman in charge had so much makeup on, I was concerned it would slowly slither down her face and stain her dress. She said the first order of business would be to pluck my eyebrows. I was trained to do as I was told. It's difficult for someone who didn't grow up in the '50s to understand that mentality. When the charm school woman began fawning over me, getting ready to pluck my eyebrows, I just knew I had to get out of there. She left for a second to go into her office and I got up and walked out. Walking out may not seem like a big deal but it was huge for me to challenge authority.

There was an article in the newspaper about it. "Should Miss Colorado Return to Charm School and Pluck Her Eyebrows?" I couldn't believe it. Radio stations were having call-ins. It was ridiculous.

I wore no makeup except lipstick. Not even during the competition. I set and combed my own hair, put on my lipstick and I was ready.

Nothing could have prepared me for my first glimpse of the Convention Hall in Atlantic City. The stage is the size of three standard basketball courts. The Hall seats 25,000 people. The runway starts at the stage and never ends. I couldn't *imagine* walking that long runway in a swimsuit and three-inch heels.

After rehearsals, other contestants would swim in the ocean, go shopping, wander the boardwalk, "pal around." I never made one friend during any pageant. I would go to my room to "center myself." Those were always the words I used. I can't believe how accurate they were. I had no understanding of my repressed memories of incest, no idea there was a night child and a day child. But that's *exactly* what I was doing, as I sat alone in my room "centering myself," trying to balance the two "selves" that lived within me. I would sit quietly with my eyes closed trying to calm myself. Then I would visualize again and again "pulling off" the next challenge. If my next event was playing the organ, I would see myself walking out on stage, seating myself, playing as if I were having the time of my life. I would play act who I wanted to be—how I wanted to present myself. It was not unusual for me to visualize this hundreds of times as I kept trying to center myself between the bad person and the ideal American girl. The shamed child was constantly pulling at me, inside, reminding me how unworthy I was. The outstanding athlete/student/outside activities/contestant was fighting to stay in the game. I never went anywhere but to rehearsals and back to my room. Alone. To center my "selves."

There are three nights of preliminary competitions. Each night a third of the girls perform in evening gown, swimsuit or talent. The next two nights they perform in the remaining categories. Wednesday night, the first night, was the easiest for me. Evening gown competition. All I had to do was walk the runway in the beautiful evening gown my father had purchased for me a year earlier for the Debutante Ball. Thursday night was a nightmare. Swimsuit. Walk down steps in three-inch heels, walk across a stage that never ends, parade and turn in front of the judges and then walk down a runway that stretches to New York City. Mother told me I had a beautiful back. I thought if I could just back in, I would win. My sister sent me a note, "Roses are red, violets are blue, flat chested girls can be beauty queens too." How could I possibly parade the body I hated so much in front of 25,000 people? There was only one way to get through it. "Act as if." I acted as if I were Miss America. I walked as I believed she would walk. It was play-acting but it worked. I was told no one had a better carriage on stage than I. I was told that I *looked* like a Miss America.

I was often asked if I had gone to Atlantic City hoping to win Miss America. My answer was the 100 percent truth. My goal was to not fall off the runway. (And to not forget my piece on the organ, but I kept that one to myself.) Winning was not my focus; surviving was.

Friday night was the night I had dreaded with all my being. Walking onto that vast stage, sitting at the organ, smiling as if I were having the time of my life while praying that every finger would remember where to go. It was the 24-hour nightmare I lived with. When I look at the video of the Pageant today, I marvel at the way I was able to smile at the audience, never watching the keyboard, looking as if I had never had more fun.

When I finished my organ piece without an error, it was, I knew, my greatest accomplishment. I had overcome enormous terror without anyone knowing. After the show, when my family came rushing into our suite, filled with joy over my performance, I was sobbing convulsively face down on the bed. Heaving, wrenching sobs. It stopped them cold. All of them went into a different room except one sister who came over to me, got on her knees, put her face near mine…"What? What? Why are you crying?"

I couldn't stop sobbing long enough to catch enough breath to answer her. The stress, the anxiety, the pressure had built to a boiling point. I just couldn't do it anymore. It was over. I had done it. It was a release of all I had held inside for so long. It is a kind of sobbing I would do often during my Miss America year.

I remember little about the rehearsal for the Saturday night television show. It would be the number one watched show of the year. (There was no Super Bowl yet). It was only the fourth year that the Pageant had been televised. All of America, literally, stayed home on Saturday night to watch *The Miss America Pageant*.

I paid no attention to the instructions during the Saturday rehearsal, about what a contestant should do if she won Miss America. All I knew is that I would never have to play the organ again. I felt an inexpressible relief.

No one knew who the final ten were until America learned during the first few minutes of the television show. When I was announced as one of the final ten, anguish overwhelmed me. I would have to play the organ again *in front of everyone I had ever known.* In front of 25,000 people in Convention Hall and fifty million people watching on television. What if my fingers forgot? That was my living nightmare. I would be completely humiliated. I couldn't do it. I just couldn't go through it again.

The two-hour show is a fog in my mind. I just remember that when I was crowned Miss America and began walking the runway, everyone stood to give me a standing ovation. When I got to the end of the runway, the music stopped. I couldn't remember what to do. Why hadn't I listened? Was there another music cue? Did I turn around immediately and walk back? I had no idea what to do so I just turned around and walked back as quickly as I could, trying to remain regal!

My family had been with me all week. The Pageant was well aware of the Van Derbur family. Mildred, my father's executive vice president, and her daughter, Miriam, were also in attendance, but they were seated apart from my family. Miriam is a year older than I. She was a brilliant pianist. She is the one who composed the arrangement, combining "Tea for Two" and "Tenderly," that I played in Atlantic City. She and Mildred had been a part of our lives for as long as I could remember.

In future years, I would learn how many tens of thousands of dollars per minute sponsors would have to pay extra, if the Pageant ran past midnight. Although I was completely unaware of time, we were coming up on the midnight hour. When I reached Burt Parks, he did something he had never done before. With the clock ticking, he called out, as only Burt Parks could, "The Van Derbur family. Where is the Van Derbur family?"

He frantically scanned the front section, where families of contestants were seated and he called out again, "Where is the Van Derbur family?" When he saw them (he had met all of us earlier in the week at the hotel), he said loudly, "There they are. Please, ladies and gentlemen, please open an aisle and let them through." The seconds continued to tick away as my family hurriedly walked down the aisle, in front of the full orchestra, to the side of the stage, up at least ten stairs and then across the vast stage to the center.

It was unprecedented. I would later be told that the Pageant wanted to show off the "ideal American family." Four sisters, two years apart. A beautiful, gracious mother. A handsome, charming, successful father. Burt introduced each sister, asked each a question and then turned to my mother. He asked her how she was feeling and she said something very telling about herself. She said, "This is every mother's dream." Well, not really.

It certainly wasn't my dream for my daughter, but it *was* my mother's dream. Soon after returning to Denver, she would begin modeling my Miss America gown (it fit her perfectly) in fashion shows and giving talks on, "What it is like to be the mother of Miss America." She was a polished public speaker and the audiences adored her.

When Burt turned to my father, he smiled warmly and proudly and said, "She's been a lovely girl all her life."

"There they are, America, the Van Derbur family."

Everyone I knew in Colorado had been watching the Pageant on television. D.D. told me later about his experience while watching. There was, of course, a two-hour difference between Atlantic City and Denver. So, as I was being crowned in Atlantic City, everyone in Denver was watching the opening of the show.

D.D. said, as soon as he saw I was one of the final ten, he dropped his eyes and uttered a prayer, "Please God, let this be." At that exact same time, a man in the control room in Denver's television station heard over the wire that I had been crowned and he had to make the decision whether or not to flash on the screen, "Marilyn has just been crowned Miss America," or let the Colorado television audience see what happened for themselves. He made, in my opinion, the wrong decision. The announcement was flashed just as D.D. was lifting his eyes from his most simple prayer, "Please God, let this be." D.D. said his mouth dropped open as he said, out loud, "Please God, not so fast!"

Larry's mother told me, years later, that when that announcement was made at the beginning of the show, Larry got up and walked out of the house. It was the only time in my life that he wasn't clapping and cheering for me. He believed I would be out of his life forever.

I was escorted to the Ball that night by the top West Point cadet, dressed in his "whites." He walked like he had a board up his back—as did I. What a perfect, stiff couple we were.

People commented on my Miss America posture. How regal I was. I wasn't regal, I was *rigid*. My physical rigidity, brought on by locking up my body so no one could get in, has been one of the most difficult and unrelenting long-term effects of incest. But my rigid, erect body was perfect for "the Miss America look."

I hadn't thought about what it would be like to be Miss America. My energies had been totally consumed by surviving the competition. I suddenly realized I wouldn't be going back to college. I wouldn't be song leader. That was good. I wouldn't have to figure out how to be a student governor. That was good. I wouldn't have to fulfill the other activities I had won or been appointed to. That was good. Nor would I ski for the University of Colorado's ski team or sing in the choir. I would miss those.

But the challenges ahead made those experiences seem like child's play. The night I won, I was told that the next morning, Sunday, there would be a huge press conference and then a police escort would take me to New York City, where I would appear on *The Steve Allen Show*. My "tour" would then begin. I would be in a different city almost daily. I would have a chaperone, who would literally never leave my side except to go to the bathroom. I would not see the Pageant people again for many weeks.

Lenora Slaughter was the Executive Director of the Miss America Pageant for 35 years. She was a tall, imposing, extremely empowered woman. Other than Larry's mother, who was empowered in a very different kind of way, I can never remember meeting or knowing a truly powerful woman. Again, remember, this is the '50s. Girls went to college to find a husband. Most girls didn't have careers. They became homemakers.

Miss Slaughter, almost single-handedly, made The Miss America Pageant into the largest scholarship foundation for women in the world, which it still is. It was her goal to be sure that young women had access to college educations. A participant can win a sizable scholarship without even winning the state title. Each year, as many as 35,000 young women enter their respective local pageants and win the best talent award or Miss Congeniality and win a $1,000, $5,000 or $10,000 scholarship. That's the major reason many girls enter two, three or four years in a row.

Even if I had needed a scholarship, I would never have entered again if I had lost. Nothing could ever make me endure again what was for me, a three-month nightmare. On the other hand, being Miss America opened every career door imaginable for me. You would never be reading this book if I hadn't been Miss America. I will always be grateful for the experience.

Before I went to sleep the night I won, I knew I was going to have to have a conversation with Miss Slaughter, the intimidating woman who ran everything. I so wanted to please her. I wanted to please *everyone*. (One of the nicest things about my life now is that I finally got over that need.) I *wanted* to tell her that I would do the best job I could possibly do, but I had to tell her, instead, that there was something I just could not, w*ould not* do. I found out that she would be riding in the limousine with me to New York City. That would be my chance. She would be with me through *The Steve Allen Show* on Sunday night. How to begin? I have no idea what we talked about for the first 30 minutes or so. I was just trying to find a way to say, "Oh, by the way, there is something I can't do…" I don't remember how I segued into it but I remember every single word of her response to me.

When I finally got the words out…"I cannot appear in a swimsuit in public. Ever again." She responded emphatically, "And you will never have to. You will never have to do *anything* you wouldn't feel comfortable doing as Marilyn Van Derbur." I believed her. I was right to believe her. There were a few times—not many—when I would say to a photographer or host, "I am not comfortable doing that." Period. End of the conversation. I knew I had her power and support behind me. I never again appeared in public in a swimsuit. I always felt it looked "cheap" to do that and I wasn't "cheap." I was a wholesome, moral, ethical young woman with as perfect a reputation as it was possible to have.

I have always felt strongly that the swimsuit competition should be dropped from the Pageant. My feelings have intensified as I have studied research on the reasons why fourth and fifth grade girls are on diets. Every day children get the message, "If you want to be popular and happy, you need to be thin." And so children, younger and younger, are developing eating disorders. Would it make any difference if The Miss America Pageant dropped swimsuit competition? Yes. Because every part of society needs to do everything possible to change the perception that thin means pretty.

I was amazed when I joined four other former Miss Americas on a network talk show several years ago. It never occurred to me that every one of them would vote for keeping swimsuit competition in the Pageant. One said, "I felt very proud of my body in my swimsuit." This isn't about how one young woman feels. This is about a very serious issue—the perception we give to young girls.

During the limousine ride, I learned that Miss Slaughter knew how to motivate. Surprisingly, motivational speaking was the career I would choose within a few years. She wasn't a "motivational speaker," but one-on-one, she knew exactly what to say to motivate me. She told me how she had struggled to find sponsors for the scholarships. She told me how hard she had worked in every single city, finding the right sponsor for the local and state pageants. After going into great detail, she "closed" by telling me that she wanted me to remember that when I arrived in a city, I *was* The Miss America Pageant. That everything she had worked for could be won or lost on how I was accepted. If I were still gracious after the 15th appearance that day (not unusual), people would love the Pageant. If I were cranky or temperamental, that would be the impression they would have of The Miss America Pageant. She said, "You *are* the Pageant, every time you walk out your door, to every person you meet you represent everything I have worked for."

I never forgot her words. On days when I was so tired I thought I would burst into tears, I remembered there was a higher purpose than my feelings. If I had the year to do over again, I couldn't have done a better job. It doesn't mean every day was perfect, but it does mean that it was the very best I was capable of doing.

My first huge test would come soon. Too soon. With police escorts, sirens blaring, traffic parting, we were driven right to the Waldorf

Astoria Hotel. My focus was on *The Steve Allen Show*. I had about three hours before I was due at the studio. As we were going to our rooms, Miss Slaughter said, "Dress as quickly as you can in your best dress. Come to the lobby quickly." I didn't even think to say "Why?" I just did as I was told. When I reached the lobby, she was waiting. She said, "Hurry, dear, they're waiting."

I said, "Who is waiting?" She said, "The National Mayor's Convention. You're going to address them." I said, "I am?" She said, "Yes."

I tried to control the intense anxiety that had instantly consumed me. Stunned, I said, "What should I say?" I will never forget her words, "Anything you want to, dear." It was assumed that I would be articulate, intelligent and gracious, once I had won the title. Trying not to sound as desperate as I felt, I said, "I don't think I can do this." As we walked into the ballroom, she said, "Of course you can, honey, you're Miss America."

I learned quickly. Very quickly. I got through that first speech by "acting as if." But what I learned was that the Pageant was never going to prep me. No help. No suggestions. Not even a critique after a talk. I was Miss America and I should know how to do this.

What was good about that (the *only* thing that was good about it) was that it *forced* me to develop ideas and a speaking style. The only thing I could think of, as an "ice breaker," at that first unexpected talk before every mayor in America, was a true experience during the week of competition. I had left my room, dressed in my beautiful, long, white evening gown, white gloves and white three-inch heels, taking great care to not wrinkle or touch anything. Since we walked to Convention Hall from our hotel, I would never have to sit in my dress; just stand until it was my time to go on stage.

As I was waiting for the elevator, a dignified, elderly lady walked out of her room with the ugliest bulldog I had ever seen. She said, "Oh, darling. You look beautiful. Good luck. You know, if you pet Mr. John (*obviously* her ugly dog), he will bring you luck." The thought of bending down to pet that dog with my spotless long white leather gloves and wrinkling my gown in the process, was inconceivable to me. She continued…"I come to the Pageant every year. You know, the last three girls who have petted Mr. John have won Miss America," and with that, I was on my knees, petting Mr. John.

Okay. It's not a side splitter but it was a way to ease my way into having nothing to say to these men and it was the beginning of my finding ways to use personal experiences as humor. You'll be glad to know I got better at it!

The other thing I learned is that my father was the only one I could turn to for help in giving speeches. In my adult years, I have heard hundreds of the best motivational speakers in America. Few have surpassed my father in being able to deliver a compelling, moving, "gotcha" message. His suggestions fit my style. That was critically important. A man could give me the best sports story in the world but it probably wouldn't fit my personality or my speaking style.

When I would arrive in a city, my host would meet me and hand me a list of events I would be expected to attend (and always be required to say "a few words"). Countless times, I would slip into a phone booth and call my father. His telephone operator would always find him for me. Instantly. My conversation would always begin the same way: "In a few minutes, I am going to address the Detroit Rotary Club and I thought we could *think together* about what I might say…"

My father would always have an idea, a story or a quote. One of the first quotes he gave me, when addressing service clubs, was "There's no end to the good a person can do if he doesn't care who gets the credit." It was a quote I could build on. (Looking back, it was ironic that when my father gave a quarter of a million dollars to the Boy Scouts in Denver, his name immediately went on the building.)

For a speech I gave to people who volunteered their time helping others, he gave me this story: "Phillips Brooks (a 1940's Billy Graham) was driving down the street one bitterly cold, snowy night when he saw a young paper boy standing on the corner selling newspapers. He had no hat. No gloves. No warm coat. As he bought all the boy's papers, he said, "Aren't you very cold?" And the boy replied, "I was sir, until you came along."

The power of one. The power of a simple act. I would take the quotes and stories my father gave me and integrate them into short speeches I would be asked to give.

One quote I never shared with an audience was one of his favorites, "I love humanity but I hate people."

My relationship with my father was complex. He was seldom at home and, when he was, he was disinterested in my activities or what was going on in my life, unless I was involved in something that he enjoyed, such as music or public speaking. I can never remember him calling me unless it was a business reason, and those calls were infrequent. Similarly, he never came to my home unless it was a holiday meal for all family members. Even then, everyone knew he would have preferred not being there. Somehow, I was able to overlook all the negatives and *only* see the positives.

As I got older, I went to extremes in my perception of him. I believed he was a great man, a wonderful father and the only person who would always be there for me. However, in my late 40's, when I voraciously read everything I could find on victim/perpetrator relationships, I found my relationship with my father during that time of my life was not unique.

Dr. Judith Herman addresses the victim/perpetrator relationship at length in her book, *Trauma and Recovery.* "As the victim is isolated, she becomes increasingly dependent on the perpetrator…The more frightened she is, the more she is tempted to cling to the one relationship that is permitted: the relationship with the perpetrator." (p. 81) "The repeated experience of terror and reprieve, especially within the isolated context of a love relationship, may result in a feeling of intense, almost worshipful dependence upon an all-powerful godlike authority. The victim may live in terror of his wrath, but she may also view him as the source of strength, guidance, and life itself. The relationship may take on an extraordinary quality of specialness…" (p. 92)

I know my chaperone wondered what I was doing on those long hours when we had cross-country flights. I didn't read or write. She saw me looking out the window or sitting with my eyes closed. I never told her but I was "centering myself." I had no idea what those words meant nor did I question them. I just knew that's what I had to do. It was almost like a meditation. In looking back over the feelings I couldn't identify, it was as if a tug of war was going in inside my head. A constant struggle to keep the day child in control. But the night child would always be there, yelling in every cell of my being, "People think you are Miss America but I know you are bad and ugly and I hate you. You promised if I would stay in the room and take his entering every part of my being, you would come back for me, but you aren't coming back for me. I hate you and I will make you miserable every day of your life for abandoning me."

In retrospect, I truly believe that is the kind of conversation that was going on, subconsciously, inside me. The night child was right. When I would learn about her, when she would surface from my repressed memories, I would hate her more than I would ever hate anything or anyone in my life. She would torment me through body pain and acute anxiety for having abandoned her.

Rage was starting to surface, manifesting itself in my body. My eyes would become engorged with blood. I wouldn't have "pink eye," the whites would turn blood red. It would hurt to open them.

One day, as Miss America, I was to be photographed for the cover of *McCall's* magazine. The Pageant was thrilled! It was the first time a Miss America would appear on a cover of a major magazine. After I was completely ready for the "shoot," the photographer got under a black hood, looked at me through the lens, and then asked the sponsor VIPs to step into a different room, and the "shoot" was cancelled. The white parts of my eyes—the inside areas–were engorged with blood. There was no possible way I could be photographed. Because the magazine was on a deadline and I was booked solid, it was over.

My blood-red eyes would be a constant source of trouble and pain for me for decades. I would go from eye doctor to eye doctor. Each would say the same thing. We can find nothing wrong and there is nothing we can give you to stop the redness.

In my 40's, I would be transfixed when I read books about the mind-body connection. Dr. Alexander Lowen wrote about blood-red eyes and the cause: buried, subconscious anger. The eyes would not clear until the anger was released. Only after my rage (anger wouldn't touch the feelings I had) surfaced, when I was 48 and 49 years old, did my eyes clear. What Dr. Lowen said had been 100 percent true for me. I have never had blood-red eyes since I worked through my rage.

Other parts of my body were erupting. I was developing a scaling on my scalp that wasn't anything like dandruff. Dandruff would have been a pleasure. It was a tough, disgusting looking crusting. For reasons I didn't understand, I would never allow a boy I was dating to touch my hair. My scalp condition made certain no one would ever *want* to touch it. And yet my hair looked perfect. It had to. My hair was central to my self-concept. When I began television work, I pleaded to do my own hair. It never occurred to me that this fetish was, at best, bizarre. I was in my late 40's when childhood memories would give me the insight as to the cause of my hair obsession. It would be more than 25 years before my life would begin to make sense.

Shortly after I was crowned, I was scheduled for an all day photography session with The Toni Company—one of the five sponsors of the Miss America Pageant. I did my own hair! They seemed pleased. I changed outfits, hundreds of times, at least that's the way it seemed. The photographer must have taken, literally, 500 to 600 pictures, which was not uncommon for an all day session.

The Toni Company would use the pictures in a variety of ways but they were looking, most particularly, for one special "shot" to use as their main picture in a major promotional campaign. Toward the end of the day, the very special lady who was the Toni representative said to me, "Do you feel we have enough pictures? Do you feel good about the session?" I said, "I think we have the picture!" I couldn't *imagine* them wanting to take any more! She continued, "Then I'm wondering if you would allow a hairdresser to pull your hair back, away from your face, for a few more pictures." No. I wasn't comfortable with that *at all* but what could I say? She had certainly let me have it my way for 98 percent of the day. "Okay." Just having the hairdresser touch my hair was very unsettling but I focused myself and tried to not think about it. I was good at that.

When I sat down for the photographer, he positioned me in a very different way and then said, "For these few shots, I'm going to ask you to not smile." I could never remember not smiling my wholesome all-American smile for a picture. Not smile? I really didn't know what to do with my face or what expression he was after but soon it was over. The Toni representative told me she would have the proofs back in a week or so and that the next time I was in New York City she would show them to me.

Two weeks later, she arrived at my hotel with about 15 of the pictures that the Toni Company and the photographer had selected. With great excitement and pride she said, "This is the one we have chosen for the major campaign. We are thrilled with it. It is *exactly* what we wanted." With a huge smile on her face, she handed me the picture. I burst into sobs. Not tears. Sobs. Heaving sobs. It was humiliating. I was so embarrassed. I had no idea why just one glance at that picture would set off such incredible emotion. I was crying too hard to even respond to her when she said, "What's wrong? What did I do? Marilyn?" She was stunned. Absolutely stunned. All I could say was, "Please don't use that picture. Please don't use that picture."

And all she could respond with was, "We won't. Of course we won't. I promise we won't." We never talked about it again.

It was not the wholesome, smiling, all-American girl I was. I perceived that the picture had sexual overtones, although no one else did. It could never be used. I fought so hard for things and never knew why. I will never forget her kindness that day. She left, I'm sure, wondering what in the world had gone on but she was so very compassionate. Whatever it was, she knew she didn't want to go there. They never showed that picture again. They used the smiling cheerleader type picture that photographers would take thousands of times during that year.

In some cities, I would give as many as ten to fifteen talks a day. I would speak at the local Rotary Club, the Women's Club, the college function, etc. Each and every talk brought on its own panic attack. It never let up. I could never get away from it.

I would spend hours going over and over what I would say. Every word would be carefully selected. My need to be perfect compelled me to over prepare. I would visualize every aspect of a speaking situation. I would be seated at a head table with four men on either side of me and about 400 men in the audience (women didn't belong to Rotary in those days). After I visualized the president standing up to introduce me, I saw myself rise, take the microphone out of the holder, acknowledge people, tell my opening, hopefully funny, personal story and then go into my message. By the time I arrived in a city, it would be a rare occasion that I had not seen myself hundreds of times, in my mind.

I heard, recently, on a "most important people of the millennium" television show that Abraham Lincoln did the same thing. Not bad company to be in, but I pity him if he lived with the same panic attacks I endured.

One of the reasons I loved being Miss America was because I often went into children's hospitals to talk with sick, even dying children. Meeting a Miss America in the 1950's was like meeting Cinderella or a Fairy Godmother. They would be told, days in advance, that I would be coming to see them. When I would walk into a ward, their eyes were wide open with awe and joy. They were meeting a *Miss America!* Nothing I did during that year brought me greater satisfaction than bringing smiles to the faces of lonely, isolated children. If a nurse had been unable to get a child to swallow medicine, I could have a conversation with that child and within minutes, the child would swallow the medicine. I could bring a smile to a face that hadn't smiled in weeks. The power of the crown with children was magical. I loved and cherished every second of those visits.

There were fresh flowers in my hotel room, always. Usually several dozen red roses. If I were going to be in a parade, I would take the roses and put them next to me. When I would see a little girl, five or six or seven—especially one who was probably never told she was pretty—I would ask the person driving my float to stop for a second. I would take one red rose and motion for the child to come to the float. Then I would hand her the rose. Sometimes I would say, "I saved this rose for someone very special. The minute I saw you, I knew it was for you." The look on each child's face is still a memory I cherish.

One of my first appearances in the fall was in Green Bay, Wisconsin, for the grand opening of its magnificent new football stadium. When we arrived, I asked the host, as I always did, "What *exactly* will I be asked to do?" He said, "Nothing. Absolutely nothing. You will just enjoy the game. The announcer will mention that we have Miss America here. The most would be your standing to wave and be recognized in the stands."

I couldn't believe it. Finally! An event where I didn't have to perform. I could have two hours to not stress out. I wasn't a great fan of football but I enjoyed the first half. Just as it was drawing to a close, I saw huge cables being readied. There was a scramble of activity on the field. It looked as if they were going to set up something that looked like a bandstand. Chairs. Podium. Microphone. I was watching with great interest when I heard, "Miss America! Miss America! *This way, Miss America.*"

Well, there was no doubt they were calling me! I wondered if I could duck under the seat in front of me. I knew instantly what was happening. I was going out onto the center of the field to sit on that stand.

There wasn't time to even think. Apparently, my original host had no idea what the plans were for half-time. I found myself stumbling over huge television cables in my high heels, climbing the three steps to the platform, and being introduced to the Vice President of the United States, Richard M. Nixon. I was seated next to him. I was quickly instructed that I would "say a few words" after Vice President Nixon spoke to *America* on network television at the opening ceremonies of the Green Gay Packers new stadium…and, of course, in front of the 40, 50, or 60 thousand (who counts at a time like this) football fans who were seated in the stands.

No one warned me that my voice would echo back to me after a slight delay. So when I said, "I'm so happy…" and I was trying to think of my next words, I heard coming back at me through an incredibly loud sound system, "I'm so happy…" It was impossible to concentrate with my voice coming back at me saying the words I had just said.

One of the great lessons I learned that year is that I could do so much more than I ever dreamed I could. Each time I would be saying inside my head, as a mantra, "I can't do that…I just *can't do that,*" but my apprehension wasn't their problem. I would fly into a city for what would be the biggest parade or conference or banquet this chairperson had ever chaired. The last thing they needed to think about was that their "star" was having an anxiety attack. So I would stand up before 500 or 10,000 people and perform. No one would know but me.

Once in awhile a college friend would track me down and I could tell by our conversation that she believed this was a year of pure joy and fun for me. It was a year of incredible loneliness, and extreme stress, which were exacerbated by not having anyone with whom to share my feelings. However, it was also a year filled with feelings of pride as I met and conquered each challenge.

My homecoming in Denver was the most memorable part of that incredible year. Denver went all out. There was a huge reception at the airport, a large parade with thousands standing on the sidewalks to watch and wave, and, of course, a press conference. The press conference was so large it had to be held in a hotel ballroom. All I saw was a sea of mostly men and what seemed like hundreds of cameras and exploding flash bulbs.

I wanted to get off to a good start. I looked over the group of reporters carefully before calling on the first person. I called on a young man—probably in his early twenties—in the back. His question is embedded in my memory. "Miss Van Derbur!" (That was my first clue. The way he said, *Miss VAN DERBUR*—kind of smugly.) "As I recall, you were nominated for Queen of Regis College last year. You couldn't even win Queen of Regis. How can you be Miss America?" What an opener. I wanted to respond, "What kind of mean pills do you take each day to make you so charming?" But, instead, I said, "I'm just grateful the judges at Regis weren't the judges in Atlantic City" and moved on as quickly as I could to the next question. The rest of the reporters were, fortunately, much more kind.

The parade, the press conference and at least six other events were held on that first day, Friday. Friday night was the big night—not only for my family and me but also for the Pageant. I had been asked to be on the Edward R. Murrow's, *Person to Person* show. A first for any Miss America to be given such an honor, such an incredible showcase.

To my horror, I learned later, the Pageant almost declined my participation in the show because Nat King Cole was the feature for the other half-hour of the show. Miss Slaughter (a Southerner) didn't want me to be on with a "Negro." Fortunately, the show went as scheduled and fortunately, times have changed for the Pageant.

The show was live from our home. The producer asked if I would play the organ—just a short selection—something different from what I had played in Atlantic City. I was too young and stupid to say "No. I really am not prepared to do that." I said, "Okay." It was the wrong answer. I only knew the piece I had played in Atlantic City. I had rehearsed it hundreds of times. I hadn't practiced anything else. How could I prepare another piece in a few hours?

Thursday night, the night before the show, the night of my arrival, I sat down at the organ and began practicing a new piece. I was exhausted. I was making mistakes. There wasn't time. It was almost midnight. I was alone downstairs when suddenly I just threw myself on the sofa and cried. One of my sisters came downstairs to comfort me. "What?" "I just can't do it. It's just too much. I just can't."

The next night, in our living room, I would play the lullaby, perfectly, dedicated to one of my sisters who was expecting her first child momentarily. The interview then continued in the basement, in the recreation room. My father played a few notes on our player piano and then the four of us sang harmony together, as we had as children. The director had put my very pregnant sister behind the couch so you couldn't see her bulging stomach. For those of you who were growing up in the '80s and '90s, this will seem inconceivable but being pregnant was not allowed on television in the '50s.

Mr. Murrow and my father were Kappa Sigma fraternity brothers and had known one another. Mr. Murrow opened with, "Good evening, brother Van" and my father answered with, "Good evening, brother

Ed." We were off and running. The show was a hit.

The next day, Saturday, there were 22 events planned. Twenty-two! The last event of that very long day was being presented at the end of the Homecoming special musical at the University of Colorado. They were very excited about presenting their own Miss America!

There was no time and no need, I thought, for any rehearsal. I arrived barely in time to be "presented." It was about 11 p.m. I was wearing my Miss America gown, the crown, three-inch heels, long white leather gloves, and the long red robe that trailed behind me.

When I was rushed backstage, I was shown a tall and obviously newly-constructed-for-the-occasion white staircase. About 15 very steep steps. No hand railing. As they were trying to rush me to the top step, I said, "Who is my escort?"

Someone quickly said, "There wasn't anyone important enough to escort you down the steps. Just walk down alone. The curtain will open, The Modern Choir will begin singing, 'Here she is…Miss America…' and the second they start, you will begin a slow walk down the steps."

He had no more than shouted all that to me when I heard the drum roll. I had no choice. I was beyond exhaustion. I held myself proud and tall, the way I always felt a Miss America should look, the curtain opened, the crowd went crazy clapping, the choir began to sing, I began my descent in front of just about everyone I ever knew. It was my moment in front of all my family and friends.

I don't know where the second step was but it wasn't where I thought it was or maybe my knees just buckled from the sheer exhaustion of it all. They weren't standard steps. They were very steep and narrow. Without actually going down face first, I somehow managed to stumble down the steps and land upright.

The crowd breathed in as if it were one person—and then gave a huge sigh when I landed upright. Then more applause. I was so embarrassed. Mortified. My father was the first one to come backstage. He said, "Well, Squirt, now everyone knows you're still just plain Marilyn." Wonderful. Not exactly what I needed to hear, but the truth!+

He might have still called me "Squirt," but everything changed the night I was crowned Miss America. Gwen, "the Countess," would forevermore be known as "Miss America's sister," and "Van," master and king of his world would be "Marilyn's father." *And there would never be anything I could do about that.*

My father seemed very proud of his new moniker. I would be stunned in the years to come as to what the ramifications would be for Gwen, having been demoted from "the Countess" to "Marilyn's sister." One of my first glimpses came after my father died. I was 47. Gwen was the executor of his estate. She was going through all of his papers, files, and rooms of "stuff." One day when she was in my father's office, she called me and said, "He had boxes of articles from your Miss America year…from all over the country." (He had many contacts nationwide because of the many national offices he had held.)

I said, "I'm so excited. I kept absolutely nothing from that year. I didn't even see most of the articles because I was in and out of town before the newspaper was out." Gwen never missed a beat as she replied, "I destroyed them." I was so stunned I didn't know what to say. I could almost understand why she had destroyed all the articles. It had to be difficult. My sisters had lives of their own and yet they were there when I won Miss America; they were in Las Vegas when I appeared at the Flamingo Hotel; back in Denver for the Homecoming festivities and the Edward R. Murrow *Person to Person Show* and back in Atlantic City when I was the outgoing Miss America. I'm sure it was disruptive and, for Gwen, who had always been "the chosen one," hard to involuntarily take a back seat when she had had always had the entire front seat. Although I was extremely disappointed she destroyed everything, I had some understanding of what her feelings were and that they were most probably subconscious feelings. The fact that she felt she needed to *tell me* about the boxes of articles and what she had done with them, gave me pause. Sibling relationships can be difficult, even under the best circumstances.

Ours, I would learn as the years passed, would be exceedingly complex. I would find myself turning to Gwen when my life shut down and she was there for me every single time. She played a critically important role in my healing process. But, unfortunately, there would be other very painful aspects to our relationship.

Almost every day during that year, I wondered how other young women had survived their years as Miss America. The pressure. The strain. I remembered Marion McKnight, who had crowned me. She would walk into a room as Miss America and say, "Hi, y'all," in her beautifully low, very southern drawl and people would almost swoon. She didn't have to give "a speech." She was just herself. She said it wasn't difficult for her. She would just say "a few words" and sit down.

I couldn't do that. I had to give the best speech they had ever heard. I had to "leave them with something to think about." I had to motivate them. Oh, what a nightmare of pressure I put on myself, trying so hard to balance the total unworthiness I felt deep inside with my new position. I was having the year others would dream of, but I was so preoccupied with dread, I couldn't enjoy it.

I called my father at least 10 times during that year when I felt overwhelmed by speeches I was asked to give on a moment's notice. As I look back, there really wasn't another person who could have filled that vacuum for me. I know that you, the reader, may find my relationship with my father to be inconceivable. One of the reasons writing this book was so important to me is because most traumatized children have complex relationships with their torturers, especially if they are their mothers or fathers. I hope to shed light on how and why these incomprehensible relationships evolve. They are common and usually very misunderstood.

The Pageant officials fell instantly in love with my mother, as everyone did. They asked her if she would consider being my chaperone for a few weeks throughout the year, to give my chaperone, Peg, a much-needed rest. They had never asked a mother to fill in before. The schedule was grueling. Every day. Every night. Dress up. Change outfits. Pack. Dash to the airport. Arrive. Check into a hotel. Beg for an iron. Unpack.

There were three main reasons for a Miss America to have a chaperone. The most important, in looking back over that year, was to keep her safe. Safe from lecherous men. I wouldn't truly understand how important that was until I moved to and worked in New York City in my early 20's. It was a problem that would send me, fairly quickly, into motivational speaking, where I would work for myself—never for a man.

As I look back, my Miss America year was the only safe year of my life—until I married Larry at age 26. There was no father invading my body; no business executive knocking on my hotel door. I never really understood how cherished Peg should have been for protecting me from the nightmarish situations I had faced in my childhood and I would soon face again when I moved to New York.

I didn't have one uncomfortable situation with a man as Miss America and no tabloid could print a story about a Miss America being involved with another celebrity because everyone knew her chaperone was *never* apart from her. Peg's job was also to be sure the arrangements were right. She kept the airline tickets, checked us into the hotels, etc. Another important job was to protect Miss America from overzealous program chairpersons who would have every second of my time planned, if allowed to do so.

Sometimes a schedule would be so tight there would be no time to go to the bathroom. It happened often. I remember being rushed from a luncheon to a parade where I was to sit on a float and smile and wave for almost three hours. I had to go to the bathroom. As I was being almost pushed out of the hotel, I said, "I really have to go to the bathroom." The program chairman said, "I'm sorry. There isn't time. The parade is ready to begin." That's when Peg stepped in and said firmly, but always sweetly, "She is going to the bathroom."

When Peg took a well-deserved vacation, Mother became my chaperone. She was incapable of protecting me, even in simple ways. Her need to please everyone superceded any compassion she should have felt for the demands of the daily schedule. She couldn't have been more exploitive of me. One night, late, we arrived in Seattle—the press and a group of people were waiting on the tarmac (there were no jet ways in those days.)

When Mother and I deplaned, many pictures were taken and then the program chairman handed Mother an outline of the next day's activities. He said, "Mrs. Van Derbur, I hope you can help me. We have a 7 a.m. breakfast, an 8 a.m. breakfast and a 9 a.m. breakfast—all are located within a block or two of each other. Marilyn will just say a few words and then we will move onto the next breakfast. (I glanced at the page to see the rest of the day similarly booked—through the 10 p.m. news.) He continued, "There was just one group we couldn't work into the schedule. I hope you will agree to what I have done. I scheduled a 6 a.m. breakfast right in your hotel. All Marilyn needs to do is just "pop in" and say a few words. Would that be okay?" My mother was supposed to say, "Are you kidding me? What do you think she is, a robot? *No one* could survive this schedule. No. She will *not* attend a 6 a.m. breakfast." That's what Peg would have said (in nicer words). My mother said, "Of course we'll be there. That will be fine."

At the parade that afternoon, I smiled and waved for over two hours. When the parade broke, I was to have 30 minutes in my room to change out of my evening gown and get ready for the next event. Mother's job was to facilitate my getting through the crowd of people that gathered wherever I was. Instead, Mother said, "Marilyn—wave to that boy. Here—these people want autographs." My insides were screaming, "*Of course* they want autographs. I've been doing that most of the day. Happily. Graciously. But I can't do it *now*. I'm ready to drop on my face. I need to change clothes. Can't you see that I am exhausted?"

Mother never met a fan she didn't love and her focus was on them, always. Never on helping me carve out a few minutes to think or change or rest. I couldn't tell the Pageant people that she wasn't doing what she was supposed to be doing. Hosts sent letters raving about my mother. How precious she was. How helpful she was. And she was. To them. I longed for her to express any compassion for the pressure of fifteen appearances in one day.

It was my father I would turn to for help and support. One night in late August, I knew that it was time for my most important call to him. I was in Detroit, appearing in a huge parade extravaganza for General Motors, with Pat Boone and other celebrities. As the floats would go down the street, I would play the organ on my wiggly float and Pat Boone would sing on his. It was late when I finally got back to my room that night. No matter how tired I was, I knew this was the night to make the call. In a few days, I would be returning to Atlantic City. The year was almost over. As I sat in my hotel room, all I could think about was the one more huge, terrifying, panic-attack-initiating-challenge that remained before me. My farewell talk. Just prior to crowning the new Miss America, I would give a three-minute talk. Whatever I wanted to say. No help from the Pageant. No hints. In front of 25,000 people in Convention Hall and 85 million people on television, I would give my final talk.

Three minutes may not seem like a long time. Unless you are in pain. Then it can be an eternity. Or unless you are standing in front of every person you have ever known or met, with no teleprompter, just a newly memorized talk coming out of a terrorized 21-year-old, trying to survive the ever-present, unbelievable pressure.

The only person I could turn to was my father. On his private line. No one had ever been allowed to call him on his private home phone except Mildred. When I became Miss America, I was given permission during that year only.

He picked up immediately. "Hi. It's Marilyn. I'm in Detroit. Huge anniversary celebration for General Motors. Long day. Anyway, I was wondering if…we…could…think…together…about what I will say during my farewell talk."

I had my pencil poised and ready to write. He knew this was coming and I knew he would have a gem for me…a thought to build on or a perfect story. I was not prepared for his response. I felt my stomach drop out of my body when he said, "This one is yours. Only you can say what this year has meant to you. You'll know what to say." He stopped. He was finished. I couldn't breathe or think. The silence had sucked all of the air out of me. I wanted to plead, "Please. I can't do this alone. Eighty five million people will be watching. *Please help me.*" But I had too much pride. So I said, "Yeah. You're right. I can do it. Well, have a good night. See you next week (in Atlantic City)."

I put down the phone and felt as if I had been completely abandoned. I had counted on him. I had depended on him. I was known as the finest speaker the Pageant had ever had. (A cocker spaniel could have had that distinction if she had worked as hard on her speeches as I did.) Now what was I going to do? What in the world would I say? I felt scared and alone. Really alone. There was no one else I could turn to. I slowly climbed into bed, turned the light off and tried to go to sleep. My mind started racing. Within a few minutes, I turned the light back on, grabbed the pencil and paper I had readied for my father's thoughts and quickly wrote my speech. I never changed one word. It was exactly three minutes and it was as good a talk as I could have given. It was *exactly* what I had wanted to say.

My father knew when to help me and he knew when it was time to pull the crutches away…and I walked, as he knew I would. My incest memories were still repressed, deep within my soul. I loved my father. I adored my father. Even after the incest memories surfaced, with all the crazy, mixed up feelings of rage, humiliation and hopelessness I would have to deal with—a part of me would still love my father until I was 56.

Something I had not thought about during my Miss America year was that, when I returned to Colorado, I was financially independent. At age 21. By the time I had paid all the taxes, given gifts to my sisters, etc. I had $50,000 cash to put into a trust. In addition, the rest of my education was pre-paid. The Pageant is a non-profit. It never takes one cent from what a Miss America earns. She keeps every penny.

My Miss America year ended with a triumphant walk down the runway. The 25,000 people stood, again, to give me a standing ovation. I felt tremendous pride as I walked the runway for the last time. I had given every minute of that year my very best effort. It was a feeling I will never forget, knowing I had overcome huge obstacles and not only survived, but thrived. The year also ended with feelings of profound respect and gratitude for the Miss America Pageant organization.

I was ready to go back to the University of Colorado and be a college student again. So ready. But would the University be ready for me?

The Toni Company wanted to use
this picture in its publicity campaign.
I broke into sobs when I saw it but had
no understanding why I had this reaction.

As television hostess for *The Miss America Pageant*, I look statuesque. Actually, my body felt as tight as piano wire. What seemed appropriate posture, was, in truth, a body imprisoned by incest.

My walk down the runway;
I was twenty years old.

After several hours of taking my
picture, the photographer asked
if he could take "just a few more"
with my hair pulled back.
This became my official
picture as Miss Colorado.

I was a guest host on
Candid Camera for ten shows.

Singing with Burt Parks, on stage
at *The Miss America Pageant*.

I was one of twelve college girls
invited to be in the first group
of debutantes in Denver. I am
in the center; Gwen is on the far right.

I developed severe ulcers as a
teenager. My doctor told me
to drink malted milks, which I did,
as you can see! My father and me
at the Debutante Ball.

For two weeks, I was the opening act for
comedian Allen King at the Flamingo Hotel.
No one gave me advice on what I should say.
I was twenty years old. My family was there
on opening night.

My father and me when I was in high school. My memories of incest were repressed, and I thought he was the most wonderful father.

Chapter 4 – Running From Love

No one had ever been happier than I was to return to the University of Colorado. I was going to be "just another co-ed" again.

I hadn't counted on photographers following me to class as I tried to blend in, nor had I anticipated what happened at the first football game. I was seated in the middle of the 9th or 10th row. Within minutes, I glanced toward the aisles and saw people lining up for an autograph. It had been comfortable and easy for me, as Miss America, to sign and smile. It was embarrassing when I tried to return to my former life.

People had wondered if it would be difficult for me to return to college. Had I changed? What had changed was *how people responded to me.* But all in all, it was an easy transition. Larry was in law school and I was dating Gary much more seriously. I had no idea why I was drawing farther and farther away from Larry.

I asked my mother to tell anyone who tried to reach me that I was back in college. Meaning, please don't call me. I had been settled in for only a few weeks when my mother called, "An advertising agency called today. They want to talk to you about being a possible television spokeswoman for AT&T." It was a short conversation. I said, "Please tell them 'thanks but no thanks.'"

That night, my father called. "I want you to rethink this. *AT&T* is calling. They have never had a spokes*woman* before. This is one of the most prestigious accounts in America. All they are asking is that you fly to Hollywood over Christmas break and do a simple television audition." My response was swift, "We are all going skiing in Aspen." My father countered, "I really think you should do this." So I did. When AT&T offered the television spokeswoman job to me, I told them that it was important to me to finish college. I had two more years. They told me that wasn't a problem; they would work around my schedule.

Television was still very new in the late 1950s. There were only three channels: NBC, CBS and ABC. *The Bell Telephone Hour* was one of the highest rated shows on television. It was strange to sit with my sorority sisters in the huge living room of the Pi Phi house and see my AT&T commercials. I was living in two different worlds.

My day child and my night child were also living in two different worlds. While reading a magazine, I saw a horrid picture of an Asian man being shot by a firing squad. It was taken at the exact second the bullets entered his body. His face was a mixture of terror and pain. I cut it out and put it on my mirror so I would remember that everyone wasn't as happy as I.

During the second semester, my ever-present need to stay busy drove me to audition for, and perform in, *Kiss Me Kate,* at our Denver Civic Theater. I drove from Boulder to Denver every other night for 6 weeks. The director gave me the part of Bianca, the wench. It required singing solos and kissing the young man who played my beau. He was shorter than I and his nervousness was obvious. He told me later that he had to have several drinks before each show, knowing he was going to kiss Miss America onstage. I didn't drink but I was easily as nervous as he, just being on stage performing.

Opening night, Larry and his family were seated in the first row. Just before the curtain opened, I ran to the bathroom, threw up, and the show began! Stage fright would not have touched how I felt before every show. How did I do that? Go to classes and then drive from Boulder to Denver for a performance and then back to Boulder. It was easy. Easier, I would learn in the years to come, than trying to deal with repressed memories and feelings. Much easier.

During the summer, I traveled from city to city, introducing AT&T's Princess phone. One of my jobs was to address installer/repairmen in the garages at 7 a.m. These men had just begun to sell phones while doing repairs, and my job was to motivate them.

I would either address the top salesmen or the least successful group. I was never told which was which but I began to discern the difference instantly. Within sixty *seconds* of meeting the supervisor I knew. If he were outgoing and positive, these would be the "winners." If he were brusque or negative, I would be about to meet the "losers." It all filtered down from the top.

When, many years later, I began addressing high school students nationwide, it would be the same thing. A positive, energetic high school principal meant a respectful and enthusiastic assembly. With a negative "I told you to shut up" kind of principal, you can imagine what I faced in the assembly!

When I graduated from college with Phi Beta Kappa honors, I had no idea what to do. Who was I? Was I a college graduate looking for a job? What job? My major was English Literature, which qualified me for zilch. Or was I a former Miss America who belonged in television or "show biz." I had been offered a seven-year movie contract but I knew I didn't want to do *that*. Going into the movies wouldn't bring me the respect I was driven to achieve. Since my only job was centered in New York City with AT&T, I decided to move there. Lendy Firestone, my college roommate, was now living in New York and she suggested we live together. She was full of fun and I felt very comfortable with her.

I was a guest host on ten *Candid Camera* Shows and a panelist on *To Tell The Truth*. I was a television host for the opening of the World's Fair and *The Miss America Pageant*, and the Cotton Bowl and Thanksgiving Parades. But the biggest night of my professional life was when I was the host of *The Bell Telephone Hour* for AT&T's huge anniversary extravaganza. Live. No second takes. No teleprompter (not in use yet). Every word was memorized. I would appear in an elegant evening gown and weave the show together as some of the finest musicians in the world gathered to perform for this major television event.

A few minutes before airtime, as I was debating whether or not I could keep from throwing up, the producer ran out to give me a message, "The entire show rests on you. Good luck." Then the floor manager began the countdown, "five…four…" and with no one to prompt me with lines if my memory shorted out, the show began. With only NBC, CBS and ABC available for viewing, an audience of millions was a given.

The show was everything anyone had hoped for. There was jubilation in the studio. I went back to my apartment and I could have written the song, "Is That All There Is?" I felt so empty. So alone.

As spokeswoman for AT&T, I did all their commercials. I was always eager to be the best and to please everyone. Perhaps that's why what happened during my third year was so perplexing to them—and to me. The Princess phone was being introduced as an additional phone for the bedroom. My "story board" for the commercial, showed me making a phone call, while sitting on the bed. As we prepared for that scene, my wardrobe assistant handed me a negligee covered by a lovely, feminine, filmy bathrobe. There was nothing "sexy" about the outfit per se, but I took one look at it and said, "I can't wear that." (I had assumed I would be in a dress.)

She left the room and in seconds there was a knock at the door. The director asked if he could speak with me. He said I would have to wear the negligee and robe. This was a bedroom scene for a bedroom phone. I said, "I know it is and I'm sorry, but I cannot wear that." He said, "This is not really negotiable. Don't you like it?" I said, "I cannot wear a negligee and robe. Only a dress." He left.

The wardrobe woman came back and said everyone was having a "hissy." They had to begin filming and I had to wear that outfit. I was hired talent and my job was to wear what I was told to wear. I couldn't articulate why I couldn't wear it. I just couldn't. Period. I had no understanding of what being in a bedroom, dressed in a negligee (even though it wasn't revealing) symbolized to me. It was so out of character for me to have the power to take a stand. It wasn't anything I was trying to analyze. I just knew that I could not, would not, wear it. The advertising agency called the executive offices of AT&T and soon an executive from AT&T arrived. He told me the same thing. I would have to wear it. I responded in the same way, "I'm sorry. I just can't."

It turned into a very difficult situation. I had absolutely no idea what was driving my adamant stance about the bedroom scene, but, ultimately, I wore a dress.

I had been told why AT&T had plucked me right out of the college classroom for this most prestigious job. An executive vice president of AT&T, Mr. Ryan, had been watching the night I gave my Miss America farewell address on Saturday night. On Monday morning, he called the ad agency and said, "Hire that girl."

I had met him on several occasions. I would see him again when we filmed on location at Disneyland in Anaheim, California.

Filming even one commercial was always an all day process. Twelve-hour days were not unusual and our first day on the set was to be no exception. Mr. Ryan had flown in from New York to be there. It was unprecedented to have an executive vice president attend an all day "shoot" but I didn't think a thing about it. Nor did I wonder why he was still there at 6:30 p.m. as we were winding down.

I was to have dinner with David, a young man I knew from California. I called the second we finished filming to tell him I was on my way to the hotel and he could pick me up in about 30 minutes.

As I was gathering my clothes and small overnight suitcase, Mr. Ryan told me he would escort me back to the hotel. As we pulled up to the hotel and I prepared to jump out, he quickly parked and told me he would help me with my things. As we approached my room, I fumbled for the key as he held my clothes. I unlocked the door and reached for my clothes as he pushed right by me into my room. I didn't have to be a rocket scientist to know what was about to happen. Mr. Ryan looked very much like my father and he was about the same age. He quickly threw the clothes on my bed and came straight at me. It happened so fast. He had his arms around me and was trying to kiss me. I was pushing him away as forcefully as I could. He said, "Just one kiss. Just one kiss," as he pushed me toward the bed.

The phone rang. I lunged for it. It was David, he was in the lobby. I said, "I'm ready. Please come quickly. Room 1102."

It was over. Mr. Ryan knew he would have to leave—and quickly. I was so shaken when David arrived, I could hardly talk. David held me gently as I poured out what had happened. It was a traumatic experience for me. I had no way of knowing that what would have been a difficult experience for any young woman, was greatly intensified by my still repressed past and Mr. Ryan's strong resemblance to my father.

I learned later that my director knew exactly what was about to happen when he heard Mr. Ryan ask to drive me back to the hotel. I told him it was unconscionable that he didn't warn me. We had become friends and I considered his "looking the other way" an egregious act of betrayal.

I was actually proud of how I handled it. I hadn't said any words that would have embarrassed Mr. Ryan. I hadn't made a scene. I felt I had done as good a job as could have been done, without injuring his pride.

He obviously didn't feel the same way. Within a short period of time, my contract was not renewed. I was told many times that I had received more fan mail as the television spokeswoman than the show had received. Herb Caen, the nationally known columnist for the *San Francisco Chronicle* had written, "The best thing about *The Bell Telephone Hour* is Marilyn Van Derbur."

I lost my job. I was angry. How *dare* he. I wouldn't play his game so my contract was not renewed. There were no sexual harassment laws at that time. The next time I was in Denver I told my father what had happened and showed him a letter I had written to the Chairman of the Board of AT&T. I had met him on a number of occasions and he had impressed me as a man of integrity. So I wrote him a letter explaining exactly what had happened. My father read the letter carefully, turned to me and said, "I'm sure you feel better." I said, "I do." And with that, he folded the letter, tore it into shreds, threw it in the wastebasket and said, "That's the end of it."

While living in New York City, I had a few dates with a very handsome, successful doctor. One night he told me we would be having dinner with friends at one of New York City's most elegant restaurants. The friends turned out to be David Susskind (who was very well known as a television interviewer in the '50s and '60s) and Jim Aubrey (the then President of CBS) and their dates. After placing our orders, I was stunned when out of the blue, Jim Aubrey turned to David Susskind and said, "Aren't you taping a show next week with some of America's most outstanding women?" David said, "Yes." Jim continued, "Marilyn should be on your show."

My eyeballs bounced from Jim to David to see what his response was going to be. I *knew* he was as surprised by the suggestion as I was. David managed to say, "Yes. I agree." David turned to me and said, "I will call you in the morning." I appeared on his show. I even remember the dress I wore. I was comfortable on the show but I shouldn't have been. I certainly didn't belong there.

The day after the show aired, Jim called. "Would you have dinner with me Wednesday night?" I was unprepared for his call and his invitation. I knew I didn't want to go *anywhere* with Jim Aubrey. Jim was a charismatic, charming man—probably in his 60's. I was 23. I knew this was not a relationship I was looking for. I said, quickly, "Oh, I wish I could but I have plans on Wednesday."

When he continued, "Okay, then how about Thursday?" I panicked. I couldn't think of a reason why I couldn't go. I said, "I have a voice lesson that night." He responded, "Really? What time?" I tried to think what time people ate dinner and I said, "7 o'clock." He continued, "Where does your voice teacher live?" Fortunately I did have a voice teacher! I told him whatever the street was. I could not, *could not* believe his answer. He said, "I live next door." Had I possibly heard him correctly? "Just come by at eight." He gave me the address. Yes, he lived in a townhouse next door.

I had the most amazing voice teacher, Herb Mayer. We adored one another. We would laugh so hard together he would almost fall off the piano bench. There is nothing sexier than laughing together. He is one of the very few married men I was involved with while living in New York who never once did anything inappropriate, said anything inappropriate or looked at me inappropriately. I scheduled a voice lesson for that night at seven and then I walked next door to the president of CBS's townhouse.

The door was slightly ajar. I rang the doorbell and I heard him call, "Come in." I walked in and heard the shower on. I sat down on the sofa and in seconds he came in wearing a white terry cloth bathrobe, towel-drying his hair. He spoke few words. He didn't need to. The message was very clear. We do *this* before we do *that*. I don't remember my exact words, but they were equally as clear. *No we don't.*

Jim Aubrey was, in my experience, a rare example of a man who understood and honored the word, "No." He used no force. Not even a hint of "maybe you will change your mind." I suggested we forget dinner—I would just leave. He said, "No, I'll take you to dinner." It was a very uncomfortable evening—and our last conversation.

My experiences with doctors were a different story. I had suffered with excruciatingly painful menstrual cramps since my periods had started. I can tell you almost every city I was in during the twelve times I had a period as Miss America. Acting as if I felt great was as difficult a challenge as I had. Many days I could barely walk.

The pain became so intense, I knew I had to see a doctor. A very prominent 5th Avenue ob/gyn was recommended to me. He was a top doctor at a top New York hospital. He examined me and told me I had a very serious case of endometriosis. He explained to me that it was as if weeds were growing inside me. He would need to go in, with his hand, and break them up. Years later, when I repeated this to other doctors, they looked at me as if I were on some kind of drug. I couldn't really be repeating what a 5th Avenue doctor, associated with a major New York hospital had said, could I? Yes. I could. That's exactly what he said.

He also told me that it would be best to see me at night because the sessions were long and painful. I'm sure my naiveté is difficult to understand, but, in the early '60s, we were brought up to trust a doctor. Always.

I was so ashamed of my body and so uncomfortable putting my feet up in those horrid stirrups. During the first session, I really didn't pay much attention to the fact that we were the only ones in his entire office. When he locked the door, the second time I came, he told me it was just to be sure no one walked in. What he did was excruciatingly, almost unbearably painful. My head would sweat; my long hair would be wet. I would have to put my head back and brace myself because it was so painful when he reached his hand into me. I would shut my eyes and try to pretend I was somewhere else just to deal with the pain. I'm not sure when I realized he had unzipped his pants and inserted himself. He was raping me. I felt helpless, absolutely helpless. I didn't tell anyone for many years.

Sometime later, a different doctor told me the endometriosis was so severe, I would need to have a D and C. In those days this procedure was done in the hospital. That first night, around 11 p.m., a good looking young man—either a resident or an intern—came into my room and told me he was scheduled to give me a complete physical. I knew there was absolutely no reason for me to have "a complete physical." I also knew that it was big news that "a former Miss America" was a patient and that this young resident/intern was going to examine me. Once again, I was completely helpless. It was one of the most humiliating, degrading experiences of my life. I had been unable to tell him what I would tell him today: "Get out!"

It was many years before I could comprehend how I could so easily protect and defend myself from an executive vice president of AT&T, president of CBS and, unfortunately many others, and have absolutely no power when it came to doctors.

When I was hospitalized in my late 40's, I would have the insight. When I was in stirrups or a hospital bed, it was as if I were a child in my bed at home; I lost all power. It was the (still repressed) night child who could not protect herself. The second I was out of "bed," the place where I had been patterned (behaviorally conditioned) so many hundreds of times, I had all the power I needed to get myself out of an uncomfortable situation. With Mr. Ryan, Jim Aubrey, and others, it was "don't even *think* about it."

During the two years I lived in New York, I worked in television. Although it was lucrative, I was working only ten or twelve days every month. I was eager for more work. One day a man called to ask me if I would be interested in being the keynote speaker for the American Mining Congress National Convention. I was stunned. I had given literally thousands of "I'm happy to be here," talks as Miss America, but I had never given a "speech." Give a keynote speech? Why in the world is he asking *me?* I had no idea what to say to him.

I responded by saying, confidently, "What date are you interested in?" He said May something. "Could you hold for a minute while I check my calendar?" I didn't have anything in March or April, much less May, but I needed time to think! I had some understanding of what it would mean to say "Yes," and that is exactly the word that came out of my mouth. Fortunately, he didn't ask what my honorarium would be because I would have had to go look at my calendar for a long time to come up with *that* answer!

I spent weeks wondering what the theme of my speech would be and many more weeks working on the text. I decided the talk would center on the importance of having a goal and a plan. It was a topic I felt passionately about.

When I arrived in Pittsburgh, I was prepared. I had memorized every single word of my 45-minute speech. I had memorized it so completely that, if you had been there, you would never have known it was memorized. I had developed an ability, as Miss America, to speak memorized words as if I were just thinking of them.

I'm not sure what I was expecting when I walked into the ballroom but the tension I had lived with ever since I had said "Yes," turned into an overwhelming, mind numbing, anxiety attack as I realized what I had gotten myself into. I was the only woman in the room. I was the only person under fifty! The five hundred men were all executives of mining companies. The absurdity of my message hit me so hard that all I could think about, as I tried to chat casually with the successful men seated on either side of me, was, *"What in the world was I thinking about when I said 'yes?' I'm going to tell these men about what it takes to be successful?"* I wanted the dais to open up like a trap door and take me into the bowels of the hotel basement.

I had done it thousands of times as Miss America. I had no choice but to do it again. Act as if it's true. I knew I had to deliver my presentation with conviction and passion—as if what I was going to say would change their lives.

I was so relieved to finally have the whole ordeal over. It was over. Finally, it was over. I quickly sat down. I was so consumed with my relief that, for seconds, I was unaware that the men were giving me a rousing ovation. Because a standing ovation is common for any Miss America to receive, I didn't give it much weight.

During lunch, I had asked the executive seated next to me how they had decided to invite me to be a keynote speaker. He said the former Lt. Governor of West Virginia had recommended me. He had heard me give a ten-minute talk as Miss America. That experience taught me that if you do whatever you are doing well, other doors will open.

It wasn't until I received personal letters from men who had attended that luncheon, asking me to speak to their state conference, Rotary Club or sales rally, that I knew I was onto something. The delegates had obviously understood I was not speaking from my vast experience, but I had drawn examples from other people's lives to illustrate basic principles.

Hundreds of people have asked me, through the years, how to become a speaker. I have learned in over 45 years of speaking that there is only one way to turn one or two speeches into a full-time career. Give a speech so powerful and memorable that men and women in the audience invite you, days, weeks or even years later, to address a conference they are chairing.

After my first keynote speech before the American Mining Congress, I had five requests from those in attendance. I thought long and hard about accepting any of them, because the terror of any upcoming speech was so extreme. I accepted each one.

Although I was living in New York, Gary was still very much in my life—as was Larry. When I was with Larry I was more loving, funny and smart. Why did I keep pushing him away? It would be two more years before I would have the answer to that question.

When I went home for Christmas, at age 22, I knew both Gary and Larry were going to ask me to marry them. I'm not sure why I believed that but I did. When Gary asked me first, I accepted.

My engagement to Gary was a front-page story. When, a few months later, I broke my engagement to him, it was a front-page story. I knew he was wrong for me, but I couldn't seem to break away. When I eventually married him, it was again a front-page story. D.D. watched my baffling behavior, knowing how deeply I had loved Larry, wondering why I hadn't married *him*.

I moved to Iowa with Gary. There is nothing to be gained from going into details as to why I knew almost immediately that it would never be possible for us to stay married. Sometimes a person just marries the wrong person for the wrong reasons. Neither of us was to blame. I was just deeply, miserably, unhappy. I cut myself off from everyone, trying to make it through just one more day.

We married in June. On the last day of August, I flew to Atlantic City to be the television hostess of *The Miss America Pageant*. I was achieving my important goal of being "the first" and "the best" when I was the first Miss America to be asked to be the television hostess immediately after my "reign."

My family again joined me for Pageant week. I told my mother first, "I am going to leave Gary. I cannot stay." She was *very* unprepared for that statement, as everyone else would be. Divorce in the '50s and early '60s was not acceptable. "How can you leave *now?* You haven't even been married for three *months!*" Her comments made me fall even deeper into feelings of guilt and unworthiness. "You need to speak with your father."

I guess I had wanted her to be a mother and say, "Oh, Marilyn, you must be so unhappy. I'm so desperately sorry. How can I help you?" Instead, I knew she was thinking about how this would look.

My father was alone in the room when I went in. "Have you made the decision to leave?" he asked. "Yes, right after football season is over." (Gary was a football coach.)

My father said, "If you have made the decision to leave, then never go back." I was stunned by the thought. Never go back? My father knew, I knew, everyone who knew me realized that Gary had a hold on me that none of us could understand. We knew that if I went back, I might never leave. I never went back. It was not a classy thing to do (that's an understatement, I know). An attorney called Gary to say, "Your wife is filing for a divorce." I am not proud of how I handled it, but it was the right decision.

Gary remarried about a year later. I am sure he now realizes what a gift I gave him by leaving. I am told he has been happily married for forty years.

News of the divorce was on the front page of almost every major newspaper in America. It was by far the darkest time of my life—to that point. Mother and I had to move out of the Waldorf Astoria Hotel in New York City because the press was hounding us. We moved to a little motel on the west side.

The Denver papers, in full front-page stories, quoted Gary as saying I had left him because I wanted to be "a star." Then it said, "Marilyn has no comment." The stories in the papers were very uncomplimentary to me and said things that were untrue. There is a tendency in divorce to want to blame. "Well, let me tell you *what he did!*" It wasn't that he was "bad" and I was "good" or vice versa. It was that he brought out the worst in me and I'm sure I brought out the worst in him. In the weeks to come, I realized the only way to combat what was being said was to just keep making what I believed to be the right decisions.

Looking back, I think, most of all, I had determined somewhere in the depths of my being that I *would never be my mother.* No matter what the cost. I would never stand for an unhappy relationship. I wouldn't live like that. I'd rather be known as the used-to-be-wonderful Miss America who was now divorced. I knew divorce was not acceptable for the "debutante Miss America." I believed no one would ever like or respect me again. The perfect record—the balance of scholarship, athletics, pageantry—it all meant nothing now. I had ruined my reputation forever and nothing was more important than respect and my reputation.

It would be many years before I could see that what I thought was the worst thing that could happen to me, would turn out to be the best. Without question, the best.

Many times, women who come from abusive homes marry into the wrong relationships for the wrong reasons and they continue to live that way until they figure out why they are making bad choices. I had made a bad choice. Again, I want to be clear. It was not that Gary was abusive or that I was abusive. Our relationship became abusive because we were so wrong for one another.

I didn't know what to do or where to go. I had no plans. No goals. I knew that Lynda Lee Mead, the former Miss America who had just completed her year the week before, was moving to New York City. I liked her very much when I talked with her during Pageant week. I called her and asked her if she wanted a roommate. She said she would love to have a roommate, so I moved into her apartment in New York City, with a suitcase filled with evening gowns and satin heels, to begin I had no idea what.

She was just starting to attend The Neighborhood Playhouse acting school. The last thing in the world I wanted to be was an actress, but I couldn't think of a thing to do so I went with her. I didn't stay very long. When we were supposed to show anger, I just couldn't. I was unable to explain to anyone why I was so tied up, walled off and out of touch with my feelings, I had no chance of emoting like an actress. To be in touch with my *feelings* would have meant opening Pandora's box.

With the divorce announced nationwide, and my having absolutely no idea what I would do with my life, I felt even more isolated. At least, up to this point, I could feel alone and isolated while constantly working toward my goal of being as perfect as my night child was imperfect. Now I had lost that. I saw no hope of that changing. Once you have lost "respect," there is no way to ever go back to reclaim it. That was my perception.

One day, while living in New York, I received a personal letter in a small envelope. I recognized Larry's handwriting the second I saw it. Why would he be writing me? I had divorced after only three months! Hadn't he lost all respect for me? Didn't he have disdain for who I was, as I knew everyone else did? I had no contact with him for well over a year. I remember his words as if I were reading his letter right now. "Of all the things we have been to one another, we have been, most of all, best friends. If I can be a friend to you at this time, please call. If not, let this letter be as a leaf in the wind."

I started crying. I read it to Lynda. She said, "Call him." I said, "I can't ever call him again. I have called him and run, called him and run. I just can't call him again." Lynda has a very soft way about her and a lovely Southern Mississippi voice. "Call him, Marilyn. He wants you to."

I thought about it for a long time and then, one night, I just picked up the phone and dialed his number. I prayed and prayed that his mother wouldn't answer. I'm sure I would have hung up.

I would have had no way of knowing that the day the announcement of the divorce was in the paper, Larry's parents were attending a convention in Chicago. When his mother read the story on the front page of the Chicago paper, she called out to his father, who was in the other room, "Noah, she's in our lives again!"

Larry fortunately, answered the phone. "Hi. It's Lynn."

"Hi. I was hoping you would call." And so it began…again.

In a few weeks, I flew home to see Larry. When I started walking down the hall to greet him, he started walking very quickly to embrace me. He will *never* forget my first words to him: "Don't touch me or I'll throw up." While in college, I had developed acute ulcers. For years, I would need to eat a little bite every hour or two to keep the acid neutralized. I always had food with me. The pain and horrible feeling of extreme nausea were with me for so many years, I still carry food with me—just in case.

As always, it felt as if we had never been apart. Larry told me what it had been like for him when I married Gary rather than marrying him. The night I married, he went to a bar and got completely drunk. Larry didn't drink. If he has four beers a year, it is a lot for him. He never drinks hard liquor. For him to get drunk was an indication of how he was feeling.

Larry continued living at home, even after law school. He told me he would go into his room, put his music on and just sit there for hours. Thinking. Brooding. Night after night, week after week. I said, "Didn't your mother ever knock on the door and say 'It's enough already. Get on with your life, for heaven's sake.'" Larry said, "No. She never invaded my solitude. She honored my feelings. She never said anything to make me feel guilty about my sadness, my feeling of loss. She knew how much I loved you. She was there to listen when I needed to talk but she never opened my door when it was closed."

Larry began telling me how he had finally begun dating again and that he was now seriously involved with Marilyn Friedman. Our conversation was suddenly interrupted by the phone ringing. Larry answered and said, "Yes. She's here. Okay. We'll be there in about thirty minutes." My heart stopped! He had told me his mother was in the hospital, nothing serious, but she would be there for several days. I wasn't at all prepared to see his mother again. I just couldn't do it. I had hurt her son so many, many times and I knew she wanted her son to marry "a nice Jewish girl." I was about as "waspy" as one could be.

"It was Mom. She wants to see us." I said, "But I can't see her. I just can't face her." Larry said, "It'll be okay. It's something we're going to have to do." I felt very unacceptable. When we walked into her room, I tried to stay exactly behind Larry so she couldn't see me. When he approached her bed, I moved a little out from behind him but still not next to him.

Larry said, "I just love her, Mom." She looked at me, shook her long, elegant index finger at me and said very authoritatively (and with no smile), "Don't you ever hurt my son again." Now *that's a mother!* Clear. Concise. It didn't matter that her son was a man now, "Don't you *ever hurt my son again.*"

We never talked about marriage during my short visit in Denver but there was no question, in either of our minds, that we would be married. I couldn't understand why we had ever been apart.

Larry called Marilyn Friedman to tell her he was sorry but…and I flew back to New York. By the time I arrived at the apartment, Larry was no longer on my mind. It was as if we had never shared those incredibly special moments together. I didn't call him and when he called me, I was distant, disconnected. He could tell by the tone of my voice that he was no longer in my life. I can't imagine the feelings he must have had. I had no feeling about it.

It was many months later that I flew home to Denver again. I hadn't been home twenty minutes before I went to the phone to call Larry. It was about 8 p.m. on a Friday night.

His mother answered. I almost hung up because we both knew that her long finger shaking at me had not stopped me from doing it again, but I said, "Is Larry there?" Not "hello, Mrs. Atler, how are you?" or "I know you can't believe it's me calling again…" Just "Is Larry there?" There was a slight pause as if she couldn't *believe* she was hearing my voice again. "No, Lynn, he isn't. He's out for the evening."

"Would you tell him I called?"

"I will."

I had no way of knowing that he was now seriously dating another "nice Jewish girl" from a fine family from San Francisco. The family had flown in for a party for Larry and Marilyn (yes, her name was Marilyn, too). Larry's mother must have been euphoric over this relationship. It was what she had hoped for. She certainly couldn't have been a fan of mine. I kept breezing in and out, winning Larry's heart and then disappearing. It seemed to be a never-ending pattern of mine. A pattern that I could not understand. An ability to almost compartmentalize Larry—to not think about him when I was not in Denver. Her heart must have dropped when she heard my voice. "Not *her* again. Maybe I'll just forget to tell Larry that she called." There is no question that she *felt* that way but what did she *do?* She called

Larry *at the party* and said, "Lynn's in town. She's trying to reach you." What a supreme act of a mother's love. Wanting not what *she* wanted, but what her son might want. I still cannot believe she made that call.

Larry called me from the party. Having no idea where he was or what he was doing, I told him I would love to see him. He made some kind of excuse, left the party and picked me up immediately. Again, it was as if we had never been apart. I fell into his arms. I always fit perfectly in his arms. Nothing else mattered. We were going to be together.

Two days later, here we go again. Larry told his soon-to-have-been fiancée, Marilyn, that he was so very sorry but…and I flew back to New York City. Larry was no longer in my thoughts. It was as if I would repress all the feelings I had for him. Feelings that had been real, true, honest. But when I was away from him, my desire to marry him was gone. I would distance myself from him, again. I didn't call him and when he called me, I was cold and distant.

When I was Miss America, D.D. had moved to the Los Angeles area to take over the huge youth ministry at the First Presbyterian Church of Santa Monica. After my year as Miss America, I flew to Los Angeles a number of times to film commercials. I always called him and my conversation would be the same. "Hi. It's Marilyn. I'm at the airport. Just wanted to call and say 'hi.'"

D.D. had felt something was wrong in my life for many years. He just couldn't figure out why he had this "feeling." I seemed to have the perfect life. Little things just didn't fit. The more they didn't fit, the more he would go back to the beginning of our relationship to look at different pieces of the puzzle.

Why had I, so consistently, come to his Friday morning class? Why had I left Larry every summer when I was so in love with him? Why had I married Gary instead of Larry? It wasn't until I divorced Gary, after only three months, that he *knew* that, for some reason, I was trying to destroy my life.

It took something as dramatic as the divorce to put the critically important piece into the puzzle. Unexplained, *destructive and extreme behavior* often gives insights into the fact that *there is something very wrong in our lives.* Finally, he knew what I was trying to do, but he had no idea why. His decisions in the next few months would change

106

my life forever. Although I wasn't aware of it, he would tuck in a few questions each time I would call, trying to get an insight into my strange behavior.

One day it just "clicked" for him. He suddenly knew that my calls of "Hi. I don't have time to see you," were calls for help. The day he realized that, he knew the next time I called, his response would be different.

A huge piece to the puzzle had also jumped into his mind as he had counseled a twenty-year-old young woman who was dating a black man. A white woman dating a black man in the late '50s and early '60s was verboten. As D.D. talked with this young woman, she told him how much she *adored* her father. As they continued to talk, D.D. asked, "Where does your family live and what does your father do?" Her response was like a smack of reality in his face. "My father is a Baptist minister in Louisiana." He suddenly knew she was doing this to get back at her father for something. It would take many more sessions before she would finally tell him that her father had incested her.

D.D. knew how much my father loathed and despised Gary. He also knew I had loved Larry from the time I first met him at age 15. When I left Gary after only three months, D.D. had an "aha" moment. Armed with new insights, as unfathomable and as incomprehensible as they seemed, he would be ready for our next "conversation."

Some weeks later when I casually called him again, he didn't even say "Hello." He said, in a very authoritative voice, *"Where are you?"* "I'm at the Beverly Hills Hotel." *"Stay there! I'm on my way."* He hung up before I could tell him I didn't have time to see him. It was about 11:30 a.m. He looked very businesslike when he arrived. The dining room was empty. He said, "Let's go in there and talk." We sat at a table in the far corner.

I have no idea how he started the conversation. He later told me that, over the years, he had broached every conceivable subject with me. As astonishing as it was to him, there was only one question left although it just didn't add up. I adored my father. But D.D. knew he had to ask the question. It was the only thing left. I was in serious trouble and he was the only one who seemed to know it.

He came at me like a one-man juggernaut, ramming through my defenses and going straight for "it." No leading questions, no gentle hints, just a straight out, get to the truth question. D.D. later called his asking "that question" a leap of faith. I remember his laser focus on my eyes as he said the words that would change my life forever:

"father…bedroom…"

I never said one word in response. I just lowered my head and began deep, racking, gut wrenching, unending sobs. Sitting in the Beverly Hills Hotel main dining room, I had no awareness that the room had filled to capacity as people talked, listened and laughed. I sobbed to complete exhaustion and then I barely lifted my head and tried to whisper just three words.

"Don't…tell…anyone."

I now know that those are the three words that almost every survivor of childhood rape/sexual violations thinks and or says. D.D.'s response to my plea was brilliant. I have thought back on it so many times. If someone had said those words to me, I would have said, "I won't. I promise." My complete despair demanded that compassion and trust. His businesslike demeanor had changed completely. With a gentle softness, he replied, "*Who* don't you want me to tell?"

That would prove to be a life-changing question and a simple one to answer. My instantaneous response was "Larry."

D.D.'s response chilled me to the bone. "Then Larry is the only one we *have* to tell." Only one word was screaming inside my head. "Never. Never. *Never.*"

The thoughts I had after discovering that I had buried 13 *years* of my nighttime life, were thrust aside at my disbelief over D.D.'s statement. That's all I could think about. Trying to take memories that had flooded me instantly and somehow juxtapose them into my almost perfect Miss America world was far too overwhelming. All I knew was that *no one else would ever know. Ever.*

We must have been in that elegant dining room for hours. When I finally became aware of the room, I realized the lunch crowd had gone. The one remaining waiter was staring at us, with a "Please *go!*" look.

I don't remember leaving the dining room. I do remember the public phones tucked back away from the lobby. How D.D. ever convinced me to call Larry, I will never know. Telling my secret was worse than dying. I had, in fact, been living an agonizing life of panic attacks and terror, fighting with every cell of my being, to never allow my secret to be known—even to me.

Incest was a "non-word " in the 1950s and 60s. The subject was taboo. Literally unthinkable. In *any* family. A complete impossibility in my family. How could I love a father who would do that to me for almost my entire life? How could he ever even think to ask me that question?

D.D. was dogmatic about my calling Larry—he never said, "How would you feel about telling Larry?" or "I can't imagine how difficult this would be but…" He said, "We'll find a phone for you to call Larry. Now." I was so overwhelmed by what I had just discovered about my life that I was in shock. I was also emotionally exhausted. Almost like a robot, I went to a pay phone and placed a call to Larry's house.

The thought of what I was about to do was so incomprehensible, I didn't even think about the fact that I had distanced myself from Larry again. I had not been in touch with him for months. As I picked up the phone to dial, Larry, his parents, their rabbi and other guests were just ready to be seated for dinner at the Atler residence.

D.D. had told me what to say. He knew I was incapable of putting a sentence together. "It's Lynn. I need you to fly to Los Angeles. There's something I have to tell you."

My call to him came out of the blue. He was obviously stunned. It took him a minute to register what I was asking. His response for the first time in all the years I had known him was cold and flat, "I've come for nine years. I'm not coming anymore. I finally have you out of my life and I want to keep it that way." That was the end of the conversation.

I hung up the phone and began sobbing again. Deep, vomit-up your soul kind of sobbing. I was crying out of despair because of Larry's response to me and I was crying out of relief that I would never have to tell him.

"He won't come." D.D. had never met Larry but he certainly felt as if he knew him.

D.D. said, "What's his number?"

"Please don't, D.D. Please don't."

"What's his number?" I mumbled the numbers and heard D.D. say, "If you have *ever loved her*, I ask you to come. *Please. Come.*"

Larry would tell me later that, when he hung up the phone the second time, his parents came into his bedroom, where he had taken the calls.

"Who was it?" Larry's mother asked.

"Lynn. She wants me to fly to California. She wants to tell me something."

I have never known Larry's highly ethical and very proper father to use a cuss word. He did after hearing that. He looked at Larry with disgust and said, "You're a damn fool if you go," and walked out of the room.

His mother said five unbelievable words to him. Words I can't imagine *any* mother saying under the same circumstances. Words that still move me to tears. "Follow your heart, my son."

I picked Larry up at the airport, the next day. He was cold. Icy cold. He said, "Hello." That's all. We didn't speak another word. I was so filled with shame and disbelief over what he was about to learn, I didn't want to talk, but I was filled with even more despair because he was so businesslike. I knew he was saying, "Ok. Let's get this over with so I can get on with my life, without you."

We walked into the large church and into D.D.'s office. It was the first time they had met. Larry, the lawyer, sat down, opened his briefcase, took out a long yellow legal pad and a pen and said, "What do you want to tell me?"

I couldn't hold it in one more second. I burst into sobs. I put my head down and sobbed uncontrollably. I couldn't look at him. It was, without question, the most agonizing moment of my life. There was no possible way I could speak one word. I just kept crying, waiting for D.D. to tell him.

Instead, I heard D.D. say, "Marilyn has something to tell you." I never lifted my head. I just said, between sobs, "I can't."

D.D. said, softly, "We will wait until you can." How brilliant D.D. was. If I had been in his position, I would have helped me. I would have found the words to tell Larry for me. But somehow, he knew, that *this was the most important first step in the healing process:* speaking the words. I had not spoken them before. I had not said one word to D.D. I had only broken into gut wrenching sobs.

I had never thought about what words I would use. I assumed D.D. would tell Larry. How do you say it? I had no idea. I just cried with my head down as far as it would go. I have never felt uglier or more unworthy in my entire life than I felt at that moment.

I knew when Larry found out who I really was, he would look at me with horror, get up, take a cab to the airport and leave my life forever. *I wasn't who we thought I was.* I hadn't been a perfect teenager at all. I hadn't been this moral, upright, ethical teenager with whom he had fallen in love. I was a bad, bad, bad person, unworthy of anyone.

All I wanted to do was get up and run out of the room. I have no memory of what I said. I only remember I used words, not sentences. And I remember knowing that when I finally said two words, he would "get it." With my head still in the shame position, I said those two words, "daddy" and "bedroom" and then I quickly raised my head. I knew, in that split second, he would have no time to process what I was saying. I would know all I needed to know by his instantaneous reaction before he could integrate what I had said.

I really didn't have to look. I knew what I would see. Disgust. Disdain. Horror. Revulsion. My eyes caught his for that one split second—and I saw only love, compassion and acceptance. He dropped his legal pad, came to me and just held me. He held me for a long, long time as I continued sobbing and then I heard him whisper to me, "I understand everything now."

It was as if the entire crazy puzzle of my bizarre actions had come together for him. No one had to explain the "why" of anything—why I married Gary—why I kept leaving Larry. I had run from him again and again because my subconscious was yelling, "If you really knew who I was you would reject me." My subconscious had been running my life and I had acted out, having no understanding of what was driving my life. I don't know how long we sat there. Larry was trying to comprehend what he had just learned and I was trying to comprehend Larry's acceptance of me.

The only other thing I remember about that afternoon was D.D.'s first comment. He said, with total sincerity, "I will marry you both—right now." That comment broke the spell for me. He had suggested more than I could absorb. I said, "I really have to get out of here. I really have to get out of here." The reality of who I was, was very difficult for me to accept. Having Larry know was more difficult. It was as if I couldn't look at myself and, now, looking into his eyes I saw love, understanding and compassion. I felt confused, exposed, vulnerable and alone. I hated me. No matter how much Larry would love me, I would hate me for decades. My most difficult and agonizing challenge in the years to come would be finding a way to accept my "self."

Larry and I spent the rest of the day together. We had a lifetime, literally, to talk about. We were discovering together a secret life that I had successfully buried. Things I had done began to make sense. I didn't have to explain to him why I had always gone away during the summers…to never sleep in my room again.

It felt like I had had amnesia and we were looking at snapshots, trying to figure out who those people were, what we/they were doing, what we/they were thinking, trying to understand how it all fit together.

The next day, Larry had to fly to Denver to go to work and I had to fly to New York for the same reason. It was so difficult to leave his arms. There was so much to talk about, so much to analyze. It was like removing cataracts and restoring my vision after looking through fog for so many years. Everything was slowly becoming clear.

I never had to tell Larry, "Don't *ever tell*." He knew that in the depths of his being. But if you had been Larry, wouldn't you have told your parents? How could he *not* tell them when he went home? What did he say to his father? He had to know that his father lacked respect for his flying to be with me—one more time. How could he *not* say, "Dad, let me tell you what's been going on. This is why Lynn kept leaving me. This is why she married Gary. She was trying to destroy her life. That's why, Dad."

And how could he not tell his *mother?* They were best friends. When Larry came home from a date, his mother would be asleep on the sofa across from the front door. She would awaken, they would take a quart of milk, rye bread, strawberry jam and cookies and have a late snack while talking into the early morning hours. Larry told me she would never pry into his life. It would never be a conversation like that. It would be a conversation of two extremely close and trusting friends, just wanting to share their lives and philosophies. A mother-child relationship that was completely foreign to me.

112

It is one of the amazing things about Larry that, out of respect for me, he kept my secret—even when he felt it brought disrespect to him. He told his parents we were getting married. We had finally worked through everything. That's all he said.

When I flew back to New York City, with this incredible new knowledge about my repressed night life, Lynda, my roommate, was there to greet me. "How was California?" "Great. The trip was great." Larry was out of my mind. The talk with D.D. and Larry was out of my mind. It was back to my New York life, as usual. It did pass quickly through my mind that I wasn't going to marry Larry.

Late the next day, I received a thick, special delivery, handwritten letter from D.D.. He started by saying that our meetings had been two of the most incredible experiences of his life. He was so happy that Larry and I would now be married. I couldn't believe what I was reading. I didn't want to marry Larry, but the last two words of that first page are forever embedded in my brain, "but remember"...I turned the page..."you will revert to your old habit patterns of repression. You must tell Larry everything you think and feel. You have no room, anywhere in your mind or body for secrets."

That's what I was doing! Again. Repressing. How did he know that? But tell Larry what I was thinking? That I didn't want to marry him? How could I possibly tell him that, again?

What I have always known is that D.D. was profoundly right. I knew what he was saying was true. It was literally my only hope of surviving. I called Larry and I told him exactly what had happened and read him D.D.'s letter. Larry said, "I understand. We'll take it a day at a time. We'll be fine. We just need to talk about it a lot."

Although we talked about getting married many times during the next two years, I just couldn't do it. I remember calling him one night, after I had emceed The Miss Texas Pageant. It was past midnight. I said, "I just can't marry you."

"I understand. It's okay."

Almost two *years* after our meeting with D.D., I was in Denver, in the car, in Larry's arms. He was gently holding me when he said, "How would you feel about *trying* marriage for a little while? We could try it for a few weeks or a few months and if it doesn't work, it's no big deal. You could just go your way."

He waited for my response. I remember thinking, "Well, that doesn't sound too bad. A few weeks. A few months. Maybe I could do that."

I said, "Yes. I think I could do that."

Oh, how wise Larry was. He knew how terrified I was of commitment. Of marriage. He knew exactly how to present it. I was willing to try.

Chapter 5 – A New Family of Choice and Love

Shortly before Larry and I were married, we went to the airport to greet his family (his parents, two older sisters and brothers-in-law). They were returning from a trip to Europe. We were a few minutes late getting there, so when we saw them, they had just deplaned and were running toward us—their arms outstretched, ready to envelop us.

I felt intense anxiety, as if I were going to be smothered. I found myself walking backward, not forward toward them. I felt this huge wave of love ready to pour over me and it was way too much for me to handle. Larry felt my "pull back" instantly and, amazingly, understood what even I didn't understand.

The next day, he went to talk to his parents. He said, "Don't touch her. Don't hug her. Don't tell her you love her. Please."

I can't imagine what they must have been thinking. "What kind of a weirdo are you marrying? What do you mean don't touch her? What's going on?"

Why didn't he say, "Listen, let me tell you what's going on. She is so filled with shame and feels so unlovable, she just can't accept love right now and this is why. Now that you understand, maybe you can just give us space until she feels more comfortable." But he never said that. He never told them my secret. They would be in their 80's before I would have the courage to tell them.

Because my sagas were always front-page news, we decided not to tell anyone we were getting married until a few weeks before the wedding. We chose (what else) Valentine's Day. In late January, we called Larry's rabbi. Larry's father had been one of the key people who had brought Rabbi Stone to Denver. Being married in Temple Emanuel was important to the Atler family. We were so excited when we walked into the rabbi's office. He was the rabbi who had been to dinner the night I had called Larry from California.

With great anticipation and joy Larry said, "We would like to have you marry us." We were completely unprepared for his response. "I cannot marry you unless Marilyn converts to Judaism." Larry was not happy with his response. "You *can't* marry us or you *won't* marry us?" "I cannot marry you unless Marilyn converts."

I said, "I will commit to never celebrating Christian holidays in our home. I will commit to rearing our children in Judaism. The only thing I cannot do is convert on demand. I cannot say words I do not believe. I can commit to everything else." The rabbi said, "I'm sorry but it's against our religious policy." It was a very short conversation. Larry was enraged. He had been bar mitzvah'd and confirmed in Temple Emanuel. The Atlers had been cornerstones of this huge congregation. It was a conversation that would impact Larry's feeling about the Temple to this day.

We were so disarmed; we had no plan B. We decided to just get away from it all and go to a movie. The second we sat down, Larry excused himself to make a phone call. When he returned, he said, "I called Rabbi Goldman. I've never met him but it occurred to me that he might be the only rabbi in Denver who might marry us. He will meet with us tomorrow."

I felt much more at ease. I so wanted to be married by a rabbi. I knew how much it meant to Larry and to his family. It would be many years before I would understand why I felt no connection with "Our Father..." or why I was so "turned off" by the religion I had been brought up in. It would be literally decades before I would lift my eyes for my first conversation with God.

The next morning we went to Temple Micah to meet with Rabbi Goldman. He was a large, handsome, imposing man with a deep, magnificent voice. He was very interested in us, in our beliefs, in our willingness to make commitments. I told him what I had told Rabbi Stone. I could commit to everything but conversion. He asked if I would be willing to read and study Judaism. I told him of course I would. I would want to. He said he would marry us.

We were married on Valentine's Day, in a cabin in the mountains. It was a snowy, winter day. Our only guests were our parents, our sisters and brothers-in-law, my one living grandmother (my mother's mother) and, of course, D.D. and his wife, Lois.

Two years earlier, when I had married Gary, 400 people had been invited to the wedding and reception. Larry was fine with the decision to have a very, very small gathering. I am ashamed to say, it never occurred to me to ask Larry's mother, Nan, if she would like to invite her two sisters. Larry was her only son. This was a wedding she had dreamed of. Why didn't she pull Larry aside when we were planning the wedding to say, "Please, Larry, please may I invite my sisters?"

She never said anything, nor did Larry. He was only interested in finally ending our interminable courtship.

Nan was in her 80's when we talked about it. I can't believe it had never preyed on my mind before. I said, "Nan, I am so desperately sorry we did not invite your sisters to the wedding." She said, "It would have been wonderful to have them there but it was fine. It was a perfect day. Don't you worry about that." Ever loving. Never judgmental.

As Rabbi Goldman began the service in front of a huge windowpane, a bluebird flew to the window and hovered there for many seconds.

I had selected one song, "One God," to be sung by a man with a mellifluous bass voice. I had heard Johnny Mathis sing it many times. It said what we wanted to say. The lyrics began, "So many stars placed in the sky by One God…so many children calling to Him with many a different name. One Father, loving each the same…"

Larry was mush. The tears had started overflowing his eyes the second he saw me walking down the very short aisle with my father. It had taken me almost six months to win his love when I was 15. He had never wavered, once hooked! He loved me. Period. His mother always knew that. I wondered how she felt seeing him marry me. If she wondered whether or not our marriage would last. She had none of the information that would have helped her to understand my erratic behavior.

I had equivocated about marrying Larry right up to the ceremony. Since the second we were married, I have never had a second thought. For 39 years, I have known every minute of every day that I have been blessed with the most ideal marriage possible. Larry is the gift I was given.

Larry's idea of a perfect weekday morning was to be at the office before 5 a.m. (My idea of a great morning was waking around 8.) Most mornings I walked with him to work—it was about three miles. Then I would take the bus home, reading the morning paper. Some mornings I would set the clocks forward and we would arrive at 4:30 a.m. He would be so happy to have such an early start on the day.

We lived only three blocks from his parents but I just wanted to be alone with Larry. I needed so much of his one-on-one time as I tried to accept and put together the day and night lives I had led. I was still uncomfortable with his family because they were so incredibly loving and demonstrative.

He asked his family to give us time to be alone. At least a year. I can only imagine their conversations—spoken or unspoken, "They need time to be *alone*? A *year*? Why didn't Larry marry some nice girl who would fit into our family?" If that's what they thought, they never let me know it.

Larry's mother and sisters, Janey and Greta, would call me every morning. The conversation was the same, "How are you? Did you have a good night?" It seemed so strange that everyone called everyone every morning. I can never remember my mother calling me on the phone or coming to see me in college—not one time. I was away from home for many years and my mother never called me to say "hello," much less every morning. My father never, ever called me unless there was something specific he needed to discuss with me. I had never seen a family as close as the Atler family, so involved with one another.

Janey always closed her daily morning telephone conversation with, "I love you, Lynn." I would respond, "Thanks for calling." One day, after her closing, "I love you, Lynn," I took a huge breath and an even bigger risk and said, "I love you too, Janey." I hoped she would not acknowledge it or make a big deal out of it. I wanted her to just say, "Bye." Instead, she said, "I've waited eight years to hear you say that." I said, "It's taken me eight years to be able to say it."

Larry's mother would call every Friday to invite us for Sabbath dinner. I would always say, "Thank you but we are going to stay home." Larry had lived at home with his parents until we were married. Larry was Nan's dearest friend. What a loss it must have been for her and yet she never made me feel guilty for cutting her son completely out of her life…at least for awhile. During this time, I needed Larry all to myself. I had way too much going on within me to even consider how this was impacting others.

When I first married into the family, I knew I didn't want to be like Nan. What did she do? Shop. Get her hair and nails done. Go to lunch. Slowly, I would come to understand that Nan was a true matriarch. While the family members were busy working and rearing children, Nan would be the one person each of us would turn to for wisdom, nurturing, counsel and unconditional love. No one ever did it better than she did. Within a very few years, she became my role model, my guide, my compass in everything that had to do with mothering and family. I knew my precious Nan for 49 years. After my mother died, I would always introduce Nan as "the mother God gave me."

Shortly after we were married, Rabbi Goldman called to ask if I would consider giving the blessing at Temple Micah in two weeks—on a Friday night—in Hebrew. I told him I would call him right back. I asked Larry how he felt about it. He said whatever I wanted to do. I called Papa (Larry's father); he said he would be very proud. So I stood in front of the congregation, a non-Jew, and gave the Friday night blessing. I have no idea how my newly learned Hebrew sounded or how the members of the congregation felt about my doing this. I always felt very welcomed into the Jewish community but I can imagine that many people felt this was very inappropriate.

I loved Rabbi Goldman's approach. He never said, "You are unwelcome unless you convert." He let me know that I was welcome and he would help me learn all I wanted to know. He gave me wonderful books to read and Hebrew to learn, but he never pressured me or demanded that I attend classes. Larry's parents joined Temple Micah to be with Larry and me. Only when Rabbi Goldman left Denver and Temple Micah relocated away from us, did we stop going. Larry couldn't bring himself to belong to his family's Temple where we had been rejected.

What we found to be hypocritical was that, after we were married, Rabbi Stone asked us to join the Temple. He wouldn't marry us, nor could we be buried together (this has changed in recent years), but we could be members after marriage and before death. If the Temple had never wanted us, I would have respected that. Not wanting, then wanting, then not wanting, was what I found to be hypocritical. (It is interesting to note that our daughter, Jennifer, was married at Temple Emanuel and is now on its Board of Trustees.)

There is no rabbi in Denver who would marry Larry and me today—unless I converted. I disagree strongly, passionately, fervently with this rule. I believe this policy excludes many from being meaningfully exposed to the Jewish faith.

That wasn't the only rule I had trouble with. Just prior to our wedding, I went to Israel with Larry and his family. One of my sisters was in her ninth month of pregnancy. Knowing the baby would be baptized shortly after his birth (she had married a Catholic), I dipped a water bottle into the Jordan River and hand carried it home with me.

When we arrived at the Church for the baptismal, my sister said, "I would like to use this water for the baptism. My sister brought it from the Jordan River." The priest said, "I cannot use that water. It's not holy water." My sister replied, "She carried the water home from the Jordan River!" His response was the same, "I cannot use that water."

I have found organized religion, many times, to be unloving, unwelcoming and divisive. I will bless Rabbi Goldman always for welcoming me, as I will always bless D.D. for his major role in my life.

During our first year of marriage, I had been naive enough to believe that once Larry and I knew my secret, I would begin to function in a more normal way. One Saturday, we were giggling in the kitchen of our apartment when Larry casually said, "Want to look at houses today? Maybe move into a house?" I went from giggles to convulsive sobbing with my head over the sink. Larry was stunned. He gave me a few minutes and then gently put his arms around me. When I was finally able to get some control over my heaving, he said, "What? What did I say?"

"I don't know. I guess it was the word 'house.' I can't live in a house. I don't feel safe in a house." And with that I began crying again.

Years later when we would move into a home, it would be a strange looking, modern, ranch style home with huge windows in almost every room. Open. Expansive. I couldn't even look at huge homes that resembled the ones in which I grew up. Too many rooms. Small windows. Dark basements. Scary attics. Tudor. Big, dark oriental rugs. Long, narrow hallways. Vines growing up the walls.

Larry always pictured himself in that kind of home. Sweeping driveways. Five or six bedrooms. Long winding staircases. We live in a home so far removed from anything he saw himself living in and I have thanked him again and again for adapting so completely to our home, where we have lived for over thirty years. He tells me, often, how bright, open and cheerful our home is but I know it isn't anything like the home he had envisioned.

Something major happened on our first anniversary. It was a weekday. Larry was at work. I was lying on the floor during our telephone conversation. I don't remember what was said; I only remember that my feelings had been hurt. When I hung up the phone, I started crying. I could see those balloons above a cartoon caricature's head—saying suddenly, what I was thinking. One of me was crying as if my heart would break, but a clone of me was giggling, laughing, jumping up and clicking her heels and the balloon-thought had one word "YIPPEE." I instantly knew what was happening. I had allowed Larry into my heart so much that he could hurt my feelings. I couldn't just shut my feelings down or totally repress them anymore. I was beginning to open up to his love. It was a major breakthrough. I was beginning to feel safe enough to trust.

I remembered a conversation we had had before our marriage. We were having dinner, sitting in a restaurant, snuggled into a back booth. Something he said just shut me down. He said, "What? Tell me what I said?" The words were so difficult to say but I knew D.D. had been right when he said the only way Larry and I could have a relationship was if I told him everything I was thinking and feeling. So I said the words I was thinking, understanding, all too well, how hurtful they would be, "I don't trust you." I will never forget the look on Larry's face. No one had ever been so trustworthy. I knew he was hurt but he quickly processed what I had said and responded, "I understand. In time you will." It did take time but it was happening.

It was like slowly peeling the layers of a huge onion. If we had known how long the process would take, I'm not sure either of us could have endured. We were taking it one day at a time.

As independent as I was in my work, traveling from city to city as a motivational speaker, I was completely dependant on Larry in my personal life. Everyone who knew us knew I never left his side.

We had been married for two years when I said, "I have something to tell you." I would say that sentence to him so many times over the next 25 years. It was always somehow connected with incest. Either something my father had done to me or what I had done or how I had felt. On this day, it was a different area of my life that I needed to "confess." The words were difficult to say, always. "I...I...I have some money in New York. I kept it there in case I had to get away." Larry's understanding and compassion always caught me off guard. "I thought you probably did. What would you like to do with it?"

"I'd like to bring it home."

"Okay."

Especially during our early years of marriage, deep grief and pain would come at the most unexpected times. We would have no warning. Movies could bore right into long repressed feelings. If a child were being terrorized or hurt, I would have to get up and leave. Quickly. I just couldn't watch it.

One of the difficult challenges Larry and I had to confront was our sexual relationship. I had spent thirteen years of my life trying not to feel anything. The goal was to completely shut down my body and not "be there."

Now I was married to the man of my dreams, the young man I had been desperately and passionately in love with since I was 15 and I was supposed to respond spontaneously? I was so ashamed of my body. I always covered myself with a sheet. It took me years to come to terms with my body. It took me years to stop waiting for a salesperson to leave the fitting room before I tried on *anything*.

At age 65, I finally have pride in my body. If a salesperson wants to come into the room while I'm trying on clothes now, that's fine. I know she's saying, "Wow. Pretty good for sixty-five!" I was finally able to replace shame with pride, but it was a long journey.

I remember as if it were yesterday, the "first time." Larry and I were kissing and hugging and giggling. We would laugh so hard together that we couldn't stop. On this particular night, we were nuzzling and instantly I realized where this was going. Larry knew exactly what I was thinking. I had just shut down when he said, softly, "It's okay to have fun." *Fun.* I hadn't even imagined "fun." It was a completely new concept for me. Making love could be *fun?* I realized, in that moment, that my relationship with Larry could be playful and completely different from anything I had ever experienced.

But as I began to learn how to give and accept sexual love, there were certain things that would shut me down. One of them was having Larry on top of me. No amount of playfulness could change my complete shut down if his weight were on me. I was feeling very guilty for the things I could not do. Larry swept that guilt out of my life with one comment, "It's okay, there are 57 other things we can do." I smiled and we began exploring. It was a very gradual process. Both Larry and I had to be very patient and gentle.We began to find a sexual relationship that was fun and satisfying, passionate and comfortable for us.

After working so hard to overcome being so sexually shut down when Larry and I were first married, we were unprepared for my shutting down again when my memories and feelings began surfacing in my late 40's. Gratefully, once I worked through the childhood memories, I could return to a very satisfying sexual relationship. It required enormous understanding from Larry.

I don't know how Larry dealt with my father. I still feel guilty for putting him in a position where he was forced to be civil to him. My parents lived only a mile away. We dropped by fairly often. I'm sure it is incomprehensible to most people that I wanted my father's daytime love as much as I have ever wanted anything. How could I possibly want my father's daytime love? It is one of the thousands of things I am grateful to Larry for—he never asked me that question.

When our behavior or belief systems are judged harshly by significant people in our lives, it adds to our feelings of degradation. It is important and validating to know that our seemingly incomprehensible beliefs are common for traumatized children. Dr. Herman writes, "...the child victim develops highly idealized images of at least one parent...most commonly, the child idealizes the abusive parent and displaces all her rage onto the non-offending parent. She may in fact feel more strongly attached to the abuser, who demonstrates a perverse interest in her, than to the non-offending parent, whom she perceives as indifferent..." (*Trauma and Recovery* p. 60)

I had no connection with my mother. Incest bars all other relationships—even with siblings, perhaps, especially with siblings. I had no relationships with grandparents, aunts or uncles or cousins. I didn't even have God because I knew the God my mother was praying to was not protecting me. My father was my only hope. I blocked out the nights and built him into a hero even though he paid no attention to me during the day as I was growing up. The truth is, all children want their father's love unless, in rare situations, the abused or neglected child becomes so filled with rage, he or she can no longer hang on to a wish for love.

Sometimes the few words my father would say would be so hurtful. Soon after Larry and I were married, he said, "Be smart. Don't ever have any children." Could that message have been any clearer? I didn't want you. That went hand in hand with my mother having tried to abort me. Only when I was in therapy and had to feel the feelings I had stuffed in my body, did I have any understanding of the overwhelming devastation of having to feel completely alone as a child. Even as an adult, I could only come to these realizations in stages, one painful step at a time.

I watched a talk show where children had been beaten, kicked, locked in a closet for long periods of time, or starved by their parents. In each instance, these children wanted to return to their abusive parents. As Dr. Herman writes, "…abused children cling tenaciously to the very parents who mistreat them." (*Trauma and Recovery,* p. 106)

Dr. Lowen wrote, "A child cannot survive without some feeling of love and acceptance…to guard her sanity, she had to believe that someone loved her, and having turned to her father, she had to believe in him." (*Betrayal of the Body,* p. 112)

My father was all I had. As destructive and as soul murdering as his attention was at night, it was the only attention I received. To believe that my father never loved me during the day, that he only used me for his own pleasures at night, would be to feel a sense of abandonment so deep, so agonizing, it would have destroyed me completely. Only when I was empowered and surrounded with love from Larry and Jennifer, would I be able to accept the truth. My father never loved me. He only used me.

Larry and I were finally married.
It had been a long journey.
Little did we know, the real
journey was just about to begin.

My father, just prior to
walking me down the aisle.

D. D. where he belongs—
in the center of our lives.

Dorothy and Noah Atler,
Greta (on the left),
and Janey (on the right).

Chapter 6 – Business as Usual

Shortly after Larry and I were married, I was to fly to the Bahamas to film a commercial for Timex. It was a wonderful account and I was excited about going, but from experience, I anticipated the prospect that the man in charge from the advertising agency might have more in mind than just the commercial. It was a gut feeling that I was learning to listen to and trust. I didn't want to undeservedly lose another job. I thought about how to handle it and quickly came up with the solution: mother. She was fun to be with and she would unknowingly serve as a shield.

When we deplaned, he was waiting at the bottom of the steps. I said, "Bill I'd like you to meet my mother, Boots Van Derbur." He looked at me with an expression I will always remember. I had been right! I was sure he would find a way to get back at me. Everyone met in the small but wonderful hotel dining room-bar for dinner. There was dancing and when he asked Mother to dance, he held her very closely, and danced with her in a sickeningly sexual way. When he seated her, he came to my other side and said, so only I could hear him, "Your mother is the most love starved woman I have ever met." I did subsequently lose the account but I had no way of knowing what role, if any, he played in that decision.

I continued to fly to New York for television appearances and traveled nationwide for speaking engagements. It was unusual in the early '60s for a woman to have this type of career. Other than flight attendants, I was the only woman I knew who traveled constantly.

I was certainly not the daughter-in-law my sweet Nan had expected. Many times, Nan would say to me, "Tell me again, darling, why do you work?" She always said it with love and with a sincere desire to understand, never with judgment. It always made me smile.

I worked endlessly on my speeches. I never wanted my speech to be good; it needed to be *perfect*. Every word had to be *perfect*. If you couldn't give me at least one example from my speech two *years* later, I would have failed in my mission. My goal was never to entertain you, it was to cause you to *take action—to do something*. My mission was to impact your *life* and anything less was not acceptable. I was 53 when I stopped memorizing and just started sharing ideas, but my mission to impact your life has never wavered!

For example: In 1993, I received a phone call from a man in Denver who had heard one of my 60-second motivational messages on a local television newscast, 13 years earlier. He said, "You gave an example of an oyster and an eagle. Could you send me that example?" *That* was a good 60-second motivational segment.

I believed every word I said. Passionately. It took me decades to realize that every speech I ever gave, I was giving to myself. One of my favorite themes was, "It isn't what happens to you that determines your life but how you *respond* to what happens to you." That was definitely my speech to me as I struggled daily to overcome the long-term trauma of incest.

The panic attacks were unrelenting. For literally thousands of nights, I would lie awake, feeling unsafe, unable to fall asleep in a hotel room or in my own bed. I would listen for the doorknob to turn. Listen. Listen. Listen. I'd get up to be sure the door was double locked. Then to check it again.

One of the worst travel nights of my life was when I flew to the east coast to address a regional conference of teachers. I flew into a small airport where I was met by the superintendent. We drove at least an hour to a small rural community. It was a hot, August summer night. Teachers would be bussed in from as far as 60 miles away for a conference before the first day of the new school year.

We were busy talking when we pulled into a large, sweeping driveway into what had obviously been a huge estate. We walked through two large main doors and into a huge foyer. Just to the right, there was a makeshift check-in area. All of a sudden, I realized how remote this "hotel" was and my first question was, "Do you have room service?" He looked at me as if I were from Mars. "No, ma'm, we don't. There's one restaurant about ten miles from here."

It was after 6 p.m. I turned to the superintendent in despair. I had had a very long travel day and I never went to dinner with anyone. Ever. I had learned many lessons while working in New York and one was: never put yourself in a position where a man can make a pass at you. I had been down that road too many times.

I said to the superintendent, "How can we solve this?" He looked at the manager who said, graciously, "We can arrange to have a dinner sent over. That's not a problem."

I thanked him profusely, gave him a simple order and told the superintendent "goodbye." He said, "I'll be by to get you at 7:45 a.m.; it will be a thirty minute drive. I'll have coffee and fruit in the car for you."

As he left, the manager pointed the way to my room. I went down a long narrow hallway to my room, at the very end of the hall. The key he had given me was one of those big, skeleton keys that fits into an old fashioned lock. If you were born after the '50s you probably haven't seen one of them. I didn't even get through the door before I looked into the room and realized there was no phone. I felt my heart sink. I dropped my dress bag on the bed and dashed back to the manager, "There is no phone in my room."

"I know, Miss, but there's one right there, in the hall. You can use that one." I wanted to say, "I don't feel safe without a phone in my room," but all I could muster was, "okay."

The manager brought dinner to my room, told me he would pick up the tray the next morning and said, "Have a good night." I steamed my dress with my travel iron, set my hair and turned on the television. When I glanced at my watch, I couldn't believe it was almost 10 p.m. I hadn't called Larry yet. As I went to open my door, I realized there was no other lock but that antique lock that other keys could easily open. No dead bolt. No sliding chain. Terror filled my body.

I opened the door and glanced down the hall. I can't explain how I knew it but I knew instantly that I was the only guest in the "hotel." There was an eerie quiet. I practically tiptoed down the hall and into the foyer. The access bar of the check-in desk was up and no one was there. There were huge doors on either side of the large, round foyer. I walked to them and found both doors were unlocked. I felt as if I were in a horror movie.

As I walked to the phone, I saw a wide set of steps going down to the basement. Very wide and long. Half way down, the steps turned at a right angle, to go down the rest of the way. A light was on over the steps and a young man, I would guess in his late teens, was standing on the landing, at a Coke machine, looking at me. He had no shirt on. Just some kind of cut-offs. He was tanned and very muscular. He didn't smile or nod, he just turned, put a coin in the Coke machine, took his bottle and went down the steps.

Every cell of my being was on red alert. I felt total dread and despair as if ten fire alarms were going off inside me. I had no idea what to do. I knew I couldn't stay there in that "hotel" for another minute. I just couldn't. I went back to my room, found the superintendent's name, went back to the phone, rummaged through the phone book and found his number. He was listed. I called. It rang and rang and rang. It was after 10 p.m. Where was he?

I knew Larry would be worried if I waited much later to call. I kept watching the steps to the basement as I placed the call. I took a deep breath. Easy does it. No problem. Everything is great.

Larry answered immediately. "Hello? Lynn?"

"Hi, Honey."

"What's wrong?"

How in the world did he know something was wrong? All I had said was "Hi, Honey."

I said, "Nothing is wrong."

He said, "I can hear it in your voice. Tell me. I want to know what's going on."

I kept my eyes glued to the steps, lowered my voice and spoke just above a whisper. I poured out the entire story. I knew as he heard my despair, he would think about how he would charter a jet to fly to me immediately. I knew exactly how he thought. I was right. He said, "I'm on my way." I said, "There is no possible way you can get here. I just don't know what to do."

He realized how ridiculous it was to think he could fly to the east coast to save me and focused on a solution. He said, "Call the superintendent and tell him you need to go to a regular hotel."

"I did. There is no answer."

"Then call a cab and tell the cab to take you to a hotel."

"Okay. I will"

"Call me right back?"

"Okay."

I dialed the operator and asked for a cab company. She said, "Lady, there are no cabs. You're in a small rural community."

"Well, is there a 'regular' hotel?"

"Not for at least thirty miles."

I called Larry back.

He said, "Call the police and hire a policeman to stand outside your door. I mean it. Do it." I said, "I would be scared of the policeman."

"Then check into a hospital as a patient. Tell them you don't feel well."

I said, "I'm going to be fine. I'm going back to my room now. I have no choices here. There's nothing I can do. I'll just get through the night."

I knew he would be awake all night. I knew how much he felt my terror. With nine locks *inside* our house (you can't imagine how many locks are on the *outside*), I still didn't feel safe at night and he knew that. He also knew that there was nothing he could do.

I hadn't taken my eyes off the steps. I went back down the long hallway, unlocked my door, entered quickly, locked the lock and started preparations.

I had a small suite so I took one of the larger tables and pushed it against the door. Then I took a chair and put it on the table. I put the tray of dishes from my meal on the chair and a spoon inside the glass. If someone opened the door, hopefully, I would hear the tray, glass and spoon fall.

Then I took my socks and put them next to the window. Although it appeared I was on the main floor, the building was built on a hill, so my room was really one story up. I put a chair next to the window so if I had to escape, I could break the glass with the chair, put the socks on my hands so I wouldn't get cut, and jump out.

Then I took the sheets and blankets off the bed and tried to lug the queen size mattress into the bathroom. The bathroom was very small but I knew if I could somehow fold the mattress together, I could get it through the door. It was a hot, sticky night and there was no air conditioning. I wrestled with that huge, bulky mattress, squishing it together as tightly as I could and managed to stuff it through the door. I did it! As I released my hold on the mattress, the door slammed shut and the mattress spewed across the floor, the top of the toilet and the tub. If I lay on the far-left side, it would be flat. Of course I hadn't thought about bringing in the sheets and blankets before the door shut and there was no possible way I could open the door. The mattress was there for all eternity. I decided I had no choice and laid down on that old yucky mattress, put a towel under my head and prepared to will myself to sleep. I had taken a sleeping pill. (My choice *every night* is to take something for sleep or lie awake all night in a deep rest.)

Hot? There isn't a word to describe how hot it was in that tiny bathroom with no air. My hair was getting wet from pure sweat. There was no way I could stay in there; it was beyond claustrophobic. I managed by sheer grit to fold that stinky mattress back together, pushing and pushing it against the wall and into the tub as I tried, with my other arm, to open the door. It was too much mass in too little space. I did it again and again. Finally, blessedly, the door opened just wide enough for me to begin mushing the mattress through it. Like a baby finally being born, with one last push, the mattress spurted out the door and onto the floor.

I was hot and exhausted. I checked the spoon, the shoes and the socks, put the mattress and sheets on the bed and vowed I would make it through the night. After lying in bed for about five minutes, I got up and did something I can never remember doing before or since. I took another sleeping pill! I've lived through hundreds of nights of night terrors and never, once, did I take more than the prescribed medication. Even with the two sleeping pills, I laid awake all night. I forced myself to rest as best I could. When the superintendent picked me up the next morning, I had decided to not tell him about my night. There was nothing he could do. It was over. I would just focus on the speech and the teachers who were gathering.

As he put his seat belt on, he said, "How was your night?" I wanted to say, "Fine, thank you," but that wasn't what came out. All the pent up feelings just poured out. The boy with no shirt. No phone in the room. I didn't go into the mattress stuffed-into-the-bathroom comic routine but he got the message.

He was very good in his response. So good. He never interrupted me; he let me pour everything out. Only when I had completely finished did he say, "I'm so sorry and so sorry I wasn't home when you called. I was in a meeting until very late. I've never stayed there. It would never have occurred to me that you wouldn't feel safe. I'm so sorry."

I felt relieved of the pressure that had built up. I thanked him for allowing me to vent and told him I was ready to move on and focus on the teachers.

138

Unfortunately, it wouldn't be the only hotel nightmare I would experience but it was definitely the most memorable.

I am amazed that, after more than forty years of travel, I was never accosted or attacked by a stranger—only by friends, acquaintances and people I worked with.

In 1968, early in our marriage, I learned something truly amazing about Larry. We learn a lot about people in a crisis situation. President Kennedy had been assassinated in 1963; Dr. Martin Luther King and Bobby Kennedy were assassinated in 1968. We were a nation in shock, horrified by the assassinations of three of our most cherished leaders.

It was during this chaotic time that I was asked to give a motivational speech at our regional Veteran's Administration Hospital. My presentation was scheduled for 10 a.m.

At 8:30 a.m. I received a call at home from the director of the hospital. He was blunt, "We have received a threat on your life and we take that threat very seriously. We would understand it completely if you would prefer to not make a presentation under these circumstances."

I said, "Thank you for letting me know. I will call you back right away." I had had threatening letters when I was Miss America. One very strange man had written scary letters for months. When I deplaned somewhere in Illinois one day, a crowd had gathered to greet me. As I glanced into the eyes of a weird man with a mohawk haircut, I knew, I just knew it was the author of those creepy letters. Several weeks later, when we returned to New York, there was another letter from him. I had been right.

Larry and I had only been married two years when a Hollywood producer I had met, kept asking me to star in one of his movies. I found him to be sleazy and strange. After turning him down many times, he called to say we were destined to be together and all he would have to do would be to arrange for Larry to be in a fatal car crash. Larry was home the third time he called, making threats and he listened on another phone. We called the FBI and, we were told, they awakened this man in the middle of the night and confronted him.

Now there was another threat but I was due at the hospital in an hour; there was little time to ponder the "why" of it. I tried to reach Larry. When his secretary tracked him down, he was in court. It was most unusual for Larry to be in court—he is not a trial attorney—but someone got a message to him that he had an emergency phone call. If you are too young to remember this time in our nation's history, it is difficult to explain the fear after the assassinations. I knew Larry would urge me to cancel. What happened next tells you as much about Larry and how he treated me as anything he has ever said or done.

Larry's response still astonishes me. He said, "What is your decision?" Isn't that amazing? "What is your decision?" Not "You're an idiot if you go" or "You owe it to me not to do this" or "Even the director of the hospital intimated you shouldn't go, didn't he?" No. Just one simple sentence, "What is your decision?" Never trying to control me in any way.

I said, "I'm going to go." He said, "I'll be there."

Larry explained the situation to a most compassionate judge and client and received a continuance. He then called Captain Jerry Kennedy of the police department and asked for police protection. Jerry apologized saying, "We don't even have police cadets available because the national mayor's convention is in town. I'm sorry, we just don't have the manpower today."

Larry immediately left the courthouse and stopped by our home to get his loaded 41 magnum pistol which he put in his briefcase and then sped to the hospital. He was still on his way when the director and I went onto the stage. It was an eerie feeling to look out at the people seated in the small V.A. auditorium, wondering if there was someone there who truly wanted to kill me. There were no metal detectors in the early '60s. There was nothing between me and two hundred people. The auditorium was packed. People were lining the walls and sitting in the aisles.

Just as I was being introduced, Larry came on stage with his briefcase. He sat down, put his briefcase on his lap and opened it wide enough to put his hand on the gun. He later told me he had absolutely no idea what he would have done if someone had stood with a gun. Shoot into the audience? It would have been comical if it hadn't been during a time in our history when violence was everywhere. About five minutes into the presentation, two men in dark suits walked in the backdoor. One went to the left, one to the right. There was no doubt in my mind that they were plain-clothes police officers. They carefully examined my car before allowing me to drive home. All was well.

There are so many things about Larry that astonish me. The most amazing is that he never told my secret. Another is that he never tried to control me—no matter what the circumstances were.

There were many times when I could not fathom why Larry's driving need to protect me did not overwhelm his ability to never try to control me. Another huge test also came early in our marriage. It had to do with my trying to find an answer for my extreme I-can't-live-in-my-body-one-more-day, body pain.

By my late 20's, my body was tormenting me so much that I was in constant pain. It didn't matter if I were standing, sitting, or trying to sleep; my muscles felt as if they were locked in that tight fetal position in which I had tried to find safety as a child and teen. It was as if I had a corkscrew in my arms, legs, low back, and buttocks, and I could feel it tightening, tightening. I couldn't stand it one more second.

I had been to back doctors since 5th grade. In my late teens, I added chiropractors and osteopaths. Massage became a part of my life and it provided some temporary relief, but it never touched the deep tightness or pain.

Early in our marriage, while skimming through a magazine, I read about a new therapy called rolfing, which is myofascial manipulation. I would describe it as deep tissue massage, although nothing about it would feel like a massage. I believed it might release body tightness. Nothing else was working. I called the national headquarters that day and asked for the name of a rolfer in Denver.

Only if you understood my shyness, my hatred of my body and my fear of a man who might want to control me or my body, would you have an insight into how severe my body pain was. The pain was even greater than my shame and fear. I went alone to this recommended man's apartment. He locked the door, which exacerbated my then extreme anxiety, I took off my clothes, except my bra and panties, and lay down on a massage "bed." There comes a point at which you will do anything to get some relief. I was there. My body pain was becoming too severe to endure.

There were 10 sessions, each working on a different area of the body. The pain of the treatments was excruciating. No one could go through any one of the ten sessions without crying out and I was no exception. I tried to keep my cries muffled, wondering what people in adjoining apartments thought was going on!

When I went home after the first session and got ready for bed,

Larry took one horrified look at my body and said, "What in the world have you done?" I was black and blue. "I tried a body therapy today called rolfing." "He brutalized you. Look at the marks on your body."

"There are 10 sessions. I'm going back." Larry was speechless. He couldn't believe what he was seeing. He knew nothing about rolfing. He knew a man had done this to my body. I expected him to say, *"No, you are not going back."* I am still astonished that he didn't say that, but he didn't. I knew he strongly, vehemently disapproved of my going, but he never tried to stop me.

Rolfing is *very* different today than it was in the '70s. It has become *much* more gentle. I have a superb, kind, gentle-but-firm rolfer, Jim Terrien. By kneading and stretching my muscles and tissues, he has helped me to release a lifetime of body pain. Rolfing is the one therapy I continue to do. Jim has played a major role in helping to free my body. Today, at age 65, I can touch my toes; something I could not do at age 10. My excruciating back pain is gone. The relief I have in my body has not been a gift, it has been hard earned.

In addition to not trying to control me, Larry has always defended me, even when I was wrong. For years, we worked out at the YMCA close to Larry's office. One day, in a class of about thirty women, the class leader said to me, in a loud voice and in front of everyone, "Marilyn, I don't think you have registered or paid for this class."

I always appeared self-assured but inside, in my personal life, I lacked any semblance of confidence. I felt so humiliated. I went to the front desk and just "lost it." I became someone I had never met before. I was literally yelling at the person, screaming like some crazy woman. Someone must have summoned Larry from the weight room because he appeared quickly and without asking any questions, he began defending me vociferously. When we left, as I sank into my car seat, I dropped my head and said, "What happened in there?" Larry said, "I don't know. Are you okay?"

He had no idea what I was screaming about. It didn't matter. His constant and immediate defense of me has been healing beyond words. I never had anyone defend me. It was as if Larry was going to make up for all the times my mother had turned away. He would defend me. Always. No matter what. What I would learn when I went into therapy many years later, is that the trauma of 13 years of incest had literally hard-wired my brain so that my stress level on a scale of one to ten was fifty. If someone humiliated me, I had no way to accommodate the additional stress, so I would go into a kind of craziness—what Freud would call "hysteria." Fortunately, it didn't happen too often before I began an intense healing process in my late 40's.

It did happen again, however, when Larry and I were in California on vacation. We were reading on the beach when, above the noise of the waves and kids playing, I heard a child screaming. I quickly sat up and scanned the beach. I saw the little girl, about four years old. Her father was holding her arm in such a way that she couldn't get away. He was holding her in the churning and spitting white water as the waves crashed. The water lunged at her and splashed all around her. She was terrified and screaming.

I jumped up, running as fast as I could, yelling, *"Stop that. Stop it!"* He looked up, stunned, as I ran right up to his face. "Let her go. Let her go *now*." It is possible that he didn't understand English but he certainly got my message. Within seconds, Larry was standing at my side. He hadn't heard the child screaming and he had no idea why I was yelling at this young, muscular man but he was there to join in with me! The man released his grip on the terrified child's arm and she ran out of the white water.

The father picked her up and quickly walked away from us. Larry never once said, "Please think before you do that. That man could have laid into me. Just think first, okay?" Larry was there to defend me no matter what.

To live with a man who, when tested, would protect me emotionally and physically was critical to my healing, but I also survived because I did my "work." D.D. had given me my first work—telling Larry. There couldn't have been a bigger risk but I did my work. Then, when D.D. said I had no room for secrets, I had to tell Larry again and again that I didn't think I would be able to marry him or, even more difficult, that I didn't trust him.

I would have no way of knowing that "the work" was just beginning. Although I was plagued with anxiety and night terrors, I was still functioning well enough to continue to excel in my speaking career.

My career choice of motivational speaking evolved over time. Hearing Dr. Kenneth McFarland give a closing keynote speech to an audience of over 2,000 people had a strong impact on my decision. He was the most electrifying motivational speaker I would ever hear. He roused, challenged and mesmerized. He brought the audience together as if we were one cohesive group. One minute we would be ready to fight for our beliefs, the next we would be laughing so hard he would have to pause because no one would have heard his next words. Most importantly, he left me with a personal challenge, not just something to *think about* but something to *do*. Weeks later, I would still be talking about his message.

It was after hearing Dr. McFarland that I knew *exactly* what I wanted to do for the rest of my life. I would be a motivational speaker. No matter how much preparation, distress or travel it would require, I knew this was my path.

I knew that Dr. McFarland was one of twelve male speakers appointed to the General Motors' Speakers Bureau. If a major organization (usually non profit, but not always) such as Rotary needed an outstanding keynote speaker but did not have the funds to pay for a top speaker, they would ask GM if it would supply the speaker, gratis. In return, the chairman would express their appreciation to GM for sponsoring the speaker. GM considered it superb public relations.

In the early '60s, there were no female motivational speakers on the lecture circuit. The same was true for audiences, they were almost always all men. That didn't faze me. I wanted to be a "General Motors speaker." I sent a letter to GM, enclosing my biography and picture. I practically sat by my mailbox waiting for their response. Days turned into weeks. There was no response.

Several months later my father called to say that Dr. Carl Winters (a GM speaker) was coming to Denver and my father was to be his host. He was going to drive Dr. Winters to a conference in the mountains and knew I would want to join them. I was overjoyed.

During our 60-minute drive, I was given ample time to casually mention the fact that I was also a motivational speaker, hoping, hoping, hoping he might suggest contacting GM on my behalf. Nothing resulted from that meeting. Zero. Zilch. Nada.

Many months later, I was flying home from Dallas, after giving a banquet speech for a sales organization. The second I was seated, I opened my overnight case and began working, working, working. I hadn't even noticed the man seated next to me who said, "Good morning."

"Good morning," I replied with a very quick nod, returning immediately to my work, which I hoped said to him, "I am not interested in any conversation. I am working."

He didn't get it. "Is Denver your home?" I responded with one word and no follow up question. "Yes." There was silence for a few seconds. I hadn't even looked up from my work and he asked no more questions.

I can become so focused on my work, especially on a plane, that I am unaware of takeoff or landing. Only when a flight attendant asked the man seated next to me to fasten his seat belt was I aware the landing gear was down and we were minutes away from touchdown. I packed up my work, turned to the man next to me and said, "So, is Denver your home?" "No. I live in Dallas." He continued, "May I ask you a question? I've never seen anyone work as hard on a flight as you did. What do you do?"

"I'm a speaker. A motivational speaker."

He responded, "Really! My company sponsors speakers."

Casually, I asked, "What is your company?"

"General Motors."

I felt the air being sucked out of me. *General Motors!* I had about three minutes before we stopped at the terminal. "Well, *Hello!* I'm Marilyn Van Derbur! I spoke in Dallas last night to a national sales meeting. I am very interested in becoming a General Motors speaker." "Well, give me your card." I didn't have a card! I quickly scribbled my name and address on a piece of paper torn from an airline magazine insert and handed it to him.

"Here's my card," he responded. "Just send a packet of information to me at my Dallas office and I will forward it on to the right people. It was nice meeting you."

"Oh, and *so nice* meeting you. So nice!"

My packet went special delivery that very day. It couldn't have been two weeks later that I received a call from Detroit, "Miss Van Derbur? I'm with the General Motors Speakers Bureau and we are interested in hearing you speak." Would I be available for an evening presentation somewhere in Michigan? I don't remember the city but I do remember that I had a talk scheduled for the Colorado Savings and

Loan League conference *the next morning* in Denver. How could I possibly give an evening talk in Michigan and a morning talk in Denver?

Surprisingly, there were many late night flights in the '60s. It would mean flying almost all night. What a deal. I accepted instantly. Larry picked me up in the wee hours of the morning, I rested for two hours, and then gave my morning speech.

Within days, GM called to book me for more speeches, with the thought of my becoming a permanent member of its lecture bureau. Twelve men, all in their late 50's or older…and me, twentysomething. I was now in the company of Dr. Kenneth McFarland. Mission accomplished! I would become and remain their only woman guest lecturer for many years, until, for economic reasons, GM closed that department.

In my late 20's and 30's, I would address at least three banquets or evening sales meetings each week, except during the summer. I did not accept speeches during July and August. No matter how busy and crazy our type A lives would be, Larry and I always took at least a month to vacation in Laguna Beach, California. Usually late July through August. We were both able to let go of our obsessive work and just play. We would swim laps in the ocean, sometimes laughing so hard that I would be unable to breathe; jog on the high school track, always timing ourselves and each day trying to break the previous day's performance; play tennis until the next scheduled players kicked us off; and then walk into town for dinner. In 39 years of marriage, we have never missed our month of August together. No client could persuade Larry; no program chairman could persuade me. It was (and is) sacred time.

Addressing youth conferences was always as important to me as business or sales conferences. During early June, especially, I would travel at a frenetic pace, addressing 4H State, Girls State, Future Farmers, etc. Many were sponsored by GM. I was always paid substantially less for youth conferences but that never mattered to me. In later years, I would begin giving at least 20 percent of my speeches at no charge, usually reserving these "no charge" presentations for student groups.

A comment after a speech to the State Student Council Conference in Texas would add a new direction to my life. I had given a talk on "have a goal, have a plan and your dream can come true" kind of talk.

146

A very intense teenager rushed backstage the instant my talk was over. There was an angry tone to his voice as he said, "I had a goal. I had a plan. My goal was to be elected president of the State Student Council and I didn't win." He just stood there, glaring at me. What I had just talked about had not worked for him.

"Can you tell me *why* you wanted to be elected president? Was it because you wanted to change school policy? Did you want to win as a sign of popularity? If you can tell me why you wanted to win, I think I can tell you how you can still accomplish your goal, although not in the way you had originally intended."

When I flew to the next city that day, I couldn't get his question off my mind. I knew that I could only communicate one basic idea in a 40-minute talk. One idea that would be embedded in their brains and souls. When a speaker tries to touch on many ideas, too often those listening remember nothing, long term.

Students certainly remembered the "goal-plan" message. Over the years, hundreds would write to me days, weeks, years later telling me about what my speech had caused them to do, but I was haunted by the teenager's question. How could I talk about all the other ideas that I believed were equally as important? His question would plant a seed that would grow into an eight-class mini-course, covering, "What is success, what is failure?" "How hard and how long should you try?" "Change what you can, accept what you cannot change," etc. While these themes were developing, I continued to address thousands of high school students.

Since GM rarely sponsored a state youth conference, I decided to find a sponsor for my youth speaking. Whenever I would be at the brink of taking another huge risk, I would remember a favorite Biblical quote: "Ask and it shall be given to you, seek and you shall find, knock and it shall be opened unto you." It doesn't say, "It shall be given to you." It says, "*Ask* and it shall be given to you..."

Larry said, "If you could choose any corporation in America to sponsor your youth speaking, what company would you choose?" I thought for a minute and then said "United Air Lines." Larry said, "Then you have your answer." Right! I would just march in to the executive offices of United Air Lines and ask them to sponsor all my youth conferences? That's exactly what I did. I wrote to the Executive Vice President, Homer Merchant, at United's Chicago headquarters and asked if I might meet with him.

A few weeks later, when I walked into his huge office, I was delighted to see a man with snow-white hair and a very warm smile. His first words to me were "Are you good?" My first word to him was, after taking in a huge breath to try to hide my shyness, "Very."

He asked if I were speaking in the area anytime soon. "Tomorrow, at the University of Illinois." Unfortunately that would mean flying to Champaign-Urbana to hear me. That's exactly what he did. The next day we signed a letter of agreement whereby United would sponsor fifty youth speeches each year in exchange for my being identified in all publicity and introduced as United Airline's Youth Speaker, a title I would hold until Homer Merchant died unexpectedly, about five years later. I would be the only youth speaker United Air Lines would ever have. The man who took Mr. Merchant's place met with me and said, "I need to know exactly how sponsoring you, as a speaker, puts money directly into United's pocket." I knew the relationship was over.

Recently, while flying on United, a flight attendant said, as she placed my pretzels and water on my tray, "I heard you speak in Florida at our state 4H conference about how important it was to set a goal. Those words really stayed with me." It had been at least thirty years since she had heard me. Those almost passing comments would affirm for me that the hassle of travel was worth it. It would be years before I would understand that every speech I gave, I was giving to myself.

Chapter 7 – A Daughter to Love

"Making the decision to have a child is momentous—it is to decide forever to have your heart go walking around outside your body." —Elizabeth Stone

I'm sure millions of women have wanted a baby as much as I did, but no one ever wanted one *more*. After a few years of hectic travel, Larry and I got down to business. At first, when I didn't get pregnant, I felt disappointment. After months and months of trying to conceive, we went to my ob/gyn. After a thorough examination, he suggested a regimen of taking my temperature daily and then at the moment of ovulation, calling Larry at his office. Larry had an incredibly demanding schedule as a successful attorney but no matter what he was doing he would come home when I called. When that didn't work, I began taking fertility pills. Each month when my period started, I would cry. As the months and years passed, both Larry and I began seeing other specialists. Ultimately, my doctor began artificially inseminating me with Larry's sperm every month.

Finally, after eight years, it worked. Every second of the journey was worth it. During my wonderful and easy pregnancy, I continued traveling and speaking. I felt no need to forewarn a program chairman. If it was unusual in the '70s to have a woman speaker for a sales rally or banquet where almost all attendees were men, it was *extremely* unusual to have a *pregnant* speaker! Ten days before Jennifer was born, Larry drove me to Colorado Springs, where I was the graduation speaker for the Air Academy High School.

Larry and I went to Lamaze classes. It was very uncommon for a husband to be present in the delivery room, but it was extremely important to me. All I needed was Larry with me and a natural delivery. No medication.

My doctor had been amazing. He had been completely involved in our quest to have a child, seeing me whenever my temperature went up, doing whatever he could, whenever he could. Four weeks before I was due, he said I didn't need to take the classes to prepare for natural childbirth—he would tell me when to breathe. That comment stopped me cold. I didn't say a word to him but when I went home, I said to Larry, "I have to change doctors. I can't go to him anymore. We have to find a doctor committed to natural childbirth." Larry said, "But he's been your doctor for eight years. He's been wonderful. What did he do?" I said, "He isn't committed to natural childbirth. The baby is in a breech position. It may be a breech birth and I won't even consider using anesthesia. I have to find another doctor."

Larry knew me well enough to know that this is what I was going to do. He suggested a man we had been in school with, Dr. Wattie Bowes. I had no understanding of the deep, underlying reason why I abruptly left my caring, attentive doctor who had been through so much with me. I wrote him a letter of explanation as soon as I figured it out but it would be years before I would have that insight. So, at the beginning of my ninth month, I began seeing a new doctor.

I asked Larry to be sure no one would be coming to the hospital. Just the two of us. Larry was Nan's only son. She had waited eight *years* for this day and she couldn't come to the hospital? I can't imagine what she thought and felt when Larry communicated that she had to stay away. No one could be anywhere in the hospital. That Larry did not try to coax me to "just allow my mother" still astonishes me. He defended me, even when it came to the mother he so adored— his closest friend before we married—even when he had no understanding of why I was adamant and unmovable on this issue.

I had no way of knowing why we kept everyone away. As desperately as I wanted a baby, this experience I was about to have, had nothing to do with childbirth. When the doctor and nurse looked at "there," they would know. There is no more vulnerable position for a woman than during childbirth. For thousands of women, childbirth isn't about childbirth at all. Even that joyous moment is taken from us by our violators. The long-term effects of childhood sexual trauma are truly incomprehensible.

Today, I am reading this chapter one more time before sending it to the publisher. Our daughter, Jennifer, is days away from having her first child. She is sharing every minute of this incredible experience with me. She has asked Larry and me to be in the delivery room, to share in the miracle of birth. If she were to tell me that I am not welcome at the hospital, I would say, "Okay, Jennifer, what ever you want," but inside I would be weeping, mourning. She doesn't want me at the hospital?

Only now can I more fully comprehend how Larry's mother must have felt. We had no information to share with her as to why we were keeping her away. And never once, in the 30 years we would share

150

together, did Nan ever mention it. Never once did she even subtly let me know what a heartache that was for her. She was and will always be the quintessential mother.

We checked into the hospital around 6 p.m. We had cards and a book; we were all prepared for the different stages of Lamaze. I was thoroughly rehearsed in my breathing technique and Larry was a superb, practiced coach! We were ready.

Just before 7 p.m., a nurse came in to check my vital signs. She called the doctor. He checked and said, "You are nine centimeters dilated." As the nurse was wheeling me into the delivery room, a man approached me from the back of my head where I couldn't see him. He said, "I am your anesthetist in case we do a caesarian." I was aghast. I threw my head back and said, "There will be no caesarian. No caesarian. We will *not be needing you.*" And then I said it one more time, just in case he had missed my point. "*There will be no caesarian. This is going to be a natural birth.*" There was no doubt in his mind or anyone else's that that was that.

As I say to doctors and nurses when addressing medical conferences, it wasn't just what I said, it was the way I said it. My response to him was adamant, almost angry. There would be no discussion about this. Any nurse or doctor present should have been alert to the probability that a much deeper issue was going on.

The nurse said, "Push! Push!" I said, "Where is Larry?" She said, "He has gone to put on his whites." I said, "I won't push until he comes back." The nurse started yelling, "Mr. Atler! Mr. Atler!" Larry returned and we began "our" job of natural childbirth. Wattie couldn't have been a more perfect doctor. He somehow let us know that he was just there to catch the baby. This was Larry's and my experience. I locked my eyes into Larry's eyes and never once looked away, nor did he. He just kept talking to me, encouraging me.

When he said, "One more hard push. Now!" I pushed. All of my training, all of the laps in the pool, the 100 sit-ups every day, eating only fresh food and gaining only eleven pounds, all of the focus and training paid off. Big time. Larry said when I pushed that last time, I almost shot her across the room. A beautiful 7 pound, 7 ounce baby girl. Jennifer. We had our baby.

I held her for a few minutes and then the nurses took Jennifer to wash her. I turned to Larry and said, "I want to walk back to my room." Larry turned to Wattie and said, "She wants to walk back to her room." Wattie knew us both very well. He shrugged his shoulders, smiled, and said, "Okay."

I don't know what I would have done if, before the birth began, Wattie had said, "It's too risky. The baby is not in a good position. We're going to be safe and do a caesarian." I would have turned into an out of control woman yelling over and over, "No anesthesia. No anesthesia."

What I wouldn't understand for several years is that I could never allow a man *to put any part of my body to sleep,* because sleep is when a man can do anything he wants with you, and you have no power and there is no one to hear you, or help you, and there is no hope of it ending…ever. That's why I had left my incredibly supportive first doctor because, although I didn't understand it, I knew he wasn't as committed to natural childbirth as I was.

When I address doctors, I suggest that my ob/gyn should have asked, in my initial medical history, "Have you had mumps, measles…were you physically abused or sexually violated as a child?" He should have asked that question as nonchalantly as he asked all the other questions. My answer would have been "No." There's no doubt about that but I would have known that he was aware that childhood violations could play a major role in our medical problems, particularly having to do with the part of us that has been touched or invaded. If I ever *had* felt comfortable enough to turn to anyone, other than Larry, my informed doctor might have been a safe choice for me. At least I would have been aware that he knew enough to ask the question, which would have led me to believe he had some knowledge about how childhood sexual violations/rape can impact our adult lives. Over the years, many survivors have told me that they have had flashbacks when seeing a dentist, hygienist, internist, or gynecologist.

If we had *understood* why even the *thought* of a C-section was so traumatizing to me, we could have dealt with it. If the doctor and I had known that the sheer terror of being put to sleep was because I had been awakened for thirteen years, teaching me that sleep was the time of greatest danger, I know I would have been okay if Larry had been able to stay with me.

If that had not been possible, then I believe if my doctor, especially Wattie, had looked right into my eyes and said, "I will never leave your side. You will be treated with dignity and respect. Our only

152

purpose here is to deliver a healthy baby into your arms. I will keep you safe," I would have been okay with anesthesia. I needed to know that he understood my terror and that he would keep me safe, no matter how irrational it may have seemed to him.

After my story of incest became public, at the request of doctors I produced two medical videos to help educate doctors and nurses about the unique challenges of survivor issues. In the video, addressing only women's issues, a woman talks about her experience of giving birth to twins. She was a textbook case, so ashamed of her body and dreading even the *idea* that a doctor or nurse was going to look at her "there." Immediately after being taken into the delivery room, *15* doctors, interns and residents came into the delivery room. They had never seen twins delivered before and it was a teaching hospital. She was horrified and overwhelmed by the situation. What did she want doctors to know? She looked right into the camera and said, "No one asked me how I felt about that."

Jennifer was several days late being born and I had scheduled a speech to a national convention, which just happened to be in Denver. Perfect! The problem was, she was born during the same week as the convention. When my picture was in the paper with my new bundle of joy, the program chairman, from Boston, called Larry at his office enraged, "What do you mean she had a baby? She is our opening keynote speaker!" Larry said, "I know she is. She'll be there. Don't worry. She'll *be* there!"

Larry told me, later, that the chairman didn't even hear his words, he just repeated, "How could she do this to us?" Larry said he decided to wait until the chairman had vented and then he would give his response again, "She'll be there." When the man finally heard Larry, he said, in disgust, "Well, she can just do a walk on." Larry said, "She will give the opening keynote speech. This is not a problem" And I did. I was given a standing ovation after my introduction.

I left the hospital the day before my speech. Nan was there. She said, "I always carry the baby down." I thought "Hmmm! I want to carry my own baby down." But I followed happily as Nan carried her only son's child down the hospital corridor. We had waited eight years for this day. So had she. Only now, with my daughter days away from her delivery, do I understand.

When Jennifer was just two weeks old, Nan called to say she was coming over to see "her baby." I'm sure she thought I would be a stay-at-home mom, like her daughters were. I wasn't sure how to phrase it, so I just said it straight out, "I'm flying to Salt Lake City today to give a speech." There was a long pause as if she could not believe what I had just said. She responded, "With *my* baby?" "Yes, Nan." There was a much longer pause. Unfathomable! Flying with a two-week-old baby! Then she said, "Just because I'm older doesn't mean I'm wiser. May I drive you to the airport?" And Nan wondered what she did that made her such an incredible mother!

Jennifer and I were in 53 cities together during her first year of life. I played with her on the plane; I played with her in the hotel room. I was only away from her for one hour while I spoke. It was the perfect mom/daughter time.

Larry supported my traveling with Jennifer but when Jennifer was two and running, as all two year olds do, I traveled with her less. We had live-in help but Larry would change his work hours so he could be home with her when she woke up and always home with her in time for dinner and playtime.

I nursed Jennifer for six months. The only reason I stopped was because I wanted to get pregnant again. I adored Jennifer; there wasn't one midnight or two a.m. feeding that I resented. I had waited so long for her and I cherished every second. Larry kept saying, "How much longer are you going to breast feed?" He wanted to be up with her. At the end of six months, he took the early morning feedings eagerly

After I stopped breastfeeding, Larry and I were eager to have another child. Although we would go back to the same routine of temperature-taking and fertility pills, I was unable to conceive again.

Until I was 39, the dysfunction I was living with was disguised as extremely successful behavior. I traveled at a frenetic pace. To give you a glimpse of my travel schedule: one day, I addressed a convention in Columbus, Ohio, in the morning—a luncheon in New York City—and a black tie dinner in Springfield, Illinois, that same night. Commercial flights could get me where I needed to be until the last leg of my schedule, then I chartered a flight to Springfield. Although three cities only happened once, it was not unusual for me to speak in two different cities in a day. This was long before x-ray machines and heightened security. Some might have called me a workaholic or a perfectionist. Isn't there always something subconscious that drives this kind of hyper-productive behavior?

As I look back, it is easy to see that I needed to keep running faster and faster to keep the volcano of memories and feelings inside me from erupting. There was no time to deal with the past. Living with me was exhausting. I was like Eveready's Energizer Bunny. I just kept going and going and going.

I would be 39 years old before everything would change.

It was not unusual to address an audience of 10,000. I was the keynote speaker for an educational conference.

When Jennifer was two weeks old,
I began speaking again. We were in
fifty-three cities during
her first year of life.

Teaching Jennifer to swim.
She raced in swim meets
through high school.

Chapter 8 – A Woman in a Man's World

I was concerned that when I addressed teens attending state conferences, that I was only reaching those who were achievers. All had excelled in order to attend the conference. What about the teens who were not excelling, who had no self-esteem, who never won an office or saw an A on an exam. Who was reaching them?

In the late 1960s, before Jennifer was born, while I was the television spokeswoman for Best Foods, I met with company executives and sold them on sponsoring my speeches to high school assemblies nationwide. (United Air Lines was sponsoring state conferences.) If I spoke in cities where I was already booked to address a chamber of commerce or sales banquet, there would be no travel expenses. I would charge them a nominal amount for each assembly and I could do as many as three assemblies a day prior to my evening business speech. They loved the idea and gave the assignment to one of their key employees. I would give her my itinerary and she would arrange for the assemblies. The only stipulation was that I didn't fly until Monday morning and I was home by Friday afternoon. The next year, I gave 229 speeches. After each and every speech, I couldn't wait for the next one.

I was addressing student assemblies during the time of school integration in America. For the first time, Black students were being bussed into all-white schools and America was seething with racial tension and violence. The woman who was booking my speeches said to me one day, "I talked to a principal in Detroit, who said, 'There is no way I can bring our 2,000 students together for a student assembly. We would have chaos.'" The woman told me she replied, "Marilyn can handle it." I wanted to say, "Listen babycakes you have never even *been* to Detroit. It's easy for *you* to send me on my way. You ought to walk into an auditorium with 2,000 teenagers booing and catcalling."

I vividly remember walking into an assembly with all-Black students in Louisiana. Can you imagine how they were feeling about a white Miss America? I was a textbook example of everything they loathed. There was booing and hissing as I walked on stage. It lessened only slightly as the principal introduced me. I stood silently before the microphone until they quieted long enough to give me an opportunity to begin. Within seconds I knew I had them because I was talking about *their* lives.

It was during this time that I knew I had to do more than one 45-minute talk. I knew I could help teenagers change their lives, if I could help them change how they felt about themselves. Too many had decided at the tender ages of 13 to 16, that they were failures. I knew I could change that mind-set.

From the seed planted many years earlier by the teenager who challenged me, I created a mini course. Eight class periods. I knew I would need to teach to be credible, especially because I was a former Miss America. That title opened some doors, but in education, you either have the academic credentials or you're not a "teacher." And there were still vestiges of an archaic perception that "beauty queens" were attractive but not too smart. I had to prove that what I was offering would bring dramatic, positive results.

When I completed the 8-week mini course, one class per week, I asked the head of the Denver Principals Association if I could address the principals with the hope that several of them would allow me to teach the course in their schools. He told me I didn't have a teaching certificate and that no teacher would give up one class period a week. He was not very encouraging, but I kept pressing the poor man until, just to get rid of me, he said he would give me 15 minutes at the next meeting. When I finished my presentation, there wasn't a principal who didn't say, "Yes. At my school." They understood what I was trying to do.

I chose three schools in different areas of Denver. When there was unanimous agreement that 8th grade students were the most difficult to teach, I asked for more 8th grade classes, although I taught the mini course in 7th through 12th.

My first class period became "What is success? What is failure?" Each class was designed to demonstrate to students that they had the power to achieve their dreams— and they were given tools to achieve them.

After each class period, I asked students to answer only one question, in writing: "What did these ideas mean to you in your personal life?" The responses were exactly what I had anticipated. They were beginning to think about themselves differently. But during the first five minutes of the first class period, one boy in one of my 8th grade classes immediately fell asleep. He was slovenly dressed and he sat slumped in the last seat in the last row. When the bell rang, waking him up, I walked back to him and said, "Why did you go to sleep as

160

soon as I started? Why didn't you give me a chance?" "Cuz you were talkin' about politics."

"I was not talking about politics. I was talking about your life. I'll make you a deal. Listen to the entire class next week, and, if you don't find anything that applies to your life, then you can sleep through the rest of the classes and I won't say a word. Deal?"

"Deal." He listened for the rest of the course. At the very end, he wrote; "You made me really want to try harder to go on to college and pass the courses even though they seem so hard. You made me really stop to think about what I want to do and have the courage to do because I don't think I can but after these classes, I'm going to give it a try."

When I addressed the teachers, I shared some of the students' comments. Within weeks of completing the mini course, I was being asked to address teacher conferences. The momentum increased when I was asked to be the keynote speaker for the National Association of Secondary School Principals (NASSP) with more than 2,000 principals. I knew my message to educators would be heard.

After sharing the concept and students' written responses, principals were saying, "We want the course in our schools." How could I possibly do that? I knew teachers wouldn't have the time to spend the hours and hours necessary to digest the examples so that they could present the material in an educational, motivational way. How could I solve that? Film. I would film the presentations, but where would I find the money to do that? There were no camcorders in those days. Film was almost prohibitively expensive.

I went to the head of one of our television stations, Al Flanagan, and told him what I wanted to do. He said, "You've got it. No charge. But you will only have enough studio time for one take. Thirty minutes to set up and thirty minutes to film." There was no teleprompter, which meant memorizing over 100 pages so completely I could present everything, flawlessly, on the first take. With, of course, my constant companion, "Miss Panic Attack," I did it. It's amazing what you can do when you have no other choices.

I would address the NASSP three years in a row. Soon after speaking to the National Association of *Elementary* School Principals, I was met in Dallas by a high school principal. He said, "I asked our superintendent twice to invite you to address our teacher conference.

Each time he would looked at me with a 'I'm sure you would like to have a Miss America so you could spend time with her' look—like I had this 'thing' for you. It was demeaning to me, and to you. When the secondary school principals heard you speak at their national convention and also requested you as our speaker, only then did he relent."

It would not be the first time, nor would it be the last, that a man would tell me how many times he had been asked exactly what the reasons were for wanting to invite a former Miss America to address his conference. Many asked how difficult it was for me, when so many were questioning their "motives." There were times, although not many, when being a former Miss America worked against me.

The concept I was presenting was very well received. After a presentation in Wisconsin, a teacher said to a principal, "I want that course to be incorporated in my class." The principal said, "But you teach math!"' The teacher responded, "First I have to teach students that they *can*. Once they know they *can,* I can teach them anything." That teacher knew *exactly* what the course was about.

I said to the principal, "If any teacher says, 'I don't have time for that mini course,' please say, 'No problem. I'll find another teacher.' Unless the teacher believes in and supports the concept, it will not have the desired results." Some teachers truly believed their only job was to teach math or science. Just the facts. It didn't matter if they called a student "stupid" or gave him F after F after F or wrote only "sloppy job," on an assignment that was being returned.

The films became so successful, I updated and reproduced them for adults *and* teens. This time Best Foods picked up the tab for the production costs in exchange for their name being at the beginning and end of each film. What a deal. One film won a national award for excellence, another won an international award.

One day, I was walking down 5th Avenue in New York when I ran into a television executive I had worked with on TV specials many years before. He said, "Marilyn! How good to see you! What are you doing now?" I couldn't wait to tell him, "I'm working with students and teachers. Motivating them…" The expression on his face changed instantly. "Oh," was his only comment but the look on his face and his body language said, "Oh, I'm so sorry you couldn't make it in the Big Time!" Little did he know that the television world that I had been a part of had filled my ego but starved my soul.

162

I was passionate about wanting to help students overcome the adversities and obstacles they faced. I wanted to help them survive and prevail. It was a huge "aha" moment when I realized I was also teaching them what *I* most needed to hear. I never wanted any student to feel as unworthy as I did.

Several years into my speaking career, a highly successful sales speaker, J. Douglas Edwards, heard me speak and asked if I would like to be his partner in presenting a series of sales seminars nationwide. I liked Doug very much. I found him to be professional and businesslike. He believed it was time to incorporate a woman into the sales circuit and he believed I was the right woman.

I accepted immediately. I went to his home in Scottsdale and stayed with him and his family as we worked on our presentations. As we left for the airport, his wife came to my side of the car and said, "Just remember—he's my husband." I was really taken back by her candor. I wanted to say, "Lady, I'm not the problem. If there is any problem, he will be it."

We spoke in thirty cities. Never once, with a word or gesture, did he make any advance to me. After our presentations, he would go to his room and I would go to mine. We each had dinner alone in our rooms. We were a solid team. He was one of the few men I worked with who treated me strictly as a professional.

My only negative experience while traveling with him happened in Tulsa. We were to give a full day seminar for an insurance company. There was a cocktail party the night before. Doug was invited. I was not. Doug told me the reason why—the president of this insurance company had not invited me because he thought I was Doug's "consort" or whatever name he used. I said nothing. As I look back, the insurance executive's behavior said more about him than me and if that were to happen today, I would tell him so.

During this time, American Salesmasters was presenting *huge* sales meetings across America. The meetings would draw as many as 5,000 to 8,000 people in each city. Two men would speak before dinner and three men would speak after. Dr. Norman Vincent Peale and Art Linkletter were two of the closing speakers. They had a group of "regulars" who would do almost every meeting, perhaps 25 cities each year.

Salesmasters' president, Hal Krause, called me and said, "I'd like you to present the Outstanding Salesman's Award at our Denver sales extravaganza." I said, "Thank you, Hal, but I'm not an award giver; I want to be one of your speakers." I almost laughed at his reply. He said "I tried a woman once and it was a disaster. I'm asking you to give the award." I said, "So you tried a woman *once*? Have you ever tried a *man, once* who was a disaster? C'mon."

He said, "Will you give the award?"

I said, "No, Hal."

"Well," he responded quickly, "you haven't heard how much I will pay you to do that." I said, "It isn't about money. I wouldn't do it no matter how much money you offered me."

When we hung up, I was proud of myself for telling him *exactly* how I felt, not trying to skirt it by saying, "I'm not available on that day."

A year later, he called me again. Same extravaganza. Same conversation. "No, Hal. I haven't changed. I'm a speaker not an award giver. Just give me one city. Just give me a chance—pick your most difficult city." To my *astonishment*, he said, "Okay. Philadelphia. Six months from now."

I booked the date, gave my talk and began the speaking circuit with "the guys." It was *wonderful!* I loved hearing each and every one of them and they were accepting of me, as were the audiences.

I knew when Hal began placing me in one of the three after-dinner slots, that I had "made it." I loved speaking with a passion. Only the constant, acute anxiety attacks kept the joy from being complete. It was as if two exaggerated, huge, opposite feelings existed within me at one time. "I can't wait to speak." "I'm going to die if I go out there and face that audience without a note. What if I forget? What if my mind goes blank?" "I *love* what I do." "I can hardly breathe when I think of going out there." Back and forth. I was driven to excel. Driven to be respected.

When the National Speakers Association asked me to address their national convention, I knew what my acceptance would mean. An instant anxiety attack that would consume me for the eight months between my acceptance and "showtime." I had just been named the "Outstanding Woman Speaker in America." 30,000 questionnaires had been sent to business and civic meeting planners asking them whom they considered to be the outstanding man and woman speaker in America. I had been chosen.

Now I would address my peers. "Okay. Show us! So, you're the outstanding woman speaker, huh? Well, let's just see." I'm not saying that is what they were thinking. That is what I *thought* they would be thinking. Only Larry would know the eight months of torment I would put myself through before that presentation in San Francisco.

To my last breath, I will remember that speech. All new material focused specifically on our profession. After my speech, I received a standing ovation. Who wouldn't excel with the need to give a perfect talk. Not just good. Perfect. It didn't take a genius to do that. For me, it required balancing the sewer-like world of my childhood with a perfect adult professional. "A coward dies many times before his death." So does a brave person if she is living in my body.

In my 30's and 40's, when anxiety tightened its grip and brought me to the brink of complete numbness, I would turn to my only resources. I would remember examples of people's lives I had studied. I would turn to them as devout Christians turn to the Scriptures—for help and hope in a time of deep despair.

As I would berate myself for wondering why others could write and give speeches so quickly and easily, I would remember Ayn Rand. She would write seven days a week for as many hours a day as she could concentrate. Once, she didn't leave her apartment for 33 days.

I had been to the Lincoln Memorial as a teenager. It was one of the few times I had ever been in awe. I was speechless as I looked at the huge marble statue of this great man. When I would question how long I would have to work to perfect a speech I would return, in my mind, to examples I had used about him.

Lincoln's Gettysburg address, which was less than three minutes, has been called one of the greatest speeches in history. I grew up picturing him reading in a log cabin. I didn't know that he had memorized long passages from Shakespeare and the Bible or that he had read all of Shakespeare's plays, some dozens of times.

Lincoln opened his speech with the word "fourscore." People didn't talk like that in Lincoln's time. A person would have said "80." But at Gettysburg, he chose Biblical words. In the Bible, it says that Abraham was "fourscore and six years old."

As I would begin to mentally flog myself for having to work so hard to do what I thought others could do so easily, I would go back again and again to my research. Abraham Lincoln and Ayn Rand worked and studied. Their accomplishments were not gifts. Their words and thoughts were friends of mine in times of insecurity and darkness. It would be almost 20 years before I would understand what was controlling my life. I had chosen a career that kept me in the eye of a tornado of terror. I would continue down this path until I made the connection as to *why* I was making certain choices. Only then, I could begin, *begin,* to make changes.

Chapter 9 – The Power of the Mind

Warriors sailed to invade a foreign land. As they prepared to advance, their commander said, "Turn and look. I have burned our ships. There is no turning back. We win or we die."

As irrational as it is, at some level I believed I won Miss America because of my long blond hair. It was the only part of me that was perfect and I kept it that way. What I wore was of little importance to me but how my hair looked was extremely important. As Jennifer was nearing her 5th birthday, I did something unthinkable. I cut my hair off. Well, most of it.

For reasons I didn't understand, while I was in Detroit for a speaking engagement, I, seemingly impulsively, rescheduled my flight home and made a quick stop in New York. Rita had done my hair for years for television commercials and she now worked in the hair salon in the Waldorf-Astoria Hotel. She knew how obsessed I was about my hair. When I sat down and said, "Please cut my hair off," she knew she must have misunderstood. She just stood there. It was such an unexpected request from me. Slowly, she began cutting it off inch by inch. I said, "Rita, please grab chunks and cut it off." She did and I left with very short hair.

I am hesitant to tell you how I felt after she cut my hair, because my thoughts were so bizarre. The only solace I take is from the story of Samson in the Bible. He felt the same way about his hair. It was his power. No hair. No power. I felt, when I boarded the flight to Denver, that people would look at me and laugh. I knew I would never get another standing ovation after a speech. I had cut off what was good about me. It would be several years before I would understand the significance of cutting my hair.

Something else strange was happening. There were times when I had to get away from Jennifer. This is the child I loved so deeply. Every day we played together. Every morning when I awakened her and every night when I put her to bed, I sang to her, nuzzled her, cherished her. Suddenly, I had surges of feelings that I had to get away from her. I would call my sister who lived close by and say, "Please come get her. Take her anywhere…to the park…to the supermarket…anywhere. Please just take her." I had no understanding of my feelings.

I knew I would have to tell Larry. I have said so many unexpected words to Larry that I believed would end our relationship forever, but never have I said more difficult words than I said this particular night. I was sobbing. That gut wrenching, doubled over, throw-up-your-guts kind of sobbing. I was on the floor. He ran to me, got down on the floor and just held me. "What? What?" There was no way I could form the words. Ever. "What? Please tell me what happened." I just shook my head "No" and cried. "You can tell me anything. You know that. Anything. Please."

I knew he would have to know but these would be my final words. After saying them, I expected that he would say, "Please leave the house now. Right now. And never come back." Every part of me believed that would be his response.

As always when I tried to say such difficult words, the words came one at a time, agonizingly. "I...don't...love...her...anymore." With that, I collapsed in sobs. I didn't love her anymore.

I waited for his response. "What do you *mean* you don't love her? Every mother loves her child. If you don't love her, then leave." But he didn't say that at all. Instead, he held me tightly and said, so quietly, "It's okay. I will love her enough for both of us."

No judgment, even though he had no understanding. It didn't matter. He loved and accepted me no matter what. My eyes fill with tears every time I think of those words I will never, ever forget, "I will love her enough for both of us." Fortunately, these feelings about Jennifer didn't come often but when they did, they came quickly and I would be desperate to distance myself from her.

Although it would be years before I would begin connecting all the dots to the incredible puzzle that would finally explain this bizarre behavior, the next experience would be the one that would, in future years, help me to understand.

It began only weeks after that anguished conversation with Larry. I was 39. I had come home from a successful speaking tour and was talking with my secretary when I felt a sudden need to lie down. It was late afternoon and even the *thought* of lying down was incomprehensible. There was so much work to be done. I kept talking with her, fighting the feelings, but it was a losing battle. I felt my entire body being forcefully pulled down as if a huge magnet were drawing me down.

Since my office was in our home, I excused myself and lay down. I always slept in a tight fetal position. I would draw my arms and legs up and into my body until I was a tightly clenched ball. But that day, I found myself lying in the position of a dead person with my legs extended straight and my arms folded across my chest.

Within minutes, I realized I was unable to move. I wasn't concerned or scared. I didn't seem connected to the experience. I went into what felt like a very deep rest, aware at all times of what was going on around me.

I heard Larry calling, "Lynn? Lynn?" The last place he would look for me would be the bedroom. Taking a nap or resting was something I had never done in all the years he had known me. It took way too much effort for me to turn my head to acknowledge him. He stood over me with a look of surprise and concern. "Lynn? What's wrong?"

Trying to form words was laborious. Without a hint of concern on my face, I barely whispered, "I don't know, but I can't move my body." Immediately, Larry reached for the phone and called his cousin, Gary Friedland, who was our doctor. He was just leaving the office and offered to stop by our house on his way home.

By the time Gary arrived, the heaviness had lifted and I was up fixing dinner. He was surprised when I answered the door. I told him I was embarrassed and sorry we had bothered him. Whatever had been the problem was over and I was fine. He was concerned and asked that we call him immediately if I had any more similar occurrences.

When Larry came home the next night, it was a repeat performance. Unable to move. Call Gary. Up, feeling fine. Gary arrives. More embarrassment. This time Gary was more concerned and said it would be important to do some tests. I didn't call him the next day as I'd promised. I knew I was fine.

The third time it happened, the heaviness in my body was so extreme, I was barely able to whisper to Larry, "Please don't call Gary. Please don't." When Gary arrived this time, I was in bed, unable to move any part of my body. He took my pulse and my blood pressure and said, "We need to get her to the hospital immediately." My blood pressure had plummeted. My pulse was in the low 40's.

Paralysis. Physical paralysis. My body had shut down almost completely. If I had to go to the bathroom just prior to a paralysis spell, the need would disappear. I would not feel hunger or discomfort. I felt

169

nothing. The spells would come and go. I could feel them beginning. It would feel like a heavy, dark cloud entering my body and within ten to fifteen minutes my body would feel like lead. I would be paralyzed. My head wasn't involved. I could open and shut my eyes. I could even talk, although speaking even a few words took incredible effort. Whispering a word or two was usually the extent of my communication. I wasn't frightened during a spell. I rarely had any thought. My mind was in limbo. Zoned out.

After two to three hours I would begin to feel the cloud lifting. I would start to feel some sensation in my body and I would know that within ten to fifteen minutes, it would be over.

One specialist followed another. Test after test. I know Larry went to the office sometimes but I can never remember a time when he was not standing by my bedside, especially when a doctor would arrive. Almost every doctor would sit on the side of my bed while conferring with us. The second he would sit down, I would feel overwhelming anxiety, as if an earthquake were happening inside my body. I could not focus on anything he said. All I could think about was getting him off my bed. Each and every time, Larry would say, "Please don't sit on her bed." Some doctors would immediately stand. Some would pay no attention to his request. Most would sit the next time they came. Larry would repeat, "*Please, doctor, do not sit on her bed!*"

One morning, I was to have a CAT scan. This was still a fairly new and very expensive piece of equipment and hospitals shared its use. I was taken to a different hospital for a 7 a.m. appointment. As Larry and I entered the hospital, we saw Papa, Janey and Don Lozow (Larry's father, sister and brother-in-law) waiting. When I returned to my hospital, they were waiting for me again. As Larry and I approached my room, I suddenly collapsed into heaving sobs. I had no idea what was causing me to burst into uncontrollable deep crying periods. Gradually, the sobs subsided. Moments later, I heard someone crying in the hallway. I asked Larry who it was. He said it was Papa. Tears flowed from my eyes. I was incredibly touched that he would feel so deeply for me. I also felt guilty for causing Larry and his family so much concern. I turned to Larry and said, "I will do everything possible to get over this."

I was in and out of the hospital for almost three months, usually for weeks at a time. My parents were in Laguna Beach, California, at their vacation home. Although they were certainly aware of my situation, they neither flew home to see me nor did they call me, Larry or any of my doctors to try to find out what was wrong. The thought of not flying to Jennifer's side if she were hospitalized for *any* reason is beyond my comprehension. That day. That minute. Other than my parents, both sides of my family were concerned and attentive. None of us had any understanding of what could possibly have been wrong.

One test required an IV. I was not in paralysis when the needle was put into my arm. The second the needle went in, I felt the kind of anxiety that sucked my breath out. My heart started pounding so hard, I knew people would hear it. When the nurse left, I turned to Larry in panic and pleaded, "Get it out. *Get it out. Please get it out.*" Larry went out to ask the nurse if we really had to do this test. "Yes we do," was her response. "But only during the day, for three days."

I began a mantra, "I can do this. It's only for 7 (5, 2) more hours. I can do this." When the first day was finally over, the nurse came in to disconnect the IV. She said, "We will leave the buffalo cap (the type of IV needle) in because the test will continue tomorrow."

I couldn't believe it. *No!* As she walked out the door, I said to Larry, "Get it out. Get it out." Larry pushed the buzzer for the nurse who was obviously in no mood to be bothered. "Yes?" she asked in a disgusted tone. "Please take the buffalo cap out."

"I'm sorry but it has to stay in."

"She would rather have the needle inserted again in the morning than to have the needle stay in all night." The nurse was brusque, "I'm sorry but the buffalo cap is to remain." She walked out. Larry took one look at me and knew it had to come out. He had no understanding of why but this was non-negotiable. He rang the call button again, "I'm sorry but the buffalo cap *has to* come out." Her angry response was, "How many good veins do you think she has? We can't put it in and take it out each day."

Larry said, "Please call Gary (our doctor). Now. Or I will." She returned and removed the buffalo cap.

Why was I so frantic? Although neither Larry nor I had any understanding, at the time, Larry never once—even with a look—said, "C'mon. You can get through this, it's just a buffalo cap. Don't make such a big deal out of it." Larry always defended me. It is inexpressible how significant it was to have Larry defend me, without question or equivocation.

The December holidays were nearing, so the doctors decided to release me for a few days. The paralysis spells were continuing to come and go but I pleaded to be released to be with Jennifer. She was in kindergarten and was about to participate in her first holiday program. Jennifer was so excited we were going to be there. She sang her songs over and over. I made sure our camera had new film and that we were among the first parents to arrive. I wanted to be sure we had good seats. The program was held in the gym where long rows of fold-up chairs had been set up. We sat in the center of the third row. The kindergartners would be the first group of students to sing.

Just as the program was beginning, I was overcome with dread as I turned to Larry and said, "It's starting." We knew we had about ten minutes to get me home to my bed. Just as Jennifer was coming out with her class, we began climbing over about 20 parents' legs, whispering, "excuse us, excuse us," trying to get home before the spell started. Larry asked a friend to bring Jennifer home when the program was over. I'm sure she wondered why we were leaving just as Jennifer's class was entering. I felt guilty and crushed that I had to leave Jennifer's performance, but I had no control and no understanding.

I was hospitalized again. On New Year's Eve, a dear friend, Leo Goto, brought a scrumptious, catered dinner to Larry and me and Janey and Don, who shared the evening with us.

After more tests and consultations, a group of doctors walked into my room one afternoon. Not one, not two, but four physicians standing literally shoulder-to-shoulder in front of my bed. Nan, Papa and Larry were in the room with me. One of the doctors turned to Larry's parents and said, "May we speak with Mrs. Atler privately please?" I said, "This is my family. Whatever you have to say, it's fine to say in front of them."

It was obvious how uncomfortable the doctors were. They knew I was not going to appreciate what they were about to say. I'm sure that's why so many came in together. They were right. I did *not* appreciate what they said, "We have done every test imaginable and we can find nothing physically wrong. We're sure you will want a second opinion, but our strong recommendation is that you see a psychiatrist."

No wonder they walked in together. They were going to tell me I was crazy and that it was all in my head. Although therapy is common

172

today, no one I knew at that time had ever been to a psychiatrist. In the '70s only weirdos went to therapy, only people who couldn't handle their own problems. I was smart, successful and very "together." I didn't have any mental or emotional problems. I was very much like my mother in this way. I was happy, bright and cheerful. It sounds strange to say it but the paralysis spells or crying episodes were simply a strange interruption in my day and not anything I thought much about. I did not welcome the doctors' report. Of courseI would get a second opinion. The thought of flying to another city was numbing but not nearly as numbing as the thought of going to a "shrink."

When we arrived at the Mayo Clinic, we found ourselves sitting on what I remember as church pews. Long benches. Waiting for our turn. After about thirty minutes, Larry had to ask the people seated on either side of us if they would mind moving and soon I was stretched out in the "dead person" position, in paralysis. I was taken from the clinic to the hospital where several different doctors examined me and then I was given a written psychiatric test. After several days, a psychiatrist walked in and in less than five minutes of conversation said, "I recommend you go into psychiatric treatment."

His brusque way antagonized me, as did his recommendation. I said, "You've talked with me less than five minutes. Give me one good reason why you feel I have any more reason to see a psychiatrist than you do." He said, "Well, I'm here and you're there!" That made me smile. I said, "Good point!"

One of my sisters lived near the Mayo Clinic. She came to sit with me each day. She was a bright spot amidst a baffling diagnosis. It would never occur to me that incest could be the cause of the paralysis.

We returned to Denver. I couldn't imagine I was going to see a "shrink." How humiliating. What did my mind have to do with paralysis? What if someone saw me?

Larry began his search. Only the highest credentialed psychiatrist would be considered. The list was finally narrowed down to three men. I would need to meet with each one to make the final decision. I just wanted to get it over with. We settled on a doctor whose office was only blocks from our home.

Although I was no longer hospitalized, the paralysis spells continued on an almost daily basis. Since I had never been in therapy or psychoanalysis, I had no idea what to expect. The only thing I cared about is that he had an "in" door and an "out" door so no one would see me coming or going. No one could ever know I was in therapy.

It was just like the movies. I lay on a couch and he sat behind me. His participation consisted of, "Uh-huh" "Uh-huh" "What did you think about that?" "Uh-huh" "Uh-huh." What was he doing behind me? He always had a paper and pen when we began. Maybe he was doing crossword puzzles. Why didn't he ever have a conversation with me? There were many times when I wondered if he had a pulse. I found the entire process to be useless.

After two, perhaps three sessions, he finally had a suggestion. To say I was startled would be a gross understatement. He said, "I want you to go home and smoke marijuana. It will help relax you." Marijuana? I had never even *seen* marijuana. To my knowledge, I had never been around anyone who had ever done drugs.

As children of the '30s and '40s, we were brought up to do as we were told and to respect our elders, especially doctors. Okay. That's what I'll do! I called a young man I knew very well, who was fresh out of college, "Do you know how to get marijuana?" There was complete silence. He was stunned by my request, not because the thought of marijuana shocked him but because I asked for it. With a definite hesitation in his voice, he said, "Yes." I said, "Is there good, better, best?" He said, "Yes." "Can you get me 'best'?" "Yes." "Quickly?" "Yes." He delivered the marijuana within the hour.

When Larry came home from work, I couldn't wait to tell him what an amazing experience we were going to have. Well, if I was square, Larry was cubicle. He rarely drank, he didn't smoke and I knew he had never smoked marijuana. The second he walked in the door, I bubbled over with my news, "Dr. Uh-huh wants me to smoke marijuana." And I showed him what I had.

Never in 24 years of knowing Larry had I seen him so angry. His face locked into a Winston Churchill bulldog rage; the veins on his neck bulged. I could almost see his brain trying to comprehend a doctor telling me to do this. His teeth were clenched, his body stiff, his face literally red with rage. I can understand why cartoonists show smoke coming out of an angry person's nostrils and mouth. Trying to control himself, he said, "Never. Never. I will *never* smoke marijuana."

"But Dr. Uh-huh says this will help me. It will help me relax."

With rage pouring out of every cell of his being, he said, "Well, that's just *fine*!Then *you* go ahead and smoke it. I'll just sit here and *watch you.*"

"Won't you smoke it with me?" With teeth still so clenched, he could hardly get his final word out, he said, "*Never.*"

I was so disappointed. I thought maybe we had found something that would help me get better, and I would do anything to get better. Larry was vehemently opposed to any form of drugs and he knew how dangerous it could be to turn me onto anything like marijuana, especially at that very vulnerable time in my life. To this day, I can't believe he didn't grab the marijuana, throw it down the garbage disposal and say *"Never!"* I remain in awe of his stand. "I will not. You can do whatever you choose. I will be with you, should you choose to do it." Above all, he would want to be there to look after me. I didn't smoke it.

Larry couldn't wait to go to my next appointment. He was still so enraged, he could barely spit out his anger at Dr. Uh-huh's *very* inappropriate and *illegal* recommendation. Dr. Uh-huh was very sorry he had ever suggested marijuana—especially to the woman married to this attorney!

The physical paralysis was inconvenient but it was a peaceful state. If I had begun smoking marijuana during this time, I *know* that I would have begged for anything stronger to make the feelings of terror, rage and overwhelming anxiety go away when they began to flood my life in upcoming years. Forget high-minded belief systems; forget the, "I would never do *that,*" philosophy. When the pain is so bad you know you will have to die, I believe most people would consider doing anything to relieve it. Anything. I am so grateful I did not choose drugs and did not add this complication to my recovery.

One of the many things that continued to astonish me about Larry was that he never told me what to do. In his incredible wisdom, he knew that I needed control, perhaps more than anything. I never had control as a child. He understood that in the marrow of his bones. Even when I would push him to the brink, as my wanting to smoke marijuana did, he never tried to control me.

The paralysis spells continued for twelve years, from age 39 to age 51. They became a normal part of our lives. When friends would come over to play with Jennifer, she would say, "Mommy's having a spell"…as if Mommy had a headache. We just accepted the inconvenience of my shutting down completely for several hours on an almost daily basis.

My doctors couldn't figure it out, nor could my highly credentialed psychiatrist. It was, perhaps, ten years before I put the puzzle together as to why my body had gone into physical paralysis at age 39. My insight may have been sparked by something a doctor said to me. One of my doctors was my uncle by marriage, Dr. Joseph Friedland. He was one of Denver's most respected, kind, loving physicians…and Gary's father. The day I was being released from the hospital, he came into my hospital room to tell me "goodbye" and, just as he was walking out the door, he turned and said, "You know, my darling, I wonder if this has anything to do with your turning forty." That comment brought a smile to my face. Maybe a Miss America was finding it difficult to age gracefully? Little did he know how I welcomed being older. I just never wanted to be young again!

One night as I was trying to find peace in my bed, I had the insight. Of course. That's why I went into paralysis at age 39. The question Uncle Joe had asked had been brilliant. The paralysis had everything to do with age. But not my age! When I was 39, Jennifer was turning 5, the age I was when the violations began. Her *age* was triggering the memories *and the feelings,* as another part of me used every ounce of energy to repress them. **This head-on-collision, this conflict, resulted in physical paralysis.**

And that's why I had cut my hair only weeks before my body went into paralysis the first time. Jennifer's age was triggering the feelings of how bad, unlovable, dirty and guilty I was. I would feel so unworthy that I would be driven to cut off the only "good" part of myself. Even as a young girl, I set my hair every night in tight bobby pins. My hair was the only part of my body that my father didn't touch or violate. It was the only part of me that was still good. Pure. Virginal. Without any conscious knowledge of why, I cut off the only part of myself that that was good; then I was all bad.

That's why I had said I didn't love Jennifer anymore. It had nothing to do with her; it was her age that was triggering all the horrific repressed memories and feelings. When I looked at her, I was feeling *me at her age*. That's why I would have to get away from her.

And that's why I had extreme trauma when a doctor sat on my bed, because that's the way my father began the nightly routine. That's why

176

I found the buffalo cap intolerable, because I didn't want anything inserted into my body. Any part of my body.

Now, when I address doctors, I suggest that a patient's *inappropriate or irrational behavior* could be a major clue to deeper issues (such as past trauma) that may be related to physical problems.

Recently, a woman told me she had been in a car accident. When the police and ambulance arrived, even though it had been a minor accident, there was concern about her back so she was put on a gurney and strapped down. She said, "The second I felt the strap tighten, the second I felt myself being held down, I began screaming, 'Don't hurt me. Don't hurt me. Don't hurt me.' At age 35, the memories of being raped were sucked out of my past and thrust into every pore of my mind and body."

I suggest to doctors, nurses and emergency care specialists that instead of thinking, "This is a crazy woman," they should think, "We'd better find out what is going on here. We are obviously dealing with a deeper issue." Talking with her just briefly, to hear her fears and gently offer comfort in an emergency situation, can be invaluable.

Larry and I would talk about how amazing the mind is; how omnipotent the mind is. As a child, my mind had split in two to protect me. Then, as an adult, it brought me down into physical paralysis as the feelings were trying to break into consciousness. Amazing. Now I knew why. That knowledge made it easier to endure.

Gratefully, it never occurred to me that if Jennifer's age were sparking the memories and feelings, then maybe her age would continue to impact me until she turned 18. If I had thought about that, I might not have survived the healing process. I always believed I would be over it in six months. I just had to make it through six more months and it would be over.

While I was hospitalized, my mind was blank most of the time. There was only one daydream that kept flashing into my mind. My father was lying in a casket and I was standing over him saying, "Too late. Too late. You died…and we never spoke of it." Over and over I would see that scene.

I knew that when I was released from the hospital I would have to confront my father…*not because I understood a connection between incest and paralysis* but because of the impact of the daydream. During non-paralysis periods, I would play it over and over in my mind: what I would say, how I would say it. Just *the thought* of confronting my father was terrifying.

During my sixth session with Dr. Uh-huh, I said, "I need to talk to my father. I'm 40 years old and we have never talked about it. I always pretended I was asleep." My need to talk to my father had become obsessive. I had to "speak the words." The Dr. made one of his rare comments. If I live to be two hundred, I will never forget his one-sentence answer: "Not for at least two years of seeing me every day, five days a week." I couldn't believe what I heard, "Not for at least two years of seeing me, every day, five days a week!"

I immediately began to count down how many more minutes I had in my exactly 50-minute session. He had totally missed three vital issues by responding to me in that way. He was not responding to my desperate need to reach out to my father. He had no understanding that he would not be controlling me and he had no clue that I had no intention of seeing him for more than a couple of months at best. I was going to figure out whatever I needed to figure out and then get back to work and life!

I left his office, walked across the street to a phone booth and called my father at his office. "I need to talk to you." "C'mon over." "No. At home" (meaning the home in which I had grown up). I barely stopped for stop signs and traffic lights. I sped to the house. I had to get there before he did to be sure the doors of the house were unlocked and open. I had to be sure I could get out quickly. Of all the feelings I had about my father, terror was one through ten.

As I unlocked the heavy, ornate, black metal, front screen door, I released the self lock, left the front door open and went into the breakfast room so I could be seated when he came home, forcing him to sit in the chair farthest away from the exit door.

He came in and sat down on the far side of the table, which had always been his seat. I'm sure the look on my face told him this was going to be a very serious conversation. I knew what I wanted to say but I hadn't thought about how I was going to start the conversation. I took a deep breath and with my eyes lowered, I said, "This is the most difficult thing I have ever done." I was unprepared for his response. He pushed his chair back, stood up and said, "I'll be back in a minute."

The staircase was near the breakfast room door where I was seated. He walked by me and went up the long, winding staircase two by two.

I listened carefully for a phone call to be made or a toilet to be flushed, but he came back immediately. I knew he had a gun. It was in his pocket. I didn't think it—I didn't wonder it—I knew it.

He had guns everywhere. In his car, near his chair in the sunroom, in his bedroom and in his office. Now he had his bedroom gun in his pocket. There was a coldness that could turn his incredibly penetrating light blue eyes into steel gray. No emotion. Just cold. Calculating. A detached meanness. I knew he could have coolly shot me or himself or both of us without another thought. Most probably both of us.

Nothing would have stopped me from talking with my father that day. It was time to speak the truth no matter what the consequences. There are many ways of dying. Dying a day at a time is the most agonizing. That's the way many survivors live—dying a day at a time. Unless and until we walk right into the terror, it becomes our life sentence. If we can walk into the terror, most of the time we can walk *through* it. It's always a risk because sometimes there are serious consequences. Each survivor has a different journey and terror is resolved in different ways. Certainly, there are safer ways.

It never occurred to me to back down because of the gun. I was 100 percent committed. Fortunately, I did not come in anger. I came in love. I know that seems incomprehensible, but my suppressed rage (certainly one of the reasons for the paralysis) would not geyser up for another eight years. If I had come in rage, I believe the consequences would have been dire.

I said, "When I say 'I love you' I want you to know I have many other feelings." I also remember saying, "You knew 16 years ago, when I was in Los Angeles talking to D.D., that something life-changing happened but you never asked me what it was." His response was brief and honest, "Maybe I didn't want to know." *He knew*! The second he said that, I knew that *he knew* what the discussion with D.D. had been about so many years earlier.

I went on to tell him the four positive things he had done for me in my life. I had them listed on a paper. I realized that everything I had listed had taken place when I was a young adult, between 17 and 24. He had supported my desire to sit with John when D.D. gave a sermon on him, helped me with my Miss America speeches and the divorce, kept my horse alive when he was too old to ride and the caretaker wanted to kill him and, most of all, facilitated the illegal abortion.

I don't remember how I phrased what his sexual violations had done to me. Maybe I didn't need to. He certainly knew what I was talking about. He never tried to deny anything. I never expected— *never dreamed*—that he would, but I now know that most violators blatantly deny any and all violations. Let me clarify. I never expected him to deny the truth *to me*. To others, he would have denied everything. That was understood. That is always understood. Does anyone really believe a father would stand in public and say, "I pried my daughters open for eighteen years." Never. If you choose to confront your perpetrator with someone else present, don't even hope for validation.

He said one thing that stopped me cold, shut me down. I have no idea what he said in the seconds or minutes that followed—until I could bring myself back into the conversation. He said, "I haven't kissed your mother for 25 years." *He hasn't kissed my mother in 25 years?* How is that possible? My mother said, on an almost daily basis, "I've had 45 years of a perfect marriage." I just couldn't find a place in my mind to accommodate that sentence. It sounds crazy now but if you grow up as a child believing something, it is very difficult to alter that belief. They have a perfect marriage! He never kissed her. My father never kissed my mother. It just didn't make any sense. In the years to come, as the truth of my life unfolded, it would all make sense. Devastating, mind-crushing sense.

The other sentence I remember word-for-word was "If I had known what it would do to you, I never would have done it." That was the sentence of the day. Those were the words I would embed in my brain, my soul, the core of my being. He never would have done it if he had realized. How desperate a child is to cling to any semblance of hope that a father really does love a daughter. That a *day time* father really does love a *day time* daughter. I clung to every word of that sentence. He wouldn't have…he would have cared enough for me not to have…it was the thread of hope that kept me going. My father really did love me, the day child. He told me so, didn't he, when he said if he had known the lifetime trauma he would cause, he wouldn't have?

To face the truth—that my father cared absolutely nothing about me, that he only used me—would have been intolerable to bear. To accept the truth that I grew up without one person loving me, without one person caring, really caring about what happened to me, would have crushed my soul completely. I was far too vulnerable, hating, shaming, blaming myself to face the naked truth of the emptiness of my childhood. I would be 56 years old before I could face that truth head on.

Our conversation was over. He stood, reached into his pocket, and pulled out the gun. If you showed me 2,000 guns, I could immediately pick out the small khaki colored gun that lay coldly in his open palm. He looked me right in the eye and said, "If you had come in any other way, I would have killed myself." His message was very clear, "If you are even *thinking* about exposing me, take a good look at the consequences."

And people wonder why children don't tell.

As he headed through the kitchen to the garage and I headed the opposite direction toward the front door, he had one last minute question, "Who have you talked to about this?" "Larry. My sisters." "Have you spoken to your mother about it?" "No." "Are you going to?" "No."

As I got into my car, parked on the side of the house, he sped by me in his black Cadillac. Always speeding. Always driving way too fast and recklessly. In his car and in his life.

Most people have no understanding of how complex the long-term effects of childhood sexual abuse can be—especially if the violator was a family member, priest, coach…trusted friend. These pedophiles weave their way into our lives. Most are charming, talented, respected family and community members. They are not the bearded, stubble faced Charles Mansons. They don't make us hate them, they make us hate ourselves. We don't want them in prison. We live a lifetime in a kind of prison difficult to describe.

When, in July, we left for our one month vacation in Laguna Beach, I knew I would never go back to therapy. I had had 53 sessions; 52 too many. Why I had continued seeing Dr. Uh-huh, I'm not sure. I think the anxiety of going to a different psychiatrist was the major reason. I hadn't made the connection yet between incest and paralysis and if he had, he wasn't talking. He didn't talk much anyway. In the years to come, when I would work with gifted, sharing, giving therapists, I would realize what a waste of time Dr. Uh-huh was.

I did not call Dr. Uh-huh when we returned. He called me. I told him I was feeling stronger and that I would not be returning. (Well, the second half of that was true!) He said it would be necessary for me to come one more time. Ever the victim, I said, "Okay." It was a very short session. He said, "If you do not keep coming, you will not get sleeping pills." Oh, he was good. He knew there were only two things that I had to have in order to survive another day, Larry and sleeping pills. The thought of not having either was truly unthinkable. I looked straight into his eyes and said, with quiet rage, "I will always find sleeping pills." I always did and I never went back to him.

There were so many times when I felt guilty, as a mother, for things I could not do with or for Jennifer, such as having to leave the holiday program before she came on stage or not being able to shop with her in the mall because the background music that played and the general hubbub of people milling around sent my stress level over the edge. My normal anxiety level, at this time in my life, was constantly on red alert. But I never felt guiltier than the night Larry was out of town (a rare occurrence) and I tucked Jennifer into her bed. She was about six. I sang to her and kissed her good night. As I walked out of her room, her words to me were, "Mommy, would you leave your door open, please?" "Of course I will Jennifer." "Promise?" "Promise."

I couldn't leave my door open. I knew it when I said it. I tried. I tried so hard. Several hours after Jennifer went to sleep, it was time for me to turn out my light. I left the door open but the terror I felt with an open door was too extreme. I had to not only close the door but lock the door. I felt so guilty, as a mother, that I would lock my bedroom door, but it was that or lying awake all night in terror.

Many soldiers who fought on the front lines during a battle still jump if they hear a car backfire or a gun being unexpectedly fired. Living with the fear of the night for thirteen years embedded in my child-teen brain that the night is not safe. It is difficult to change what is bored into the core of a child's belief system.

I managed to still give speeches during this time but my schedule was greatly reduced. Each year my life would shut down a little more, as hysterical sobbing increased, usually with no understanding of why I was crying. As night terrors took over the nights even heavy sleeping pills wouldn't knock me out. I would lie awake, watching the door, knowing that if I didn't watch the door, I would die. The feeling was far beyond an intense foreboding of impending violence and doom. I believed I would literally die.

During this time of recovery, I wasn't remembering the memories and feelings, I was living them. When memories and feelings are split

182

off and stuffed deeply within the body, it is necessary to disgorge them and feel them as if they are happening in real time. This was not a voluntary decision. When the memories are triggered by a child's age, a medical procedure, a sexual experience, sound or smell, the memories and feelings are instantly felt and no amount of willing them away or decision to "just get over it," will work.

D.D. knew about my terror of the night and, in my late 40's, he gave me what was, perhaps, my greatest challenge. (I seemed to have so many of those.) D.D. said, "Every time you close and lock your door you are re-patterning your belief system that you are not safe. You need to stop doing that. Tonight when you go to bed, leave the door open. Just do it!"

"Okay, I will." The words were so easy to say. The prospective deed incomprehensible…but I was determined to do the "work" of healing. Peace. Joy. Calm. Healing. These are not gifts. These are hard earned blessings.

When I went to bed the night of his ultimatum, I left the door unlocked and open. I was in bed perhaps thirty seconds when I jumped up, closed the door and locked it. Within moments, I knew I would hear it, the scuff of footsteps in the hallway leading to our bedroom (similar to the long hallway to my childhood room). The terror of the night was still running my night life. My father wasn't coming to get me any more. I knew that in my brain, but no amount of intellectual reasoning comes into play during flashbacks. Every night, when I went to bed, I lived in flashbacks. If my father had raped me in a barn every single time, I would never step foot in a barn again, but I couldn't avoid the scene of the crime because it was always my bedroom.

I was determined to break the conditioning. The next night I tried it again. Same results. The third night I made a commitment to do it, no matter what. I left the door wide open and during the entire night, I rested deeply while watching the door. About every 60 seconds, I would quickly open my eyes to look at the doorway. One of the amazing aspects of surviving a childhood of torment is the coping skills we develop. I had learned how to think of nothing. The *feeling* was terror but, as a child, I had learned how to keep my mind blank. I had done it! I hadn't closed the door. I felt enormous satisfaction. I was also exhausted from not sleeping. The fourth night, I watched the door for about two hours and then I said something to myself, words that would become my mantra—words that I had lived by on previous occasions. But somehow actually saying the words, in my head, had an incredible impact. I rolled over, turned away from the door, locked my body into the tight fetal position and said, "If I die, I die but I don't want to live this way anymore." That was as powerful a statement as I had ever said to myself. My belief system—the *feelings* were that if I didn't watch the door, I would die. I don't ask you to understand that. I do ask you to honor the fact that those were my *feelings.*

I had made a deal. I might die. I understood that but I was dying a night at a time doing it this way so I made the decision to risk my life to break the chain of terror. I knew the only way I could break the pattern was to walk right into it.

The first few nights were difficult beyond description, but little by little, week by week, I began to find more peace with the door being unlocked and wide open.

I have had many nights since then when I have, for a variety of reasons, been thrown back into that night time terror. I had a night like that not too long ago and, as I began watching the door, I caught myself and repeated the phrase, "If I die, I die, but I'm not going to live that way anymore."

It was the same feeling as when I confronted my father and knew he had a gun. Although I didn't say those exact words, it was what I was feeling. Whatever the consequences, I am going to do this because I cannot live in this nightmarish world forever.

I now sleep with my door open, at home. That is an enormous victory for me.

When writing this book, I spent many nights alone in Vail. One night I heard noises that sent that old terror back into every pore of my body. I caught myself immediately and knew I wouldn't honor the fear by getting up and checking. My commitment still stood. I wasn't going to play the nightly game of checking, ever again.

I wish I didn't have to tell you what happened in the spring of 2002. I would like to have survivors know that every single bit of anxiety and fear ended for me because I did the work of healing. There are still times, however, when situations are uncomfortable. That became true in Vail during the spring. The ski season had ended and no one—not one person—was staying in our condominium building. Most of the restaurants had closed. Vail felt like a ghost town.

At night, even with the "white noise machine" I always use, I was listening, knowing I was the only person in the entire building. Even the sleeping medication I take at night so I can fall asleep, didn't work so I called the off site manager and asked to have huge dead bolts put on the inside of the front door and my bedroom door. He asked how large. I said large enough so that no one could get in without breaking the entire door down. He said, "The fire marshal will not allow ones that large because then they can't get in, in case of fire." I said, "Those are the ones I want. Please." He said, "No one has ever tried to break in…" I said, "Please don't tell me how safe the building is. This has nothing to do with rational thinking. This has to do with my perception. I have to perceive that no one could get through those doors without big axes."

He knew "my story." He said, "I'll have someone put them on right away." Now, when I go to Vail during the off-season, I feel safe and sleep well. It was a simple way to give me peace. Do I feel like a failure because I'm more comfortable with huge bolts on the door? No. Do I feel like I should go back into therapy because when I am alone in a building, I feel safer with dead bolts? No. I'm sure there will always be times when I will take an extra precaution for whatever reason.

I remember reading that Barbra Streisand was too terrified to sing in front of live audiences so she didn't for twenty-two years. She finally walked right into the fear and gave concerts we will never forget.

For survivors, the *only* path to sanity, peace and healing is to face our fears. I used to say to Larry, "All I ask is to feel just thirty seconds of peace within my being." Now I live with a calm that is difficult to describe. I know there is light at the end of the tunnel for survivors who are willing to do the work of healing because I live in that light now.

Chapter 10 – Putting Feelings With Memories

After spending almost three months in three different hospitals and 53 visits with Dr. Uh-huh, I once again began the frenetic schedule of speaking engagements and the production of ten motivational films. I wrote every word of the text for the ten 30 minute films, found over 500 visuals (film footage or photographs), and secured the release for the use of each. I was still needing to do more, be more and run faster—and I loved every minute of working on the films.

Without question, the most memorable part of writing the text for the educational, motivational films was the time I spent with Jennifer and her friends. They were my adorable, nine-year-old research sources and guinea pigs. They would tell me which examples touched their lives and which ones didn't. Eight to ten girls would come to the house and I would read them at least twenty different examples for each class. These were almost always examples of people's lives. Then I would ask them to write down which ones they remembered and why. It was fascinating. Not only which they chose but why the examples had been significant to them. We did this over many weeks.

Now in their 30's, many have told me that listening to and sharing their own ideas regarding "How long and how hard should you try?" or "What determines whether or not one is successful?" impacted their adult lives. Although I hadn't made a connection with what was driving my life, I needed to give them what I never had, someone to say, "You can do it. You can get through one more day—or one more night. You can overcome shame. You can be okay in the world."

During the same time period, I scheduled an appointment with the manager of one of our major television stations to ask if he would insert a one-minute motivational segment into the local news. He said, "Yes." As I researched, wrote, and timed, to the second, 130 television segments, I began to wonder, "How do I come up with 130 different ideas?" And the answer came, "One at a time." I even typed the text onto the teleprompter. The only thing I didn't pay much attention to was what I wore. That was short-lived. My sister-in-law, Janey, began choosing outfits; fortunately, she has impeccable taste.

I felt a coldness each time I went into the newsroom to work. I was grateful when the anchorman was honest with me, "I don't like what you are doing. I don't want it on my show. I have only 22 minutes for news, weather, and sports. Now you have taken another minute away." I understood his feelings. Fortunately, the responses to my segments were so positive, the station manager decided to rerun all of them.

When Jennifer's middle school asked me to address 125 teachers and parents at the annual dinner, I was just beginning a free fall into a despair that was unfathomable. Jennifer was in 8th grade. How could I say "No?" Everyone knew this was what I did at least three times a week in other cities. Other parents volunteered their time to run the auction and organize events. But in other cities no one knew me personally. At Jennifer's school, everyone knew me. That made it a far different speech than one I would give in Omaha or Dallas.

Two to three months before the speech my anxiety became so intense I hired a hypnotist to come to my home every week to try to hypnotize me into believing: "You will feel calm. You will feel peace. As you walk into the banquet, you will know they want to hear your message and that will be your focus…" Again and again he tried hypnosis. The thoughts I had were, "I will die if I go." "I cannot do it." "I won't be able to breathe."

The presentation went perfectly; the price for me was way too high. It would be years before I would understand that they would introduce a former Miss America, Outstanding Woman Speaker in America, but I would know who I really was. Totally and completely unacceptable. Unless and until I could change my perception about myself, the inner fear would continue.

One day, when Jennifer was a toddler, I stopped by my parents' house to pick up something. My father said, "Get that snotty nosed kid out of here." Mother would always try to ease the situation. She said, "He just doesn't like small children."

It was during this time that something happened that would drastically change my father's life. My father had always been a bully. He took what he wanted when he wanted it. He backed down from no one. I learned an invaluable lesson about bullies from my father.

He was 73 years old when it happened. He was driving his car into the alley. He put the electric garage door up, drove in and started to get out of the car. He was carrying papers in his arms. Quickly, a masked gunman rushed into the garage and demanded his money. My father threw the papers in his face and began to tussle with him. He looked up and saw another man with a stocking covering his face, holding a gun. My father quickly let go, headed for the door and yelled, "Go on, God damn it, shoot me." And one of them did. He was shot through the leg. The gunmen ran. My father opened the door to the house and yelled, "God damn it, Bootsie, come here." Mother ran to him and saw the blood streaming from his leg. He said, "We're going to the hospital." My father drove.

The next day, in big black print, the newspaper article was entitled, "Van, feisty, says they didn't get anything." Oh, but they did. They took something far more valuable than money. They took something irreplaceable. His confidence. His cockiness. His arrogance. My father had never known what it was like to be a victim. He wasn't scared of anything or anyone. He was tough. Until he was shot—and then he became fearful. He went yellow-belly. It totally changed his life. Whereas before he had guns in many places, he now had guns *everywhere*. Doors were locked and double locked.

One night the family met for dinner. For some reason, Mother had not joined us. As we left the restaurant, I said, "Would it be okay if I drive behind you until you get home?" Before the shooting he would have been insulted by that question. Now he said, "That would be fine." After the shooting, his alcohol consumption increased and he started drinking during the day. He began staying at home in his bathrobe, stretched out in his big lounge chair. Many days he didn't shave. He finally knew what it felt like to be a victim and it turned him into a coward…depressed, unmotivated and even more anti-social.

My father stopped going to the office and was becoming depressed and inactive. I called every day to ask him if he would go for a walk. I was worried about him and tried to encourage him. He rarely spoke to me when we walked together. I'm sure he went just to be sure his beloved mean chow dog, Ching, would get a walk. It is astonishing to me how I could have blinded myself to his rudeness and dislike of me. He couldn't have been more blunt. I didn't or couldn't acknowledge that.

I was becoming unable to function even minimally. I knew even people who loved me (never Larry) were saying, "Get over it!" Why couldn't I "get over it?" A dear friend stopped by one day. She couldn't have been more loving but her words cut me to the bone. "Lynn, it's a beautiful day. You have Larry, Jennifer, this wonderful home, an incredible career, you need to let this go now and move on with your life." Not one word had been said with malice. She had always been supportive of me but her words were so hurtful. If only she knew how desperately I wanted to move on. The feelings and emotions had become more than I could suppress or control anymore. The recovery process has nothing to do with willpower or choice.

I wish I had known that many—if not most—adults, sexually violated as children, *are in their 40's* before they begin to deal with their childhoods. Just knowing that this is "normal" for many survivors would have helped me cope with friends and family members who were saying, "This happened a long time ago. Just move on with your life."

I remember the first time someone said to me, "You need to feel the feelings." I thought, what is she talking about? What does that mean? But when the feelings started coming up, I never asked that question again.

Background music in a restaurant or beauty salon could tap into such overwhelming anxiety, I would have to leave. Immediately. Jennifer's music, which always emanated from her room, would make me feel as if I were going crazy. The fast beat would cause feelings of hysteria. We stopped going to movies. No radio in the car. No mysteries or suspense shows on television. We adapted. Sort of. Too many times, I would lose control.

Watching a television commercial could send me over the edge. One began showing a child in bed. We saw her bedroom door slowly open and the black shadow of a huge man quietly entering her room. The sponsor was a home security system with an 800 number. I grabbed for the phone, dialed the number and began screaming (and I do mean screaming) into the phone, "Stop it. Stop it. Don't ever show that commercial again. Stop it." My anxiety would cross the line of even semi-normal behavior.

A neighbor was hammering and sawing for what seemed like weeks. One day, I just couldn't stand the noise one more second. The distress took over. I opened the window and just screamed, "Stop it. Stop it. Stop the noise." My ability to find a more civil way to express my feelings was not possible. When anxiety crossed the line into hysteria, I said and did things that I look back on with embarrassment and incredulity.

When Jennifer turned 13, huge waves of anxiety would so fill my body, I would feel like a child trapped in a corner by a Doberman pinscher, snarling as he began to close in. As summer approached and free time surrounded me, feelings of terror engulfed me, much as if I were on an elevator that started on the thirty-fifth floor and suddenly dropped, as if the wires had been cut, to the basement. I couldn't stop the adrenalin from surging. Now, at age 46, *Jennifer was mirroring me as she began puberty.*

Everything began to quickly change. These were now the much more exaggerated feelings of my father prying open a daughter whose sexual feelings were far more intense. It was the beginning of almost six years of believing I would die from the pain or burst apart from feelings my body could not contain as I was forced to dredge up *feelings* I had buried. I have no words to even attempt to describe those feelings. Just take a minute to vividly envision a child or teen you love, being pried open and penetrated in every part of her being for 13 years, and you will get a sense of it.

Just as all this was beginning, I received a phone call from D.D. After 25 years of living in California, he and his wife Karen (D.D. had remarried after his wife, Lois, died) were moving back to Denver. I liked Karen instantly and found her to be brilliant and funny. In the months to come, D.D. would call this unexpected return, "God's grace."

He would return just as my life was shutting down completely. The four of us began meeting three to five nights a week. I would count the hours until they would arrive for our "therapy sessions." They were my only lifeline and I would tax them to their maximum when it came time to try to make contact with my night child. Although I would see many therapists in the years to come, none would have better insights than my "team."

One morning, Larry and I took our usual 6 a.m. walk. Traffic had not yet begun in our quiet neighborhood. Suddenly, in the middle of an intersection, I began sobbing hysterically and loudly, "My daddy's dead. My daddy's dead." I wailed it over and over again. The deep heaving sobs were so emotionally exhausting, I slumped down in the intersection; Larry thought he might have to carry me home. This was one of the few times Larry had appointments he could not cancel. He called D.D. who responded, as always, "I'm on my way."

By the time D.D. arrived, the bottled up, stuffed in, mashed down feelings started to pour out of me. Obsessively, I began to tell D.D.

191

how wonderful my father was. I listed the four things he had done for me. D.D. knew the list well. I knew how hard it was for D.D. to listen to me extolling what I considered to be my father's virtues but he listened, as he always did, as I went on in a state of near hysteria. I didn't realize it at the time but *the closer I came to the terrifying feelings of rage* I had for my father, the more frantically I would steel myself from them by loud protestations of love. If I confronted the truth about my father—that he was a truly evil man—the entire world I had constructed would implode.

While extolling my father's virtues, my night child was screaming at my refusal to even acknowledge her, much less comfort and love her. She was like the child who goes into the kitchen and says, "Mommy can you help me with this?" And the mother replies perfunctorily, "In a minute." "Please now, Mommy?" "I said in a minute." The child pulls on her mother's dress. The mother ignores her. The child pulls harder. Finally, the child pulls down the cookie jar, it splinters into hundreds of pieces. She now has her mother's attention.

My night child kept her part of the deal. She had "taken it" until I was strong and secure enough to come back and rescue her. Now, instead of gratitude for her sacrificing herself, I loathed, despised and blamed her. Well, she had *no intention* of staying locked off in the night anymore. My night child, that part of myself that I blocked out, walled off, and pushed down, was enraged. The feelings that part of me held inside for so long were coming out of me like a garden hose hit by a machine gun. Everywhere.

There was no question that tapping into the rage I had for my father would be the most important step now. My team chiseled and hammered at my defense mechanisms but we couldn't find a way in. "I love my father" would be my consistent response.

After meeting with Larry, D.D. and Karen several nights a week for almost a month, one Friday in September I was in total despair. I felt as if I needed to put both hands around my head and try to hold it together. For the first time, I understood the words, "lose my mind." I knew hospitalization was a possibility. Not the hospital where they do tests and body scans. No. The hospital where they lock the door behind you. I wouldn't. I couldn't. No one could know.

Before D.D. left that Friday night, he strongly urged me to stop seeing my father because my anxiety, obviously caused by him, was so dangerously consuming me. No matter how my father had rejected me as an adult, I came back, so obsessed was I, the day child-adult, with earning his love. No matter what I did, no matter what award I won, or what special dish I would cook for him or how bright or witty my conversations might be, he rebuffed me.

Larry and D.D. knew that the crazy feelings I was having, the extreme stress, the paralysis...all of it was directly related to my fight to keep from admitting to anyone (mostly myself) the extraordinary pain and rage I had for my father. They knew that I was self destructing because I could not let myself acknowledge the truth of what the buried feelings really were. I would destroy myself before I would destroy the fantasy of my love for my father.

Larry had a brilliant idea. He called my sister Gwen, who was living in San Francisco. "Lynn is in acute anxiety. I'm not sure she can hold on much longer. We believe she could tap into her underlying feelings if you would fly here and tell her the details of the incest with your father. We think she would be so angry by what he did to *you*, it would lead us into her anger." Gwen said, "I'll take the first flight tomorrow morning." Larry said, "I'll have a ticket waiting for you at the counter."

Gwen was incested from age 8 to age 18. She survived very differently than I. Rather than repressing and burying, she defiantly fought her way through the reality of it every day and every night.

I had flown to talk to Gwen as soon as my repressed memories surfaced, when I was 24, but we had never talked about any specifics. All she had said was, "Oh my God, I thought I was the only one. I never should have left you. It's my fault." No matter how many times I told her that she couldn't have done anything, she still believed she could have stopped it.

I was transfixed and dumbfounded as Gwen shared her story with Larry and me. I could barely process the information she was giving us. I will share only those things Gwen has spoken publicly, said to an author for a book or given me permission to share. The most shocking thing she said was, "I had all the power." I could barely integrate those five words. I responded, "You had all the *power?* What power could you possibly have had?"

"I could have told. He knew that at any moment I could have told."

"And who would you have told?"

"Gaba." (My mother's father)

"You had a close relationship with him?"

"Yes. Very close. I would take three busses to go stay with them for the weekend."

Gwen continued, "I could have told Gaba. He would have stopped it. The reason you didn't spend weekends with them was because you were the fourth child. They were "grand-childrened" out by the time you were old enough to spend the night." Then Gwen said, "I still have the power. He named me the executor of his estate. He used me. I'm using him."

There is no doubt in my mind that this is one of the major reasons why Gwen and I responded so differently. She *perceived* she had power. She *perceived* she could stop it.

A national expert on how trauma impacts brain hormones said recently, "Perception is the key. People who feel some control over their lives, even under stress, cope better." [1] .

But Gwen didn't tell our grandfather or anyone. Nor would she have. (Even as an adult, Gwen never confronted my father.) Most children don't tell because they are so ashamed and frightened. But if Mother had chosen to protect us, there is no question my grandfather would have welcomed Mother and her four children into their very large home.

My belief was that I had *no* power. There wasn't a soul in the world I could have turned to. I had no way out. That was *my* perception as a child, and I could not have been more right. Looking back as an adult, I had no one. Incest cut me off from everyone except my father and we had been conditioned to never "tell." Sexual abuse is a mind game, as well as physical torment and humiliation. Perhaps more importantly, I was terrified of my father.

Gwen never pretended to be asleep. When she told us she *talked to him* at night, I could barely breathe. Some of the things she said to him were inconceivable to me. She refused to let him think she was frightened by him or that he controlled her. On the other hand, I was immobilized by his power over me.

---

[1] Esther Sternberg, director of the National Institute of Health research on how brain hormones affect disease. *USA Today*, May 4, 2000

Gwen was defiant. She defied Mother openly. One day when Gwen was 12, Mother asked her to do something and Gwen said, "No." Mother said, "I told you to do it." Gwen shouted, "No!" In complete frustration, my mother hit her across the face and Gwen hit Mother back. I cannot *imagine* hitting my mother in the face nor can I ever remember another instance where my mother physically hit any one of us.

It was at that point that my father decided to send Gwen to boarding school in Kansas City. My father would then fly to Kansas City and take her to the Muelbach Hotel, then the most luxurious hotel in Kansas, for weekends. Even when Gwen thought she might have escaped, my father had the last word. He had all the power and he exercised it time and again.

The same Friday night Larry had called Gwen to fly to Denver, he called a highly regarded psychiatrist and left this message, "My wife is in *acute* anxiety. She may need to be hospitalized. Could you see her right away?" The psychiatrist finally returned the call on Monday. I met with him on Tuesday. I'm amazed I was able to drive myself. I hadn't seen a psychiatrist since Dr Uh -Huh, seven years earlier. That was when I had the luxury of paralysis spells, keeping everything locked deep inside me. The spells were peaceful.

I had no way of knowing that an earthquake was now in the beginning stages of awakening. Now, the ground was shaking with anger. I was in serious trouble. I wasn't living on the brink of hysteria, I was in the epicenter. I had to vomit up sewage from the depths of my being.

Rationally, it seemed incomprehensible for me to tell another person what my father had done, but emotionally, it was like trying to hold down spoiled milk. I just had to get it out. I thought I would burst as I waited. I wanted to break the door down and scream a scream that would stop people's hearts from beating. I wondered if I could wait until I sat down in his office to let it all pour out. When he opened the door, I rushed in. It was obvious I was in an emotional emergency and that I would burst wide open if I couldn't start vomiting feelings immediately.

The psychiatrist paid no attention at all. He began a recitation of his billing process. A lengthy dissertation. I would have to give seven days notice if I wanted to cancel an appointment. If I didn't, I would be charged the full $105. I would need to pay in advance. "Now."

When he said, "Now," I realized he meant *right now*. I was to take out my checkbook and write him a check for $210. How could I possibly focus on his billing procedures?

I rummaged around for my checkbook and a pen, wrote the check and handed it to him. I had not said one word to him.

We sat facing one another. At least I would know he wasn't doing crossword puzzles while I lay on a couch as he sat behind me as my last psychiatrist had. Finally, I knew I could start. I didn't start, my entire being burst open. Not with sobs but with convulsive, heaving sounds with no words spoken. It was more like dry heaves than crying. It took me several minutes to compose myself enough to even speak in words. Sentences were out of the question. "Father. Night. No hope. No help. Can't do this…another day…

Must die…"

When I had exhausted myself, I became quiet. His first words to me were, "I don't think incest is such a big deal to have caused all this." That should have been my first clue. But I had seen his many plaques in the waiting room.

Having *anyone*, but especially having a reputable psychiatrist, invalidate my pain was like a huge, lead wrecking ball hitting me in the head. It would be a sentence that would ring in my head for years. If he said that to me today, I would get up and walk out after such a flippant, outrageous, unprofessional and uninformed comment—but I was vulnerable and defenseless. I couldn't even begin to deal with what he had just said. I needed to continue getting the pain up, puncturing the vastness of the excruciating feelings I had stuffed for so many years.

The only other memory I have of that first session with this highly credentialed doctor, was trying to tell him my unspeakable story. As I dropped my head in shame, sobbing while searching for words to continue a sentence, he interrupted me and said, "Your time is up." I was far too stunned to even raise my head. My time is up? In the middle of that sentence, my time is up? I raised my head to look at him. I must have misunderstood those four words. No one, not even an animal would respond to a human being in so much pain, with those four words. My precious little mutt, Benji, would have come to me and laid his head on my lap or licked me. I had unzipped my soul and it was out there raw, naked and in pain. The look on his face confirmed what he had said. My time was up.

I stood and walked to the door. I fumbled with the doorknob and walked out in a complete daze. I was so filled with unresolved energies and feelings, I couldn't even think of taking the elevator. He left me completely opened and incapable of knowing how to stuff the feelings back in. How do you do that? Run. That's all I could think of to do. Run. And run. And run. I ran down the cement staircase, ten flights, to the parking lot. It was raining. I ran past my car and just kept running around and around the parking lot. Running faster and faster. My innards, my guts, my decades of feelings were spilling out all over the parking lot and I didn't know what to do.

If that's what he learned in medical school, he should demand a refund. When a therapist just stares at us as we relate horrific things adults have done to us, it makes us wonder, "Maybe it isn't such a big deal. He certainly doesn't think it is." That cavalier attitude is abusive. It violates us again. As inconceivable as this may seem, the indescribably painful feelings he left me with were far more destructive than the rape I experienced by the 5th Avenue New York doctor. It was, perhaps, the most traumatic moment of my recovery.

I was so out of control and my anxiety was so acute, I knew I had to make a choice. Go back to him or be hospitalized. I just couldn't go to a psychiatric hospital. No one could know. It would end my life. I certainly did believe that. I don't remember the next session two days later (which I had prepaid) but I do remember leaving the session knowing that I had to talk to my father again. I was now 47. Our one conversation seven years earlier had not been enough. I hadn't even begun to access the feelings when I talked with him. Then, I had had no anger or tears. Just cerebral facts. Now I had to tell him what I was *feeling*, and he had to tell me how sorry he was. He never said he was sorry. I had to ask him questions. I needed answers. *I had to talk to my father.*

I chose Sunday morning, three days after my second visit with the psychiatrist. I called my parents' home. Mother answered but I heard my father pick up. He always picked up and listened to every conversation. I would talk to Mother but I knew my father would hear what I was saying.

Mother said, "You haven't been over to see us in ten days. Is something wrong?" I said, "Yes, Mother there is. I'm seeing a psychiatrist." Going to therapy was unheard of in my parents' generation. I had never told them that I had seen a psychiatrist years earlier. I was now *emotionally connected* to my childhood trauma. With my words, I was lighting a blazing red flare.

If Jennifer called to tell me that something was wrong and she was seeing a psychiatrist, I would be in my car before she could finish the sentence. But, of course, Mother didn't respond to this new information in any way, she went right on with the conversation as if she hadn't even heard what I had just said. She talked about the weather and her new car and what they had for breakfast. It didn't matter. I wasn't saying anything for her to hear anyway. I knew what her response would be. Nothing.

I was talking because I *knew* my father would know exactly what I was saying. "Help! Please help me. I'm really in trouble and we need to talk. You can help me get through this." But I also knew my father knew I was "speaking the words." For the first time, he knew I was telling someone other than family. He knew that it would be difficult to keep Denver's outstanding business and civic leader, and Colorado's Miss America's explosive secret, a secret.

I was reaching out to my father as I had never reached out before. In despair. I know he heard how much trouble I was in, how much pain. I wanted him to go upstairs, close his door, pick up his private telephone and say, "Let's talk." I needed to talk about it. To try to find some resolution. I needed him desperately.

Do you know what my father did for me that day? He died. There will never be any doubt in my mind that he made a choice. Reach out to me or die. It should have been no surprise to me what his choice was.

Four hours after I called, Mother called, "Come quickly. I've just dialed 911." My father had taken his chow dog for a walk around the block, come home and fallen just inside the front door. He asked Mother to help him crawl up the stairs. Mother pushed him up and then, because he had lost control of his bowels, Mother took his pants down to the basement to wash them. About ten minutes later, she called 911.

Larry, Jennifer and I were there when the ambulance arrived. We followed the ambulance to the emergency room and then waited and waited and waited. I kept sobbing to my sister, "I killed him. I know I killed him. He had to die because he knew the secret was out."

I knew I would break the door down if a nurse came out and said, "You can't see him." I had to see him. I had to talk to him. A doctor finally came into the waiting room, turned to Mother and said, "He's dead." That's all he said. Just "He's dead."

Then a compassionate nurse came out and said, "You can say goodbye to him now, if you wish." Mother just put her head inside the door and said, "Bye Poppy." One of my sisters walked in and said, "Bye Daddy." Then it was my turn. Larry went in with me and stood behind me. My father's light blue eyes were still open. His face was still warm. His pure white hair was soft. I had never touched his hair. Hesitatingly, I touched his face and his hair and sobbed, "I love you Daddy, I'm so sorry. I'm so sorry. I'm so sorry. I love you. I'm so sorry." I must have repeated those words more than a hundred times. I can't even imagine how difficult this was for Larry. As much as he felt pain for my feelings, I know another part of him was thinking, "Finally. He's dead." But he would never have said anything like that to me.

I sobbed and said those words over and over and then I realized, suddenly, that we were not alone in the room. A nurse was standing in the far corner. I said, "I'm sorry I'm taking so long." She said, "Take as long as you want. There's no hurry." And I did stay. For a long time. It was agonizing to say goodbye to my father. I had no more time to try to win the only thing I ever wanted from him—his day time love. He had dominated my entire life. He would continue to dominate my life long after his death. The long-term effects of childhood sexual abuse are incomprehensible.

My father died in early September. Only weeks earlier, while on vacation in Laguna Beach, California, I had had a premonition of his death. I had visualized him dead, lying in a casket. What was so incredibly eerie and strange about the "vision" I had, was that he was lying in a small viewing room in one of his other buildings, not where he had his office.

There would have been no question that the service for any family member—especially my father—would be held at the main mortuary. He owned four mortuary buildings and yet, in this strange premonition, I had seen my father lying in a casket in his newest mortuary, in the third room, a small, unimportant room.

In my premonition, I had seen his entire funeral. Rather than having an organist playing music as everyone gathered for the service, I had arranged for a tape of his music to be played. Anyone who knew my father even slightly knew he played the piano and would instantly recognize his unique style. Then during the service I had heard a tape of him reciting his poetry, which would be played over the sound system.

I had chills for days, when, after my father died, I learned he had been taken to the new mortuary and when I went to see him, he was in the third small room and would remain there until the large drawing room was ready. I stood next to the casket, looking at him. His hands were across his chest. Suddenly, my blood turned cold when I looked at the fingernail on the middle finger of his left hand. It was filed off. All his other nails were exactly the same. Well manicured, well rounded. But not the middle finger. The nail had been cut down to the quick. I knew the second I saw it. I wasn't the last one. He had never stopped. I could barely breathe. I had to not think about it. It was literally unbelievable to me. I never thought about it again until I was 56.

His obituary was on the front page of our paper and many of my friends began sending cards of condolence. One friend started her letter to me with this sentence, "I know exactly how you feel." How could she possibly know how I felt? I had no idea how I felt. One part of me was grieving while, at the same time, rage was just beginning to slowly drip through a newly punctured, tiny pinhole.

The day before the funeral, I asked Larry to go with me while I expressed my anger at my father for the way he had treated Larry and at myself for having allowed it. But I had known, all too well, that if I had said, "Either you treat Larry respectfully or I'll leave," he would have said, "Go. I didn't ask you here anyway."

Allowing my father to treat Larry disrespectfully—by just ignoring him—is something for which I will never forgive myself. When I tell Larry that, he responds, "How you survived and kept your sanity is more than I can understand. How I felt wasn't important. If I had expressed my rage for your father or mother, it would have exacerbated your problems. You always come first."

One of my sisters had been working at the mortuary for years and I met with her to discuss the funeral plans. She just stared at me when I told her I had our father's music and poetry ready to go. She couldn't believe the suggestion of his music and poetry. I couldn't believe that she didn't know this was the way it was going to be. I had already seen

200

it, as if it had already happened.

My father's funeral was huge. He was, in his death, as he had been in his life, in charge and on center stage. He would have loved his part in the service. People hearing him play and recite, one last time.

It is the custom for the immediate family to close the casket after the service. I said to Mother, "Mildred and Miriam will need to be with us." Her eyes turned cold as she said, "After everyone has gone." I repeated, "After everyone has gone." Seven of the women in his life closed the casket. He had impacted our lives in very different ways but he had been the driving force behind each of us. If only his death had ended my pain. He died as I was just beginning to face the truth of my life.

His interment was on the mountain he had purchased years earlier, near the 400 foot lighted cross. When the long black limousines arrived at the top of the mountain, the skies opened up. Never have I heard such loud thunder or seen so many bolts of lightning. It was as if God were enraged that it was now His turn to figure out what to do with this man.

My father was buried in an elegant casket with huge flower arrangements everywhere. There was standing room only.

When the four sisters and brothers-in-law gathered at our family home the next day, Gwen said, "If you gave anything to him that you would like to have back, just tell me and it will be fine for you to take it." Two or three sisters or brothers-in-law mentioned several things. Larry said, "I would love to have the 12 gauge shot gun that I gave your father." Gwen said, "Marilyn is not to have a gun" and she gave the shotgun to a brother-in-law.

When we left the house, I said to Larry, "I am going to Gart's Sporting Goods store now to buy a gun." He didn't say, "That is ridiculous! You will never use a gun, just let it go." He said, "I'll go with you." We drove downtown. I went straight to the gun department, pointed out the pistol I wanted to buy (I had never held or shot a pistol) and we went home. The second we walked in the door, I called Gwen and said, "I have a gun." And that was the end of it. It was the beginning of my empowerment within my family.

Two days after my father died, I went back to the psychiatrist for my third session. My feelings were so mixed and overwhelming. We both sat down without saying anything. He said, "I would appreciate a check for this week's sessions before we begin." I said, "He died." He said, "Who died?" I wanted to say, "His obituary was on the front page of the paper, you jerk," instead, I said, "My father. The funeral is day after tomorrow." And then with anger beginning to build, I said, icily, "Will I have to pay for the missed session?" He mulled that over for a long time before he said, "I guess not." I never went back.

But during that last session, he summed up my father's feelings about me. He said, "What did your father leave you in his will?" I was taken aback by the question. I said, "What does that matter?" He replied, "It was his last statement to you." I responded, "I was told that until a year ago, he had left nothing to us. Only during the last year, when he was losing his grip on life (after he had been shot) did his attorney say, 'Van, you just can't do this. You need to leave your daughters *something.*' Only then did he decide to leave us anything at all." That's when the psychiatrist said, almost casually, "He didn't care very much about you, did he?"

It would be more than a year before I would have the courage to see another therapist, a woman psychologist. My first words to her were, "Please never say these words to me, 'Your time is up.' Please *never* say those words to me. Say, we have ten more minutes or we need to begin winding down now. But never say, 'Your time is up.' No matter what the circumstances are."

Many months later, Larry and I were playing a game with several family members, to whom I had disclosed the truth. A question is asked, usually having to do with ethics. It was getting late. Someone said, "One more question. Lynn, this one will be yours." He picked up the card and read the question, "If you could ask anyone, living or dead, one question and there were no ramifications from the question or the answer, what one question would you ask, and to whom would you ask it?" He put the card down and said, "Well, that's an easy one. The question would be to your father and it would be one word. It would begin with a 'w' and end with a 'y.'" Very slowly I answered, "You're half right. The question *would* be to my father, but the question would be, 'Did you ever love me?'"

He said, "Well, I'll never understand *that.*"

How could anyone understand that? I so wished I could think the way everyone wanted me to think. Did I love my father? Hate my father? Did everything feel so horrid? Were there times when he made my body feel good? I knew no one could understand the complex

202

journey I was on. Except Larry. He said, "If you take the white covering off of a golf ball, you will find hundreds of rubber bands. It isn't possible to separate them, they are so intricately intertwined and pasted together. And so are your feelings. He was your *father.* You have love and hate, disgust and despair, pleasure and rage..."

It was more than a year later, when, in therapy I would cry out like a mother wailing for a dead child, "He didn't love me. He never loved me. He didn't give a damn about me." The truth would sear me with pain.

Chapter 11 – A New Mother Daughter Bond

D.D. and Karen continued coming over for our frequent sessions. I always sent Jennifer to her room. My constant sobbing, bursts of emotion and our stark conversations were not appropriate for any 13-year-old.

The weeks melded into months. Larry, Jennifer and I had always done everything together. Now, suddenly, she was asked to stay in her room as we began to lock her out of our lives. It took a simple question from our precious child to finally make me realize what we had been doing.

We were scheduled for our annual week of entertaining friends and business associates at Black Lake. I couldn't imagine engaging in conversations, climbing mountains, or laughing by the fire. The most I had been able to do in a day was drag myself to therapy. I thought we would have to cancel, but as the time drew near I felt focused enough to try to pull it off.

Soon after our arrival, I asked Jennifer if she would like to go with me to make an important call to a family member. The closest phone was two miles away but it was a slow drive down a one-lane dirt road. By the time I hung up, I was crying. Jennifer said, "What's wrong, Mommy?" She had asked that question so many times. "It's okay, Jennifer. I'll be okay."

As we started back to the lodge, we were both silent. Family issues were so intense and upsetting, I could barely focus on the road. Jennifer was very quiet. She just looked out the window. How could I keep shutting her out of my life? I was driving my beloved daughter away and I knew it. I could hear Jennifer saying to friends who came over and walked by me while I was in paralysis on a sofa, "Mommy's just having a spell." Like "Mom has a migraine."

The second we drove up to the lodge, I caught Larry's eye. I never had to say anything to him. He could tell, by one glance, when I was upset. Others would never notice. He came over immediately and we walked down toward the lake.

"She keeps asking, 'What's wrong, Mommy?' I have shut her out for too long. Jennifer needs to know the truth."

The look on Larry's face will always haunt me. I saw the thought of his only child, his cherished daughter knowing about a father's lasciviousness—evil—betrayal.

When Jennifer was growing up, no mother we knew, traveled—much less traveled every week. And certainly no lawyer-father stayed home to make his daughter a peanut butter, grape and mayonnaise sandwich. And few, if any, fathers of our generation arrived home before dinner so they could get a pizza and go swimming or play pitch and putt or just wrestle and giggle with a daughter. He was and has always been the quintessential father.

He was also very protective of her. When Jennifer was a baby and toddler, there had been a bed in her room, in addition to her crib. When she was sick, Larry would sleep in her room to be sure she was okay. He slept on the floor. He was concerned that if he slept in the bed, he might sleep too soundly to hear her.

If she went to a friend's house to play, he would drive her there—even if it was only a few blocks away. Jennifer was Larry's precious little girl, his only child. How difficult it must have been for *him* to allow perversion and a father's violation of a sacred trust into the world he had so carefully crafted for his most special daughter. He had, as always, thought about this long before I had. His response was immediate but deeply sad. He said, "It's the right thing to do now."

Why didn't I ask him to be a part of the conversation? How could I not have included Larry? I look back and wonder how I could have been so thoughtless but I also realize that it would have been a different conversation if anyone else—even Larry—had been there.

The next morning, I asked Jennifer if she would go with me again to make another phone call. I knew this was a conversation we wanted to have with absolute privacy. As I drove down the dirt road with aspen branches gently brushing on the car, I couldn't think of one word to say, so we drove in silence. When we got to the rickety old cabin where the phone was housed, I asked Jennifer to sit on the weathered wooden steps with me. I lowered my head and the sobbing began. I believed, with all my heart, that when I told Jennifer, she would say, "I don't want you to be my mom anymore." I knew I would be as unacceptable to her as I was to myself.

If you are not a survivor of childhood sexual abuse, I'm sure it is difficult to understand that kind of shame but it is very real. We feel so unworthy and we believe, each time we disclose, that we will be shunned, no longer wanted. Sometimes our fears are confirmed. I will always remember what a close friend said after she told her husband that she had been raped by her father, "He never looked at me the same way again."

I'm not sure how long I cried before I began trying to speak even one word to Jennifer. What are the words? How do you explain incest to a 13-year-old? Jennifer hadn't even had her first kiss yet. I could *never* have said the word "incest" and, if I had been able, I'm sure she would not have known what I was talking about.

I searched for words, hoping she would understand without my having to be explicit. She did understand and she began to cry. She was the only person who had ever cried for me. It was one of the most profoundly moving moments of my life.

She put her arms around me and began gently rocking me. We sat there and just held one another, surrounded only by aspen and pine trees, blue sky and a gentle breeze.

Silently, we slowly got into the car and started down the road, back to the lodge. I kept my eyes straight ahead, willing the heaving sobs within me to be still, but unable to stop a steady stream of tears from pouring out of my eyes, down my cheeks and onto the light blue shirt I was wearing.

Jennifer's window was down and she was looking out, thinking. She was the one to break the silence with slow, pensive, but spontaneous words: "You know, Mom, you've changed so many people's lives with your speeches. Think how many more lives you could change if people knew *this* about you."

I was so stunned, I stopped the car. For the first time, I looked right into her eyes and said, "Well what if *your* friends knew, Jennifer?" She replied, without a moment of hesitation, "They would respect you more."

It was a life changing moment. If I were ever asked to list the five most important moments of my life, this would be one. I believed if her friends knew, they wouldn't want to be friends with her. Boys' parents would forbid them to ask her out and the university she dreamed of attending wouldn't even consider her—if they knew. That's part of the viciousness of what my father did to me.

In that instant, my young, innocent, beautiful child set me free. Not a hint of shame in her voice. With no preparation or tutoring, coaching or counseling, she removed the invisible gag from my mouth and in a matter of seconds, my worst fear was over. My daughter was not ashamed of me. *My daughter was not ashamed of me.* Inexplicably, Jennifer had become one of my healers. Her wisdom and support in the years to come would have unparalleled significance. Her complete acceptance of me, as unfathomable as it was to me, was one of the key pieces to the puzzle I was so trying to put together.

Several months later, however, Jennifer asked me a question that stopped me cold. I couldn't breathe. For many seconds, I couldn't think. I never thought she would ask me *that* question. She began, "Mom, I need to ask you a question. I know your answer will be 'No' and that's okay. It really is. I just need to ask, but you need to know that saying 'No' is okay."

"Mom...(long pause)...Mom...(long pause)...I was wondering if I could tell Kaia and Carey (her two best friends). It's okay if you say 'no' Mom."

I couldn't believe she was asking me that. Tell two *thirteen* year olds? Then *everyone* would know. They would tell *their friends* and then *their friends* would tell *their friends* and then everyone would know. It was my biggest nightmare. Never. *Never.* Those were my thoughts.

Fortunately, I said none of that. I tried to casually suck in a breath to ease the anxiety that had gripped every part of my being. "Of course you can, Jennifer—I have my support system and you need to develop a support system for yourself. You can tell anyone you feel you need to tell."

When she left, I couldn't believe it. Now everyone would know. I also knew I would have to call Kaia and Carey and forewarn them so they would know *what to say* to her. I could help prepare them.

I'm so glad I didn't do that either. I couldn't have scripted it better. Jennifer and her friends really knew how to care for one another. They didn't say what I thought they were going to say, "Ugh. Yuk. Ew." Jennifer later told me that when she told Carey, Carey started crying. "Oh, Jenn. I love your mom so much. I'm so sorry. Please tell her I love her. What can I do to help?" Kaia had responded in a similar way. They were and are so special and remain dear to my heart. At an early age, Jennifer had surrounded herself with loving, nurturing friends, something that had been denied me because I could never share my secret or myself.

That summer, I gave a "thank you" party for D.D., Karen, Larry, Jennifer and seven other people who had supported me. I had made it! I had survived my father's death and I was going to be fine. It was over. I was going to be "back to normal." I had no idea I was standing on the brink of a huge, crumbling cliff, just weeks away from falling off and into the darkest cavern I had ever known.

One year after my father's death, I resolved to get on with my life and my career. I was 48, Jennifer was 14. In late September, I was booked to be the closing keynote speaker for a convention in Dallas. Over 900 insurance executives from the United States and Canada. Because there was no back stage area, they asked me to come in from the back of the room, walk down the long aisle and up onto the stage after my introduction.

I always had a very confident way of walking—it was part of the "act as if" philosophy I had developed. But as I walked to center stage, I was suddenly flooded with feelings of terror. I had no notes. My entire presentation was completely memorized although no one would have known it. I usually stood in front of a podium; instead, I quickly planted myself behind the podium and immediately grasped the sides with both hands. I always lifted the microphone out of the holder and held it as I turned my head from side to side, looking at individual people.

Not that day! As I held onto the podium, I kept hearing an inner voice inside me *screaming*, "I can't do this anymore! I can't do this anymore!" Over and over again. I knew I was going to have to scream those words out loud but, quickly, like an echo, a second inner voice would reply, "Of course you can. You've done it a thousand times." And my real voice began the speech. The voices kept this inner dialogue going for what felt like forty-five minutes but I realized I had only finished the first example—about two minutes. My first inner voice said, "There's no way you can keep this up for an hour." The other voice chimed in, "Of course you can..." While the third voice kept giving the speech.

Only years of experience and the mastery of appearing confident, while feeling terror, got me through that presentation. As they rose to give me a standing ovation, I wasn't sure I could let go of the podium and walk off the stage, much less get into a cab that would take me back to the airport. I felt that if I didn't take my hands and literally hold my head together, it would come apart; that I would "lose my mind."

If I had had pills to take, I would have taken them. I had a better understanding of why some people take drugs—because they can't stand the extreme anxiety one more minute. That was one of the three or four times I believed I would have to be hospitalized.

I found a telephone in the lobby and, in despair, I called D.D. I knew if I called Larry, he would have tried to charter the Concorde. He would have been beside himself. I told D.D. I was going to try to get to the airport and board my flight. Could he meet me? But he couldn't say anything to me. Not anything. Not one word. I would not be able to talk or listen. I had never felt such extreme panic. I remember nothing about the flight home. As I got into D.D.'s car, he said, "What happened?" I shook my head, saying, in essence, "Please don't talk to me. Please."

Larry was waiting for me when we arrived home. He spent a few minutes with me and then he said gently, "I am canceling the rest of your speeches. All of them." He didn't ask me. It was the first time I could ever remember him telling me what I was going to do or not do. I have no idea what he told the program chairman, with the publicity out and a thousand people scheduled to attend four months from then. She has pneumonia and they expect it to last for four months? She broke her leg? She's crazy? Crazy would have been the accurate word for how I felt. Completely unable to cope.

Because I had dissociated the thirteen years of the nights of my life so completely, I had not worked through them. I had split the feelings off. Now Jennifer's teenage years were triggering the feelings and once the lock had been blown off, there was no way to stuff everything back in. I could either get stuck forever in the tar pit of feelings or I could feel them, experience them and then, hopefully release them. But I couldn't just pretend they weren't there. They were ruling my life. If I didn't find a way to address them I believed I would lose everything and everyone I held dear.

During these years, I wonder how many times I didn't return a phone call from a friend or invite someone in who "stopped by." How many invitations did we turn down from friends asking us to dinner? If I were able to get myself together enough to attend a school function,

210

how many conversations did I avoid because my entire focus was on just trying to look normal while distress was screaming out of every pore of my being?

I was told, several times, that Trudy or Sally or Cindy felt I should have been more involved in the community and given more of myself. When I was quietly funneling money to survivor causes, some were asking why I wasn't giving more to *their* causes. I learned to be careful in judging other people because we rarely understand what is going on in another person's life.

During the almost six-year period of my recovery, I would never have been able to hold a job. Not even a part time job. Not even a part, part time job. I realized how easy it would be to lose everything. I am much more generous with street people now. If one person is "scamming," I would rather err on the side of being scammed than not helping someone who has fallen on hard times.

When the memories and feelings surfaced it wasn't that I was remembering the feelings or the experiences, I was actually reliving the feelings as if they were happening to me in present time.

Vietnam vets have had the same experiences. When something triggers a flashback, they are suddenly in the battle. They aren't remembering it. They are there. The terror is real. This disorder has a name: Post Traumatic Stress Disorder (PTSD). It is common among solders who have been in battle and among children and adults who were sexually traumatized, particularly if the abuse started when they were young.

Dr. Herman writes, "Traumatic events appear to recondition the human nervous system. Long after the danger is past, traumatized people relive the event as though it were continually recurring in the present. They cannot resume the normal course of their lives for the trauma repeatedly interrupts...flashbacks...nightmares...memories...often return with all the vividness and emotional force of the original event...traumatic nightmares can recur unmodified for years on end..." (*Trauma and Recovery,* p. 37)

Larry was right to cancel my future speeches. When I returned from Dallas, my anxiety was so intense, my despair so deep, that for the next five months, I did not speak to anyone on the phone, open my mail, or go anywhere—not even to the store for groceries. Just the *thought* of talking to anyone would send off an earthquake in my mind. The only thing I could manage was a few nights a week of trying to work through the feelings with Larry, D.D. and Karen, in our home.

It is difficult to find the words to describe acute anxiety. It felt like an experience I had once when an older boy playfully held my head underwater as a child. He held me under too long. I couldn't breathe and I couldn't break away. I had to get up. *I had to get up.* I had to get a breath. I began fighting to get up but he held me down. Those feelings are similar to the feelings I had for six years. Never letting up.

I was told that in order to get through the extreme dysfunction I was experiencing, I would need to feel the feelings. What did that mean, "just feel the feelings?" One way to describe it is to give an example of Carolyn, a friend of mine whose memories of childhood sexual abuse had also been repressed. When hers began erupting, she was diagnosed with Multiple Personality Disorder (MPD), now called Dissociative Identity Disorder (DID). For those of you who do not believe it is possible for someone to have different personalities (alters), all I can say is, once you are in the presence of someone who is struggling with this disorder, you know it is real.

Carolyn split into a number of alters. One was named Dena. She split Dena off when she was only six years old because something happened to her that was so traumatic she literally could not hold it in her mind. Her father had told her that if she cried when he sexually violated her, he would kill her cat. She cried. In front of her, he killed her cat. A six-year-old cannot accommodate something this horrid and so her mind had to split the experience off. Dena carried only that memory.

When Carolyn, as an adult, went into therapy to integrate the different alters into one personality, she had to become the child alter and experience her father killing her cat, in her adult body, in order for her to integrate Dena into her adult self.

She found that each alter had different terrifying experiences. As a child, when she literally could not cope, she would dissociate what was happening to her and form another alter who would retain the experiences. So, in therapy, her challenge was to find a way to access that alter and then have the courage to let her adult self know and feel what the child had experienced. That's what it means to "feel the feelings." You actually experience what you had to wall off as a child.

212

For years, the feelings so overwhelmed me, there were many days when I felt as if I would have to die because I didn't think I could accept—allow—feel—the extreme anguish one more minute.

Dr. James Chu writes, "Any therapist who has experienced a patient's full-blown flashback has felt the forceful pull into the actual experience of the events along with the patient. The reliving of the trauma is experienced as a real and contemporary event...she feels the experience in the present..." (*Rebuilding Shattered Lives,* p. 34)

I finally realized I would have to find another therapist. Not because "my team" (Larry, D.D. and Karen) wasn't doing everything that could be done. In the years to come, I would work with therapists who had special techniques or skills but none would have more insights or better intuition than Larry, D.D. and Karen.

But for so long, Larry had been dropping everything to care for me, talk to me, listen to me go over the same story. He would never tell a client that he was canceling the afternoon meeting to come home to listen to me talk and cry about the same childhood experiences. Endlessly. Why didn't he scream, "I can't listen to this one more time," or, "We've been over it and over it. Can't you let it go and get on with your life?" Freud called it the "repetition compulsion."

Survivors need to talk about it repetitively, which in many cases, including mine, means over and over, year after year. And we don't stop talking about it, talking about it, talking about it, until we don't need to talk about it anymore. Somehow Larry knew that the pain was so woven into the fabric of my night child that it would be a miracle if I could ever free her. He was saintly patient.

I scheduled appointments with a woman psychologist, Jane O'Carolyn. Oh, the agony of telling the story again. Would it ever get easier? Because I was in such emotional upheaval and because her days were heavily booked, we agreed to meet as many mornings as I could function from 5:30 to 7:30. That would allow me to get home in time to see Jennifer off to school. She said the work would be far too draining to meet every day. I doubted her. She was right.

She gave me homework assignments. One assignment that I did several times was fascinating. Each time, it would be an insight into my subconscious. I was to go to a store where they had at least 50 different magazines and then, without thinking about it, quickly select 15. Then, buy a huge poster board, 44" x 28", go home, sit on the floor and rapidly begin looking through each magazine. I was not to think about it—just quickly glance at every page, tearing out anything that caught my eye. It didn't matter whether I liked it or not. If my eyes pondered it, I was to tear it out. Then, without thinking about it, I would put the torn pictures or words onto the large poster board. Quickly. With no thought.

This process would take me from two to three hours to complete. I would work without stopping. What would emerge, in each instance, were themes, with pictures and words surrounding them.

On the first one I did, a large picture of Elizabeth Taylor was in the center; the right side had picture after picture of young girls. The left side was of a man surrounded by violent words, knives, and guns. Then, as we would study the picture, she would give me her analysis of what she believed my subconscious was saying.

There was no question about Liz Taylor. She was the strong, earthy mother who would protect at all cost. The mother I needed and never had. The man was to be killed violently. Just looking at the messages my subconscious mind was sending helped me to better understand the feelings I was having trouble accessing.

But the healing process wasn't going fast enough for me. I wanted the memories to return faster so I could end the nightmare and get on with my life.

One day, I read a fascinating article about a sodium amytal (more commonly called "truth serum") interview. Coincidentally, I saw a fictitious show on television where a woman had wanted to recover all her memories and she had had a successful sodium amytal interview.

I walked in the door for my next therapy session and said, "I want a sodium amytal interview." I didn't just *want it,* I was going to have it. The psychologist could see I was all business about this and we began discussing it at length. She said only a psychiatrist could do it because it involved medication; she could not. She would make some calls. I was grateful she didn't try to talk me out of it.

An appointment was made with a woman psychiatrist. Her answer was simple. "No." My question was also simple, "Why not?" "Because a sodium amytal interview can bring up memories without feelings. It's true, you will get a quick route to repressed memories but days or weeks later, all the feelings can begin coming up. It can be like a bad LSD trip. Way too overwhelming. Too much for you to handle.

214

Now, your memories are coming up the way they are supposed to. Your subconscious knows when you can handle more memories and it would be very wrong to force the process."

I was not happy with her response. I wanted to get this *done*. Give me all the memories. I'll deal with them. She obviously knew my thoughts because just as we were leaving, she said, "And no doctor in Colorado will do this."

She left no doubt that no doctor in *Colorado* would do this, but that didn't mean I couldn't find a psychiatrist in another state. Now where would *you* look for a doctor to perform this procedure? Right, Beverly Hills! I began calling. Yes! Found one! He would do it. Now I had "the answer" as to how I could quickly complete this horrid process. I'd rather have one huge, heavy dose than wade through the muck month after month.

I was ready to make the airline reservations. I had kept Larry appraised of what I was doing and who was saying what. He knew how dangerous the truth serum could be and he was 100 percent, completely, totally, opposed to my doing it, but never once did he say, "You can't do that." He must have known there were risks either way—trying to control me or allowing me to find my own way.

In retrospect, I think it was *because* he didn't try to tell me what to do that I acted responsibly. Maybe if he had said *"No,"* I would have gone just to show him no one was ever going to control me again.

I knew if I did it, there was a strong possibility that the feelings would so overwhelm me that I would need to be hospitalized. I visualized Larry standing over my bed—again. Hovering over my bed—again. I knew I couldn't risk it. I decided against it for his sake.

A survivor told me a wonderful story about this. Two men wanted to explore the jungles of Africa. With the natives, they had carefully laid out a map of where they wanted to go and how long the journey would take. With the natives leading them, they reached their first goal much more quickly than they had planned and urged the natives to keep going. The same was true of the second day. The third day, having gone almost twice as far as planned, the natives sat down and would not go another step. Struggling to understand them, the lead guide said, "We have come too far. We must wait, now, for our spirits to catch up."

It can be true for those of us in recovery. We can push too hard to integrate memories and we can be overwhelmed with too many feelings. There is no question in my mind, now, that the truth serum would have been exceedingly dangerous for me. At that time, I was barely coping with the memories that were ever so slowly, seeping into my conscious mind.

I had only had a few sessions with Jane when she asked me if I would be interested in going to a self-defense class. My answer was simple and direct, "No." It wasn't open for discussion. The thought of anyone touching me, the thought of *any* personal contact brought overwhelming anxiety. I wanted to stay in my head; I didn't want to get into my body. Ever. It was the first and only time I can remember not doing anything that was suggested to me that might possibly contribute to my healing.

Several months later, in the spring, she asked me again. I had worked so hard and had made huge gains. This time, my answer was, "Yes." Although I wasn't nearly as assertive with my "Yes" as I had been with my "No," it was still "Yes." Gut level, I must have known how terrifying it would be to get into my body and try to protect my "self."

There were seven women. It was just a local, neighborhood self-defense class, meeting one night a week for 10 weeks. Each of us had been sexually traumatized. Incest, sexual assault, or rape. We knew it but we didn't talk about it.

I always needed to role model, motivate, encourage everyone. I was the first one volunteer for whatever. I'm "up for it." I could always get everyone laughing when it came to my favorite move. "The attacker" (the woman instructor) comes straight at you, puts her arms around you like a massive bear hug. We were taught how to bring our arms up quickly, while bringing one knee up as hard as possible, ramming the man's balls up his throat. Loved that move. Wanted to practice it all the time. Always made everyone laugh with my enthusiasm and zest for ramming. Although there were serious moments, moments that triggered some of the women's memories by mimicking ways they had been attacked, there were other fun moments when we could laugh together. No matter what the instructor asked us to do, everyone always knew, "Marilyn will do it!"

But one thought kept recurring. On the first night we had been told that during the seventh session, "the man" would come. "The man" was our attacker. Our violator. The person who took our freedom

216

away, rendering us helpless. The man who had total power. The man who murdered our souls. The man who ripped our secure, fun, trusting world and turned it into nights of horror, nights of flashbacks, decades of nights of reliving being pried open, decades of nights of stuffing—burying—primal screams into the depths of our beings.

On the seventh night, for the first and only time in our lives, we could defend ourselves. We could fight back. We could kick and hit and wail from that deep place within, "NOOOOOOOOOOOOOOO." Over and over. "No." "*No!*"

We always grew instantly silent when our instructor talked about the seventh session and "the man." Each of us was terrorized even thinking about it. It would take every ounce of courage to confront our violator. To confront is to die. That is our belief system. And now we were going to be put to the test. Stop him. Hit him. Kick him. Thoughts that seemed incomprehensible. Hit my *father?* He would kill me. I could never hit him. He would beat me senseless. He had all the power. I had none. *None. None!* Stop him? No one could stop him. Ever. Scream over and over with a loud and commanding voice, "*No.*" "*No.*" Scream "No" to my father? No one *ever* told my father "No." It would be like telling a six-year-old to hit Mike Tyson.

I was in the deepest throes of recovery. "The man" would take us back in time. I wouldn't remember how I felt as a child, I would experience in real time, the feelings of a six-year-old or a twelve-year-old or (worst of all) a seventeen-year-old. But as the classes progressed, I became more empowered. I knew that, for the first time in my life, I would have power in my father's presence. I would have the power to scream, "*No! No more! Never again!*"

Two women didn't show up that night. No one asked why. We all understood that for some, actually confronting the perpetrator—even in play-acting—was far too overwhelming.

No one was talking that night. The instructor merely said, "His name is Gregg. He will come in now." Boy, was I ready for "him." I couldn't wait to take him on. I would be first, as always. I knew exactly what he would look like. Stubble. Slovenly. Sneering. Mean. Gregg walked in. As I looked at him, it was as if my brain short-circuited. He wasn't mean. He didn't have stubble. He was soft and gentle. Handsome. I don't remember anything that happened from the time I first saw him until I heard my name being called. Loudly, "Marilyn. *Marilyn!* Everyone else has taken her turn. It's your turn

217

now." Her voice snapped me back into reality…the present.

I stood like a robot and walked over to him. He said, "What would you like me to do?" I said, "Grab me from behind." He did and I quickly broke his hold. I said, "Now from the front." The women were waiting for me to ram him. He had protective covering on and we were told not to worry about hurting him. He was protected. I could ram his balls through his eye sockets. He faced me. My arms were down at my sides. He put his arms around me, as the women waited for me to do my favorite move. I knew exactly what to do. Raise my arms. Quickly. Ram my knee. Hard.

But I couldn't move even one muscle. I was frozen solid. It was as if my arms were tied to my body. All I could think of was wanting to hold him. I wanted to lift my arms and put them around him. I wanted to put my arms around him as much as I have ever wanted anything in my life. What would the women think? I have to ram him. But I want to hold him. I was completely immobilized.

I heard a voice. A loud voice. "Marilyn. Marilyn. Open your eyes now. *Open your eyes, Marilyn.*"

My eyes felt as if they had been glued shut. I finally forced them open. I felt dazed. The instructor said, "We'll take a break now."

The women formed a circle to talk about their feelings from having confronted "their rapist." I sat down in the circle. For about five seconds. Then I got up, went out of the room and began looking in all the different rooms down the hallway. I had to find Gregg. He was sitting in a corner room, studying. He was a graduate student. His girlfriend had been raped and he wanted to do something to help women feel safe.

He lifted his eyes as I walked over to him. "Would you hold me?" "Of course."

He gently put his arms around me. There were no roaming hands, no hot, pulsating fingers, just a warm, gentle, loving embrace. I lifted my arms and put them around him and then the sobs erupted. He didn't move a muscle. He just softly held me while I sobbed convulsively for a long time. I said, "Thank you," and went back to the class. I sat down in the circle but found myself getting up again, going back to Gregg.

"Would you hold me again?" "Yes." I sobbed as if my heart would

218

break as he held me so gently. Then Gregg said quietly, "Did this happen recently?" His question jolted me back to reality. Gregg was not my father and I was not nine or ten or twelve. I was a 48-year-old woman. I didn't answer. I just managed to say, "Thank you, Gregg."

It was one of the most intense emotional experiences of my life. I never wanted to let him go. I never wanted to let go of that *feeling*. My father gently holding me, like a father should hold a daughter. It was what I had always longed for and the play-acting was so real that night, I felt a part of the empty pit in my soul had been filled.

Survivors ask me to hold them, often for a long time. Many times, we say very few words. Some have told me that when I held them, it was the first time they had ever felt safe or loved. I understand. Gregg had held me during one of my darkest hours and it felt real.

Although talking to therapists was an extremely important part of my recovery, other more unconventional therapies helped me access the feelings. Self-defense therapy had the most impact. I will always be grateful to the woman psychologist for suggesting it. It helped me to access the *feelings* of the child I was judging so unmercifully. The night child should have been able to stop him; she should have fought to the death. That night opened a tiny crack in the wall of disdain I felt for her. Until I could have some compassion for the night child, I could never integrate her. For decades my judgement of her was lethal.

Healing is a process we must actively go through and participate in. For some of us, there may be times in our process when we feel blocked and unable to move forward. Sometimes experiential techniques can be useful. I got stuck trying to figure everything out in my head. When I finally stopped seeing therapists who only asked questions like, "And how did that make you feel?" and started seeing therapists who would have conversations with me, I began moving ahead. I needed therapists who would give me their feedback and insights and walk me through scenarios.

I was in therapy with Jane for a year. I made tremendous progress. When she told me she was going to be moving to Texas, I knew I would be fine and would stop therapy.

One of the activities I could not do, during the six years my life shut down, was run with Larry and "the guys." I was always "one of the guys." Larry and I did everything together. Running in the morning was an important part of our daily life. Skiing was an important part of our winter weekends. Neither would be possible for me. The emotional energy needed for coping with the feelings drained my physical energy completely. For the first time in our 23-year marriage, Larry would go running without me. It was one of the ways Larry coped with the stress of his life.

Recovery is an agonizing time for a survivor but it is also extremely difficult for the support person. Going to bed had its own rituals. Larry had to be with me. It didn't matter if he wasn't tired or if he wanted to read. He had to go to bed when I did. It was just a given. Everything in our bedroom had to be closed up tight. No light or sound. No movement. Larry knew that if he moved and awakened me, I would be unable to go back to sleep.

For his own survival, Larry began keeping a journal of his thoughts. I know where it is and I will never read it. I used every resource available to me to get better. I know the most difficult part of this excruciating time for Larry was wondering if it would ever end. Would his wife and best friend always be this way…barely able to hold her mind together…unable to free her body of overwhelming pain? I don't know how he was able to continue to give me unconditional support and love.

We live in a ranch style home. Our bedroom has windows that face the backyard. Above the windows are smaller windows that also open. Even though there is heavy, ornate wrought iron grating protecting all the windows, I had boards made for the lower windows. It never seemed strange to do that, nor has Larry ever said, "Could we please remove the boards from our windows?"

Nor did he ever say or do anything to make me feel guilty about our non-existent sexual relationship during this time. I'm sure this is true for most survivors, during the most agonizing time of our recovery, when we feel our perpetrator's invasions as if the trauma were happening to us, in real time, we don't want to be touched. Anywhere. Ever.

One day I was lying in bed with a paralysis spell that was so deep, I knew that if I could slow everything down just a little bit more, I could go into nothingness. I never thought of the word "death," but that's what nothingness was to me, at that time. Larry sat on the floor and put his head close to mine. The spell was so complete, I could only whisper one word at a time. Very slowly I said, "I'm…slipping…away." It was the first time he thought it was

220

possible that I would not make it through recovery. After about three hours, the spell begin to lift and I could begin to slowly move my body. That was the only time the paralysis spell had been scary. All other times—and I had had hundreds of spells—it was a time of peace, almost serenity. I felt absolutely nothing.

For literally hundreds of days, I felt as if I were a huge balloon. Someone attached a hose to the opening of the balloon and pumped in sounds and feelings so loud and intense, I knew my entire body would have to explode as a balloon would when too much air was injected.

I began to understand why a person would get into a car, push the gas pedal down until the speedometer read 100 miles an hour and then drive into a post or a mountain or off a cliff, because there was no place to put the feelings.

I told Larry I needed to go back into therapy. He made some confidential phone calls and I was put in touch with a woman psychotherapist, Bobbi Furer, who lived nearby. A grandmother. When I drove to her home she had a garden and a fence. Normal. Good.

When I rang her doorbell she opened the door and was taken aback when she saw me. She said, "I need to tell you I know who you are, and have socially met members of your family. Do you want to work with me?"

I said, "I'm in so much pain I can't even think about that. Let's go to work." I had worked with her for almost a year when she called one day to say she was going to start a small support group that would meet once a week for four months. Five women. Would I come? I lost it. Big time. I yelled at her, "How could you possibly ask me to come where there would be other people? I would *never* go where there was anyone else." Didn't she know how scared I was that "people" would find out? Of *course I would not come.*

The only times I yelled or screamed were times when my anxiety was pushed beyond my ability to cope. I was getting wise enough in this process to know that the thing we are most terrified of is the thing we must do. I had told Larry and Jennifer again and again that I would do *anything* to get better but I never thought that would mean allowing anyone else to know my secret. That was my greatest fear, that Colorado would learn that their Miss America was an incest survivor. That would be the end, forever, of my life.

I knew healing was not a gift. There was only one route and that was doing the work and remembering my mantra, "If I die, I die, but I don't want to live this way anymore." It had never occurred to me that this might mean disclosing to strangers, but I called Bobbi and said, "I'll be there."

It was a freezing cold night in February. I was 49. I arrived at exactly 7 p.m. There were several cars parked in front of her house. I sat there and looked at her house. I couldn't go in. I just couldn't go in. So I asked myself, "Why can't you go in?" It took a minute before the answer came, "Because I don't want to be one of *them*." And I responded to myself, "But you *are* one of them." I opened the door and slowly walked across the street.

When Bobbi let me in, she said, "Everyone is here except a young woman I have never met. She called to ask if she could come. I'm going to wait here for her. Why don't you go downstairs and join the other women?"

That was not an option for me. I said, "No. I'll wait here with you. I'll go down when you go down." In a few minutes the doorbell rang. When Bobbi opened the door, I was stunned to see her. Long blond hair. Blue eyes. Levis and sneakers. A sophomore at the University of Denver. She was me when I was in college. The look on her face told me this was the first time she had ever reached out and I vowed I would do everything possible to role model for her.

We sat in a circle and told our first names and ages. When I said I was 49, I could see the look of despair on Sara's face. I turned to her and said, "Sara you won't have to be here when you're 49 if you do the work now. You can do the work now or you can do the work later but you will have to do the work of healing."

At the conclusion of the that first session, Bobbi said, "Next week, please bring a doll to represent your inner child." I burst into rage. "You know how I *hate* dolls, Bobbi. You can stick things in them and pull on them and they can't protect themselves. I *hate dolls!*" Bobbi said quietly, "Marilyn will not be bringing a doll."

I left knowing that I would have to get a doll. How could I expect Sara to do the work if I wasn't willing to? I also knew that the things I most strongly resisted were the most important things for me to do.

I hated shopping—for anything. I ran into Kmart to buy a doll. Just any doll. Who cares? Just grab one and get this over with. I looked at rows of dolls. Just grab one. But I couldn't. I looked and looked and couldn't find one to buy. I ran into a huge toy store expecting to quickly snatch up a doll. Get this done! Who cares? More rows of dolls. Couldn't pick one. Ran out of there and into Target. Looking, looking. "There she is!" I found her.

At our next meeting, it was startling to see the dolls the different women had selected. I had no idea why I had picked the doll I did. Nor did I understand why I couldn't take any of the countless dolls I had seen. Bobbi pointed it out. I didn't even realize the significance when I held her up. She had no body. Her head was a small, square baby pillow. Little black fabric shoes had been sewn to her head. No body. Then without even realizing what I was doing, when I got home, I took liquid white out and took off her mouth, later realizing so nothing could go in her mouth, and then I took a black pen and drew tear drops running down her cheeks. All of this had been done without one iota of recognition of what I was doing or why. Another woman had brought a doll that had different compartments so she could hide things.

Bobbi said, "I'm going to ask each of you to put your doll in front of you and tell her what happened to her." One woman had been so traumatized, there were many sessions where she could not utter one word. She just sat with a look of horror frozen on her face. I managed to get a few sentences out and then it was Sara's turn. Sara was sitting on the floor with her legs crossed, her head down. She was silent. Bobbi said, "Sara it's your turn." Sara didn't budge. Bobbi said, "Sara please put your doll in front of you and tell her what happened to her." Sara didn't move an inch. Bobbi said, "Sara please put your doll in front of you and tell her what happened to her." Nothing. Bobbi said, "The reason I can't tell my doll what happened is because..." Nothing. Bobbi repeated the statement: "The reason I can't tell...." Sara lifted her head ever so slightly and she whispered, "because then I would know it was true." And she never came back.

Bobbi later told me the only thing she knew about Sara was her older brother had been her violator. I grieved over Sara. When she has her first sexual relationship or when her daughter is six or eight or ten or when someone punctures the vastness of her pain, she will have to do the work of healing. It's so much more difficult the longer we wait.

During this agonizing time, one of the most important things Larry did for me was to interpret to Jennifer. When Larry would come home and find me lying on the floor doubled over with sobs or lying in bed in paralysis, he never once said, "This again? How long is this going to go on? Get up and get on with your life." He would turn to Jennifer and say, "Your mother is the most courageous woman you will ever know." How easily a family member can undermine another. Larry supported me like bedrock.

It was during these darkest months of my life that D.D. learned that a woman was going to speak publicly about incest. There were very few books about incest in the 1980s and no one was talking about it on talk shows. It was still a taboo subject. Although it was challenging for me to even get dressed, Larry, D.D. and I decided we would go. I was terrified someone would see me there so I was grateful when we walked in and found only a handful of people had gathered. My gratitude turned to angst when I saw Dottie Lamm walk in. Colorado's First Lady. I wanted to be invisible or crawl under the chair but the room was too small to ignore her so I nodded a hello.

Several weeks later, she called. I wasn't answering my phone but her message asked that I return her call so, reluctantly, I did. She asked if I could come to the Governor's mansion for lunch the following week. I thanked her for the invitation and thought up some excuse as to why that would not be possible. There was no way I would be emotionally strong enough to get dressed, drive to the Governor's mansion and have lunch. I wasn't prepared for her response, "What day could you come?" Thoughts flashed through my mind, "I'm sorry but I have the measles and I won't be well for at least six months." "I wish I could but I fell on the ice and broke my leg and I will be bedridden until summer." My thoughts returned to her question, "What day could you come?" I stammered. Unable to think of anything remotely reasonable, I said, "I could come a week from Wednesday." Dottie said, "I will look forward to seeing you."

I knew why she wanted to meet with me. A prestigious women's organization had been asking me to join and I knew Dottie was the chosen person to ask me one-on-one. I already knew my answer, "I am swamped right now with traveling and speaking. I would love to belong but the timing isn't right because I am away so much."

Dottie met me at the door and we walked onto the patio where a small table was beautifully set for the two of us. My anxiety was so acute, I tried to remember to take deep, slow breaths. We exchanged a few pleasantries and then Dottie said, "What did you think about the woman who talked about incest. Did you believe her? I'm writing a column about her talk and I'm interested in your perception." Well, I was 100 percent totally and completely unprepared for that. I had no defenses. I hadn't put my armor on. I stared at her as if I had been frozen, like a dog resting so peacefully until he hears an unfamiliar sound; he instantly perks up his head and ears and doesn't move a muscle.

I quickly melted, my head dropped and tears flowed so freely, they dripped onto the tablecloth. Dottie was stunned. "What? Marilyn, what did I say? I'm so sorry I've upset you." She sat in disbelief as I tried to stop the tears and raise my head. I was too out of control of my thoughts to be embarrassed. Without raising my head, I said, "Yes. Me, too." I don't remember the rest of my time with her other than her kindness and compassion. I don't remember saying, "Please don't tell anyone. Anyone. Anyone." I somehow knew she would be protective of me and my vulnerability.

Later that year, I returned home from the Tattered Cover bookstore having purchased a book on incest, one of the few books then available. Jennifer said, "Were you embarrassed to buy that book, Mom?" "Yes, Jennifer, I was. So embarrassed and ashamed and afraid that anyone would find out." Jennifer responded, "Why, Mom? You didn't do anything wrong." It was a sentence she would say often. Why couldn't I remember that? I would try to look at my child self through her eyes. I didn't do anything wrong. I was not to blame. I was not a bad person. Although Larry would use every opportunity to help her understand and see the recovery process in a positive light, Jennifer was born with an "old soul." She has innate wisdom and a love that has always spilled all over me.

I was unable to work, travel or function for any period of time during Jennifer's 8th through 12th grade years. If I had been able to *crawl* to the airport, I would have been traveling, speaking, trying to be "important." Instead, during those most significant years of Jennifer's life, I was home with her. We spent hours talking, laughing, "hanging out," or sometimes going to the Denver jail to bail out two troubled boys I was working with. I always tried to schedule therapy at a time when she was in school. When she would come home from school I would be waiting for her, sometimes crying, but many other times we would laugh so hard together we would literally drop to the floor. Jennifer shared her inner most thoughts on issues that were important to her. I didn't share the details of what my father had done to me or the issues I was currently struggling with, but she knew she could ask me any question. There were no more secrets.

Just as I had reached the top of my career, my life had been stopped. To my dying day, I will bless my Higher Power for knowing that the only way I would stay home would be if I were literally unable to go. The reason Jennifer and I have the incredible bond we have today is because I opened up my life and my truth to her and because I was home with her during her junior and senior high school years when she needed a mom with whom to share her life. I wanted to be there for her, to be part of her life and the lives of her friends. When we would go to Vail for ski weekends, she always took friends with her. We played games, took walks, cooked together, shared thoughts. I took full advantage of every opportunity to be the best possible mom. During the times when my internal turmoil took control, Larry and his family, one of my sisters or Jennifer's friends were able to help fill the void.

But there were times when my recovery took a heavy toll. When Jennifer was in 8th grade, the head of her school called and asked if I would meet with him. Just getting dressed seemed daunting. As I sat down, he said, "I've asked to meet with you because we are concerned about Jennifer. She has always been such a happy child and recently we haven't been seeing the joy. We're concerned." He hadn't uttered one more *word* before the tears flooded my eyes and began streaming down my face and onto my dress. During our entire conversation the tears never stopped. I said, "I know and I'm grateful for your concern but the problem is mine, not hers. Whenever there are major difficulties in a family, I'm sure children are affected. I wish I could change that." It was very obvious how much pain I was in and that there was no possibility I was going to share more than I just had.

He said, "What can we do here at school to help?"

"Just give her all the support you can."

With continuous tears streaming down my face, I drove home.

Later that year, parents panicked when we learned one of Jennifer's classmates had disappeared on a Friday. By Saturday night there was great alarm. Although she wasn't one of Jennifer's friends, we all knew her. Her parents were extremely successful professionals. She had begun distinguishing herself by wearing clothes that were unusual, and by dying her hair purple. This was very uncommon behavior for the girls in Jennifer's grade. At her age and in her school, they tended

226

to dress the same. On Sunday night, we heard she had returned or "been found" and she was to be back at school on Monday. Evidently she had run away.

Although I had absolutely no right to do so, and as difficult as it was for me to do, because I was very fragile emotionally, I called the head of the school in anger. "How can you just let her back in school? She wore clothes that were different, she dyed her hair purple and then she ran away. She is crying out. Can't you hear her? She is screaming for help. What's left for her to do? Kill herself? You cannot just pretend this didn't happen. You must demand that she be seen by an independent therapist—not one that her parents choose—before being allowed back into school."

Looking back, I'm surprised he didn't say, "Excuse me but this is not your business," but he didn't say that. He assured me that he hadn't thought about it in that light and that they would require that she see a therapist (not chosen by her parents) before being allowed to return to school. I was told that, upon making that request, her parents withdrew her from school. I never heard anything more about this student. It is possible there was nothing seriously wrong but what I began to understand is that no matter how closed down and withdrawn I would be during the recovery process, I would have a voice if I felt a child were in trouble.

When Jennifer began her freshman year at Duke University, I learned that one of her former middle school classmates had been sexually violated in her home. Although my constant living nightmare was that "people would know" about me, I knew I had to write the administrator who had been concerned about Jennifer. He was now in charge of a large private girls school in another state. Although I was not yet aware of how pervasive sexual abuse is, I knew he was seeing girls every day who were or had been sexually violated. My intense fear of being known was overshadowed by my need to have him understand the problem. He was far away from Denver and I would urge him to keep my secret.

I remember every second of writing that letter. What was so difficult was actually dropping it into the mailbox. My hand wanted to be a "slinky" and roll into the box and retrieve it. Telling him that I was "one of them" was an extremely difficult disclosure. At least I didn't have to look at him as I searched for words.

It would take two days for the letter to reach him and two days for his return letter. On the fourth day I began waiting for the mailman. He usually delivered mail by 11 a.m.—so by 10:45 on Monday morning, I was watching. Watching. There was no letter from him. Well, I had mailed my letter on a Wednesday so maybe he didn't get it on Friday, which meant I wouldn't have a response until Tuesday. His letter would arrive on Tuesday.

But it didn't arrive on Tuesday or Wednesday or Thursday. I knew why. I had always known why. He would never want to have anything to do with me again. He confirmed all the things I knew. I was unacceptable. He can never know how hurtful and damaging his lack of response was to me. It ate away at my already devastated self-image. I should never have told. I would never tell again. Anyone. Ever.

But I couldn't get his apparent dismissal or condemnation of me out of my mind. One day I read an article by a local columnist. She wrote about a co-worker who had been raped. When the woman returned to work, her peers had decided the best way to handle it was not to talk about it. Just never bring it up. They realized, later, how wrong they had been. How much this reinforced this woman's feeling about herself that she was now unacceptable. The point of her column was that their non-response had only intensified her feelings of unworthiness and her pain.

I cut the article out and slipped it into an envelope with my name and return address on it. No note. Just the article. I mailed it on a Monday. I waited for the mailman on Friday. And Saturday. And Monday.

It took several years and my evolution from victim to survivor, before I realized that his non-response had nothing to do with me. It had everything to do with him. It's possible that he is just extremely rude but that was inconsistent with his general personality, so I ruled that out. What I now believe is that he is either a survivor of childhood sexual abuse himself, a perpetrator or somewhere very close to one of those choices. He may not even know why he cannot respond but it has nothing to do with me.

When my story became front-page news for many days in Denver, I knew this private school administrator would read about "my story." Perhaps then, after a number of years, he would respond. But he never did. And once again I am reminded of a well-known quote, "What you do shouts so loud, I can't hear what you say." Or in this instance,

228

"What you *don't do* shouts so loud, I *can hear* what you say." It was only the first time I would be aware that what happened was more about the other person than it was about me.

Similarly, after my story became public, I was asked to give a keynote speech to the National Association of Juvenile and Family Court Judges. I volunteered to produce a video to educate offending teenagers and families about the long-term effects of an older child sexually violating a younger or less powerful child. It would be appropriate for educating baby-sitters, camp counselors, Boy Scout leaders, etc.

I sent one to a Boy Scout executive in California to watch. I was interested in his feedback. He didn't respond. After six weeks, I dropped him a note. His response was, "Please forgive me for not having responded to you. The video has been on my desk for six weeks. I have not been able to watch it. When I was a boy, my uncle…"

His non-response had nothing to do with the video or me. It had everything to do with him. I will always be grateful for his honesty. Honesty educates. The truth educates and sets us free.

I learned this lesson again and again. Two years before my life began shutting down, Sharon, a young woman I was close to, asked me to address her sorority's initiation of their pledges. I accepted immediately. When I arrived at the banquet, I was told that she had not made her grades. Had not made her *grades*? She had grown up in Denver. She had always been an A student. Unbelievable. She was so embarrassed. I chalked it up as an adjustment phase.

But the next time I was speaking on the east coast, near her college, I made of point of going to see her. There was something that wasn't right. I couldn't put my finger on it. She was bouncy and gorgeous, full of fun and smiles. But it didn't feel right. My gut told me all was not well. I had nothing other than that to go on, but it was enough. I told her I thought something was wrong in her life. Would she share it with me? She laughed it off and said, "I'm fine. I love it here." I didn't believe her but I didn't know what more to do. It was at least three months before I saw her again, when she came home for Christmas. I had the same feeling. It was so strong that I asked her if we could talk the next day at my house.

She came over and I said, "I know something is wrong. I don't know what it is but I'm going to pull out my ace. I'm going to tell you something about my life." I told her about my father. I was crying so hard, I had told almost no one, at this point in my journey. I couldn't look at her. She didn't say anything. So I looked up. She was crying as she whispered, "I didn't think there was anything worse than rape."

She had been raped, at knife point, her freshman year in college. Outside the library, about 8 p.m. while walking back to the dorm. She burned the clothes she wore and never spoke of it. To anyone.

Sharon wasn't attending class, and hadn't been for many weeks. Her roommate and her friends had no idea that she wasn't attending class, much less, that she had been raped. She was staying in bed or wandering around. She was destroyed inside. She was never going to tell anyone and, slowly, she was destroying her life.

I put my arms around her and just held her. Later that day, I told her she would have to tell her parents and her boyfriend. She said, "Never." I said, "Never is not an option." She looked at me the way I must have looked at D.D. when he told me I would need to tell Larry. Incomprehensible. She would never tell. Anyone. Ever.

It took time to convince her to tell her boyfriend. She did. He didn't put his arms around her or say anything and she was devastated by his lack of response. Her boyfriend was also in Denver, so I asked if Larry and I might meet with the two of them together before they left town. After very few pleasantries, I went right to it.

I said to her boyfriend, "Sharon is upset because you didn't say anything after she told you." He said, "I was so devastated. I had no idea what to say." I said, "Maybe you could say something to her now." He was so sweet and so in love with her. He tried to help her understand how intense his feelings were and how much he hadn't known what to do.

Sharon told him the feelings she had had. It was a critically important meeting for both of them and one that could only have taken place in front of a third party—a therapist, someone like D.D., or someone who loves her as much as I—and who has "been there."

She then had to tell her parents. She said, "I know my dad will never look at me the same way again." Oh, I so understood that. *She* was the one who carried the shame and the guilt. It was so easy for me to know that this was not her shame and yet I could not rid myself of mine.

I had met her parents but I didn't know them personally. I prayed they would respond supportively. They were seated together as Sharon sat on the floor sobbing, trying to get the words out. When they understood what she was trying to say, they both reached out for her. Her mother began crying with her, her father held her tightly, telling her how sorry he was.

Now my role was over. I knew I should not force any more "work" although I felt *strongly* that she should be in therapy and read the few books then available on rape and healing. That was *my* journey. It might not be hers. It is not unlike the non-drinker who wants to reform the drinker or the spouse wanting to moderate the compulsive eater.

It is *very* difficult for me to stay uninvolved. Very difficult. But I do. I see her whenever she is in Denver. It is never discussed. She knows she can come to me at any time and that's the way it needs to stay.

I learned that lesson again and again. There were several teenagers I had been extremely close to. The most painful lesson involved a college girl, "Jody." When I was at the deepest, blackest time of my recovery, before I could speak the words, I knew I had to disclose to her. Just as I had needed Jennifer to know me, I now needed to know whether or not I would be acceptable to her. I wrote to her and poured out my heart. When Jody didn't respond, I was devastated. Just as I had believed Jennifer would say, when learning the truth of my life, "I don't want you to be my Mom anymore," I believed Jody would say she didn't want me in her life anymore. I concluded from her unresponsiveness that I was right. She didn't want me in her life anymore. I was no longer the woman she had so respected and loved.

I waited for two weeks. I thought about picking up the phone but I could never have *spoken* the words. Writing the words was difficult enough. Even the *thought* of speaking them was too overwhelming. So I wrote to her again. When she didn't respond to my second letter, the message was reinforced. It was very clear. So very clear. I was unacceptable.

When this happens, when we are in recovery, rejection is 1,000 times more devastating than it would be at any other time in our lives because we are often the child seeking the approval and acceptance of others, rather than a mature adult. I could not have hated myself any more than I did during this time. I loathed and despised my night child, and Jody confirmed my belief system.

It was a year later when I realized the truth. I was standing in my kitchen, washing vegetables, thinking about nothing, when I had the epiphany—the insight. It hit me hard and I knew it was true. I never questioned these kinds of insights because they came with such clarity. Of course, *this has happened to her.* That's why she turned away from me. I didn't *think it.* I *knew* it. This was not about me. This was about her. Several months later, when Jody was home from college, she came to see me. Bubbly. Happy. Oh boy, did I know *that* cover. It was as if she had never received letters from me. The second she sat down, her bubbly self shut down, as she saw the look on my face. All business. And compassion. I minced no words.

"I know something about you, Jody. This has happened to you." It took a second for my words to register and then, instantly, her entire being collapsed into deep, wrenching sobs. I held her and told her how very sorry I was. She sobbed the way I did when D.D. asked me that question—about my father, night time, my bedroom—whatever words he used.

She told me bits and pieces. Very little information. But enough to understand what she had been through. She was unable to speak about it, in any depth. I understood. She went back to college the next day. I began writing to her. I sent her a book about healing. I knew I could help her. She didn't respond. It didn't matter. I kept writing to her. I knew how much support she needed and I was the only one who knew her secret.

And then…I heard through a mutual friend, that she never wanted to speak to me again.

That shook me to the core. I was struggling so hard, during this time that I could barely focus on anything other than getting through another day. I wrote her immediately and asked her what I had done but there was no response. I was cut off from her completely. About two years after my story became public, I was finally able to force a meeting with her.

I began our meeting with an apology, "I'm so very sorry, Jody. I should never have forced my way into your life. I'm *not* sorry that I confronted you about what happened to you—I would do that again because that's what saved my life—someone loving me enough to ask me the question, but I am deeply sorry that I kept trying to help you by pushing you to confront your past. So many people have turned to me for help and I have been able to give them information and support they have been unable to find anywhere else, at this time in their recovery process. The *huge* mistake I made is that you did not come to me for help. I injected myself into your life. I did it for the right reasons—because I never wanted anyone else to go through the years of pain I had gone through—I wanted your journey to be easier and I believed it could be if you started at a younger age, but I was very, very wrong."

I continued, "Each of us has our own personal journey. It has been very difficult for me to learn that people don't heal on *my* time schedule. Some people are not ready to begin the work. Some may choose to *never* do it. I am deeply sorry. I was out of line. Doing the wrong thing for the right reasons still makes it wrong. I hope you can forgive me." We hugged, talked about other things for a few minutes and then went our own ways. We had been so very close. Our love had been so strong—even though our age difference was great. Unfortunately, our relationship will never be the same.

It was one of the most important lessons I have learned. When someone is in pain, because of childhood issues, I believe it is mandatory to reach out, as D.D. did with me. But then the ball should remain in their court. To let them know we are only a phone call away if they want to talk but not to pressure them to do what *we believe* they should do.

I want to take every child, teenager and college student in pain for rape or sexual abuse, and walk the journey of healing with them— trying to make their lives easier than mine has been. And then I remind myself that most of us, fortunately not all, confront our childhoods in our late 30's to late 40's.

Don't pray for an easy life. Pray to be a strong person.

An example of the montages I did by quickly tearing out pictures from magazines.

Chapter 12 – What I Needed to Heal

When Jennifer was 14, she invited two girls and three boys to join us for a week during our vacation in California to celebrate her graduation from 9th grade. I was feeling stronger when we invited them months earlier. I always knew this recovery process was going to be over soon. Soon. Maybe a few more months. It was one of my coping mechanisms, believing the craziness was in the final chapter of my healing process.

Since the five teens were our guests, I had all of our paper airline tickets. When I handed them to the boarding agent, she said, "I'm sorry but the tickets from Denver to Orange County have been pulled from every ticket. I cannot board any of you. You don't have tickets. The return tickets are here but not the departing tickets." Well, she took one look at me and knew we would have to figure something out. My normal stress level during this time was off the chart. High stress would send me over the edge. After a very short conversation, with my obvious hysteria close to overflowing, she said, "I will board all of you now."

Immediately upon our arrival at the condominium, my body was suddenly gripped with pain. I couldn't sit. I felt as if an ax had been embedded in my anus. The pain was excruciating. And my body felt as if it were bulging and bloating, ready to explode. Too many feelings to try to contain. I could understand why people jumped off high bridges. I didn't know what to do. I tried so hard to appear normal to the kids but I ran upstairs, grabbed a phone book and quickly flipped the yellow pages and called the first woman therapist's name I saw, Phyllis Rubalcaba, a hypnotherapist. I was surprised when she answered. "I'm in acute anxiety. I don't think I can make it." She said, "Come immediately." I couldn't believe that in Southern California where everyone seems to be at least forty minutes away, she was only three *blocks* away. The ten minutes I waited for her seemed like ten hours. The waiting room was filled with green plants with long tentacles. Maybe thirty. I felt as if the room was closing in on me and that the tentacles were going to crawl all over me like an octopus. I had never felt so claustrophobic.

When she came out to greet me, I was taken aback by her looks. She wore a flowered cotton summer dress, and her hairdo was a throw back to the '50s. I wanted a *real therapist* not someone who bakes cookies every day. When I went into her small office I just couldn't hold it in anymore. Before I was even seated, I burst into heaving sobs. I managed to get a few words out—"father, incest, thirteen years…Larry…" With very little background, Phyllis said, "I am going to use hypnosis." I sobbed, "Hypnosis doesn't work for me. I have tried hypnosis with three different therapists over the years." She said, "Are you willing to try again?" I was so out of control of my emotions, all I could say was, "Okay."

She instructed me, as the other hypnotherapists had done, to close my eyes and picture myself going down, down, down in an elevator: 10…9…8…Then she said, "You are going to the beach where you can completely relax." I had tried to do that so many times. Usually I tried to mentally go to a place I love in the mountains but every time I would close my eyes, I would be consumed by not feeling safe. No matter how remote the area, I still had to stay alert and aware because someone would come and touch me and hurt me. Why was she trying this? The entire hour would be consumed by my listening and looking with my eyes closed, watching, waiting. Anxiety surged through my body. I had to watch for danger. Instead of feeling more relaxed, I felt overwhelmed. I always had to watch, even if my eyes were closed.

Then Phyllis said, "As you are closing your eyes, you see Larry coming to be with you. He is sitting very near you, protecting you as you begin this journey." I wanted to scream with joy. Yes. Of course. Why hadn't anyone else thought of that? Why hadn't therapists with all their degrees and certificates on their walls, thought of that? I can go anywhere and do anything if Larry is with me. I could now work unafraid. After the session, I said, "How did you know to have Larry come to protect me?" She said, "I spent five minutes with you."

Although I don't believe I was ever hypnotized, I was able to go into a deep state of concentration to do the work. I saw Phyllis four times a week during our month stay. Each time when she would gently probe the area of my talking to or being with my night child, I would shut down. Coming to terms with my father, mother, or other members of my family would never be my biggest challenge. The night child was. She *should have died.* No one could persuade me differently. There was an all out war in my psyche over this as she demanded to be heard. She was obviously hearing how desperately I hated her and she would have her say by shutting down my life by paralysis, night terrors and body pain.

I could never believe that Larry could accept what I could not accept, that there were nights when my body had responded. Without question, the worst night of my life was when I had to remember that my father could bring my body to orgasm. How could I have allowed that to happen? I had tried so hard to shut everything down. Tight. Let nothing in. When my father would tell me to "just go with it…just relax," I would tighten everything even tighter. How could Larry not be disgusted by the sight of me? The first time I told Larry, he responded by saying, "You must bless the night child for finding a way to not shut off all feelings. If she had shut down, you and I may never have been able to have a sexual relationship. I thank her and bless her for finding the way."

I was reviled by my night child. Larry wanted to scoop her up in his arms. I raged at her. He tried to comfort her. He was filled with wonder that she found a way to live. I condemned her because she didn't die.

Although therapists were extremely helpful, I couldn't reason my way through the body pain. The first thing I always talked to therapists about and kept talking about was the body pain I endured. I would cry out for help to ease the tightness that kept me enslaved to my own body. One day, someone (not the therapist I was seeing) suggested I look into bioenergetics. I had never heard the word before. I went to The Tattered Cover bookstore, and asked a woman for a book on bioenergetics. She said, "You will find them in that section, and she motioned to shelves of books. I couldn't believe it. Dr. Alexander Lowen had written book after book and there were multiple copies of all his books. I bought *Betrayal of the Body* and then scurried home. With each page, I would cry out inside my head, "He knows me! He knows what I'm feeling. He knows what I mean when I cry out, 'my skin is screaming!'"

I read, underlined and yellowed the book in two days and then went back for more of his books. He had studied under William Reich who had studied under Freud. Dr. Lowen had written books for years. Oh, if only he were still alive. I called the Bioenergetics Office in New York City and asked if there was anyone in Denver who was trained in bioenergetics. In my conversation with the woman who answered the phone, I had a feeling he had not died! I said, "Is Dr. Lowen *still living*?" "Oh yes. But he isn't taking any new patients."

Oh, that woman did not know me or understand my body pain. She had no idea what I was living with day and night. He would see me;

there was never a doubt in my mind that he would see me. I wrote him a personal letter and he wrote back suggesting I fly to New York at my earliest convenience. I left almost immediately.

He was in his late 70's and I had instant confidence in him. He knew I was an incest survivor and that my muscles were unbearably constricted. He did many "exercises" with me but the one that had the most impact was also the most bizarre. He told me exactly what he was going to do. He didn't need to. I had read every word he had written and I knew exactly what the exercises were.

I was to sit in a chair. He would stand behind me. He said, "I'm going to start hitting you. All you have to do to stop me is to say 'stop' or raise your hand up. I will stop instantly. I will begin hitting you lightly. If you don't stop me, I will hit you harder. I will hurt you. All you have to do is say 'Stop' Do you understand?" "Yes." I understood.

He began hitting me. My mind shut down completely. I had no ability to lift my hand nor was I able to form even one word, not even the simplest "No". He kept hitting me harder and harder. It hurt. I kept leaning forward in the chair until my head was almost on my knees. I was slumped completely, in a total victim position.

Other than self-defense classes, nothing a therapist had ever done or said, had put me in touch with how I *felt* as a child. I knew I was tough and that I could ride wild horses and ski fast runs. I kept searching for ways to understand why I couldn't say "No" to my father. Why couldn't I say "No?" I could never have empathy for the night child nor could I ever integrate her into me believing, as I did, that I was strong and powerful and that I should have been able to stop him. I could never have come to understand that through logic. Only when I could *feel* how powerless, how completely powerless I was, could I begin to have compassion for the child who had to just "take it." Just "take it." It was the second most powerful experience I had in the many different therapies I tried over the years.

What changed, during recovery, was not my childhood. My childhood would always stay the same. What changed was my *perception*. I needed to change my conviction that I should have been able to stand up to my father. No amount of reasoning could shift the blame from me to my father. I was stuck. I had to seek other therapies because what I was doing wasn't working during this critical part of my recovery.

If you have ever had a loved one with cancer or AIDS who was told, "There's nothing more we can do for you," then you can better understand why I desperately searched for anyone who could help. I know women with cancer who flew to Europe and Mexico for "alternative treatments" after their doctors had told them there was nothing more they could do. They weren't going to just give up. As bizarre as Dr. Lowen's approach was, he was masterful in helping me find a way back into my childhood.

Shortly after seeing Dr. Lowen, I remembered a picture I had purchased when I was living in New York. It was the only poster-size picture of any kind I bought in my 20's or 30's. The memory came like a flashback. I could see the picture. It was of a child about five. She was street smart and quick and gutsy. Just as I had been as a child. That's why I couldn't understand why I hadn't stood up to my father. I had to find that picture. I had given it away. I hadn't wanted it anymore. Now I needed to see it again because it was a picture of me. I finally remembered to whom I had given it many years earlier, and asked if Larry could pick it up *immediately*. My subconscious had purchased that poster before I had any memories of incest.

I was so unprepared for what I saw. She wasn't tough and street smart, she was profoundly vulnerable, completely alone, trapped and scared. So very scared. Only when I could begin to understand how I really was as a child, could I ever begin to have compassion for the one I hated most, the night child. My perception of her had to change or I would never be able to find resolution. It was *her* skin that was screaming. It was *her* terror that was keeping me awake at night. It was *her* feeling of hopelessness that I would struggle with during my recovery. She was the key and I knew that unless I could integrate the night child with the day child, my nightmare would continue. Unless we go back, find the truth and confront the terror, our subconscious memories will run our lives, choose our relationships, dictate our career choices...control us.

One morning, I woke up with a sudden compulsion to go through the house I had lived in from birth to 10 years of age. That huge, old, terrifying house. It had been the only house on the block. It had a dark, dank basement, a scary attic and way too many rooms. Larry and I had driven by it many times. Once we rode our bikes by the home and the caretaker (a really scary looking man), who was living there was on the porch. I asked him if we could look inside. He left no doubt that

that would never be even a remote possibility.

But now I *had* to go through it. I had to go back to the place where I had been traumatized. And I had to go *immediately*. I called D.D. and Karen and asked them if they would meet me there right away. I grabbed a framed montage of childhood pictures off the wall, stopped at the bank to have a $100 bill changed into one hundred *one-dollar* bills, and sped to the house.

D.D. and Karen were there. I asked Karen if she would come with me and then I turned to D.D. and said, "I need you to stay in the car and wait for us. If we aren't back in ten minutes, I want you to get the police. I feel as if I'm going to die if I go into that house. Do you promise to get help if we aren't out in ten minutes?" D.D. never made light of my panicky feelings. He knew I was confronting very real childhood fears.

Karen and I went to the front door and rang the bell. The strange caretaker cracked the door open a few inches. "Yes?"

"Hello. I grew up in this house." (I showed him the montage with the picture of the house in it) and it's worth $100 for me to come in and walk through the house right now."

I waved the one hundred, one-dollar bills, where he could see them and I waited for his response.

"You're Marilyn Van Derbur, aren't you?"

"Yes and it's worth $100 for me to come in now. May we?"

He looked at me and then at the wad of money, opened the door, said, "Come in," and took the money.

There were old boards and junk everywhere. In the living room, I was stunned to see the old, funereal dark-violet velvet drapes that had hung there when I was a child. It had been almost forty years since we had lived there and the same dreary drapes were still there! I felt such fear as I walked up the winding staircase—the staircase my father had held me over as a five year old—by my ankles. I remembered my bedroom and the big window where the child's rocker sat with the doll who had watched everything.

I didn't stay upstairs very long. I felt like I had to get out—but not before I had gone through every room. I had no memory of the room where we must have spent the most time, the breakfast room. I had completely forgotten the entire room. Nor did I remember the sunroom or the pantry. I remembered the dining room and the small round buzzer that was under the table near my mother's chair. When she wanted the maid to come in, she would put her foot on it and it would buzz in the kitchen.

The caretaker had not accompanied us. Karen and I said nothing as we walked through the big house with too many rooms. As we slowly walked back down the steps, the man was waiting. He said, "How do you feel being back here?" I felt very fragile and said softly, "I find this house extremely depressing." He said, "I do too." I left feeling compassion for him and grateful to him for allowing us in.

I was going to therapy four days a week, desperately trying to get through recovery. As helpful as it was, however, I was unable to alleviate the body pain. So I turned to "alternative therapies" long before most people had ever heard those words. And some (certainly not all and I tried many) were the most helpful of anything I did. The process is risky. There are charlatans out there ready to offer us magical, instant remedies and some are dangerous; some could easily compound our injuries. As I look back, I can say that for me, credentials and degrees are not what helped me. In fact, I was further traumatized by some highly credentialed professionals. I have found that it is not easy to find safe, gifted healers but they're out there.

Many of us don't need to be smarter to figure it out; we need to get out of our heads and into our bodies because our bodies have memories. Our bodies have their own stories to tell. Because my body pain was so excruciating and unrelenting, I began to read medical journals and books trying to better understand what was causing my body to torment me.

I began to understand that the sexual energy and the energy of rage, humiliation, helplessness and terror had had no conventional means of expression. Most sexual encounters end with a release of energy. Incest forces that energy to be internalized. Nor was I able to release rage through screams or confront feelings of helplessness with hitting and kicking. Equally as importantly, the second my father first opened my body, my reaction was to try to close my body tight. This started a muscular holding pattern that I would invoke thousands of times until my buttocks, arms and legs lost their ability to release the chronic muscular contractions. Living with this body torment and chronic insomnia have been the two most difficult parts of my recovery.

Reading medical journals where this process was described in detail gave me comfort, knowing I wasn't crazy. It also gave me hope that if experts could describe the process that drives the body pain, then perhaps therapists could find ways to help me release it.

One day, I heard about a new treatment—from two very different sources. I took that coincidence as a message that maybe this therapist, this treatment, could help me to rid my body of the unrelenting tightness that I have lived with for as long as I could remember.

I told the therapist that I knew what the tightness was about. When I would hear my father's felt slippers lightly scuffing on the linoleum floor, I would pull myself into the tightest possible fetal position. But there were entry places I couldn't cover, like my buttocks so I would just tighten, tighten, tighten.

All I remember about my meeting with this new therapist was standing, facing him with my body posture tall and erect…as always. Authoritative. In control. And then he asked me a question that no one else had ever asked. A question that bored right into "the truth." One profoundly simple question. "Do you really want to let go of the body tightness?" What a stupid question. Of course I want to let go of my body tightness. Why couldn't I just say that? "Yes, you idiot, that's why I'm here. Because I want to let go of the unrelenting tightness." But even more tactful words wouldn't come. My mind shut down. Two radically different thoughts were coming at one another like 747s in flight, but no words would come. Slowly, my body began collapsing into the victim position. Shoulders slumped, back curved, head down. I just stood there—caved in and unable to speak. Finally, I whispered in a childlike voice, "It's all I have."

They are moments of incredible insight…when the truth is spoken. Everything becomes clear. The only way I could try to protect my body was to tighten everything up and in. It never worked, but it was all I had and I could *never let go of the only thing I had to protect me.* Deep within my soul, I *didn't want to let go* because, after years of conditioning, I still didn't feel safe enough to trust that I would not be invaded again. Only after making that connection, could I begin, *begin,* to release the contractions.

But, without question, the most powerful insight I have *ever* had, came when I went to the Gioretto Institute. Gwen had urged, cajoled, pleaded with me to fly to San Jose, California, and go to the Institute with her. Survivors, perpetrators and non-offending mothers of

244

survivors were brought together for education and healing. Gwen told me she believed it would help me. Several years later, I learned what she really wanted was for me to be the driving force behind establishing a similar healing center in Denver.

I was in the depths of recovery. I felt as if an avalanche had smothered me with anxiety so severe, I couldn't breathe or extricate myself. I was in full-time therapy. My career had been shut down. I was in no shape to get dressed, much less travel, but Gwen was extremely persuasive. So I went.

We were to attend a night meeting where survivors, perpetrators and wives of perpetrators sat around a large circle together. There were 30 people in the circle and no one had a relationship with anyone else, so a survivor could rage at someone else's mother who had not protected her daughter. The perpetrators were all men who had been court ordered to attend. All had served time in prison. I always pictured perpetrators as being big bullies, unclean, with bulldog faces. I was caught off guard when a short, lean, shy man, who looked like he might be an accountant, spoke. He had been convicted of raping his daughter and had served a long prison sentence in solitary confinement, because it was common knowledge what other inmates do to men who rape their daughters.

He talked about his loneliness. He had a job at a Kmart or Wal-Mart. He said that during his breaks he would stand in a phone booth or a small closet because it was the only place he felt normal.

The insight I had the second he said that was so strong, it physically moved my upper body back into my chair. I understood, in one flash second, why *I had always chosen to put myself in positions of terror.* Whether it was racing down the mountain in a fast college ski meet or speaking in front of huge audiences without a note, I had *chosen a lifestyle* that would place me in a position of terror because that's what felt *normal to me.* I had grown up in terror. We choose what we know. This was the information I needed. I couldn't change what I didn't understand. This was the connection.

Through research, we are beginning to understand that a child's brain can become programmed so that *terror becomes the normal state.* "The early brain can become hard-wired to deal with high fear states," says Dr. Jay Giedd of the National Institutes of Health. "Its normal state will be to have a lot of adrenalin flowing. When these children become adults they will feel empty or bored if they *aren't on the edge.*"

We repeat the same situations we grew up in—we create the same *feelings*—unless and until we make the connection as to *why* we are doing what we do.

Although understanding the connection was the critically important first step, it would be several years before I could change my perceptions, my choices, my behavior and the underlying feelings that were a result of my belief system.

God, please give me patience. But hurry.

When, in my late forties, I found the picture of the little girl I had purchased in my early twenties, I was unprepared for what I saw.
(Credit: Keane Eyes Gallery)

Chapter 13 – Not All Mothers Protect Their Young

Until a year after my father's death, I had never felt a need to talk with my mother about what had happened in our home. Although it may have *started* with a need, it quickly grew into a driving obsession.

While on a walk one day, I began to feel an anger I had never felt before. It was inside my head, inside my body. It grew into a seething rage, a blood-red rage directed at my mother. I had to talk to her and find out why she didn't protect me. But a constant concern kept bubbling up. If I confronted her, she might die from the pain of her betrayal of me. I knew that *she knew,* the night she was within steps of my door and then chose to turn away. Now my mother was 72. I didn't want to hurt her, but my need to confront her had become obsessive. It was all I thought about and I had come to believe that, many times, the thoughts that keep coming into our minds are an inner wisdom, guiding us into the next step of our recovery.

When D.D. and Karen came over for a session, I told them my concerns. I felt that if I didn't talk with her I would die from the pain and the rage but, if I did talk to her, she might be crushed from the pain of having to confront her real life. I didn't know what to do. We discussed it at length and, finally, Larry and D.D. said at almost exactly the same moment, "You need to talk with her."

I spent hours thinking about what I would say; how I would broach it. It had been eight years since that one conversation with my father. I would return to the same breakfast room table; my mother would be seated at the opposite end of the table. My chair was always the same.

I had some understanding of how overwhelming and devastating what I was about to say would be to my mother. Although there has never been a question in my mind as to whether or not she knew, I also believed she had put all that information somewhere in the deep recesses of her mind.

Confronting my mother was far different from confronting my father. When I spoke with my father, eight years earlier, the *feelings* of his hands everywhere on my body were still deeply, deeply buried. I had an adult, rational conversation with him. The feelings of rage and despair and unending terror had not yet begun to surface. The physical paralysis had been my final, desperate means of pushing everything down while hot emotional lava was pushing up. It was a battle I would lose, as the buried (but still very much alive) feelings my father had made my child body feel and the incomprehensible experiences my mind had no way of computing, began to erupt.

The force that drove me to confront my mother was rage—a red-hot, destroy-everything-in-its-path rage that was erupting with increasing intensity. The emotions of deep shame, humiliation and despair were ever present but it was the anger of hearing her footsteps turn away; her abandoning me forever, that drove me to speak to her.

I, a 40-year-old adult, had spoken to my father. When I went to speak to my mother, I was in the throes of recovery. I wasn't *remembering* my father turning the doorknob; he *was* turning the doorknob *every night now.* I was the child, finally doing what people would later tell me I should have done, turning to my mother for protection, understanding and, most of all, rage against her husband who had, for 18 years, violated her daughters in unspeakable ways. I had some understanding of what I was asking. Acknowledging 18 years of incest would forever change her past, present and future. I was dying inside, fighting to cope with facing one more day. When she saw the incredible pain—when she actually saw it—wouldn't she be willing to do anything to help me?

I remember how I started. I was looking at her. My head was not yet lowered into the shame position. I told her I was in very deep pain—that I was in trouble and that she could help me. I told her I was going to ask her to do something that would be extremely difficult and excruciatingly painful. I then asked her—if my arm had been severed from my body and if—for example—I would die if I didn't get another arm, would she be willing to give me her arm? Would she, literally, be willing to give me a part of her "self" if it meant saving my life? She looked at me with a what-in-the-world-are-you talking-about expression.

I tried again, "If my life depended on your giving me one of your kidneys, would you?" She gave me a blank look. My metaphors were going nowhere. I decided to try one more time. "A mother bear will protect her cubs with her life. A lioness will protect her cubs with her life. I am going to ask you to give me a part of your life. I need, so much, for you to give me a part of your self. It will be painful. I wouldn't ask if I didn't need you, right now, so desperately. I have to tell you something. It isn't even that I *want to*. I have to. I feel as if someone forced me to drink a quart of sour milk; I have to throw it up. I have held it down as long as I can. I can't control it anymore. It's coming up from my gut. It's in my throat, my mouth. I can't keep it down for one more minute." She said nothing. She just looked at me, perplexed and emotionally disconnected from my obviously overwhelming feelings.

I had no idea how to form the words. I had thought through "Would you give me a part of your self," but I hadn't thought through what words I would use after that. How do you tell a mother that for 13 years, her husband routinely, brazenly, invaded her daughter's bedroom late at night and entered and violated every part of her daughter's body. Where are the words? I could never have said the word "incest."

Deep, heaving sobs took over. I found myself doubled over in my chair. The sobbing was loud and uncontrollable. I remember the thoughts I had, as I tried to control myself so I could try to form words, "Why is she just sitting there? Why isn't she holding me? Comforting me?" I didn't look up. All I could do was to say words. I don't remember what words I spoke. I do remember knowing that when I said two specific words, she would get it. "Daddy, bedroom."

Still not looking up and still crying, I waited to feel her arms around me. I waited for her to comfort me. I waited. Finally, I looked up. Nothing could have prepared me for what happened next. She was sitting straight up in her chair with her arms folded across her chest and she said, coldly, "I don't believe you. It's in your fantasy."

I have never been as staggered by anything anyone has ever said to me. I felt as if I had been hit by an 18 wheeler. I was so aghast, I stopped crying. It was as if she had slapped me, hard, across the face. I said nothing. She said nothing more. Stunned, I got up and, in a daze, walked out the door. I have no idea how I managed the short drive home.

As I came in the back door, the phone was ringing. It was my sister, Gwen. I burst into sobs again. "I'm so sorry. I just had to tell her. She said she didn't believe me." Gwen said, "I know. She just called me. She told me you were making it up. I told her you weren't. She asked me how I knew that and I told her 'because it happened to me, too'. I told her about your meeting with D.D., your telling Larry."

Gwen continued, "I wish you had told me you were going to tell her. I would have told you this would have been her response. I'm so sorry." I hung up the phone and, almost instantly, it rang again. It was Larry's sister, Janey. I didn't let her even begin a sentence. Through tears, I said, "I really can't talk now, Janey, I've just had a very difficult conversation with my mother."

Now it was Janey's turn to stun me. She said, "Really? She just called Nan. They've gone to the deli for a corned beef sandwich." Mother didn't miss a beat. She couldn't even cry for me for ten minutes. I had thought that if I told her, she might kill herself. Instead, she went to the deli for a corned beef sandwich.

About two hours later, D.D. called me. He knew I was going to talk with her but I hadn't called him. I was too devastated to call even Larry. I was so exhausted from having sobbed for so long, I just sat, blank, as if someone had emotionally eviscerated me.

D.D. had energy—positive energy in his voice. "Bootsie just called me. She wants me to come over as soon as possible. I am so grateful she has turned to me. I can help her through this. I can help her to help you. I'm leaving now."

Less than an hour later, D.D. called again. "I just met with Bootsie. I am in shock. She welcomed me graciously. You know how charming your mother can be. I followed her into your very formal living room where she had placed two straight back chairs facing one another right in the center of the room. Her expression changed completely when we sat facing one another. I had never seen an expression like that on her face. It was cold, businesslike, almost a stare. I was caught completely off guard. I thought she would be crying, asking how she could not have known, searching for ways to help you. She had only two words to say. She had only one question to ask me: 'Who knows?'

"I was really unprepared to answer that question. For a few seconds, I was speechless. I said, 'Well, your other daughters.'

'Anyone else?'

'I guess their husbands.'

'Anyone else?'

'I don't think so.'

"She then ushered me to the door and I left. That's all she wanted to know. In all my years of being a minister, I've never seen anything like that. She was a completely different woman. Clinical. Flat. Uncaring. All she really cared about was herself—needing to know who knew so she could begin damage control, I guess. I have never been as surprised by any conversation. I would never have believed it if I hadn't been there."

Even though my mother had walked down to my room that one night and then not had the courage to open the door to my bedroom, she *could have* become my mother that day if she had put her arms around me and cried with me, from the depths of her being.

I wanted her to grab the nearest kitchen knife and say, "We're going to slash and rip up the life-size oil painting of your father. *Now.*" If she couldn't think clearly enough to say it to me that day, then I wanted her to call me six months later or two years later and say those words. She never did. The full-length oil portrait of my father hung, with pride, in her beautifully decorated pink bedroom, until she died. As a society, we believe a mother will always protect her child. We are so wrong.

It is important to me, as it is to my two middle sisters, that I say more than one time, that I am speaking of *my* relationship with *my* mother, not their relationship with their mother.

Many factors played into how different our relationships were with her. One was the fact that two sisters moved away from Denver at age 18 and never returned, except for brief visits. Siblings who live within a few miles of their aging parents often have a more complex relationship. And none of my sisters was ever in a position where she needed to test her relationship with Mother. When my life shut down and I became obsessed with talking to her, I needed her desperately and she turned away.

Although the following analogy is not comparable to the trauma I endured, I liken it to a couple who had been married for 30 years. They had devoted friends. Each week they had barbeques, played cards, went to the beach together. Then they got divorced and the wife learned that some of her friends really *weren't* her devoted friends. They were her *husband's* devoted friends. They felt they needed to make a choice and she was not chosen. I tested my mother and she did not choose me. Mother would not acknowledge what I had endured. She chose the life she had built in her mind. Perfect wife. Perfect mother.

Before telling Mother I wondered, should I tell her? Was it fair to her? Would it have been better for me to keep the secret, "stuff" the emotion? Suppress the rage? No matter what the cost to my health, marriage, family, my life?

The answer to that question became crystal clear to me when a survivor, wrote, "I am an incest survivor too, but I can't tell my mother. I don't want to hurt her. She's in her 70's now and I just can't hurt her." I wrote back, "The most hurtful thing Jennifer could do to me is to keep me out of her life. The most hurtful thing Jennifer could do to me is to keep me from knowing her." The movie, *The Bridges of Madison County*, was then showing in theaters. I asked her, if she hadn't seen it, to please see the movie and then write to me and tell me what the movie was saying about this same issue.

In the movie, Meryl Streep plays a married woman, who lives a secluded life on a farm and has a passionate, brief affair with a photographer who was traveling through town. At the end of the movie, after she dies, her children are going through her memorabilia. In a box, she has written them a long letter describing this incredible affair—the passion, the love she felt for this man. Why would she want her children to know she had been an adulteress? Because she wanted them to *know her* and it would not have been possible to have known her life without knowing this significant event.

The bond I made with Jennifer when I told her "my terrible secret" came because I allowed her to know *me*. Not just the me I was proud of. Not just the me that I knew she would love but *all* of me.

The richness of Tchaikovsky and Rachmaninoff comes not just from the high notes but from the lowest notes as well. I wanted Jennifer and me to share all the notes of our lives and for this to happen, I would have to role model and reveal my life to her.

Survivors of childhood sexual abuse will tell you that what happened to them was *the* defining moment of their lives. No one can know us without knowing "this" about us.

When I told my mother, I gave her a chance to know me. Unfortunately, she turned away and continued to make hurtful comments that were dismissive of the pain I was in.

One night when Mother, Nan and Papa were over for dinner, I was in the kitchen with Larry, doing dishes when Mother came in. The subject of religion came up. My mother turned to me and said, "The reason you don't have a stronger faith in God is because you have never been tested." Larry froze. I knew he feared I was going to hit her in the face with the pan I was drying. I said nothing. I just kept drying. He was bursting with emotion but he followed my lead.

I was learning to "put my armor on," before being with Mother. That meant being on guard at all times when I was with her, so she couldn't catch me in a vulnerable state. Expecting hurtful comments, being prepared, made it easier for me to hear the words she said, but not allow them to penetrate and hurt me. The armor helped but many times, her words cut me to the core.

I also began drawing boundaries. I made a vow that I would not betray the night child by saying things that were not true. Our bodies *do* react to our beliefs and thoughts. That fact can no longer be questioned. I was put to the test when I went to the hospital with Mother. She needed to have surgery and although it was not serious, she would need a general anesthesia. I was the only family member with her. When she was taken to the surgical area, her doctor and nurse came to accompany her into the operating room. As they were leaving together, Mother said, "I love you, Marilyn." I knew the drill. I was supposed to say, "I love you too, Mother." Because the doctor was there. It would not have been important if we had been alone. The easy route was to say, "I love you too, Mother," but not at this time in my life. I said, "I'll be here, Mother. I'll be waiting for you the minute you are out of the recovery room. I know it's going to go well." I was proud of myself for being there for her but, also, for not betraying my *self.*

Another boundary I set had to do with church. Mother asked me if, on Mother's day, I would go to church with her. That request pushed every button I had. It threw me back into not wanting to pray to "Our Father…" and having to say "hello," to every available person as Mother showed off her family. I said, "I cannot go to church with you. I would be happy to cook a special dinner, but I cannot go to church with you." Not "playing the game," was empowering for me. I was learning how to be with Mother while not giving her the power to devastate me.

But one day, I obviously forgot about my armor. Mother called and asked, "How did you sleep?" I always said "fine" to anyone who asked that question, but now that she *knew why* I couldn't sleep at night, I decided to tell her the truth. "I had a terrible night, Mother. Terrible.

The sleeping pill didn't work, I had night terrors; it was terrible." In a voice verging on cheerfulness, she replied, "Now I've told you this before. I want you to do it tonight. Take two Tums." I felt rage surge within me. I had held it in check for months, as almost each time we spoke, she would say something that made light of what I was going through which always increased the agony of my recovery. I heard myself say, in one of the very few times I ever raised my voice to her, "I cannot speak to you again. I'm hanging up the phone now. I cannot speak to you again." And I didn't. For weeks.

Gwen called from San Francisco. "Did you get the mail today?"

"Yes."

"What did you think?"

"What did I think about *what?*"

"About the check from mother."

"Oh. I tore it up and threw it away."

"It was for $10,000."

"I know."

"Why did you throw it away?"

"Because I don't want her money. Why did she send it?"

"Because she wants to reach out to you and she doesn't know how."

"Well, that isn't the way."

Gwen said, "Please, won't you keep it as a gift from her?"

"I certainly will not."

Gwen tried one more time: "I'm coming to Denver next week. Will you at least meet with her if I'm there? At least let her try?"

"Okay."

I was very apprehensive about going. I was far too fragile to have Mother hurt me again.

We went into the same breakfast room where I had confronted my father when I was 40 and my mother eight years later. I tried to explain to Mother that as the repressed memories and feelings flooded every part of my being, I was not a 48-year-old adult. I was a child of six or eight or ten and I needed a mother to stand up for me, protect me, cry for me, hold me.

She said, "All I want is peace. I will do anything for peace." That did it. I found myself doubling my fist and ramming it into the table as I rose to my full height and raged, "That's what got us here in the first place. You were willing to do anything for peace. Don't rock the boat. Don't open the door. Don't raise your voice. *Sometimes you have to go to war to have peace, Mother.* Sometimes you have to stand right up to someone and cry out, *'No more. Stop!'* Sometimes there's fighting and bleeding in order to have peace."

She looked frightened. She had never seen me enraged or forceful. I was ever the dutiful, good child and adult and all those feelings that I had buried in every cell of my being were now crying out for expression. She had stoically and clinically heard me. I left knowing I might as well have been talking to a wall.

The next week I received another check in the mail from Mother for even more money. I couldn't believe it. She hadn't heard a word I had said. Since Gwen was the executor and watched over every check Mother wrote, I called her.

"She did it again. She just doesn't get it."

Gwen said, "Well, she had written a check to a sister so after our talk, she wrote the other three of us checks for the same amount, because she wants to treat us equally."

"This is *not about money.* Why can't she hear me?"

"I'm sorry. I keep telling her what she should say to you but she won't or can't."

Originally, I thought Mother was trying to protect my father. I finally realized that she was totally immersed with her *self*, to the total exclusion of anyone else. Her only concern was protecting *herself. Her* image. Her place in the community. She needed to believe she was a perfect wife and mother and incest didn't fit in that picture.

I began to see our family as a Hollywood set. We looked like a beautiful picture but if you walked through the front door of our set there was just rubble and trash. Mother was busy, busy making sure no one would ever see behind that door.

One of the most difficult parts of my recovery was coming to terms with my mother. Not only was she not empathizing with me, she was undermining me at every turn. She devastated and enraged me but I believed, with all my heart, that she would ultimately understand, turn to me, and be my mother. However, her actions continued to show me that this would never happen.

At the depth of my despair, Mother invited Larry's mother and one of his sisters to her condominium in Laguna Beach, California. They had the most wonderful time. Nan and Janey came home raving about my precious mother and how distraught she was over me and how much she loved me. That was one of the hardest parts of my journey. The Bootsie other people saw and adored was not the woman I saw. I have never met anyone, who was as good as my mother was, at playing the different roles.

The Atler family had always been my safe place. Nan and Papa and the rest of the family were so grounded, so loving, so accepting. Nan and Papa were in their 80's. Although I still felt too much shame to disclose incest to them, they had become the parents I never had and Mother knew that. I never realized the lengths she would go to, to poison the well of love I had found with the Atlers until one day when Larry and I were visiting with Larry's parents. We were having a nice visit when Nan's face turned serious. (I had been in paralysis for about three hours the day before.) Nan said, "You know, my darling, these paralysis spells are so difficult for Larry—and especially for Jennifer. She needs you so much. Bootsie just told me what causes these spells. *Greed* over the estate." I will never forget her saying that word. Other than 'incest,' I had never heard an uglier word than "greed." "Darling, you and Larry have enough money to live very well. I'm hoping you can find a way to let this go."

I took one look at Larry, which meant "get me out of here as quickly as you can." As we were walking down the hallway, I said to Larry, "I can live with them believing I'm crazy but I can't live with *that.*" I began to understand how sweetly vicious my mother was when it came to sacrificing me to save herself. We turned right around and went back. Nan and Papa were still seated together on the sofa. I sat on the floor in front of them.

I said, "I never thought I could say these words to you but I will tell you what it's about." And then the tears, as always, started. I felt such shame. I felt so dirty and bad. They had had such respect for me—such love for me. Now they would know who I really was. I was approaching 50 and I still could not rid myself of that belief system.

That was my biggest challenge and I certainly had not conquered it yet.

I really don't know how I got the words out through the shame and the sobs. I do know that once they understood what I was trying to say, Papa rose from the sofa in rage and said, "I will never speak to your mother again. Had I known, I would have put Van in jail." Had I ever heard such beautiful words? Finally. Maybe it was genetic. The people who had responded so incredibly to my secret were Larry, Jennifer, Janey, Nan and Papa.

Do parents want to know what to say? What to do? Oh, my Papa knew exactly what to do. He was enraged. *Enraged.* And he wanted to protect me. My father had died. There was nothing he could do to him—although he *would have*. There is *no doubt* in my mind, he would have. But he could rage at Mother who had become, after Nan, one of his best friends. Yes, Papa, those are the words I needed to hear. I will never forget them.

My response to Papa was, however, "This is not about you and Mother. I want you to remain friends. She is fun to be with and you are good friends and companions. (She was the only one who could still drive.) This is between my mother and me. I just needed you to know the truth."

Nan sat in shock. She literally could not absorb that a father could do that to a daughter. That my father could have done that to me. She was devastated and truly speechless.

I left feeling so much stronger. Even though they knew my deepest, darkest secret, they hadn't looked at me differently. Each held me close. The first words spoken were of protection and accusation, but not at me. Papa's accusation was directed at my father and at the one who was complicit, the one who started down the stairs and then turned back around and left me. Without hope. Forever.

I had a mother and a father, Nan and Papa. The woman who gave birth to me was trying to destroy that relationship to protect her perfect picture of herself. I had seen Mother do this before but trying to alienate Larry's parents from me this was her most egregious, selfish act.

I have often thought about who might have stood up to my father. Larry's mother or father could, and would, have stood right up to my father and confronted him straight on. I cannot think of another adult of their generation who could have or would have done that. There was a strength and a power that both of Larry's parents had. Just being in their presence, you knew you would be safe. They would fight to the death to protect you. A feeling I had never known as a child.

Larry's father had been featured on the cover of *The Colorado Lawyer* magazine as one of the top lawyers in Colorado. In all the years I knew him, I never once saw him compromise his integrity. He was a commanding man with a deep, resonant voice. He was physically strong, and even into his 70's, he could ride a horse with anyone.

Nan told me that the first time she heard my father say to my mother, "Get up and let's go, stupid," she was astonished to hear those words come from my father's mouth, but much more shocked that my mother got up and went! She said, "I would *never* allow *anyone* to speak to me that way." Nan was regal in her carriage and empowered in her ability to stand up to anyone, if it were necessary.

During this period, when I was having a very difficult time with Mother, Nan said something to me that intimated that maybe I could try a little harder in my relationship with my mother. This is not a reflection on Nan. It reflects how incredibly skilled Mother was as deceiving almost everyone. Jennifer was in her junior year in high school. I was to accompany Larry on a very important trip to Israel in which we were to be hosts to members of the U.S. Congress and other dignitaries. Days before we were to leave, my paralysis spells became overwhelming. I would lie for hours, unable to move.

When Jennifer came home from school, I said, "Jennifer I need you so badly. I need you to go on this trip and be a 'host.' I cannot go. Will you go in my place?" It was the first time I had asked her to fill in for me. Jennifer really didn't want to go. It was a time for her to study for finals and these final grades would count heavily on what college might accept her. She didn't hesitate, "I'd love to go Mom. We'll have fun."

I was unable to get out of bed most of the 10 days they were gone. Nan called and said Mother had been crying to her, saying how worried she was about me. (My mother never once cried for me, told me she was sorry for what I was going through or in any way acknowledged—to me—how my adult life had been brought down by a nightmare childhood.) She told me that perhaps I was being hard on Mother. It was a Sunday. I dragged myself out of bed, threw some

260

sweats on, and drove to their home.

They knew I had come with something serious to say. "You can judge me on anything except my relationship with my mother. You intimated that I am not a good person because I don't try hard enough with my mother. You don't see what she does or hear what she says to me. If you were to judge me on my relationship to my mother, you would label me 'saint.'" Nan said, "I think we should stop seeing your mother. It's too hard on you. We just won't be with her anymore."

"This has nothing to do with your relationship with my mother. This is between my mother and me. I want you to continue being friends. I know Mother is fun to be with. I just ask that you stop judging me in regard to her." I think they understood what I was saying although, at that point, they had never seen the mother that I was talking about.

After Larry's father passed away, Mother and Nan became inseparable—having breakfast together every morning and dinner together almost every night (usually at our house). Finally, Nan *began* to see things my mother would do and say that were unconscionable.

Nan was most concerned about my deep sadness over the estrangement from one of my sisters. She and I had been best friends, as adults. She had stopped speaking to me a year after my father died. I believed that I had done nothing to cause the excruciatingly painful rift and I wanted a meeting with her desperately. Nan would say, "Bootsie, why do you let this go on? You could stop this. You know you could stop this. Why don't you stop this?" It was inconceivable to Nan that a mother could sit back and allow two sisters, who had dearly loved one another, to not speak for twelve years!

I got one of those aching insights one day when Mother said to me, "As long as you speak to me, that's what's important." I wanted to shriek, "*No Mother,* what you *should* be saying is, 'I don't care if you ever speak to me again but you *will speak to your sister and your sister will speak to you. The two of you need to work this out. Now!'"*

Finally, I just couldn't take it anymore. Since I had asked and asked, I decided to write Mother a letter so she would better understand the seriousness of my simple request. I asked her to ask my sister to meet with me just once. She didn't have to require any results or even a second meeting. Just one meeting. I went on to say in my letter, that if she did not request this meeting, she would not be welcome in our home again.

At this time, she was having dinner with us at least four nights a week. No one else was taking her to dinner. Another sister would have breakfast with her and be attentive during the day. (My other two sisters lived in other states.) I knew she couldn't deny me because we would have Nan without her and then Mother would be alone every night.

But Mother wouldn't do it. With that sweet smile, she would just shake her head "No." No explanation. Just "No." I backed down. Our lives went back to the usual, dinner four to five times a week and still no contact with my sister. When talk shows would come on about sisters being reunited after having been separated at birth or by war— whatever the reason, I would burst into tears. I grieved daily.

Before this happened, if someone had said to me, "I haven't talked to my sister in ten years," I would have said, "Grow up. Talk it out. Work through it." Today, I would say, "I'm so sorry. So very, very sorry."

It was during this same time that my psychologist, Jane, told me that I needed to find out what my childhood was really like. She said, "You made up your life. You made up a belief system that you were a happy child. You need to find out the truth. You need to interview at least five people to see what your childhood really was."

I had vowed to do every bit of work she suggested. I was willing to do anything to "get well," but interview five people? Was she kidding me? Who in the world would I interview? Everyone else believed my family was who we appeared to be. *No one* would know about my childhood. I drove home completely perplexed. She had given me an impossible assignment. Just as I was pulling into the driveway, I knew! Norma! Maybe Norma would know something.

Norma was only 16 when she moved in to take care of me, a newborn and my sisters two, four, and six years of age. She lived with us on the second floor until I was seven. She had the maid's quarters with her own bath and a private staircase that led down to the kitchen.

I was 48 and I had not been in touch with Norma for *decades*. It was Veteran's Day, a year after my father had died.

"Norma. It's Marilyn."

"*Marilyn!* How wonderful to hear your voice."

"Norma, I need to talk to you. It's very important. Could I come over right now?"

"Well, of course! I can't wait to see you."

It was wonderful to see Norma again. She looked the same as I had remembered.

I looked very different from what she expected, I'm sure. I was in sweats. Larry later told me that my face had changed: it had a pale, drawn, anxious look.

We sat at her small kitchen table and I went right to it. "Norma. I need to know about my childhood. I need to know what my life was like when you lived with us."

She beamed and started right in. "Oh, your beautiful, precious mother..." I knew instantly we were going to get nowhere. It was going to be a complete waste of time. Just another perfect-Bootsie litany.

I stopped her. It took as much courage as any disclosure I did. This one was rough. Not only because I felt so ashamed but, also, because I knew how she felt about my parents.

"Norma. Let me tell you why I need to know..."

After the initial complete and utter shock, I could almost see her mind working—like a computer going back to memories—way, way back to memories. Her first words were hesitating and slow, "You know, I thought it was strange. One of my jobs was to wake Gwen up around 10 p.m. and take her to the bathroom. She wet her bed even into her teens. It was strange." Her voice just drifted off as she tried to fit that memory into any slot at all. Norma's eyes had been looking into space as she remembered that. I waited for her to make eye contact with me before I said, "It's common for children who are being sexually violated at night, to wet or even defecate in their beds. Sometimes it is because they want to make their beds as unwelcoming as possible. Because my father usually came in after 10 p.m., he was obviously trying to avoid a wet bed."

I wanted, most of all, to know about my mother. It was much more difficult for Norma to talk about my mother than about my father. She *loved* my mother.

"Did Mother hold me, rock me, sing to me, read to me?"

Norma smiled a bit, for the first time since the jolting truth, "Oh, your mother *adored* you. We would put on little plays for her. We would rehearse and rehearse. She loved them."

"That's not what I asked you, Norma. Did she ever rock me, brush my hair, sing to me, or cuddle me?."

"Oh, she truly adored…"

"Norma?"

Norma's face changed completely. Her look was more than contemplative—it was sad. It was so difficult for her to say that one word. So difficult. "No."

She quickly changed the subject. It was obvious how uncomfortable she was saying anything about Mother that wasn't positive. "Your father was never home for dinner. Maybe 'never' is too strong a word, but I can't remember a night when all of you ate together. Sometimes a Sunday brunch, after church (your father never went to church) but never dinner. He didn't come home until after dinner—until the four of you had been fed and usually were in bed." She was much more comfortable talking about my father. "He really didn't seem to care about any of you. He didn't care if you talked or walked. He just didn't pay any attention to you. He slept late, almost always getting up after the four of you were dressed, fed, and off to school."

"What does the name Mildred mean to you?"(Ultimately my father's Executive Vice President.)

"Oh. That name means a lot." It was, perhaps, the most shocking thing she said to me. I had no idea Mildred had been in my father's life from the time I was born. "Did they have dinner together every night?" "Yes, they did." Stunned, I continued, "What did my mother think about Mildred?" It was the only time Norma laughed during our discussion. "Oh, she only worried about what *other people* thought about Mildred!"

That fit. Perfectly.

She told me my father paid her, and the other household help, Ruth and Virginia, as little as he could get away with. It was clear, however, that she had liked him, that she had been charmed by him, as most people were.

Norma smiled as she recounted a story about us when we were about two, four, six, and eight. It was a Sunday morning. Mother was seated in the first row at church with us, dressed exactly alike. Norma was seated alone in the back. During his opening remarks, the minister looked down at our family and said, "I must comment on Mrs. Van Derbur and her beautiful family. Some people tell me they just can't get to the morning service because there is so much to do. If Mrs. Van Derbur can get her little girls fed, dressed and seated for the service, it should inspire others to know they can do the same." Norma said, "I almost laughed out loud. Your mother had done nothing. Ruth and Virginia had fixed breakfast as I scurried to get all of you dressed and ready."

Norma and I talked for two hours. She filled in some important pieces for me. The most important piece was validating what I already knew—Mother had never nurtured me. We had never made that incredibly important connection that society expects all mothers and children make. The bond was never there—even in my earliest years. Immediately after my conversation with Norma, I called my sisters to report what I had learned.

Another lesson about Mother was to come several weeks after my visit with Norma. She called me during the third week of December. I was surprised she would share with me what she did. "I just received a Christmas card from your mother. May I read what she wrote to me?"

"Please."

"It's been so many years since we have been in touch, Norma, but I have thought about you so many times and always so fondly. I'm sorry to tell you that Marilyn isn't doing well. She's had a complete nervous breakdown. I hope the Holidays are happy for you and your family. Love, Bootsie."

That would have been enough for me. I was not prepared for what she said next. "And she enclosed a check for $200." Mother was good! I was just getting a glimpse of how good she really was. I learned later that one of my sisters had mentioned to Mother that I had been to see Norma. This was several months after I had first disclosed to Mother. She would use any way she could to keep things under wraps. Money was usually her weapon of choice. I felt a knot in my stomach.

If my sister Gwen had not come forward, it is very possible that I would have been involuntarily hospitalized for many months at the request of my mother. Mother would have driven to the hospital bringing beautiful flowers while saying to the nurses, "Isn't it just terrible—so sad—that Marilyn has lost her mind, that she has these delusions!" She would cry for the nurses and then the door to my room would close and I would see a very different woman. She was so good at her deception.

A woman gave birth to me. She gave me some wonderful qualities. A sense of humor. A positive attitude. A strong body. A medical history that is clear of dreaded diseases, *but* she was not my mother. When, in mid-life, I was strong enough to accept love from Nan, God gave me Nan to be my mother. She had absolutely no idea what she did that made her the incredible mother and matriarch she was. It just came naturally to her.

Most people believe it is a natural instinct for a mother to protect her young.

For millions of us, that is not true. Many of our birth mothers seem like such wonderful mothers but behind closed doors, they are, at best, disconnected, uncaring strangers who vanish when they are most needed.

"Silence is the voice of complicity."—Dr. Emmett Miller

Chapter 14 – Mike Was a Gift

I lived most of my life believing that the way to accomplish a goal was to establish a plan, diligently implement it, and, if obstacles were encountered, then knock the door down, if necessary, to accomplish it. I'm not talking about doing anything underhanded or malicious, just not letting any disappointments or setbacks discourage you.

In recent years that belief system has turned 180 degrees. I now believe you set a goal and work to achieve it, but if there is no energy behind it, if the doors keep slamming in your face, stand back and consider the possibility that this isn't what you are meant to do, or that the timing or methodology is wrong.

I share a belief with many that we are given clues and synchronistic windows of opportunity to guide us on our journeys. Our challenge is to recognize these events as they are given to us.

Never did I learn this lesson more clearly than when I met Mike. We could have lived on different planets; our lives were so different. Our paths would never have crossed if I hadn't gone to see Norma. As I was leaving Norma's apartment, she said, "I have a question for you. I have a grandson who is in trouble. He is in a revolving door, going from different schools to being a drop out, to being confined in juvenile detention. Do you know any way I can help him?" I don't remember my answer to her but there was no place in my mind that day to even begin to hear her request of me.

One year later, I called Norma. I wanted to thank her, again, for her help. This time I heard her, "Do you know how I can help my grandson, Mark?"

"Would you like me to meet with him?" Norma replied, "I was so hoping you would be willing to do that." She told me more about him and then I said, "I will need to meet with him alone."

The following week I drove to Norma's apartment and met Mark. Norma left so I could speak with him privately. He had an orange mohawk, was dressed slovenly and his attitude was not welcoming.

"So," he said, "Whadya want to see me for?"

I knew that I represented everything he loathed. He saw me as wealthy and, ugh! a former Miss America. There wouldn't have been anything I could have added to that list that would have made me more unacceptable to him (except debutante!).

"I don't know, Mark. Let's just talk for a few minutes and see. Are you willing to do that?" "Yea, I guess."

"Tell me, Mark, if you could change anything in your life, what would it be?"

He didn't have to study that question for an answer. "I hate the school I'm in. It's an 'alternative school' for dummies and drop outs."

"So, where would you *like* to be in school?" Our discussion continued as I began to figure out how I could help Mark get from A to B. As he told me about his life and his horrid mother (which Norma confirmed), he began to talk about his best friend, Mike. How Mike had helped him survive. Mike, who was two to three years older, had been the only person in his life, other than Norma, who cared. When things became intolerable, Mark would go stay with Mike in his apartment.

When I went home and began planning a strategy to help Mark, I decided to thank Mike for all the help he had been to Mark. All I knew about Mike was that he was 17 and living in an apartment with no phone. I went to the supermarket, bought two bags of groceries and knocked on Mike's door. We were very unprepared to meet one another. Mike had absolutely no idea why this woman with groceries was standing at his door and I was equally surprised by his appearance. He was about 6' 1", very muscular, his head was shaved and he had a swastika tattooed on his arm. It was obvious that he was a raging skinhead (a hate group that targets minorities) and that was confusing to me because his skin was light brown.

I hadn't planned what I would say so I just smiled and said, "You must wonder why I'm here!" That was an understatement.

I told him I was grateful for the friendship he had extended to Mark and that I wanted to thank him so I bought some groceries. He continued his quizzical look and then said, "Would you like to come in?" "Yes, I would. Thank you."

At that moment, I entered a world that was as unfamiliar to me as mine would be to him. There wasn't one stick of furniture. Nothing. When I walked into the kitchen and opened the refrigerator door to put the groceries away, there was nothing in there. No butter. No milk. Absolutely empty. When I opened the cupboard to put cereal away it

268

was completely empty.

I turned to go back into the starkly empty, very small living room and Mike said, "Would you like to sit down?" I said, "Yes" and quickly sat down on the floor. Fortunately, all I was wearing during this dark time of my life were sweats. "May I take your coat?" He hung my sweatshirt on a hook in the closet and we began to talk.

"Tell me about yourself, Mike." He didn't tell me very much but I liked him the second I was able to get past the skinhead identity. When it was time to leave, he said, "May I walk you to your car?" I would have been terrified of him if I had met him at 11 p.m. at a 7-Eleven. He would have wanted me to be. In part, that's what his identity was all about. But I found him to be articulate, warm, gracious, thoughtful and very likeable.

As he closed my car door, I put my window down and said, "Mike, I would like to be a part of your life. I have no idea what that means but if I can ever 'be there' for you, I would like to be."

I saw, quickly, that he did not immediately dismiss that comment. He said, "Well, I have to go to court next week. I don't have a job and I have no way to get there. Would you want to go with me?"

"Yes, Mike, I would."

This was occurring during my late 40's when I was so shut down I could barely drive to therapy, but somehow I knew I could go with Mike, so he wouldn't be alone.

As we were driving to court, he told me that he had broken a policeman's arm and smashed in his windshield with his black combat boots. Hmmm. That got my attention but for some reason I had no fear of him. He looked menacing but I didn't find him to be what he appeared.

I had never been to court before and, for some reason, this was not the juvenile court (where I would, in the future, go with Mark countless times). This was the adult court. I felt anxiety and discomfort as I walked in and took a seat in the far back row of the small courtroom.

I saw a young woman with long blond hair turn and look at me as Mike and I walked in together. When Mike approached her, I realized she was his public defender. He had told me about her. Linda. He liked her. They talked for a few minutes and then Mike walked over to me with somewhat of a quizzical look on his face. He said, "Are you famous?" I could barely contain a smile. "Why do you ask, Mike?" "Because Linda said you are and that you're the best thing that has ever happened to me and that I'd better not screw this up."

At that moment, the judge walked into the courtroom and sat down. I was the only one in the courtroom other than Mike and Linda. Maybe there was a guard of some kind but I was the only "guest."

Judge Soja looked at me and then at his docket. He motioned for Linda to approach. They talked for a few seconds and then the judge said, "I would like to see you, Mike and Mrs. Atler in chambers."

I almost fell off my chair. He wanted to see *me in chambers?* I could barely breathe. I couldn't imagine why he would want to talk with me. I stood up like a robot and walked, with Linda, to the judge's chambers. He wasted no words. He said, "Mike has a very serious offense and I almost always take the recommendation I am given as to the penalty. The recommendation I have is two years, hard time. But because you are here, Mrs. Atler..."

I wanted to stand up and plead, *"No judge! Not because I am here. I have just met this kid! I am not a part of this procedure!"* but the judge didn't ask me any questions. He continued, "Because you are here, I am going to give Mike probation."

And it was over. Our conference was over. He stood up and left. I was so dazed I could barely get up. I now seemed to be in charge of a skinhead with no job, no phone and no transportation. He had been kicked out of high school and was going to be evicted from his vacant apartment. I would have had no way of knowing what a gift he would be in my life.

As Mike and I walked out of court, I had absolutely no words. I was bewildered by what had happened. Mike said, "I might have been better off in prison." I wanted to say, "You'll be fine, Mike. We'll figure this out," but I said what was honest, "We'll take it a day at a time, Mike."

And so my journey with Mike began. I asked him what he wanted to do. He said, "My dream is to graduate from high school. I want to do that more than anything but I was expelled because I took a knife to school. There is no way they would let me back in school."

"Where were you in high school Mike?"

"Manual."

I said, "Well, let me see what I can do."

Jennifer had just started attending Manual High School. Mike had been expelled the year before. I called the principal, Linda Transou, and said, "What would it take to get Mike back into school? He only has two classes to complete before his graduation." She couldn't have been clearer: "He will *never* be allowed back in this school. *Never. Under any circumstances.*"

She left no doubt in my mind about that! I began making phone calls to see what other route we might take. I wanted Mike to have another chance. Although he was very slow to tell me about himself, I did learn that his father was African American, his mother Caucasian. They had divorced when he was very young. When Mike was 12, his mother was beating him, as usual, but this time he just couldn't take it anymore and began breaking furniture. He never struck her. The police were called and Mike was taken out of the home. In the police car, he was told that he would be placed in foster care or in The Denver Children's Home.

Mike responded quickly, "My Dad will take me. He's a police officer, too. He's married and they have a child. He'll take me." Mike told me they went to court and his stepmother said, in front of the judge, "It's me or him." His father chose his wife and Mike was sent to The Denver Children's Home to live.

Mike's father, a policeman, had been on the third floor above the courtroom when the judge was prepared to sentence Mike to "two years, hard time." Mike would be in jail several times in the years to come and his father would never once be in contact with him. I now had a better understanding of why he attacked the police car and aggressively resisted the policeman who had tried to restrain him. It also explained something else Mike did that I couldn't understand. He kept talking about how he hated "those Mexicans." I wondered how he could hate any minority considering his own background. I didn't wonder that anymore when I learned that his stepmother was of Mexican descent.

When I talked to a good friend of mine, Judy Fruland, a counselor at a neighboring high school about Mike, she suggested I look into a correspondence course. I tracked it down and then called the principal of Manual back. "Mike can take these two courses by correspondence.

If he does and if he passes, will you accept them as credits and allow him to have his high school degree?" Linda was not receptive. She finally said, "That's not my decision. You'll have to call an administrator for the Denver Public Schools." I did. He seemed meek and indecisive but he finally said, "Well I don't like the idea..." I said, "I'm not asking you to like it, I'm asking you to accept it. Will you?" He said, "Well, I suppose if he passes the courses we would." I immediately typed letters with copies to everyone I could think of confirming his weak acceptance of this plan.

Mike and I had a deal. I would pay for his rent and his phone if he kept his job and studied. With every passing day, I would learn more about him. I called him one day. There was no answer. A few seconds later, my phone rang. It was Mike, "Did you just call me?" "Yes, Mike. How did you know?" "Because as I was walking in the door, my phone was ringing and you're the only one who ever calls me."

I realized that Mike only existed for a few people. I had helped him get a job in a gas station. I called family members and friends and asked them if they would mind driving out of their way (for some of them, *way* out of their way) to buy gas where Mike was working. "Would you ask for *Mike* please? He has a *name*. He needs to be called by his *name*." (This is before all of us were pumping our own gas.) Soon BMW's and Mercedes were driving into a distant gas station and beautifully groomed women began asking for Mike.

During this time, Larry was the chairman of the regional board of the Anti-Defamation League, an organization that fights hate and bigotry, and it was members of the Jewish community who would always end up giving Mike jobs. The problem was—he was a skinhead. You didn't have to ask him, you knew it when you looked at him.

One day I said to him, "Mike. We have a problem. You know I love you just the way you are but you look like a skinhead (he didn't act like one anymore), and that is becoming an employment problem. Would you consider growing just a little bit of hair so you don't look like a skinhead?"

He stared at me intently and then he said, in a soft voice, "Then who will I be?"

His simple question told me so much about his isolation and loneliness. He didn't belong anywhere so he joined with others who didn't belong anywhere either. Although it would cost him his self-identity, he began growing hair.

I knew Mike wasn't studying very much so I would pick him up and take him with us to Larry's law office on Saturdays. Papa was also there. He was the epitome of a gentleman attorney. Just the way he carried himself demanded respect. He was as honorable a man as I would ever know and you would know that the minute you met him. He had a majestic quality.

Papa was in the car one day when I was driving Mike to an appointment with his probation officer. As I let Papa out and he shut the car door behind him, he stuck his head in the window and said to Mike, in the back seat, "Be a good boy." As we pulled away, Mike said to me, "Did you hear what Mr. Atler said to me? He said 'You're a good boy.' If Mr. Atler said I'm a good boy, it must be true."

I said, "It's true, Mike" and I felt my eyes cloud with tears as I realized how vulnerable and unloved this menacing man/boy was. We were more alike than we were different as I would learn time and time again.

I told Papa what Mike had said and every time Papa saw Mike after that, he would always leave saying, "You're a good boy, Mike."

When Mike mailed his first biology test to the grader, it came back with an F. We were in trouble and biology wasn't my strong point.

Early in our relationship, Mike had talked about how much he had loved going to high school and how much he remembered his biology teacher, Donna Holmes. She had always treated him with respect, even though she failed him in the course. Fortunately, that night, I had written her a letter, telling her I was sure she would remember Mike; that I knew he had been a problem in her class but that he had remembered her as one of the few people who had treated him with respect, as if he were "somebody."

A few weeks later, I found myself picking up the phone to call her. "I need your help so badly. Mike is taking a correspondence course in biology and he's failing. Would you even consider tutoring him?"

"Anytime. Any day." She was one of the gifts of my life. She tutored Mike on Sundays and when I gave her a check she said she wouldn't accept payment. I did manage to compensate her, but she never asked for nor did she expect payment.

He passed both courses. We were euphoric!

A few days later, Mike called me, "I want to march." My heart dropped. I couldn't believe it. All I could think of was Skokie, Illinois, where the skinheads had recently marched. I was speechless. Slowly, I asked, "Where do you want to march, Mike?" And then I held my breath.

"In my graduation. I want to march in Manual's graduation." I was so surprised, "But Mike, your class graduated two years ago." "I know but I want to march with the class this year."

I couldn't believe I was going to call Linda again. She had made it very clear how she felt about Mike. And I understood her position. But I fervently believed Mike could make it in the world. Here I was, barely able to face my own days and I was fighting for Mike.

"Linda, Mike has passed the courses and the most important thing in his life is marching in the graduation exercises." Her response was brief. "No." I continued, "He did the work. Please hear what I'm saying. This is the most important thing in his life. I am pleading with you to bend the rules a bit here. Please. What harm can there be in him walking in the procession? Please."

I could feel her giving. As much to get me off the phone as anything. "I don't like it, but okay." I couldn't wait to tell Mike. I knew how significant this was to him. I had never heard him so excited but, as we continued to talk about it, he suddenly changed the conversation completely. He said, "There is one more thing I want, more than anything else." I had no idea how huge this next request was going to be as I answered almost casually, "What is it Mike?" There was a long pause and then with an incredibly sad, soft voice, Mike said, "I want my mom to be there."

Whoa. I was caught off guard by that request. It took a few seconds for me to respond. I said, "How do I find her, Mike?" He answered, "I don't know where she is. I haven't spoken to her since I was twelve. I don't know how to find her." "Okay, Mike. I'll try."

I only knew how to find his father. It was the one phone call I never wanted to make. I already knew everything I ever wanted to know about him but I had no choice. I had no other leads.

"Hello. My name is Marilyn Atler. I am working with Mike and I wondered if you could put me in touch with his mother."

"No I couldn't." He was turning out to be everything I had expected. "Well, could you tell me what her name is? I know she isn't using her married name."

"Her name is Bruin. I only know where she works." I felt a surge of energy. "Could you tell me the name of the company?"

She was working on the outskirts of Denver. I found her! I called, got the address and quickly wrote her a letter asking her to call me, telling her only that I was working with Mike. I wasn't optimistic that she would respond. Mike's father had said, "She wants nothing to do with Mike. She will never return your call. Leave her alone. She hasn't talked to Mike in years."

When I answered my phone about a week later, I was filled with disbelief by what I heard. "Hello. This is Patsy. I'm Mike's mother." I was so surprised to hear her voice I didn't say anything for a minute so she continued, "What are *you* doing with Mike?"

I said, "You have a fine son, Patsy." She said, "Yeah. I'm sure he's told you *all about me.*" I said, "Let me tell you what he's told me about you. He is going to graduate from high school and the only thing he wants is for you to be there. Will you come? Please?"

"He's *graduating?"*

"Yes. In two weeks. Will you come?

Long, long pause. "Yes. I will." I told her where and when and then scurried to call Mike. "She's coming, Mike! Your mother is coming!" I knew how incredibly important this was to him. We both hung up elated.

He called me back instantly. "I want you to go with her." I knew what *that* was about. "Maybe you don't love me, Mom, but I am lovable. See? Marilyn loves me."

I called Patsy back. We agreed to meet ten minutes before seven at our huge coliseum. I told her what I would be wearing. She said, "I'll know you."

I knew how much I was *not* going to like her. As I approached our designated meeting place, I saw her watching me. I liked her instantly. We went in and sat down in row ZZ or QQ, it was certainly high up. Thousands of people were there as the students began to march in. Patsy hadn't seen Mike in six years. As the students began filing in I

275

saw her fervently scanning, looking for Mike.

As Mike entered (with black combat boots on!) I saw him looking up into the vast numbers of people. Suddenly, Patsy stood up and began frantically waving and shouting, "Mike! Mike!" As Mike was scanning, he saw her. With all the other students walking solemnly ahead, he waved to his mom. I saw an instant connection in that one second. I didn't know what had happened when Mike was a boy but I knew they had loved one another. Deeply. He tapped the boy's shoulder who was walking in front of him, pointed to us, and said three simple words I could lip read, "That's my mom!"

As the principal said, "We thank the parents who have worked so hard for this day," Patsy reached over, took my hand and said, "And our special friends."

I had seen a small gift that she was carrying. As she saw me looking at it, she said, "I really have no money to buy Mike an expensive present. This is a Thesaurus."

A Thesaurus! Of course! Mike loved words, long, huge words, "I saw a somnambulist the other day. He looked malevolent." He would talk like that! Only when I knew what her gift was did I understand another bond—their love of words.

As a student's name was called to receive his or her diploma, friends and family members would cheer and call out his or her name. I suddenly realized there wasn't going to be anyone to cheer for Mike. My heart felt heavy when his name was called until I heard a huge cheering section to my right. Of course! Jennifer had organized a group to cheer and call his name. He beamed his megawatt smile when he accepted his diploma.

After the commencement, Mike looked up at us, as if to say, "What now?" I motioned for him to jump the railing and come up to us. He weaved his way through the people milling in the aisles. When he reached us, he never looked at his mother. He put his arms around me (it had always been very difficult for him to show any affection) and said, "Thank you for tonight. Thank you for tonight. Thank you for tonight." And then he turned and said, "Hi. Mom." I was mush. His mother told him how proud she was and then said, "Mike, I'd like to take you out to dinner tonight."

Now it was Mike's turn to reject. He said, "Oh, Mom, they're giving a party for me. Thanks anyway." No one was giving a party for

Mike. He had two friends. When Mike left, his mother said, "I know you won't understand this but please don't tell Mike where to reach me." I said, "I won't."

Something happened not too long after his graduation that opened a locked door for me. He had been arrested again. When he deserved to be arrested I would let him sit in jail. When he did *not* deserve to be arrested (and I was never really sure), I would go down and bail him out. Sometimes Jennifer would come home from school and I'd say, "Jennifer would you go down to jail with me?" She would always say, "Sure, Mom." We had entered a new world!

This time I went alone. As I was waiting for Mike to be brought to the area where I could see him, a policeman saw me and said, "Marilyn! What are you doing here?" I said, "I'm waiting to see Mike Bruin. He said, "He's a bad seed." I seethed inside as I responded, "There is no such thing as a bad seed." His warm smile changed completely and he turned away.

Mike had been locked in solitary confinement. He was handcuffed and leg cuffed.

His dad was once again three floors above, never to be seen. I was able to talk with Mike only through a restraining glass. It was devastating to see him this way. I'm sure he pretended to be tough and mean in the "outside world," but to me, he showed how alone and vulnerable he was. He didn't try to "buck up." He allowed me into the pain of his world where no one loved him or cared about him. He even shared his shame. He said, "They made me sit in my own excrement." And his head dropped low. I wanted to break through the restraining glass and just hold him and let him know that he wasn't alone.

The special connection I had felt for Mike the first time we met, had turned into a deep love for him. I felt love from him in return, although I'm sure that's not the word he would have used. His face would light up when he saw me. As would mine when I saw him. When we looked for an apartment for him and then found the perfect place, he communicated utter joy. No matter how desperate his situation was, he seemed able to extricate himself and see the bright side. I can never remember him being depressed for any period of time.

When I went home from seeing Mike in jail and told Larry what I had seen, I burst into uncontrollable, gut wrenching sobs. "His father's three floors up." "Solitary confinement." My sobbing was deep, like throwing up all of my insides. Suddenly I was aware of a split screen. Mike in his isolation cell. Me in the isolation in my bedroom. His father three floors up. My mother down a long hallway. I suddenly realized that, for the first time in my life, I was crying not only for Mike but also for myself. Something had finally broken through all my defenses. It was the first time I had ever been able to connect with and cry for my night child. It was an enormous breakthrough.

No matter how many times I had gone to talk therapy, I couldn't find a way to connect with the night child I had abandoned. I just hated her. I had no compassion for her at all. I was finally understanding that I would be stuck in the muck of dysfunction until I could find a way to stop judging her so unmercifully. So many times, when I wasn't making progress in talk therapy, situations would synchronistically arise that would break through the walls I had built. Mike had helped me find my way to my "self."

One mid-December night I learned that Mike was back in jail. This time I felt his sentence was too harsh for what he had done. Larry knows me so well. He said, "I can tell there's something on your mind." "Yes. There is. Mike. I want him out of jail before Christmas." Larry said, "What will it take to get him out?" I took a breath and then said, "$7500." Larry said, "Seventy-five *hundred dollars?*" "Yes but I'll get every penny back if he shows up in court at his assigned time."

I continued, "You invest in IBM. I invest in Mike." Larry smiled. I never had to have Larry's "consent" about what I did but I always wanted him to know—and in this instance, to agree.

Mike later told me that that was the day he knew I really cared about him. That I was willing to risk $7500. There were so many times when our minds ran on different tracks. I wanted to say, "Mike—that's only money. That's the easy part. I show you how much I care about you by calling, showing up, being with you…"

When Jennifer turned sixteen, we went car shopping for her. Everywhere we went, I was also looking for a used car for Mike. Mike was twenty. He had never owned *anything* of value and he was doing so well. When the car salesman talked to us about a car for Jennifer, I said, "We're going to buy a car for her but what would you sell *that* car for?" He said, "I don't know. Someone just drove it in. I have no idea if it's a good car or not." "What do you *think?*" He said, "I don't know but my guess is, it's probably a pretty good car. I would sell it to you

278

for $600."

I can never remember anyone as filled with joy as Mike was with his new "old" car! He never wanted to get out of it. He couldn't believe he had his own car. We talked about car insurance, never drinking and driving—the things parents talk to their children about.

He had owned the car for about two months when I heard through my grapevine that Mike had a DUI. The second I heard it, I said to Larry, "I'll be back in about thirty minutes." "Where are you going?" "To get the car." Larry said, "I'm afraid to have you confront Mike." I was grateful Larry didn't say, "I need to go with you." This was between Mike and me. I said, "I'll be fine."

I drove to Mike's apartment and rang the doorbell. When Mike answered, I said nothing—I just held my hand out—palm up. He knew exactly what that meant. He reached in his pocket, pulled out the car keys and gave them to me. I sold the car that day. It's one of the more difficult things I had to do. I had some understanding of what a car meant to him. I also knew there were some things that required immediate action. He knew how strongly I felt about endangering another person's life. I knew it was the right thing to do but that didn't make it any easier.

A year before my story of incest became front-page news, I managed to tell Mike some of my story. He showed so much compassion when he saw how painful it was for me to try to find the words. It never seemed to get easier.

In therapy, my psychiatrist felt it might empower me if a man held me down while I physically pushed him off me while crying out, "No. No. Stop." I agreed instantly. I knew Mike hadn't been taught to never be aggressive with a woman, so I asked him if he would do it. It was agonizing for him to forcefully hold me down as I screamed, "No" and tried to push him off. It was my hope that this experience would impact him so strongly that he would never be forceful with a woman.

I was an integral part of Mike's life for eight years, as he was a part of mine.

He would take three busses to personally hand me a birthday card. I loved and adored him and I would tell him so. I knew how unlovable he felt. Oh, how I understood those feelings.

He moved to Seattle and began working on a fishing boat, earning incredible money. Mark also moved to Seattle. I spoke to Mark recently and he seems to be doing well.

I only wish that were true of Mike. Two years after he had moved to Seattle, Patsy called. She said, "There is no easy way to say this. Mike hanged himself."

I couldn't believe it. I just couldn't absorb what she was saying. Mike would never do that. No matter how "down" he got, he was always positive. Always a smile on his face. His mother continued, "He left a note. He only mentioned two names. His girl friend's name and yours. He wrote, 'I'm sorry Marilyn.'"

Several days later she called to say there was going to be a memorial service in two hours. It was a very last minute thing. Could I come? "I'll be there." There were only three of us on one side of the aisle. Patsy, one of her friends, and I. On the other side of the aisle were his father, stepmother, stepsister and two or three other people.

The minister was dreadful. He no more knew or cared about Mike than any stranger. I came very close to standing up and saying, "Excuse me, Reverend, but I will talk about Mike." But I sat quietly. His mother turned to me and said, "Is Mike in there?" She motioned to what looked like a vase on a small stand. I said, "No." In a few more minutes, she whispered the question again. I gave the same answer. Finally she said, "Are Mike's *ashes* in there?" I said, "Yes."

Whenever some pious person says to me, "The Lord never gives us more than we can bear," I think about Mike. Sometimes the pain of such a devastating childhood *is* too much to bear.

Chapter 15 – Still Searching for Answers

In his 80's, round-shouldered and jowl faced, Winston Churchill gave an entire graduation speech in just nine words, "Never give up. Never, never, never, never give up."

As I was writing this morning, I was interrupted by a phone call. A request that I call a woman in Texas who was in despair and wanted to talk with me. I called her immediately. She is in her late 40's and about to return to her childhood home to talk with her parents. She had been violated by her father and unprotected by her mother. She asked what she should be prepared for.

I was so grateful she called *before* she talked with them. I wish someone had prepared me for *my* parents. We talked for about an hour and a half. After our conversation, she said, "I know your time is valuable. What may I pay you for your time today?" I broke out laughing. It had been a very serious conversation and it was nice to have that break. "I wouldn't think of charging you anything. Please write me after you see them and let me know what happens. You are in my thoughts."

I hung up and thought about Anthony Robbins, guru to the stars…invited to the White House by the President. A big time motivational speaker: Infomercials, conferences, rallys.

A good friend had called me during the time of my greatest despair. She knew what I was going through and told me Tony Robbins was coming to Denver for a seminar. She knew he could be helpful to me and wondered if I would want to meet with him personally.

I was in my late 40's, spending my days in the throes of dysfunction. Memories and feelings made me feel totally crazy and out of control. I was in full time therapy, unable to work at all. It was going so slowly. Guru. *Of course* I wanted to see him. She called back to say it had been arranged. A one-hour meeting was scheduled the morning after his evening seminar. I knew I had finally found the person who could help me. This was "my answer."

I called D.D. and asked him if he wanted to go to a seminar with me that ended with people going outside to walk on hot coals. I said participation was voluntary. D.D. was always game to go anywhere with me. He asked if he could invite his daughter, Megan.

It was one of the few times I didn't mention an evening commitment to Larry. In fact, I can never remember not telling him, in advance, if I were going to be away but I knew this was something he would *not* want to do. And that was an understatement.

That morning, I casually mentioned that I was going to an evening, motivational seminar with D.D. Larry was very protective of me. I knew he would go with me if D.D. hadn't already committed. Larry surprised me by saying, "I'll go too." Quickly, I said, "I'm not sure this is a conference you would enjoy." He asked more, "Is this a participatory seminar where we have to *do* things?"

"No."

I knew that wasn't a completely honest answer. It was so unlike me to ever be even slightly dishonest with Larry but I had to go to this seminar. Maybe Tony would have the magic that would lift me from my craziness. When traditional medical doctors cannot help us cope with pain or extreme dysfunction, many of us believe there must be a "miracle cure" out there just waiting for us. Tony had suddenly become that hope for me. I was desperate to end the acute 24-hour-a-day panic attack I was living with. Larry and D.D. didn't *have* to participate. They could just sit there.

Larry said he would meet me there. He would come directly from work. I called to charge one more attendee to my charge card. It was a *very* expensive seminar but I knew it would be worth every penny!

There was a long line in the hotel lobby waiting for the doors to open for the conference. Larry was surprised by how many people had signed up. As he stood in line with me, he saw a table with a stack of papers on it. People were picking up the papers and signing them. Larry went over to pick one up. It was a liability waiver. When Larry learned that there was going to be a "fire walk," he was as angry as I have ever seen him, even angrier than when the psychiatrist had suggested we smoke marijuana. He was *enraged.* He stormed out of the lobby, got into his car and burned rubber. He thought I had trapped him into a participatory meeting. Few things anger him more than feeling trapped and I had not been honest with him. Although no one *had* to participate, everyone did.

D.D., Megan and I went in and sat down on the side—in the front row. After about 20 minutes, I saw Larry standing in the back. I motioned to him to bring a chair and put it next to me, in the aisle. He was still very, very angry but I knew why he had come back. He knew I was going to do the "fire walk" and he wanted to be there, as always, to protect me in whatever ways he could. He didn't come back to try to stop me. He never tried to stop me from what I wanted to do or *had to do*. He never tried to take my power away.

We sat through a four-hour seminar, learning the words we would say as we walked on the hot coals, "cool moss," while focusing our minds. Our thoughts. Getting ready. The idea was that if you could do *this*, then you should certainly be able to conquer your fears and achieve your goals. If you could walk on fire, then you could certainly ask your boss for a raise or, as I prayed, not live in out-of-control anxiety and unrelenting body pain anymore.

It was close to midnight when we were told to take off our shoes and go outside. There was snow on the ground and it was freezing cold. There were about 200 of us who elected to "walk." We saw this huge fire—flames licking high up into the air and someone was shoveling coals from the heart of the fire and spreading them in two different pits, each approximately eighteen feet long.

Two lines were to be formed as each person waited for his or her turn to walk on the red-hot coals. As we were walking to the coal pits, a woman began yelling, "Don't do this. I did and I burned my feet. Don't do this." She just kept screaming at us. Larry knew I would do it no matter what anyone said because I had to find a way to conquer the terror I was living with. As each of us stared at the huge fire and pondered what was ahead of us, Larry ran ahead to be first in line. He wouldn't try to stop me even though he thought this was an outrageously *stupid* and dangerous thing to do. He would go first to be sure it was safe for me. Unhesitatingly, he stepped onto the red-hot coals with his bare feet, completed the "walk" and then he ran back to me. I was about 15th in line. He said, "It's okay to do. Just don't stop. Step lightly and quickly."

As the person before me was just finishing the walk, Tony said "*Stop* the line," and he motioned for the man who brought hot coals off the flaming fire to bring fresh hot coals. He knew exactly who I was and he made me wait and watch fresh red-hot coals being put down where I would walk.

"Why are you doing this to me Tony?"

"It's your turn." And he motioned for me to go. I thought of the word I was to focus on, "cool moss," and then I walked lightly and quickly across.

D.D. was 68 at the time, what did he need this for? He was in line right behind me and he walked the coals. What an incredibly special man D.D. is in my life. Megan also walked on the coals and it turned out to be an extremely positive and empowering experience for her. It may be a stretch to say it was a life-changing experience for her but it was close to that.

I slept very little that night. I knew the next day would bring some semblance of peace into my mind. Tony is tall, imposing and charismatic. During my hour with him he was sensitive and compassionate but he didn't do anything that any therapist hadn't done at one time or another. He tried to convince me that today would literally be the first day of the rest of my life. According to Tony, that was my life-changing day. I could put the night terrors, panic attacks, feelings of complete despair and the conviction that I would have to die behind me.

I thanked him profusely and genuinely for taking time out of his busy schedule to meet with me. Nothing could have prepared me for what he said next: "My payment for an hour session varies. Usually, I charge $3,000 to $3,500. I never accept more than $3,500." (This was in the 1980s.) Stunned would not even begin to describe how I felt. Aghast. Why hadn't he told me there would be a charge? Why hadn't I thought to ask? In the world I lived in, if someone of national stature could be of help to someone also respected and well known, it was done gratuitously.

I was a completely unprepared, naive, powerless victim. During our healing process, when we are forced to actually live and feel the feelings we shoved so far down into the core our of beings, we *are* victims and never was I more of a victim than when Tony said, "I charge between $3,000 and $3,500." Why didn't I say what I would say to him today, "Get a life! I'll pay you because I was too stupid to know you would charge but I will pay you the same as I would pay a top notch psychiatrist and not a penny more." The victim paid thousands. I can't tell you how difficult that is to write. I was vulnerable and he took full advantage. Unfortunately, that day was no different than the day before. The "guru to the stars" had made no difference in my life at all. I tried, he tried, but there was no magic.

When the woman on the phone this morning offered to pay me for our phone conversation, I thought of Tony Robbins. I believe it is unethical to charge people who are in despair exorbitant amounts of money. It is similar to someone trucking in gallons of fresh water to an earthquake-decimated city and then charging them a hundred dollars a glass. Those who can, will pay, because they are desperate.

Telling Larry what I had done was incredibly difficult. I knew how exploited I had been and I knew Larry would say, "How could you be so *stupid* as to *pay* him that? And you *allowed* that?" But Larry didn't say that. He just put his arms around me and held me.

I would return to the day-to-day struggle of going back, digging into memories and feelings; just another day back in the psychic muck. Another miracle cure dashed into nothingness.

Although Larry and D.D. felt rage at my father, I was unable to find the anger. I knew it was there; I just didn't know how to access it. "Okay, anger, it's time. Please show yourself." I began to understand the process of recovery, I just couldn't figure out how to do so much of it. I wanted to get better on *my* timetable, which was always *now*. One of the frustrating aspects of healing from childhood sexual abuse was knowing what I needed to do but not being able to control the timing.

When I had gone to group support meetings and the therapist, Bobbi, had asked me to try to find the anger, I would beat a pillow, but there were no feelings of anger. So I would turn to Susan, raped by her brother, and say, "Susan, will you get angry for me?" She was walking rage. She would stand up, her face purple with anger and hit and yell. She was looking for a way through her anger; I was trying to find mine.

Just as working with Mike helped me access the feelings of isolation and loneliness I felt as a child, it took another unexpected event to access my anger.

I had been watching television at home the first time the story was reported on the noon news. Gary Hart, our Colorado U. S. Senator, who was then running for President, had allegedly been having an affair with a woman "young enough to be his daughter." There was a picture of him with a young woman, Donna Rice, sitting on his lap, taken on a boat called "Monkey Business." I felt rage coming out of every pore.

When Larry came home that night, the evening network news was about to begin. He found me very different from the woman he had been married to for 23 years. I was frenetic and my newly found anger was spilling out like an open fire hydrant. The television sound was blaring as I spurted, "I'm going to be screaming at the TV. Go into another room and watch."

He looked at me quizzically and quietly sat down. It was the lead story; "Gary Hart has been having an affair with a woman young enough to be his daughter." When the words, "young enough to be his daughter," were said, I shrieked at the television set. In the days to come, every time those words were said, I would scream them back. "Young enough to be your daughter. Young enough to be your daughter."

When Hart later said that his children were upset because he was dropping out of the Presidential race, I screamed at the television, "Your children are upset because you can't keep your pants zipped up." I must have screamed that a hundred times knowing that this really wasn't about him. I was aware of what was happening and I did nothing to try to stop it. Larry was also aware. Gary Hart had become my father. I couldn't rage directly at my father but I could rage and rage and rage at Gary Hart, which I did for months. I had finally found a conduit that allowed me to begin to do the work of addressing the rage I had so successfully buried as a child. It was a huge breakthrough.

I also raged at his wife when she said, "If it doesn't bother me, why should it bother anyone else?" Although I had begun to access the rage at my mother, Gary Hart's wife gave me another means and I used it.

Peace of mind is not a gift to a survivor of childhood sexual trauma. Healing requires work so agonizing, it is difficult to communicate with words. Accessing and then working through the rage was incredibly challenging for me—and for Larry.

One thing I had going for me (one of the few things at this time in my life) is that Larry and I had grown up together. He knew I was tough. When it was a red flag day at the beach, meaning very dangerous waves and rip tides, I'd say, "Let's go," and we went. We would jump on horses that hadn't been ridden all winter and ski black diamond-straight-down-the-mountain-trails. He also knew I was persistent. I would stay with something that was important to me until I accomplished it—no matter what. So when in my mid-40's I would say, "I don't think I can get through another day," he wouldn't say, "You have to try harder," because he knew if I said it was hard, it was hard. He knew if anyone could get through it, I could. Many times I thought how much more difficult it would have been if Larry and I had not had such a long history before my entire life unraveled.

My body pain was unrelenting. It never changed. It never let up. I would sit on the floor and extend my legs, trying to stretch the taut piano wire in the backs of my legs, as I tried to find relief for my body. I had tried at least sixty sessions of acupuncture, acupressure and deep massage. Nothing brought relief. I was in despair. There was, however, one thing I hadn't tried—biofeedback.

I found an expert in the field who was willing to see me on a Saturday morning. I couldn't wait to have her hook me up. I was in acute anxiety as I waited for her. She walked into the room and looked at me with surprise. "You're Marilyn Van Derbur!" "Yes." I was in no mood to talk about what it was like to be Miss America!

"I'm so thrilled to meet you." Why didn't my pain show? Why couldn't people see how sliced and burned, scarred and mutilated I was inside? I said, "My arms and legs are so tight. I am trying to find relief."

Appearing light and chipper, she hooked up my right arm first. She looked at the machine and said casually, "Look at the read out. Your arm is peaceful. There is no tension." She seemed very pleased that she had found nothing wrong. I couldn't believe what she was saying. I said, "Then try my left arm. It's even tighter." She said, "Look. No tension." I burst into tears. I cried out to this woman who knew nothing about why I was there, "Then what do I do? Where do I go? What can I *do*?" She stared at me in disbelief. I left in despair. It was my last hope for peace in my body. No one could help me.

When I drove home, my niece and nephew, Debbie and Mike Horwitz were there, visiting. Mike was a top doctor at Cedars Sinai Hospital in Los Angeles. I was crying, "I can't live in my body anymore. I just can't do it anymore." Debbie said, "Michael, are you hearing Lynn?" Mike had heard me. Mike had always heard me. He said, "I want you to come to Cedars and check into the psychiatric/drug rehab ward for thirty days. I work with a brilliant psychiatrist. I think he can help you." I trusted Mike implicitly, but 30 days? 30 days? What about Jennifer? It was the fall of her senior year. I had tried everything else. I really couldn't live in my body…one…more…day. We flew to Los Angeles and Larry checked me into the ward where they lock the door behind you and then flew home to be with Jennifer.

I was told that I needed to get off of Halcion—a sleeping medication that my doctor had given me for sleep. He said coming off Halcion would be extremely difficult; they would use medication to help me.

The psychiatrist said he was going to put me on an anti-depressant for sleep. I said, "But I'm not depressed." He said, "Trust me on this one."

The first night was horrible. They gave me a pill but I didn't sleep for one *second.* Staying in the hospital, in a bed, where I couldn't lock my door, evoked all the feelings of my childhood. I would have to watch the door all night.

The next morning, my doctor came in. "You slept well, last night."

"I didn't sleep at all."

"Yes you did."

"No. I didn't."

"But Inga, the night nurse, said she checked on you every hour and you were sleeping." I said, "I know she checked. Tonight, I will wave to her every hour." And I did. Inga would open the door and, with my eyes still closed, I would raise my hand and wave.

The next day, I had a roommate. A woman in her late 60's, who was hooked on Xanax.

I didn't want anyone else in my room. How could I ever be safe? Her first night, she got up to go to the bathroom. She couldn't find it in the dark and she was groping. She groped my leg. She was *very sorry* she had done that and she *never* did that again!

The nurses knew I was an incest survivor. I could never understand why a nurse didn't come in and say words that I needed to hear, "I can only imagine how difficult it must be for you, to be here at night and how unsafe you must feel. Is there anything I can do to help you feel safer?" Just those words—that acknowledgment—would have meant so much.

Loved ones or family members were to come to the psychiatric ward for special sessions after we had been there one week. Larry flew back to Los Angeles to spend the day with me and two doctors. I would have no way of knowing how devastating that time was for him.

288

When he flew home, he said to Jennifer, "I think we've lost her. If she does come back, she will never be the same. It's as if she is living in a different world now. I'm afraid she isn't going to come out of it." Larry later told me that this was one of two times when he thought he had lost me forever.

All patients *had* to stay 30 days—because the insurance coverage was for that period. I had been there only 16 days, when, after waiting in a single line for 40 minutes to use a phone, Larry told me Papa was dying. Papa, my precious father-in-law. My real father. How I adored him. We shared a special relationship. During Nan and Papa's later years, I would cook Friday night dinner, load it into the trunk of my car and drive it over to their apartment for the Sabbath dinner. He would always grin when he would see me. I made him smile. He filled my life with such joy.

I packed my overnight bag and waited until morning. When my doctor came into my room, I was like a caged lioness. I said, "My father-in-law is dying. I am leaving now. I am walking out that door. Right now." And then I added, "Please unlock it for me."

The doctor slowly and carefully weighed my words, looked at my Churchill-bulldog face and said, "You will still be feeling the after effects of having been on sleeping pills for so many years. Please stay in touch with me by phone." And so I left. The change in medication would be one of the most significant events of my healing. Within two weeks of being on the anti-depressant, the night terrors stopped. Insomnia would continue to plague me but not having night terrors was a *major life-change* for me. Finally, at age 51, the night terrors were over.

Research has now confirmed what I have always believed to be true. Years of trauma change children's brain chemistry. Our brains become hardwired differently. The good news is that there are some medications that can help bring about a more normal brain chemistry.

The doctor had given me one more prescription. He had said, "You aren't making much headway in therapy, are you?" I wondered how he knew that. "No." He said, "That's because your terror is so extreme. I will give you a medication to help bring down that wall of terror and you can go back into therapy and look inside." He prescribed the first and only daytime medication I would take. Within nine months, I had weaned myself off of it, but it played a significant role in my therapy.

Larry picked me up at the airport and we went directly to the hospital. Jennifer was there. She left school every lunch hour to be with Papa, her most precious Papa. He was 88 and he was dying. He knew it was his time and he was ready. He died as he had lived, with courage and dignity. He was my father; he had accepted me and loved me as if I were of his flesh and blood. It was an honor to be loved by him. There isn't a day that Larry, Jennifer and I do not think about and miss him.

I had been home for two weeks before I called the doctor in California. I said, "I've gained ten pounds in two weeks because of the medication." He said, "Are you having night terrors?" "No." "So?" I said, "Thank you." The ten pounds have stayed with me and my response continues to be, "Thank you."

I had no intention of going back into therapy. I was feeling stronger, I wasn't crying all the time, the paralysis spells were becoming less frequent and the night terrors were gone. But the psychiatrist from Cedars Sinai called and said, "You must have your blood tested at least once a month while you are on this medication. You will need to see a psychiatrist to have him monitor your blood and your progress." Would it ever end?

I can't remember how I selected the fourth male psychiatrist. The first two had been beyond dreadful. The third, Dr. Lowen, had been a rare gift. I would soon learn that the fourth was a superb choice, but I was now much more empowered. I was no longer Marilyn, the victim. When I went to see Dr. James (not his real name) the first time, I said, "If you are going to call me 'Marilyn,' then I will call you 'Bob.' If you want to call me 'Mrs. Atler,' then I will call you 'Dr. James'. Which would you prefer?" He looked at me for a long time before answering, "Bob is fine."

I could never figure out why a therapist, whose main job is to empower the patient, immediately sets himself up as having more power. I am Dr. and you are Marilyn. There is already a power differential. The women therapists I had seen didn't have a problem with first names. The men did. I wanted to make it clear from the outset that he would not win this subtle battle. Larry had understood, minute one, that having power and control was paramount in terms of my recovery. Now, when I address psychiatrists, I talk about how our very first encounter can trigger our most important issue—power.

I also had therapists who said, "You cannot go to any other kind of

290

therapy or work with any other therapist while you are seeing me." Oh really! Well forget that! I will see whomever I want, whenever I want. That's what I always said to myself as I was being told what to do.

There were two experiences that were particularly memorable. One day, I was sitting in Bob's waiting room and my eyes closed. It wasn't as if I needed to rest, my eyes just closed. When I tried to open them, they wouldn't open. I tried again. They wouldn't open. When Bob opened the door, he said, "Marilyn, please come in." I said, "I can't open my eyes." He said, "It's okay. Take my arm. You know where the chair is. Don't worry about it."

I sat in the large lean-back chair and struggled to open my eyes. I said, "Why can't I open my eyes?" He said, "What do you think?" I knew I was becoming more empowered when I said, "I'm asking *you*. I'm paying you $105 for fifty minutes and I want you to tell me why I can't open my eyes."

He said quietly, "The night child is here."

I pride myself on being smart. It's amazing to me how ignorant I can be about my own self. How obvious could it be? Of course.

My eyes stayed closed during the entire session. The next few times, I had the same experience. During the fourth session with my eyes closed, the night child needed to have a physical closeness with Bob. A healthy father-daughter closeness. As I moved to sit on the sofa and he sat next to me, he said, "We need to watch our boundaries when we do this work." I remember nothing more about that session other than the anger that began to seethe inside me the second he said those words, "We need to watch…" It continued to build until the end of the session. As I was walking out the door, I turned to him and said in an angry voice, "I had no safe place as a child and now you are telling me that I'm not safe in here? That I need to take responsibility for being safe? If you can't guarantee my safety, then you need to get a different job." And I walked out the door. I knew it the second I said those words—the night child was morphing into me. Bob had been talking to the child part of me when we were in session and I had held him accountable.

Bob began the next session by saying, "You were absolutely right. You can do or say anything in this room. I will keep you safe. I have complete responsibility for the boundaries and for your safety." The vulnerable, powerless part of me was finally becoming empowered.

Finally. It felt so good.

My paralysis spells were becoming less frequent. It was during this time that I realized what a gift the paralysis had been. I had given hundreds upon hundreds of speeches. How could traveling to give hundreds more compare with establishing a life- long bond with my daughter? The paralysis had forced me (and it took physical paralysis to do it), to pay attention to the chaos I held within, the chaos that also impacted everyone I loved.

That experience helped shape a new way of thinking. Maybe the goal I strive so hard for isn't really what is best for me. If I want something (such as wanting to stay on the lecture circuit), and it doesn't happen, maybe it wasn't right for me. At the time, I could never have been convinced that paralysis spells were in my best interest.

When Jennifer left for college, I missed her so much. We had spent time every day together. Other than Larry, she was my best friend. The first few weeks, she called me every day. I always waited for the answering machine to pick up, so her message would be recorded. Then I would quickly ask her what was going on in her day. Most days it was, "Oh, Mom, you're never going to believe how incredible this is…" Or "Mom! I met the cutest boy today." Or "Today was so fantastic…" What I would not know was that she would call me every day while in college, in law school and when she was an intern for our Congresswoman, Pat Schroeder. By the time she moved home, I had saved at least 60 messages from Jennifer. When she was 30, I put them all on one cassette tape and gave them to her. It was like listening to an album of "audiographs" as each telephone conversation brought back her experiences from the eight years she was away.

My unusual ideas were not always as well received. When Jennifer came home from college the first time, I spent hours thinking about what I could do to make her homecoming special. I called ten people she knew and I hired a band. Well, maybe it wasn't a band. There were four musicians; two played trumpets. We were going to form a semi-circle so the second she stepped into the airport, we would cheer and the trumpets would blare a "welcome home." I was beyond excited.

As we walked on the moving walkway, toward the concourse, I suddenly saw her moving toward us on the opposite moving walkway. I was horrified. How could her plane have been so early? I yelled, "What you are doing here so early?" Then I turned and cried out,

"Start playing. Start playing." And with that trumpets began blaring as we passed one another on the moving walkways. To say that Jennifer was mortified would not even touch her reaction. She could not believe what was happening. When we got into the car, Jennifer said, "Mom, promise me...*promise me* that you will *never* do that again. I want to hear you say, 'I promise.'" I said, "I promise."

When she came home for Christmas break, I arrived at the gate early. Just as her flight was pulling into the gate, I saw a clown. A thin, tall, colorful clown with a big red nose. I had no idea why he was there, nor did I ask. Impulsively, I went up to him and said, "...She's about 5' 9", thin, and she will be carrying a back pack...." Jennifer emerged from the jet way, saw the clown, and instantly began sprinting over chairs, between people, and down the concourse. Later, she said, "Mom. How *could you?*" It didn't matter that I hadn't hired him. It didn't matter that it was a spur of the moment decision and I have never done it again!

It was during this time that another major change was occurring. I began to be obsessed with being known. I was 51 years old and only a few people knew my secret. I felt as if I had been living a lie to those who did not know. When my life shut down at age 45, I had become reclusive. There were weeks when I didn't return phone calls. At Jennifer's school activities, many times I would leave in the middle of an event. Only very close family members knew I was in therapy. Some people knew about the paralysis but not what caused it.

It had been difficult for me to have the wide circle of close friends many women enjoy. Traveling constantly, being frenetically successful, having disabling dysfunction and needing time with Larry and Jennifer had taken a toll. Fortunately, I was blessed with family and friends who accepted my friendship on the limited basis in which it was offered.

I had disclosed to very few people before my late 40's. The first person I needed to tell was my sister-in-law, Janey. From the day Larry and I were married, Janey was my sister and I wanted her to know me—and no one could ever know me unless they knew "this" about me. I was in my early 30's when I drove to her house unannounced. She could tell by the look on my face this was going to be a serious conversation. We sat down and then I searched for the words. That was always the most difficult part. I hadn't thought of what words I would use. My head suddenly dropped into the shame position and I began deep sobbing, trying to speak one word at a time. She couldn't have been more shocked or more compassionate. I had chosen wisely. It would be 20 years before I would tell Nan and Papa. Janey kept my secret all those years.

My next disclosure was to my nephew (by marriage), Mike Horwitz. He was only a teenager but he and I were incredibly close and he was wise beyond his years. That day our closeness became a steel bond that nothing would ever bend or break. My trust in him gave me the courage to go to Cedars Sinai.

Sometimes years would pass before I would feel compelled to disclose to other family members or friends. I had been living a lie. I wasn't who people thought I was. Would I be acceptable to them? I remembered the quote, "And then the day came when the risk to remain tight in a bud was more painful than the risk it took to blossom." (Anais Nin) I knew I was there. No therapist suggested that I disclose to carefully selected people but somehow, toward the end of my very long recovery, I knew I had to confront shame. I also knew this could not be done in talk therapy. Disclosing was like climbing Mt. Everest, barefoot, every time I did it. The tears always flowed and the words always came slowly.

I was 51 when I felt compelled (obsessed would be a more accurate word), to disclose to eight people who were not close friends. I didn't consciously choose them. While I was cooking or driving, they kept popping up in my mind. I was intrigued and puzzled but I believed some inner part of me was directing my recovery—if I listened carefully. My only goal was to get well, have the craziness stop and find peace. I would do whatever was necessary to accomplish that, even mortify myself by telling acquaintances words I'm sure they puzzled over for days. They were people for whom I had the ultimate respect. My thinking must have been, "Maybe if they can accept me, then maybe I am 'acceptable.'" Now, mercifully, in the final stages of doing the work of healing, I was confronting my shame. One acquaintance to whom I disclosed, asked me the key question, "How can I support you?" My spontaneous response clarified this process for me, "I just want you to know me."

For me, there was not one therapist or even one type of therapy that could have helped me through the entire process of healing. I needed Larry, Jennifer, D.D., Karen, psychiatrists, a psychologist, psychotherapists, rolfers, massage therapists, group therapy, self-defense classes, acupuncture and acupressure. I also tried neurolinguistic programming, Alpha-Theta Brainwave Neuro-Feedback and EMDR (eye movement desensitizing and reprocessing). I even resorted to healing touch. My body pain was so intense and unrelenting, I survived another day by believing someone out there could help me.

I needed different approaches at different times and sometimes in combination. The journey is different for each of us; it is a *process* that we must discover for ourselves. Some therapists are safe, some are not. Some are skilled and compassionate, some are not. But remaining a victim is intolerable. Recovery is treacherous but the peace and contentment that awaits us is beyond description. Trust your gut. Stay the course. There is no greater gift you will give *your children* than confronting your demons, because dysfunction permeates a home and all who live there. Patience and persistence are basic tools.

Chapter 16 – Messages From a Higher Power

I had never prayed. I didn't want a more powerful father and I knew, deep inside, that the Father my mother was praying to when I was a child, wasn't protecting me.

But when I could see the light at the end of the tunnel, when my need to sob was subsiding, my rage was diminishing and my need to constantly, *constantly* talk about it was decreasing, I knew I was nearing the end of the agonizing journey.

I was so sick of being sick. I was so tired of being tired and paralyzed, frenetic and crazy. I knew I was ready to get on with my future life rather than staying stuck in the past. There had never been any doubt in my mind that I was going to plunge forward and go on where I had left off that horrid day in Dallas when I heard myself screaming inside my head, "I can't do this anymore," in front of 900 insurance executives. Now I could return to the business of motivational speaking.

I was stunned to realize that I could never go back to my old life. A scene had flashed into my mind of a soldier in Vietnam. He had been brutalized and held in prison for years. I saw him as he managed to escape and make his way to the airport. All he wanted to do was get on a plane, fly to America, sweep his family into his arms and hold them tightly. He had to get home. Somehow, he had to get home. Just as he dashed onto the concourse to run up the steps to a flight that would take him to freedom, he realized he had information that could help the other prisoners escape. He had no choice. He had to go back.

That's how I felt the day I knew I was "almost home free." I knew I could never just go on with my life. If the pain of my childhood had been no worse than the unending nights of terror, the body pain and the paralysis spells, I could have moved on—but the experiences I had during recovery (the six years between age 45 and 51) were so excruciating, I had to do something to help others who were fighting for their lives.

I just didn't know what to do or how to help and still remain anonymous. That was the key. Although I had been disclosing to one person at a time, "people" could never know my secret. If the general public ever found out, the life of being respected and honored would be over forever.

I didn't know where to turn for answers and so for the first time in my life, I literally looked up and said, in language my daughter and her friends used in high school, "Okay. Here's the deal! I want to help but I don't know how. If YOU will show me the way, if YOU will give me assignments, I will do them. I will do whatever YOU ask me to do. I will never back away."

I had read *The Celestine Prophecy*. The message of the book had had a profound effect on me. Ask for guidance and then listen carefully for clues. You *will be given clues.* The tricky part is to be open to the simplest, synchronistic event such as a conversation you have with a stranger on an elevator or a comment made by a friend you meet unexpectedly. Our lives are influenced by a Higher Power and our job is to recognize the clues.

It's like the story of the man whose home is about to be buried by a flood that has overtaken his village. A man in a boat comes by, "Get in quickly. I can take you to safety." The man replies, "I'll be fine. God will take care of me." A few hours later, as the waters are seeping into his house, a helicopter hovers overhead and he hears a man screaming, "We will throw a harness. Put it on carefully. We will take you to safety." The man yells back, "I will be fine. God will care for me." The floodwaters wipe his home away and the man drowns. When he gets to heaven, he says to God, "Where were you? Why didn't you save me?" And God replies, "I sent a boat and I sent a helicopter. You didn't listen."

I began to believe that my Higher Power worked through people. I believed after my "deal" that I would be given assignments. I just didn't know where or when or what.

My dear friend, Karen (D.D.'s wife), was in a psychiatric hospital. She had repressed memories of horrific childhood sexual abuse, which had suddenly erupted into her consciousness. I thought no one could have a more barbaric journey than I had but Karen lived a nightmare I'm not sure I could have survived. I have been in awe of her courage.

Karen and I learned something about being locked in a psychiatric ward. You don't exist for your friends anymore. If you're in a regular hospital, friends visit, call, send flowers. If you're in a psychiatric ward, nothing. No one. D.D., Larry and I were Karen's only visitors.

When I buzzed the buzzer to be allowed into the ward one day, a new head nurse greeted me. "Marilyn! How wonderful to see you." I had known her through our respective daughters who had been on swim team together. Swim team moms see one another often during the swim meet season. It had been at least ten years since I had seen her and those years had been, without question, the most difficult time of my life. She would have had no way of knowing that. I looked "together" and I was now finally feeling stronger, more empowered, less like a fragile victim.

Karen had a new roommate, Susan. I said "Hello" to Susan but focused my attention on Karen. Karen was at the bottom of that very black pit. She felt unacceptable, unloved, worthless and despicable. The fact that I visited her was very meaningful to her at this time in her life. She didn't want me befriending anyone else. I understood.

Only when a nurse came in to talk with Karen did Susan say anything to me. She appeared to have an eating disorder. She was bone thin. Pasty. Expressionless. With carefully selected words, she let me know that she was an incest survivor and a flight attendant. She knew she would never be able to return to work. Her life was over. She would never survive the memories.

When I walked out the door, I knew I had been given my first assignment, Susan. How could I tell Susan I was an incest survivor? I never thought an assignment would include my having to disclose my secret to a stranger. Why had I made that deal, anyway? I should have put a few qualifications in the deal. At least I would have time to think about it. I knew I couldn't talk to Susan as long as she and Karen were roommates.

A few days later, when I visited Karen, I learned that Susan had been moved to a private room. Why couldn't I have been given longer to think about it? After visiting Karen, I walked down the hall to see Susan. I told her that I was also a survivor and that I was going back to work. I had "been there." I assured her that if she continued to do the work of healing, she could move beyond the pain and the dysfunction. She stared at me. She told me it was difficult to believe I had ever been locked in a psychiatric ward. I left knowing I had responded to my first assignment. I never realized how hard this assignment would be.

My worst nightmare came true the next day. When I buzzed the buzzer, my friend, the head nurse, opened the door. Her face was serious. I couldn't believe I was hearing the words she said to me,

"You can't imagine how much you helped Susan yesterday by telling her about your life. You gave her so much hope." I don't remember saying one word in response. I was irate that Susan had told my secret. Worse yet, she had told someone I knew. Now the nurse would tell other people and soon everyone would know. The monkey chatter that went on in my head as I walked to Susan's room had become a cacophony.

I had planned on visiting Karen first but I passed her room and approached Susan's door. I suddenly stopped in the hallway. A change in thought had stopped me cold. I remembered that this was my first assignment and that quieted my fears. I knew that supporting and sharing with Susan was what I was meant to do and I was peaceful with that. I just wouldn't think about the consequences for me.

My next assignment was much more difficult. The Miss America Pageant was having a huge reunion, the 75th. Almost all former Miss Americas would be there. The thought of going back as Miss America was daunting and irrelevant to my life. Yet what could be more powerful for me than to have my night child there with me. "Here she is, too, Miss America!" I would be the only one who would know what that meant but I knew that standing on that stage would be a major step for me. When I had been crowned Miss America, I hadn't known about my night child.

When I suggested selecting an evening gown from the basement closet, my sister-in-law, Janey, winced. Not a chance. She made sure I was dressed "to the nines." Everything new! Fabulous, jeweled evening gown. Perfect long earrings. And, she insisted someone go with me to do makeup. I couldn't imagine taking someone with me just to do makeup. What an extravagant waste of money! I never wore make up. Lipstick and eye brow pencil, that was it. Well, maybe she was right. Maybe this was the time to prove to myself that I was strong, empowered and pretty. I had felt weak, ugly and bad for too many years.

Janey knew exactly who should go with me, Barbara. Barbara was in her early 30's and had never traveled to the east coast. She was thrilled beyond words to go to The Miss America Pageant.

We were the last ones to arrive late Friday afternoon and we went directly to Convention Hall. I would be introduced on the Saturday night telecast. It had been many years since I had been there as the television hostess for the national telecast. Barbara was wide eyed as one person after another said, "Marilyn! How wonderful to have you back." Just before showtime, she scurried to her seat to watch the parade of former Miss Americas walk the runway in front of that massive audience.

Sunday morning, while speeding down the freeway from Atlantic City to the Philadelphia airport, I said to Barbara, "So, tell me about yourself. How long have you been a makeup artist? Are you in a relationship?" Barbara said, "Well, my life isn't great right now. One of my best friends, Beth, has come to live with me. She's really having problems. She was molested by her father and she's having a really hard time dealing with all the memories."

I almost drove off the road. I knew the second the words came out of her mouth that this was my second assignment. How could I be asked to do this? Barbara looked at me like I was Cinderella. How could I be asked to shatter that? I just couldn't tell *her*. I just couldn't. I don't remember if Barbara continued; I stopped listening when she said the words, "father" and "molest." But I did remember my deal. There was never a doubt in my mind that this was my second assignment.

With my eyes looking straight ahead, I said, "Maybe I can help Beth. I was too. From age five to age 18." I couldn't believe I'd said the words. Well, I hadn't said *that word*. I just couldn't say *that word* ("incest"), but she understood. I couldn't look at her. I knew what she would be thinking about me. I tried to keep breathing normally.

Barbara didn't say anything. I kept driving. She still didn't say anything. Finally, I glanced at her and saw tears flooding down her face. Knowing I had looked at her and without looking back, she said softly, "Three. Three. Two brothers and an uncle."

It was difficult to assimilate. Now my tears were flowing. "Oh, Barbara, I'm so sorry. So sorry. I can help you and I can help Beth." We never stopped talking, sharing, crying, all the way back to Denver. Barbara later told me she stayed up all night with Beth. Their healing process had taken a huge step forward. It had been my second assignment and it had gone well. I was grateful to be able to reach into her life and give her the most precious gift I could give: hope.

It would have made the most difficult time in my life so much more bearable if only I had had hope. If only an empowered, centered, peaceful, joyous woman had come to me and said, "I've been there.

You can be where I am—*if* you do the work of healing."

I would have no idea the day Barbara and I flew home from Atlantic City that it would be the beginning of a lifelong friendship.

Gwen had been pushing me for years to start a healing center in Denver. That's why, a few years earlier, she had urged me to fly to San Jose, California, to go to the Giorretto Institute with her. It had been an agonizing experience but even in the midst of my out-of-control emotions, I was very aware of the important work they were doing with survivors. Now I knew it was time. I called Gwen and told her I was ready to form a program to help support adult survivors in Denver. We would create the place and the program that would have made my healing so much easier.

The Kempe National Center for the Prevention and Treatment of Child Abuse ("Kempe") had an outstanding national reputation for research and treatment of sexually violated children. Maybe Kempe would be willing to start an adult survivor program. It would mean telling the leadership that I was a survivor and although that meant only two or at the most, three people, I didn't believe I could do it. Shame was still haunting my life, but I also knew there was a higher purpose than my shame. So, Gwen, Larry and I made an appointment to talk with the Kempe executives. They agreed to start a new program if we could come up with the necessary funding of $250,000. Were they kidding? Larry and I would contribute as much as we could but I couldn't imagine raising $250,000. Gwen had already solved that. I had forgotten that she was the one with "all the power" of my father's estate. It was just the beginning of my learning about how, since my father died, Gwen had taken his place in telling Mother what to do and when to do it. Although I had a superficially positive relationship with my mother, Gwen had never liked Mother and she had never made any bones about it. She had disdain for Mother and why wouldn't she? Gwen's bedroom had immediately adjoined Mother's bedroom and Mother had to have been aware of what was happening in Gwen's bedroom for so many years. Now, Gwen was in control of Mother and she relished her position. It would work against me in future years but at this time it was welcomed.

We set up a dinner meeting with Mother, Gwen, Larry, me and Howard Torgove, Chairman of the Board of the Kempe Foundation. Howard is handsome (important to my mother), charming (important to my mother) and articulate. He presented a five-year treatment and research program. The adult survivor program would begin with ten survivors and slowly add more. Mother was charmed by Howard but she couldn't have cared less about the program. She didn't even want to be there. Gwen had ordered her to be there and, after the presentation, Gwen told Mother that she should give $250,000 to fund the new program. It was a done deal. A search would commence for a psychiatrist who would be the director of the program.

It took almost two years to put the program in place. Dr. Tom Roesler, a psychiatrist from Seattle, was hired to begin networking with psychiatrists in Denver. I went to Kempe one day to talk with him about a friend of mine. One of the major reasons I wanted a program was for her to have a safe place to begin her healing process. She had had a complete breakdown many years earlier and there was no doubt in my mind that she had been another one of my father's young victims.

In the process of talking with Tom, he mentioned Mother. He was concerned that if Mother kept contributing money to Kempe, this association might puncture her defense system, leaving her devastated. I told him there was no way her name was going to be associated with the program and that nothing would penetrate her defenses. He pressed it. In essence, he was questioning my sense of responsibility to my mother. I replied, "I don't think that should hinder the process of setting up this program. We do what is responsible, in the best way we can."

He pressed it again. His point was becoming clearer. I should take more responsibility for my mother. Finally, I said, "You know, there is a part of me that says, if she has to take responsibility and some consequences for not doing anything for 18 years, then that's the way it will be." He looked at me as if he were disappointed in me—that I wasn't as "good a person" as he had expected.

I left knowing I had *allowed him* to make me feel guilty. I was angry, angry, angry that I couldn't say, "Don't even *think* of trying to make me feel guilty. Just stop it."

Later that day, I typed in my journal, "I can protect other people. Why can't I protect myself? I should have had my armor on. I went in unprotected. If you can't feel safe at Kempe, with a psychiatrist whose entire profession has been helping incest victims, then where can you feel safe?"

The program was ready to begin in the spring. I was 53. I didn't want to be directly involved with the program. Everyone knew how strongly I felt about not participating. I also had a firm commitment from every single person I had spoken with that *no one* would share my secret. No one. I had such a peaceful feeling knowing that other men and women, just beginning their journey of facing buried memories and feelings, would have support; that they would not feel as isolated and hopeless as I had during my healing process. The program was to be announced on May 8th at 7 p.m. I was still seeing a psychiatrist four days a week. The worst of recovery was over but chronic insomnia, body pain and shame were still invading every day and night of my life.

Tom had told me about the meeting but I had paid little attention. Something about having networked with psychiatrists—each would bring a survivor, 36 people total. He was going to fly one of his former patients from Seattle to talk about the importance of a support program. Great. However he wanted to do it was fine with me. We had given him the money and the reins. My part was over.

Ten days before the scheduled meeting, Tom called. Could he run over and talk with Larry and me that night? Sure.

I was unprepared for what he was going to say. He got right to the point. "It's because of you, Marilyn, that the adult survivor program has come into being. I'm wondering if you would stand before these 36 therapists and survivors and tell them why it was so important to you." Had I heard him correctly? "You mean, tell them I'm a survivor?" "Yes."

The thought knocked my brain out of commission…took the breath out of my body. I sat expressionless, unable to comprehend what he had said. But that's what he had said. I would say, "I'm an incest survivor" in front of 36 people. In public. In front of people I had never met. Would I do that? Never.

But I didn't say, "Never." My mind was saying "Never." My soul was saying "Never." I looked at Larry who, wisely, offered no counsel. My mouth opened and I heard myself say, "I'll call you in the morning." That was it. No "goodbye, can't talk anymore." Tom knew enough to leave.

I don't remember what Larry and I said to one another that night. All I remember is calling two of my sisters. Gwen, of course, was adamantly supportive. I should have said, "Then *you* fly to Denver and say *you* are an incest survivor," but that thought didn't occur to me. I'm sure my sister in Palm Springs would have preferred, understandably, that I had not accepted this talk but she said she was 100 percent supportive of me, as she always had been and would continue to be. I called my two Van Derbur nieces, Julie Wham and Debbie Griffin who lived in Denver. Not only were they with me, they would come to the small meeting to support me.

I couldn't believe what I was doing. It flew in the face of my entire life. Fight to the death to keep the secret. Never let "people" know. Tom had assured me again and again that this would be a private meeting—that psychiatrists were honor bound to never repeat what they had heard and I would tell them to never tell. My secret would be safe.

It never occurred to me that this was my third assignment. My mind was far too overwhelmed to allow such an extraneous thought. Some part of me picked up the phone the next morning and told Tom I would do it. Small, secret meeting.

I thought about nothing else during the next nine days. I typed my thoughts out what seemed like hundreds of times. Over and over. Change a word. No. Don't say that. Use this word. Never tell them that. How do I say this? Playing the organ in front of 85 million people on network television was child's play compared to this.

May 8th was a Wednesday. My text was ready. About 30 minutes worth. Honest. Direct. I was even going to say "that word" for the first time ever. It is such an ugly, six-letter word. I had it in the text. I would speak it out loud. I would hear it. I remembered Sara in the support group I attended. She had said, "If I say the words then I will know it was true." "My name is Marilyn Van Derbur Atler and I'm an incest survivor." That said it all. That's all you ever need to know about me because that's what comprises the marrow of my bones, the center of my soul, the emptiness of a huge part of my heart.

Jennifer was home from Duke University. She had just completed her sophomore year. How grateful I was to have her with me. When I was with Larry and Jennifer I felt so incredibly and unconditionally loved.

All of Larry's family would be there. Nieces and nephews from both sides of my family would be there. Nan. I needed Nan there. And

I wanted Mother there. How could I ever get her there? I knew exactly how to do it. It was one of the few times I was devious rather than candid.

On Monday night, when Nan and Mother were at our home for dinner, I talked about the meeting. I had primed Jennifer and Nan. Jennifer said, "I'll be there for you, Mom." Nan said, "You know I'll be there, my darling." It was at that point that I turned to my mother and said, "I want you there too, Mother. It's easy to stand by me in the good times but I want you there for me now in the tough times." I knew what Mother's answer would be. I knew she would say "Yes" because Nan had said "Yes" and what would people think if Larry's mother were there and she wasn't. I knew exactly how she thought. She said she would be there.

In future years, I wouldn't want her to come to my speeches because I always felt muzzled—unable to speak the truth about how difficult she had made my recovery. I still wanted to avoid hurting her, so I would choose my words carefully; but I couldn't betray myself either. I had finally come to understand that the only thing that would set me free was the truth. It was a tightrope I would walk often.

I had been losing weight during those nine days of anxiety and preparation. When I finally weighed myself again, I found that, within that two-week period, I had lost ten pounds.

On the morning of my speech, I was mentally prepared. I had gone over it and over it in my mind. Walking in. Standing at the podium. Looking out at the 36 people (I had forgotten that with Larry's and my family the group would grow to almost 50). Now, I would just have to wait.

Do you remember being outside on a beautiful summer day, not a cloud in the sky and then, within minutes, the dark clouds came, the thunder cracked and the rains poured—endless, drenching rains? That's what happened that afternoon. The thunderclap was the ringing of my phone. Someone from Kempe, I don't remember who, but I do remember the exact words he said: "A reporter is coming." Four words. Four simple words. It was as if I couldn't assimilate what he had said. Finally, I responded. "A reporter? A newspaper reporter?" "Yes." "Are you sure?" "No, but we think so." *"You think so?* I need to know. Please find out and call me back."

He didn't call me back. A woman did. The head of the public

relations department of the University of Colorado Health Sciences Center (of which Kempe is a part). Now *they* knew! How could Kempe have told *them?* What a nightmare. She said, "I'm sorry but it's true. The reporter's name is Carol Kreck. *The Denver Post.*" "How did she find out?" "We are told she saw the Kempe bulletin that mentioned the announcement of a new program. She writes on women's and children's issues. She wants to know more about the program. She's coming

"Does she know that I'm the speaker?"

"No but she does know it is a celebrity. She doesn't know it's you but she will—even if you don't speak tonight. Too many people know it's you. She will find out."

The woman continued, "I would like to come and meet with you right now. May I come over?" I don't remember what time it was. Sometime in the afternoon. We were only hours away from the start of the meeting. I felt completely numb.

"Okay."

She didn't come alone. One of my closest high school friends, Ann McAdams, came with her. Ann was her assistant. I could only remember five people working at Kempe. It had never concerned me that it was a part of the huge organization, the University of Colorado Health Sciences Center. Sadly, Ann wasn't just a high school friend. I had learned years earlier that she was one of the seven women (that I know of) that my father had violated decades earlier. Ann had lived one block from our home. She was stunningly beautiful, a brilliant pianist, and my entire family had adored her, especially my father. How incredible that she would be back in my life at this moment. Ann could talk to me the way someone I had just met never could. Ann put it right on the table. She said, "Here's the way it is. Carol Kreck will be there. There is no way you can keep this a secret any longer because many people are now involved. If no one shows up to speak, questions will be asked. It is known that a high profile celebrity will be speaking as an incest survivor and it won't take long for the paper to find out it's you.

Now, here's what I strongly recommend you do. Give us your text. We will go to the editor of the *Post* and make a deal. If we tell them who you are, they will guarantee us that they will print *your* words, not Carol's interpretation of them. What can happen is—if you aren't speaking until 7 p.m., the second she sees it's you, she will run to phone in a story that we will have no control over. We can have control if you will give us permission to go down and negotiate. Don't you want your words to be used? Don't you want your message to be presented the way you present it…or do you want a few sentences phoned in at the last minute?"

I felt like a patient who had just been diagnosed with a life threatening disease. The doctors said, "You either go in immediately for an operation or you will die." I felt as if I had no choice.

They left the house with my text, promising to have it back by 6 p.m. I have no idea what happened during the next three or four hours. The next thing I remember is walking into the room about 6:59 p.m. with Larry and Jennifer. Our families filled the first two rows. As I approached the front of the room, a woman seated on an aisle, stood up and said quietly, "I'm Carol Kreck. I'm with *The Denver Post*." I said, "You're the last person I want to see tonight," and I walked to the podium.

This was going to be the end of my life. That's what I had always believed. That's one of the most devastating aspects of childhood sexual abuse. We believe in the marrow of our bones that we are ugly and bad and that people will look at us with disdain. If we are violated as children, we must keep the secret. With rare exception, all of us feel that way.

If I ever looked up from my text, I didn't see anyone. I felt robotic. I just read the words on the page—at least I tried to. Sometimes I would get to a word I just couldn't speak. I should have said the words out loud again and again to allow my lips to form them and my ears to hear them. I should never have spoken the words for the first time in public. Many times I had to stop, try to get a grip and go on. I knew it was going to be hard. I had no idea it was going to be that difficult. It wasn't the reporter. I had eliminated her from my mind. I really couldn't think about her or the ramifications of her being there. My challenge was to read the words I had written to fifty people.

I don't remember anything more about that night. I don't remember driving home or trying to sleep. No memories. The next morning my new life would begin. Just as my childhood was split into day child-night child, my life would forevermore be split into before May 8th and after May 8th.

Chapter 17 – The 2nd Day of the Rest of My Life

It was the morning after the first day of the rest of my life.

I knew it would be a major story in the newspaper. I had no idea *how* major. There was a front-page picture and then inside, there were full-length *New York Times* size pages…pictures of me as Miss America…pictures of my entire family. My text was quoted, as promised. There was an article about Kempe, including what to do and whom to call if you were a survivor.

Many days later, I went to *The Denver Post* to meet the managing editor, Gay Cook. I wanted to thank her personally for the way my story had been written—with respect and compassion. She told me they had, in essence, stopped the presses and that she had stayed at the paper until she had seen and approved every picture, every caption, every sentence.

My mother had no idea what she would encounter when she awakened that day. My only thoughts, at dawn that morning, were of her. I knew Mother would react according to the way other people reacted. Because Mother always slept late, drove to the same restaurant for breakfast and would then read the paper, I knew I had a couple of hours.

My first call was to the retired head of The Miss America Pageant, Lenora Slaughter. Lenora was living in Scottsdale. There was no doubt that Bootsie was her favorite mother of a Miss America. She had told me—and Mother—and anyone else who would listen about her "precious Bootsie."

The horror of what I was about to tell her seemed suddenly insignificant compared to helping Mother through this public disclosure. I don't remember how I told her; I do remember exactly what I asked her to do: "Please call Mother now and tell her you are so proud of her for the family coming forward with this story. Please! Now!" She said she would. I can't imagine how crushing and mind-blowing this information must have been to Lenora.

I then called a man universally respected by all Coloradans. A contemporary of my father who had been his close friend and associate, Don Seawell, the founder and head of the Denver Center for the Performing Arts (DCPA). My father had contributed over $250,000 to the DCPA and had been a member of the Board. I can't imagine how difficult this news must have been for Don. All of that paled when compared with what Mother was going to face in the next few hours. "Please, Don. Would you call Mother and tell her how proud you are of her for the family coming forward with this story?" He, of course, agreed.

I had one more call, to Eunice Richardson, an elegant woman and Mother's contemporary. They had reared their children together. Mother would have said she was her best friend; however, Mother didn't really have close friends. She was even more isolated than I was. She might have spent four days a year with Eunice, and that was because my parents entertained one weekend a year in their mountain home. "Eunice. It's Marilyn. Have you read the morning paper yet? Would you call Mother, please?" She was almost too stunned to speak but she said she would call her right away.

If Mother believed people saw this in a positive light (wouldn't that be a miracle!), it would be easier for her. What I did *not* know is that an angel would be sent to help Mother at least an hour before she would get these calls. Mother told me her doorbell rang at 7 a.m. She awakened, put on a robe, and opened the window upstairs to see who was there. She recognized him immediately. "I'll be right there." It was a man she had been in a civic theater play with many years earlier. He had played her son. Mother said that when she opened the screen he threw his arms around her and said, "Thank you, Bootsie. I was raped as a young boy. This will bring so much healing. Thank you." She had, of course, no idea what he was talking about. She would learn quickly and that first encounter would set the stage to help her through the next days.

I had learned, so painfully, what was important to Mother. I had known it all my life but nothing would shake the foundation of her life—or mine—as this breaking story would. She cared about one thing: what people thought. Several years later when Larry and I were being given a significant award at a major black tie dinner, I urged Mother not go to. It was another banquet and it would be an effort for her to go because she was in her 80's. She had one question. "Is Nan going?" "Yes." "Then I will go. What would people think if she were there and I wasn't?"

I felt I had done all I could for Mother. Suddenly, a wave of anxiety

310

swept over me and brought me back to the reality of *my* life. It was over! What would my new life be? I was sure many people would not speak to me or would avoid me. At age 53, my belief systems that had been formed as a child were still very much intact.

I looked at the front page and scanned the other pages. It just seemed so overwhelming. Our back doorbell rang. It was one of my very favorite friends of Jennifer's, Katherine Rickenbaugh. I adored her. She had just returned from her sophomore year in college and she was standing at my back door, holding a bouquet of fresh spring flowers. She had a precious smile on her face as she handed me the flowers. That moment meant the world to me. We hugged each other. I don't remember any words—sometimes words aren't necessary. That's the way my new life began.

Ann called. She was now assigned to help handle the nightmare world in which I found myself. "How are you doing? We're going to have to schedule a press conference." My response was quick and easy. "Never." She could make me hear when no one else could and she knew the magic words: "They will call your mother and your sisters if you don't give an interview." I said, "What time is the press conference?"

Larry, Jennifer and I walked in together. It was the three of us, always. I can't imagine how people go through difficult times without the solid support of loved ones. From the day I married Larry, I never again felt alone. He was my rock. Jennifer may have been only a college sophomore but she was self-assured and committed to the three of us as a family…and to our future…whatever that involved.

I had had a lifetime of experience with press conferences so I knew exactly what to expect. There were about 20 reporters; still and television cameras. I have a snapshot in my mind that I cherish of one of our local television newsmen. I saw everyone juggling to get a better shot, ask the next question, probe deeper—but I didn't feel that when I looked into his face. His facial expression seemed to say to me, "I'm so sorry for what you are going through. So sorry for what you've been through. So sorry." He asked a superb question but it was his compassion that meant so much me.

Some of the veteran reporters had known my father. I knew it must have been like trying to put a square peg into a round hole. It just didn't fit. My father was charismatic, handsome, successful and he had given so much time and money to our community. I soon realized that's what my major role would ultimately become: helping people understand that violence and sexual abuse can happen in even the most (seemingly) perfect families. To believe my father would penetrate his daughters for 18 years was impossible for anyone to fathom.

I would never have shown up for a press conference if I hadn't been told that the press would get the story, if not from me, then from my mother and my sisters. Although friends would be protective of my mother, I knew reporters would ask her: "Where *were you*? Why didn't you protect your daughters?" I had to keep the press away from her although they were questions I had asked myself thousands of times. "Where *was she?*" Unfortunately, the answers were heart wrenching. Although I would reach out to survivors from that first day, I was not returning phone calls for individual interviews.

Sometimes, most times, what changes our lives is not some huge, earth-shattering event but a simple, chance experience that turns us in a different direction. That's exactly what happened to me the next morning—the third day.

I received a phone call the previous afternoon—soon after the press conference—telling me that a reporter was calling my sisters. How naive I had been to think I could divert reporters by having a press conference. I called my sister, Gwen, in San Francisco and said, "If you want to go public with this, please do it in California. Please do *not* give an interview to a Denver reporter. We're never going to get off the front pages." That morning, a picture of me and a headline covered the entire front page of *The Rocky Mountain News*. Gwen said, "I will need to do what I think is right."

Early that night a friend called saying, "A newspaper reporter has Gwen's story." I called the paper and spoke with the night editor, Chris. "Please don't run the story. Haven't we said enough on this? Please don't run the story." He said, "It's an editorial decision that I will have to make."

The next morning, Gwen's story was on the front page but they didn't use her picture. They used mine. I couldn't believe what was happening. The phones never stopped ringing. I needed to run away from it all, so Larry, Jennifer and I drove to a nearby high school track to jog. As we were jogging, a woman arrived with her two dogs. She came often and we always exchanged quick "hi's" as we passed one another. On this day, however, she stopped me. "We're so proud of what you're doing, Marilyn, and I'm so grateful Gwen came forward this morning." I said, "Really! Why?" Her casual response would change the direction of my life, "Because yesterday on a popular radio talk show, people were calling in and saying 'why should we believe her?' Now that your sister has come forward, they will have to believe you."

I was *astounded.* It was something I had never even considered! There were people who *didn't believe me?* How could that be? Who would lie about such a shaming thing? I looked at her and said, "If people don't believe 53-year-old me, then who, dear God, is going to believe *a child?*"

I felt galvanized. I felt like a 747 with all jets burning. Suddenly, I realized everything had changed. Everything. I knew in that split second that my job was to advocate for children. I went home and called both newspapers and four television stations and said, "Here is my unlisted home phone number. Today is the first day of the rest of my life." Within a few weeks, we had bumper stickers that would be seen on hundreds of cars, saying, "BELIEVE THE CHILDREN."

I accepted my first satellite television interview that day. I had done hundreds of television interviews in my life but never through a remote where I sat in a room alone, with someone talking to me through an ear device that wouldn't stay in properly—while I looked into a black box. I only remember her last question (whoever "she" was): "Would you be talking to me today, Marilyn, if your father were still alive?" As I stared into that little black box, I felt as if she had taken all the letters of the alphabet and scrambled them so nothing made sense. I remember her question. I have no idea what answer I gave. I know what my answer *should have been.* "No, of course I would not be speaking to you today if my father were still alive."

If my father had still been living, Gwen would not have told my mother to give $250,000 to Kempe to start an adult survivor program nor would Dr. Roesler have asked me to speak.

As I gave more interviews, I knew I was making observations some people didn't want to hear. "I loved my father." They had expected to hear, "I hated my bestial father." Although the words were difficult to speak, I gave information that I knew would cause some people to judge me harshly. I knew "I was five years old" was a safe answer. The response to that was, "Oh, you were only *five.* A precious little child. I'm so sorry." But no one wanted to hear, "18." I knew exactly how people felt about *that* because that's the way I felt about it too. Only

Larry kept me from dropping into a black pit of despair so deep I would never be able to rise. I would sob it, cry it, rage it, *I was 18. I was 5' 8" and 130 pounds.* And then I would crumble into heaving sobs. "Why couldn't I stop him?" Quietly and gently, Larry would hold me and say, "Because, like Pavlov's dogs, you had been conditioned as a child." If Larry had judged me harshly, I'm not sure I could have survived. It was one of the most difficult confrontations I would have, again and again, with myself. There was no one who could ever judge me more harshly than I had judged myself.

When I walked into a television studio one day, I practically ran into another person as we both turned a corner. I had taken her by surprise. She looked at me and stopped dead in her tracks. What she needed to say was far more compelling than her concern that someone was with me. She just blurted it out, "Thank you for saying you were 18. My brother raped me when I was 17 and all I have heard is 'how could you have been 17?' Thank you. I don't feel as guilty anymore." The truth was difficult and painful but it is the only thing that sets us free.

When hockey star, Sheldon Kennedy, came forward at age 27, to say that he had been sexually assaulted about 300 times by his coach from age 14 to age 19, I was astonished by his courage. He knew that his revelation would be met by many saying, or certainly thinking, "Why did an athlete, obviously capable of protecting himself, allow a coach to sexually assault him when he was 17 or 18?" He had never told anyone. The only reason he came forward was because he saw his former coach with young boys and he knew, in the depths of his soul, that the coach was sexually violating them. He couldn't have lived with himself if he hadn't done everything he could to save other boys from what he had endured.

If I thought "18" was going to be difficult for people to understand, I could only imagine what people would think about the fact that until I was 24, I didn't remember my father coming into my room for 13 years. Not only did I not have research to back me up, I had never met anyone who had repressed all knowledge of incest. Gwen had never repressed her memories. It would be weeks before I would make the time to begin reading the research. The facts are incontrovertible. What I know now, is that dissociation is a very common response to childhood trauma.

No matter where I turned, someone would stop me to tell me his or her story. The more interviews I did, the more people would write, call, stop me or ask if a friend could call me.

Susie Erikson from Longmont, Colorado, told me that she was standing in a supermarket checkout line, when she glanced at the front page of a Denver paper and saw the words "incest" and "Miss America" on the front page. She quickly bought the paper, left her groceries in the basket, ran to her car and sobbed uncontrollably as she read the whole article. She said, "By the time I reached my home, the feelings were so confusing and terrifying, I called my therapist. After hearing what happened he said, 'Susie, this is important. If you can get angry with Marilyn's father, then you can get angry at your own father.'"

The question, "what is my life going to be now" was no longer significant. My insomnia and body pain were suddenly irrelevant. Within hours, my life had changed from "me, me, me" which is what the life of therapy tends to evoke, to responding to hundreds who were coming forward for help and support. I called my psychiatrist (whom I had been seeing four days a week) and said, "I have to cancel my appointments for this week."

I cancelled the following week, as well. The third week I called to say I would not be returning. That chapter of my therapy was over. Shame had been the Mt. Kilimanjaro that I could never seem to conquer. Having everyone know my secret, and having most people accept me, had picked me up and jetted me to the top of that huge obstacle where I could finally see the truth. It wasn't my fault.

The phones at Kempe never stopped ringing and, understandably, they were totally unprepared. They had been expecting to work with ten survivors. Their question to me was, "What do we do with all these hundreds of people?" I had the answer. I called D.D., who was then a retired Presbyterian minister in his 70's, and recited one of my favorite Biblical quotes, "'Gird up your loins.' Hundreds and hundreds of people have called Kempe for help and support. We need to find a way to respond to them. I will respond to the people who are calling me but we have to find a way to help to those who are reaching out to Kempe."

D.D. said, "I'm on my way," and he immediately went to Kempe for a meeting. If I ever want to check his pulse and be sure his emotions can still go over the top, all I have to do is remind him of this meeting. D.D. said to Tom (Dr. Roesler), "We need to find a large facility and begin holding support group sessions. Immediately." He continued, "I know the adult survivor program is ready to go. We just need to exponentially enlarge it." Tom said, "Our original agreement was to begin a support group with ten survivors. We have our *ten* and you have all the rest." (This is where D.D.'s blood pressure exploded.) When D.D. relates this story, he always shows me the arm gesture that went with that statement. Tom brought the back of his hand up to his face (elbow bent) and then with a sweeping gesture as if he were going to begin leading an orchestra, he dramatically indicated to D.D.: "…and you have all the rest."

D.D. said, "The Van Derburs gave you *a quarter of a million dollars*. You can't just pretend nothing has happened here. Everything has changed. You don't have *ten people*, you have hundreds upon hundreds." Tom repeated, "We have our ten. That was the agreement. And you have all the rest." D.D. was dumbfounded. He truly could not believe what he was hearing. Then, D.D. said, he was handed a stack of hundreds of phone messages.

There was never any doubt as to why so many survivors in the greater Denver area had come forward immediately for help and support. It was because of the newspaper and television coverage. During the first few days, when my story was front-page news, *The Denver Post* and *The Rocky Mountain News* told my story with accuracy, compassion, respect and honesty. They would refer to me as "a woman of courage." Every local television reporter gave me the same respect.

Sandy Gleysteen, an exceptionally efficient and engaging producer for Maria Shriver, spent several days with Larry, Jennifer and me; Maria flew to Denver to interview me. The result was a dynamic, nationally televised segment that thousands of survivors watched in disbelief. An incest survivor was shown as a woman to be admired. With the exception of one local columnist, the media never questioned the validity of what I was saying. For the first time, survivors began to think that maybe it was safe for them to come forward. I will be eternally grateful to the editors and media reporters who treated me with the utmost respect. The media was the catalyst that helped to free thousands of men and women from their secrets and their shame.

We quickly created a new organization, which D.D. named Survivor United Network (SUN). D.D. said, "The Lord will provide," and it was true. Kempe apportioned a small fraction of the Van Derbur donation to help us get started and other funds miraculously began arriving. Survivors came by the hundreds but not only for help, some also wanted to donate money. One woman, Janet Curry, read my story and eventually moved from Seattle to Denver. She is an incest survivor and knew she needed to be near SUN. Her father (a well known judge in Kansas City, who denied Janet's allegations and became active in the False Memory Syndrome Foundation) had given her $50,000, which she called "hush" money. She donated it to SUN.

Adele Phelan, an extraordinary community leader, arranged for SUN to favorably lease a large, old building. With my sister-in-law, Janey, at the helm, family members, friends and survivors created a beautiful, safe place for survivors to gather. Almost immediately, we were welcoming up to 500 survivors each *week* for as many as 32 different support groups and programs. Everything for survivors was free.

One of D.D.'s first and most important decisions was hiring Sharon Lions who developed and implemented all of the groups and programs. In addition to survivor programs, SUN had the largest voluntary participation of therapists in the Denver metropolitan area. As many as 100 therapists met monthly for educational programs. Many therapists donated their time to put on workshops. We had a huge volunteer pool for our hotline and phone support, as well as a media response team for local, national and international phone and television interviews.

Lyda Hersloff called. She is an incest survivor and when her parents died, they left her money. She said, "The money is contaminated. I don't want it. I will never accept anything from my father." She met with D.D., toured SUN and donated $50,000.

Other people touched me deeply with their contributions. Vickie Bane, the *People* magazine reporter who would ultimately tell my story, contributed. Individuals who were not survivors but who were experiencing the incredible reaching out and healing that was happening in Denver wanted to be a part of it. Later, I was shown a list of friends who had contributed to our new program. It became a pulling together of a caring group of family, friends, associates and strangers…the entire community was involved.

The first week after my story became public is a blur. I remember specific events but some have no chronology in my memory. An extended family member called: "One of my best friends, Cindy, just called me from Los Angeles. She just read your story. I had no idea she had been raped. She was crying hysterically. She is getting on a plane *today*. She has to talk to you. Will you spend time with her? I can't believe I didn't know; we were inseparable all the way through school." What my family member would *not* know (but would soon learn) is that she knew the boy (now a man) who had raped Cindy. It was the older brother of a mutual friend. They had all grown up together. He was "the nicest" boy from "the nicest" family. She was 13, he was17.

Cindy arrived at my door late that afternoon. Sometimes, many times, there are no words. I just held her as she sobbed. She was 26 years old. Other than telling my family member a few hours earlier, she had never told anyone. With her head down, she struggled to tell me her story. We talked for almost an hour and then I suggested we go for a walk. Cindy was emotionally exhausted. I hoped fresh air and sunshine would help calm her. There was no traffic in our quiet neighborhood except one car in the distance. I paid no attention as the car passed us nor was I aware that the driver, upon recognizing me, stopped and backed up. Then we were both aware of her!

She was driving a new Jaguar. As she rolled down the passenger side window and leaned over to say something, we saw a middle aged woman dressed up and flashy in the best sense of the word. With a smile on her face, she said, "Thanks, Marilyn. I'm an incest survivor too. Great work!" No hint of shame. No whispered words. Cindy looked at me in disbelief. If I had planned it, it couldn't have been more effective. The fact that this woman could come forward so freely was very powerful. Cindy was beginning to learn that we stay ashamed by acting ashamed.

That morning, before Cindy arrived, another local newspaper reporter had called. During our conversation she said, "The day after your press conference, when every channel was broadcasting your interviews, I couldn't believe what was happening in our newsroom. As reporters sat at their desks watching, I saw two women with their heads down on their desks. Others seemed unable to make eye contact with anyone. It was as if they were walking in a fog. When I went to the ladies room, another reporter was lying down in a stall in the fetal position, crying. No one had to tell us about statistics that day. I could see it on reporters' faces as they struggled to work."

A local reporter called me within days after having interviewed me for a news story. He was distraught. He had just learned that his sons—little boys—had been sexually violated. He had no idea what to think or what to do. He was bewildered. He had gone from a compassionate reporter, witnessing my pain during those first few days, to a parent facing a nightmare of unimagined agony. No one ever believes it's going to happen in his or her family.

A producer from a national television show called. Could she interview me the next day? When she arrived, she introduced herself and the man and woman accompanying her, explaining they were both from Denver. Still overwhelmed with what was going on in my life, I paid little attention to them as they set up. The woman, who was in charge of sound, attached the microphone to my blouse and very quickly, we began the interview.

After the interview, I noticed that the soundwoman was trembling. Her breathing was difficult. Having had a personal relationship for decades with panic attacks, I wondered if this was what she was experiencing. I asked if I could get her a glass of water. She shook her head "No." I felt very strongly that she didn't want me to ask her any more questions. She and the cameraman left quickly.

The following week, I received a letter from her. She told me that as she was putting my microphone on, she noticed a book on the table next to me. In large print, the title said, *Cry Uncle*. (A survivor, violated by her uncle, had written the book and given it to me.) As the interview began I talked about sexual violations, which reminded her of her uncle violating her as a child. She wrote that she had no idea how she managed to work the dials as she recorded the interview. These disclosures were happening on a daily basis, *everywhere* I went.

Three years later, I spoke to a group of teenage girls during a high school class period. After I shared my story, I asked them to write down what my presentation had meant to them. A girl wrote that her uncle had sexually violated her. She signed her name and told me her mother had had the same experience. *It was the sound woman's daughter.* Adults who violate children never stop. Believe it. Count on it. Don't hope that your violator is the rare exception.

The mail arrived in bags. Pages typed on a computer. Pages written in tiny handwriting—almost unreadable. Pages written in pencil on a yellow legal paper. Almost all of them said, in different words, "I have never told anyone this but…"

I remembered my letters to Jody, one of the first people to whom I had disclosed—long before my story became public. Jody, a close friend of Jennifer's, had been like a daughter to me. She hadn't responded either. I knew I was unacceptable—even to her. I knew what it felt like to disclose for the first time, or the second time, or the twentieth time. The letters had to be answered *immediately.* Each letter had to be read—every word—and answered as if it were the only letter I had received. Point by point. Feeling by feeling. No secretary could help me. I knew every single person who had written to me was watching his or her mailbox as I had done so many years earlier.

The first few days, I set my alarm for 6 a.m. Then 5 a.m. Then 4:30 a.m. There was no other way to keep up with the mail. I was up before dawn every morning. I thought the mail would begin to subside but it didn't. What I was completely unprepared for was that survivors to whom I had responded wrote back immediately!

Almost every friend of mine, local or national, called me at least once to say, "A good friend of mine just called. He or she has just told me…he or she wondered if you could take just a minute to…"

Our long breakfast room table became a second office. Mail was stacked; some letters had been opened and read, others were still unopened. One morning, as I was responding, I saw a new Mercedes park in front of our home. I didn't recognize the woman. She was wearing an elegant suit, high heels and large gold earrings. Our curtains were wide open but she never glanced at me as she put a letter through our mail drop. She quickly walked away.

Her letter was heartbreaking. She was an incest survivor, still filled with shame and secrets. I will never forget her last sentence, "Since you have had the courage to speak your name, today, I will at least have the courage to sign my name." I recognized her name immediately. She is one of the most successful women in Colorado…on the outside. Inside she was crumpled, stomped on and ravaged, but she had taken her first step, she had written the words. The next step would be speaking the words. It would be one full year before she would be able to do that.

I took a break one day to dash into a specialty grocery store. Jennifer loved one of their prepared salads so I rushed in, saw some wonderful fresh strawberries which I quickly put into a sack, went to the deli, took a number and tried to be patient while waiting my turn. As I stood looking in the display case, I was unaware of the woman standing next to me, until she quietly said, "I heard you speak." That sentence *could have meant,* "I heard you speak ten years ago at a sales meeting in Detroit," or it could have meant, "I heard you speak last week at the small meeting where the reporter had been." Although the look on her face told me all I needed to know, I was still pretty new at this so I asked, "Where did you hear me speak?" "At the Kempe meeting." I put down the sack I was holding and put my arms around her. "I'm so sorry," was all I said as I held her. "Thank you," she managed to respond. At that moment, I heard my number being called and my attention was diverted back to the deli. I placed my order and then turned back to talk with the woman but she was gone. I quickly looked around the store to find her but she had disappeared without a trace. As the man behind the counter handed me my order and I turned to leave, the woman reappeared holding an arm full of fresh flowers. She handed them to me with tears in her eyes. There were no more words. We had spoken volumes to one another.

A couple of days later, I decided to dash into the mall. I needed a pair of new jogging shoes so badly that I made the time to buy them. As I came out of the shoe store, I saw a woman standing right across from the door. I was beginning to recognize what I would see hundreds of times in the months to come. It is difficult to describe "the look." It is a mixture of fear, shyness, shame…and expectation.

She was just staring at me. I stopped my hurried pace as if a huge hand had reached out and stopped me cold. I went from the start of a fast walk few people can keep up with, to slow motion, to a complete stop. For a moment, we just locked eyes. Knowing eyes. Then, very slowly, I walked over to her, stopping a few feet away, being very aware of not invading her physical space.

I said, "I'm so sorry." She said, "Thank you." I waited. Did she want to tell me more or did she just want me to know that she had been sexually violated? I stayed very still and quiet. Because she didn't move away, I knew she wanted to say something to me. It was one of the first times I would hear what I would hear hundreds of times in the years to come. "It was my brother. I've never told anyone." She stopped. I said, "May I hug you?" With her head down, she nodded "Yes." I put my arms around her and we just held one another. She seemed empty as if her insides had been taken out years earlier. She said, "I can't cry. I can't feel anything." I said, "If you will begin to do the work of healing—if you will begin to speak the words, the tears will come." She had just taken her first step. It was enough for now.

In the first few days, I had been asked to go from television studio to television studio. Several female news reporters who interviewed me, said either before or after the interviews, in different words—and yet the words are all the same—"Me, too." Not necessarily incest but sexual violations.

When I read the statistics, I know how wrong they are, how underreported sexual violations are. I know because for twelve years I have been stopped thousands of times and, with very rare exception, not one man or woman has ever reported.

I do remember one woman who did. She stood in line to talk with me after a speech—as I recall in St. Louis, Missouri. She was in her early 30's. She told me she had told someone (as a teenager) about her father raping her. That person then reported her father to the authorities and before the police could apprehend him, he hanged himself. She had found him. The words came out of my mouth before I could stop them. "It was his final violation of you. His final, selfish violation of you. Do you feel guilt over his death?" She had obviously done *much* healing work. She said, "Not one bit."

Within a week of my story becoming public, D.D. called to say, "We have to call a meeting. We have hundreds of survivors who need to hear from you. Now. The pain is palpable. If we announce to survivors only that you will be speaking at the church (where D.D. had been my youth minister) will you speak?"

"Of course."

The meeting was called for the following Wednesday at 7 p.m. The sanctuary holds 1,100 people. We anticipated 200. When Larry, Jennifer and I walked up the long cement stairway leading to the front door of the sanctuary, we were talking casually and quietly. The second we opened the door, we just stood there, unable to speak. It was about 6:55 and every seat was taken. There were 1,100 men and women sitting in complete silence. Shame hung over the sanctuary like heavy, wet cotton. The lights were low, heads were down. No one was looking at anyone else. It was a night that would change many lives, including Jennifer's.

I knew survivors would need to see Larry and Jennifer that night. Survivors tend to have common beliefs. No one will love us enough to stay with us during the very long recovery process and our children will be "screwed up" and alienated from us. So I asked Jennifer if she would be comfortable introducing me. She said, "Of course, Mom." I never once asked her what she was going to say. She seemed very comfortable with her assignment. I asked Larry if he would speak as well. People who had read the articles were stopping me to say, "Is Larry real?" I wanted everyone in pain to see how real he was and how a marriage can not only survive but also thrive when two people are pulling one heavy load *together*.

I'm sure everyone expected me to give the same talk they had read in the newspapers two weeks earlier. The newspaper had quoted directly and extensively from the talk I had given to the original 50 people who had gathered for the announcement of the new Kempe program.

My talk could not have been more different because something had happened the day before that had changed my life forever. Something I believed would *never* happen. I was on the telephone with a local reporter. He said, "Marilyn it's been almost two weeks since your story was reported. What has changed for you personally during that time?"

"What had changed for me personally?" I was trying to think of an answer when suddenly I realized something *had* changed. *Everything* had changed. Never again would I know such a change. "I just realized that something incredible has changed. Actually, everything has changed. I've been talking about incest all day today and I feel no shame. *I feel no shame.*"

It was *the* life changing moment for me. It was over. Shame was what had kept me tethered. Chained. Mute. Imprisoned. Shame, for over 50 years, had torn at the fabric of my being, ripped and pulled until I thought I couldn't hold myself together one more day. Now it was over.

That became the theme of my talk. It was the core issue for every survivor whose head was down.

I had seen the remarkable statue of "Prometheus Bound" so often when I was living in New York. A huge statute of a man struggling against chains that held him prisoner. Public exposure, public disclosure and the public's incredibly healing response had ripped my tethers away. I was free. Free at last. I felt like Julie Andrews singing *The Sound of Music* as she ran across the meadow, completely open and unafraid. The chains that bound me had been broken.

I couldn't have given a more powerful talk than to stand before a thousand people still bound in shame and say, "My name is Marilyn Van Derbur Atler. I am an incest survivor from age five to age 18 and I feel *no shame*."

They were incredible words to say and incredible words to hear. "How could she not feel shame?" Oh, I knew the question. I had lived with that question for five decades and I knew the answer because I finally stood in the light, in the truth.

I knew survivors would come to the meeting filled with shame. The letters, phone calls and personal experiences I had had with hundreds of survivors in just two weeks left no doubt in my mind about that. So I ended my presentation with a question, "Tonight, after the meeting, won't you come and tell me *your name*…with pride."

What happened next stunned every person in the sanctuary. With the lights dimmed and the quiet of a tomb, people began lining up. For three hours, Larry, Jennifer and I talked with men and women who waited quietly as the line slowly snaked along. No one was in a hurry. Each person reached deep inside for words most had never spoken.

Although many of the over 1,100 people were unknown to us, many who stood in line were friends or acquaintances. Jennifer will never forget the sight of one of her favorite teachers (a man who, we would learn that night, had been violated by his mother). People didn't look at one another or speak to one another. It was a seemingly endless line of men and women in a room filled with hundreds, each isolated by shame. Many would finally reach me and be unable to speak. Some would be unable to even lift their heads. I understood.

When I spoke with the last few people in line, I glanced up for the first time, to look at the sanctuary. Scattered throughout, were men and women sitting alone. One was in the very last row. Another was about halfway back, sitting on the far aisle. Others were sprinkled throughout. Each alone. Each one looking. Watching.

I was physically and emotionally exhausted but I knew these were people who could not even stand, much less line up. Very slowly, I approached the first woman, seated in the middle of a row. Before taking one step into her row, I asked, "May I talk with you?" She knew I was there but she had not raised her eyes from the bowed head position. With barely a head motion, she nodded, "Yes." I left a wide space between us as I slowly sat down. She didn't move a muscle. I waited for what seemed a long time and then said, "I'm sorry tonight was so difficult for you." She sat stone-like. I waited. It was obvious she was unable to move or speak. I motioned for Larry and subtly moved my right hand, which he instantly knew meant I needed a pencil and paper. He handed me one of his cards and I wrote down my address. I laid it on the church pew and said, "I am leaving you my address. I hope you will write to me the words you cannot say. I'm so sorry." Very slowly, I stood and proceeded to the next person. And so it went, until almost midnight.

When Larry, Jennifer and I left that night, Jennifer turned to me and said, "After seeing the pain in this room, I know I have to work to improve the lives of children and families." She had found her mission as a college sophomore. She would never waiver.

A reporter from *The Rocky Mountain News*, J.R. Moehringer, had been there. Since I had never met him, I wouldn't have known him even if he had sat in the front row. He had been one of the few reporters who had not been friendly or sympathetic. He believed I had given the story to the other Denver paper (*The Denver Post*) and he was very angry. No matter how many times I explained, in detail, exactly how the story had come about, he couldn't seem to let go of his anger…until that night. It is difficult to understand the pain and shame of sexual abuse survivors but he later told me he had stayed for over an hour after my presentation and watched the people line up.

He had been converted into one of our staunchest supporters. In the weeks and months to come, he would write supportive, insightful articles. He exemplified the type of reporter I have always had so much respect for, the one who is willing to come, listen, and stay as long as necessary to understand, as much as possible, what the story is.

One of the stories printed the next day was titled, "Dad Threatened Suicide If Incest Exposed." I couldn't believe it! I called the woman reporter (who had obviously been there) and I said, "That's not what was important last night. What was important was the fact that 1,100 people came. That was the story. Not my father threatening suicide." She said, "I agree. I don't choose the headline, an editor does." To anyone who was there, the 1,100 people who came together *was* the story. It was, I believe, the largest group of survivors ever gathered together in one room, from one city.

There was another theme to my talk that night. One that carried as much importance as not feeling shame. The theme was "I did my work." As I would relate the different therapies I had tried, I would close each example by saying, "I did my work." The terrorizing confrontation of my father and agonizing disclosure to my mother, "I did my work." Going to individual and group therapy and self-defense classes, "I did my work." If survivors were only going to remember one sentence, I wanted the sentence to be, "I did my work." Recovery is not a gift. No one gets through it without doing the work of healing. The work may be different for each survivor but the work means confronting issues while feeling despair, hopelessness, anger and shame.

So much happened in the days immediately following my story breaking that I almost forgot a commitment I made months earlier: to give the graduation speech in only ten days for East High School, the school from which Larry and I had graduated. There would be 3,000 people in attendance and, I was told, I would be the first woman speaker. (I always wondered why anyone would tell me that. How could they not have had a woman commencement speaker in so many decades?) One of my dearest friends, Judy Fruland, a gifted counselor at East High, called to tell me something she heard the superintendent say to a school administrator, "Marilyn should *not have done this!*" Oh, the message was clear. I was not acceptable as their commencement speaker now. I knew it. She knew it. Maybe everybody knew it.

This would be my first public appearance since my secret had been disclosed. I arrived just in time to sit on the dais. There were at least twenty other dignitaries on the stage, including the superintendent. I avoided eye contact with her. Finally, it was my turn! Anxiety had invaded every pore of my being. A student began by saying, "Our speaker tonight is Marilyn Van Derbur Atler." Before she could utter another word, 3,000 people stood, almost as one, to give me a resounding standing ovation. It took a minute for me to register what was happening and then I turned to look at the superintendent as both of us were beginning to understand that perhaps I was acceptable after all.

But sometimes a comment would sting. A friend pierced my armor by saying, "Why did you want to ruin your father's reputation?" It reminded me of the day the serial murderer, Ted Kaczynsky—the Unibomber—had been caught. His brother had turned him in. Someone said, "How could he turn in his own brother?" The man said,

"Because he was murdering people. He was the Unibomber!"

Only one columnist in a local Denver paper began attacking me early on. It's never a fair fight when you respond to a columnist because he will always have the last word. He can write whatever he wants, whenever he wants. Survivors, by the hundreds, were wondering what was motivating him. As I was able to stand back (which took awhile) I realized what he was doing and saying said much more about him than it did about me.

He had known my father and my family for many years. He instantly became abusive toward me in his column, the first of which was entitled, "Abuse allegations: Truth or revenge?" He opened his column with the word, "Assassination." That was just his opener! His closing sentence was, "It usually comes down to one person's word against another's or, in Marilyn's case, her word against a father who is dead and unable to respond to the accusation."

What he was writing was not only mean, it was absolutely untrue. Two days after my story was printed, my sister, Gwen, who never repressed her memories, came forward on the front page of the paper to say that she was also an incest survivor from age eight to age eighteen. My mother (she finally had no choice but to do so) had come forward to acknowledge the fact that incest had occurred in her home for eighteen years. And not one member of my very large family ever denied or questioned what Gwen and I were saying. It was *not* one person's word against another's—as he charged.

He had also written that we should remember the good things my father did, like his support of the Boy Scouts. I could not believe what I was reading. I would have expected him to express rage that a father could rape daughters—especially the respectable, honored, highly visible man he had known for so many years. Whatever his motivations were for trying to discredit me, with no truth on his side, I wasn't about to sit there and take it. I had to lie there and take it from my father. I wasn't about to sit there and take it from him. I sent him an angry letter, as did many other survivors.

Notwithstanding, he taught me a very important lesson. There will always be people who will not believe survivors of childhood sexual abuse. Always. Just as there are people who say there was no Holocaust. When we know our own truth, we must stand strong and not allow people to blame or shame us. But I also know that if he had been the *only* voice from our Denver papers, I would have been devastated and thousands of survivors would have stayed locked in their silence and shame. Fortunately, he was the only reporter who tried to discredit me.

Being attacked by a highly regarded columnist served a very positive purpose. Most survivors are attacked by family members or friends. The attack may be, "I don't believe you," or "Stop lying," or "Don't ever say those words again..." By a columnist attacking me, survivors saw that even in the midst of being believed and accepted, I was also being accosted. Not only did he not stop me, he energized me. Now, those who try to discredit me no longer get to the heart of me; I feel they help define one of the most important purposes of my life: to stand strong and tall for those who simply cannot, yet, oppose the bullies.

Letters from movie producers began arriving. I knew I wanted to help survivors in their recovery but I also knew a "movie of the week" wasn't the way! Fifteen credentialed movie producers contacted me within that first year. One was particularly persistent, Suzanne Somer's husband, who produced the movie of the week of her life. He just wouldn't take "No" for an answer. Finally, one day he called and listed twelve reasons why it would be positive for me to do a movie of my story. He was good! Every reason he listed was positive. I knew better than to try to debate him on each reason. I said what was true and incontrovertible, "It just doesn't feel right." He said, "Someone will tell your story with or without your involvement. If you want it to be done right, you need to participate." I gave the same response, "It just doesn't feel right."

It was the next day that I was hit hard by what he had said. A reporter I had spoken to at length called. She had asked me earlier in the week if I would be interested in collaborating with her on a book about my life. I did not equivocate, "I'm not interested in doing a book." She called back to say, "You only have five weeks to get a book out. If you don't, someone will write an unauthorized biography or a story thinly disguised—maybe five sisters instead of four and a Miss U.S.A. instead of a Miss America. Think about it."

I felt like I had been backed into a corner. My head felt like it couldn't deal with one more issue. I was on overload. The thought of someone writing whatever they wanted and then calling it an "unauthorized biography" was overwhelming. I hung up the phone and walked out the back door. I walked and walked, not my usual "I bet you can't keep up with me" pace but a slow pace. I have never been an avid student of the Bible and yet, frequently, during these difficult times, a quote from the Bible would flash into my mind, as it did on this walk, "Having done all, stand." I would do what I would do and let others do what they must do. I couldn't control others. I could control my decision and my decision was no book. I felt peaceful when I walked back in the door.

Every June, Larry and I entertain five couples in the mountains. Our invitations had been extended weeks before my story became public. I knew it would be a breath of fresh air for Larry to be away from the mail bags and phones that never stopped ringing. After driving an hour, we approached the cut off to Silverthorne, a very small mountain community. We usually drive through it, but as soon as we approached the cutoff I said to Larry, "Could we stop for gas?" Larry has known me since I was 15-years-old. We finish one another's sentences. He said, with no pleasure in his voice, "What is the *agenda*?" I said, "I just need to stop for a couple of minutes at the gas station. I'm meeting a survivor there. Just for a couple of minutes." I could feel his blood pressure rising. He said, "We have four cars behind us. Executives. Eager to get where we are going." I didn't play fair. I said, "When I knew I was going to disclose to you, it was the most important moment of my life. She has never told anyone." He began to melt. "I'll make it short, I promise."

I quickly glanced at different cars and then I saw the door of a huge truck open, as a woman, dressed in high heels and a beautiful dress, struggled to gracefully step down. I couldn't help it. I started laughing. No one wears heels in Silverthorne. She thought she was meeting Miss America. I had on Levis, hiking boots and a turtleneck. It certainly broke the ice. I said, "I forgot my crown!" She started laughing with me. And then, quickly, the mood changed as she haltingly began to share her story. I put my arms around her as she cried and searched for the words.

Within days of my story going public, I received a letter from the Chairman of the Board of The Miss America Pageant. He said, "We hope you have seriously considered your motivations for coming forward with this story." I felt anger surge through my body when I read that sentence. I didn't respond. I didn't need that kind of judgment.

A few weeks later, I received another letter from him in which he asked me to be a celebrity judge for *The Miss America Pageant* in September. I knew the celebrity judges had been invited months earlier. I knew what had happened. Grass roots America was telling the Pageant that I was more than just "acceptable." They now wanted me. I wrote back saying, in essence, that my dance card was full and I was unavailable. He wrote again. Would I reconsider? I picked up the phone and called him. I would come if they would introduce me as a "former Miss America/incest survivor." That idea obviously stopped him cold. We negotiated. We agreed on the exact words which I immediately confirmed in writing. What an incredibly symbolic night it would be. A Hollywood script could not have portrayed such an oxymoron, "former Miss America/incest survivor."

Celebrity judges judge only the final competition on Saturday night. The judges had a short rehearsal late Saturday afternoon. As the full orchestra played and the sound system blared, Patrick Wayne, John Wayne's son, was introduced. Then I walked across the stage, listening carefully to the words that would be used in my introduction. Not one *word* of what we had agreed to was used. As the run through continued, I quickly said in a very authoritative voice, "Excuse me! Stop! Please!" I walked over to the head of the Pageant and said, "We agreed on the exact words that would be said but those words are not in the script." He said, "Well, we're going to use the text that's already been prepared and approved."

I had an NBC camera focused on the two of us. Maria Shriver's producer and her camera crew had accompanied me to Atlantic City. The Pageant executive was well aware we were being filmed. I continued, "We agreed on the exact words." He looked at me and then at the camera (which was rolling film) and he said, "All right. We'll change the script."

Pageant officials had asked if I would like someone from Clairol, a sponsor, to comb my hair in my suite, just before the show. I naturally said, "Yes," and they sent their best. As I was making idle chatter, talking about the script changes, she said, "What's that about?" I said, "I'm an incest survivor. I want that word to be more speakable. I want that word said tonight."

She instantly burst into sobs—not tears—sobs. Sobs so wrenching, my mother came in from the other room to see what was wrong. A survivor. Another survivor in so much pain. She had to stop completely and cry it out before she could continue.

When I flew home from the Pageant the next day, a survivor from a nearby city had driven to Denver to personally put a letter in my mailbox. It read, "As you were introduced as a former Miss America, incest survivor, a huge chunk of shame slid away from all of us."

Chapter 18 – It's Never Too Late

It happened on Sunday, June 3, 1996. Jennifer and I had been out for an early morning walk. We stopped by the hospital to see Mother who was experiencing breathing problems. She was awake and animated. I told her I had a ripe honeydew melon. It was her favorite.

Jennifer and I walked home, I cut up the honeydew and drove back. She relished every bite as she sat in a chair while talking with my sister and me. While my sister was talking, I saw Mother's head slowly fall to the side as she exhaled completely. I couldn't believe what I was seeing. With that last, slow exhale, Mother died. No wide-eyed stare of fear, no gasp for air. I had never seen anyone die before. I still cannot imagine death can come so easily, so painlessly, unexpectedly, quietly.

We asked the nurse if we could leave Mother in the room until other family members were called. All four sisters happened to be in Colorado at that time, although one sister was two hours away. It was 10:30 in the morning and during the next few hours, sisters, brothers-in-law and grandchildren came to sit with us.

I overheard someone say, "You know she wanted Ching (her beloved chow dog) to be buried with her." Another person said, "Yes. I know."

Shocked, I said, "Are you thinking of burying Ching with Mother?"

"Yes."

"You're going to kill him and bury him in the casket with Mother?" I was trying to stretch my mind enough to envision what that would look like.

"Well, we're not going to put Ching *in the casket.* He will be cremated and the *ashes* will be buried with her."

And so it was.

There is no question Ching was very old and that he was ailing. He hadn't been well or alert for a long time. *No one* would have questioned that it was "his time." I had just never heard of a dog being buried with its owner. It was quintessential "Bootsie."

The night before the funeral, I asked Jennifer if she would go to the mortuary with me. For years as a teenager, I had worked in the mortuary as a receptionist. I would take family members to the room where their loved one was lying in a casket. Sometimes, when people came alone, they would ask me to go in with them. I assumed they were looking for closure. I wanted as much closure as possible. Mother was in a beautiful casket in a large room at Horan & McConaty Mortuary. She was surrounded with gorgeous baskets and arrangements of fresh flowers. Jennifer went to the far corner of the room and sat down. I went to the casket and looked at Mother. I had no feelings at all. Over the 58 years of my life, my mother had drained me of all the caring and respect every child should feel for her mother. Like the women of old who used to put their big heavy carpets on long clotheslines outside and then beat the dirt out with a stick, my mother beat every ounce of love out of me, one beat at a time.

I just started talking. My words seemed flat and stiff, devoid of energy, "We never had one conversation of any substance, did we Mother? We never knew one another. If I have any sadness, it is for what never was. We never held each other and spoke from the depths of our souls as Jennifer and I have done so many times. We never even shared the joys of life. We are strangers, still." The tears had begun to flow and suddenly, I found myself crying over the mother I never had. Not once in my entire life had she been maternal. My last words to my mother that night were, "We're going to do it one more time, Mother. Tomorrow, we will be the perfect family and you will be the perfect mother. I will do it for you, Mother. One last time."

I suddenly became aware that Jennifer's head was down and she was crying over what I had never had. My mother had no relationship with her mother, nor had I with mine. Incredibly, Jennifer and I shared our lives completely.

At the mortuary the next day, the four daughters and our husbands sat off to the side in a family room. Twelve grandchildren, their mates and great grandchildren were seated in the first four rows. The room was packed. A side section had to be opened to accommodate more people.

I had envisioned her funeral so many times; talking to the minister as he planned what he would say. "If you say she was a wonderful mother, I will stand up and scream, 'No she was not!'" I had envisioned that at least fifty times but, of course, it didn't happen that way, nor did I need it to. I had become relatively peaceful with my relationship with my birth mother.

The minister talked about our perfect mother and how she had devoted her life to us. I sat quietly and respectfully. After the funeral, we formed a line to talk with and thank friends who had come. One of the first women to speak to me said, "I have never seen a more loving family." I wanted to say, "Some of us haven't even *spoken* to one another in twelve years. There has been anger and bitter rage." But I just smiled and said nothing.

At the mausoleum, on the mountain, each of us was given a beautiful red rose to place on her casket. I so wanted to stand up for myself and *not* take the rose and *not* place it on her casket but, robotically, I placed the rose. As we drove away, I said to Larry and Jennifer, "This finally ends the most painful relationship I will ever know." Seconds later, I recalled something a gifted spiritual counselor-psychic, LuAnn Glatzmaier, said to me only two weeks earlier, "Your family is gathering as it will never gather again." I felt a chill.

Mother died on a Sunday. On Monday, I called the sister who hadn't spoken to me for 12 years and asked, "Could we have dinner together tonight? All of us?" My heart stopped beating as I waited for her answer. It was the answer I had longed for, "Yes."

It took my mother's death to open the door for us to become sisters again. There isn't anyone outside our family who would comprehend the fact that my mother never tried to help her daughters resolve a severed relationship for twelve years. Very few people saw the mother I knew. What I realized, yet again, after her death was that I'd given her so many chances to be "a mother." Each time, by word or act, she declined the opportunity.

Two of the most egregious examples happened while I was in recovery. One day when Jennifer and I walked up the winding staircase in my parents' home, Mother was walking out of her bedroom, which was to the right. My bedroom was to the left. As we reached the top step, Mother said to me, "Why don't you go down into your bedroom and relive some of your childhood memories?" If Jennifer had not been with me, if she had not heard Mother say those words, I'm not sure I could have believed or remembered such an inexplicable, hurtful statement.

The second example was one of the most gut wrenching moments of my life. It happened in my late 40's when I was in the depths of experiencing memories and feelings that were overwhelming me. My mother had stopped by, unexpectedly, to pick up something. Cheryl, a woman who was working for me at the time, let her in. I was seated at the breakfast room table doubled over, deeply sobbing. When crying overtook my body during those six endless years of recovery, I had no control over it. I would cry to limpness. I didn't look up when Mother came in. When I was able, I lifted my head. She was sitting at the end of the table and she said, "I have no tears for you. I can feel nothing for you." It wasn't said with meanness, it was just factual. It was one of the most painful moments of my life.

When Mother left, Cheryl came into the room and held me while I sobbed in her arms, "I just want a mother. I just want a mother." It is difficult to remember that we are not adults when repressed memories and feelings take over our lives. We are thrown back into the childhood feelings as if they were happening to us in the present.

About 45 minutes later, a close relative came by. She had always been one of my most loving supporters. I was still crying…sobbing, "I just want a mother." She put her hand on my arm and in a few minutes said, as if to herself, "I will never judge you again." I knew she had a glimmer into the blackness of my life. Few people saw the raw pain as she did that day. Usually, I was able to get myself together before seeing someone.

One huge lesson that I learned between the time I first spoke to my mother about incest and when she died, ten years later, is that,*it is never too late to be a mother…or a father.* She had so many opportunities to be my mother. If, at any time before her death, she had been able to genuinely cry for me or with me…if at any time before her death, she had been able to say, from the depths of her being, "I am so deeply sorry. Where was I? Why didn't I know?", I would have had a mother.

I spoke to The New England Conference on Child Sexual Abuse, which is a multidisciplinary group of chiefs of police, district attorneys, social workers and child advocates. I've had literally thousands of question and answer sessions during my 42 years of public speaking. I can never remember going blank when asked a question but when a man asked, "Why wouldn't a mother believe her child?" I said, "I don't know how to answer that. I just don't know." Of *course I knew!* His question had, unexpectedly thrown me back into my mother saying, "I don't believe you. It's in your fantasy."

There are many reasons why a mother will deny her child. The first reason shocked me when I was first confronted with it. Amy and I had

336

been close friends for years. There were so many things I admired about her. Foremost, I admired the way she mothered her children. She was kind, nurturing, devoted.

One day she called to say that she couldn't meet with me, because her 4th grade daughter, Billie, had written a suicide note. A counselor had asked her to come to school immediately. Amy said, "She does this because she's fat. The kids make fun of her. That's why she writes these notes."

When Amy called the next day, she told me in a flat voice that a physician had examined Billie and then told her and the social worker that Billie had been raped. The little nine-year-old girl would not speak. They could not get her to respond in any way to their questions.

Amy kept probing until she finally figured it out. Billie had been raped by her 14- year-old cousin, Richy. Amy confronted Richy and told him "to never do that again." Billie remained mute. Amy told me Billie had one counseling session and that she was fine now.

I was shocked, "She's 'fine' now?" I asked without any desire to hide my disbelief.

"Yes," Amy responded.

This was during the time when D.D. and Karen were coming over for our evening sessions, to help me try to wade through the psychic quicksand of my childhood. I was being sucked down and they, along with Larry, were my lifelines. I asked Amy if she would come over on Saturday night so we could talk. She agreed. She knew Larry, D.D. and Karen would be there.

It was as if someone had painted her face with shellac. She was expressionless. Her eyes seemed vacant. I had expected her to be doubled over, crying, despondent. I couldn't have been more wrong.

D.D. gently explained how important it was that Amy talk with Billie, ask her questions and encourage her to talk about what happened. "She needs to speak the words. Secrets will keep her locked in shame. You need to find out if this happened more than once; where it happened; if any other boy has ever violated her—you need to get her to talk about it."

I was completely unprepared for Amy's response, "I don't want to know." She *didn't want to know?* How is that possible? How could a mother be so dispassionate about her daughter's rape? How could *Amy* be so dispassionate? She loved her children so dearly—at least I always thought she did. Was I so wrong in my assessment of Amy as a mother? Even D.D. had been stunned into silence by her cryptic "I don't want to know."

I broke the silence. "Amy would you allow me to talk with her?" Amy said, "Sure." It was as if I had asked her if I could talk to her daughter about what she did during spring vacation. I was grateful but baffled. She apparently didn't care about what had happened to her daughter.

The phone rang the next morning shortly before 7 a.m. It was Amy. Her words came slowly, very slowly. "The reason…the reason…I don't want to know…about what happened…to Billie…is because…" She struggled to finish the sentence "…when I was nine…it was a man on our block…everyone knew him…" There was silence as I waited to hear if she wanted to continue. She did. It was a sentence I would hear from others hundreds and hundreds of times in the years to come. "I've…never…told…anyone."

How quickly things fall into place when the truth is known. Of course she didn't want to know. Billie's rape vividly thrust Amy's childhood rape back into her life. For Amy to be able to share her daughter's pain, she would have to deal with her own agonizing past. It didn't take me long to realize Amy wanted no part of that. I told Amy how sorry I was and that I was available to her at any time if she wanted to talk about it. She let me know she did not want to talk about it now, or ever. She is a single mother who has a stressful, full time job. It would be easy to say, "You need to deal with this now," but facing past trauma was, I felt, more than she could cope with at that time.

"Thank you for allowing me to talk with Billie." Although Billie was my immediate focus, I hoped Amy would eventually meet with me, or a therapist, to begin to release the painful memories she intuitively knew would be too overwhelming. There was little doubt that the memories were and still are in Amy's body. She suffers every day with arthritis. It would be years before I would hear thousands of survivors talk about the physical pain they live with as a result of "stuffing" memories and feelings. Many survivors of childhood sexual abuse would put this puzzle together before most doctors had even considered the connection.

I called Billie to ask if I could pick her up after school the next day.

338

Billie and I had been "pals" for several years. I knew I had to find a way to help Billie understand that her inability to talk about it was normal for those of us who had been so horrifically violated.

How could I help Billie understand she wasn't the only one, that she wasn't bad, and that she could survive this ultimate betrayal of her mind, body and spirit? How could I help her understand that I knew it was wrong for her mother to just tap her cousin on the hand and say, "Musn't do that again." Or how devastating it was when her mother didn't communicate an understanding of what a childhood-ending experience this had been for Billie. I wanted her to know that not all families just shrug off the rape of a child. It was also urgent for Richy to go into therapy so *he* understood how violently, how catastrophically, he had changed Billie's life. He needed to learn how to vent his anger or get his need for power met without hurting another person.

Suddenly, I knew exactly what to do to help Billie. I hurriedly called bookstores until I found one that carried the audio cassette of Maya Angelou reading her autobiography, *I Know Why The Caged Bird Sings*.

I knew that no matter how much affection and respect Billie had for me, she still saw me as white, affluent and, most of all, as "Miss America." She needed a Black role model. She needed to know, as a 9-year-old Black child, that another Black child, Maya Angelou, at 8 years old, had experienced the same life altering experience. Most of all, she needed to know that this raped child had grown into a woman of respect, enormous success, even fame. I had read Maya Angelou's book so I knew exactly what I was listening for as I fast forwarded the cassette to the place I wanted Billie to begin listening.

When Billie and I arrived home, I briefly explained who Maya Angelou was, and then without telling her that she had also been raped, I turned on the cassette. Billie had no idea what she was going to hear. She started listening with her head up but as Maya began to talk about the time Mr. Freeman (her mother's boyfriend) raped her. Billie dropped her head.

I wanted Billie to know that when we are violated by someone in the family or someone we know well, sometimes there can be good feelings as well as bad feelings. When Mr. Freeman began being sexual with Maya (before the rape), she wrote: "Finally, he was quiet, and then came the nice part. He held me so softly that I wished he wouldn't ever let me go. I felt at home. From the way he was holding me I knew he'd never let me go or let anything bad ever happen to me." (*I Know Why the Caged Bird Sings,* p. 61)

I wanted Billie to hear Maya talk about her feelings after her first experience with Mr. Freeman. When he held her close while he gratified himself. "I didn't want to admit that I had in fact liked his holding me or that I had liked his smell or the hard heart-beating, so I said nothing…"

But then Maya talks about her second experience with Mr. Freeman. It was difficult to listen to her words as she told her own story, "Then there was the pain. A breaking and entering when even the senses are torn apart. I thought I had died…"

There was another part I wanted Billie to hear, "Mr. Freeman was given one year and one day, but he never got a chance to do his time. His lawyer got him released that very afternoon…" I kept the cassette player going because I wanted her to hear three more sentences: "A tall white policeman came to the door and said, 'Mrs. Baxter (Maya's grandmother), I thought you ought to know, Freeman's been found dead on the lot behind the slaughterhouse…Seems like he was dropped there. Some say he was kicked to death.'" It was the first time I saw Billie's face lighten a little. She didn't smile but she certainly didn't seem sad about his fate.

When I stopped the cassette recorder, I gave Billie the only other gift I could think of that might help her. I told her about my father. One would think that telling a child would be easier than telling an adult but it wasn't. Every word was agonizing for me. When Billie understood what I was saying, she moved for the first time. She got up from her chair and put her arms around me. I stood and enfolded her in my arms. Neither of us said another word. We left the house and I drove her home in silence. As I pulled up in front of her home, I said, "Billie—you know this is not your fault. You are not to blame. We're going to talk about this again. It is very important that you not try to pretend this never happened. It's important to talk about it." She nodded, opened the car door and walked into her house.

Billie seemed to be doing fine. Even I had hopes that she was finding ways to cope with the myriad of feelings every child and adult has after being raped. My hopes were dashed when she sent me a poem she had written. She was a sophomore in high school. Her poem was pure rage. Even her handwriting was rage. She was a talented

340

writer even though it was difficult to read what she had written.

I called to tell her how moved I had been by her writing and asked if she would allow me to submit her poem to the major survivor national newsletter, *The Healing Woman.* She said, "Yes." I knew having her words published would be extremely significant to her. It was a way of validating that what she felt was important enough to share with others. Most importantly, she would know that she was being heard and that others would "bear witness."

I received a phone call from *The Healing Woman* asking if they could use her name. Billie's response was exactly what I had expected, "Use my name!"

During the work of healing, there comes a time for many of us when we want to be known. We may still carry the shame but we don't want to carry the secret one more day. That is, perhaps, the most significant day in our recovery. Wanting to be known more than wanting to keep the secret.

Billie wanted to be known. I can only imagine the pride and satisfaction she felt when she saw her published poem. Now, maybe others could understand her rage.

I knew Billie had taken major steps in her healing process when she asked me to address her high school class, after my story became public. There were about 20 students. Before I shared my story, I thanked Billie for inviting me and told the class that she was one of the most courageous young women I had ever known. After class, when the principal accompanied Billie and me to my car, the principal said, "Would you address our students again?" I responded, "If Billie asks me. I would do anything Billie asked me to do." I smiled at Billie and drove away knowing she had taken another major step in her healing process.

Why doesn't a mother believe her child? Why doesn't a mother cry for and with her child? Amy was a textbook example of one reason. Whether she realized it consciously or not, for her to cry for Billie she would have had to open up her own pain and feel the feelings that she buried so many years ago. Unwilling or incapable of doing this, Billie was motherless during a defining time that would shape and impact the rest of her life.

That experience enabled me to understand why some people would respond to me in one of the ways they did when my story became public. Some people would literally turn away from me because I was triggering their conscious or repressed memories of abuse.

A second reason why a mother will deny a child's truth, if the father is the perpetrator, is because that forces her to choose between her child and her husband. The husband will, 99.9 percent of the time, deny any sexual abuse and the mother needs to choose whom to believe. In most cases—as in my mother's case—the mother chooses the husband.

But not always. In my late 40's, when Gwen and I went to the Giorretto Institute in San Jose, we were allowed to sit in on a session, although visitors were rarely allowed. At an evening therapy session, about 30 survivors, perpetrators, and mothers of survivors sat around a circle *together*. No one was related. The men were court ordered to attend. My anxiety level was way over the top as I tried to sit quietly, appearing composed.

Just as the leader was beginning the session, a woman in her 30's *burst* into the room, crying hysterically. Not caring that she was interrupting the session, she cried out, "I left him. He sexually abused all three of my daughters and I left him. We all left. I have nothing and nowhere to go. And I still love him."

I was stunned. My shock overcame my intense shyness and I broke in from across the room, "You mean you're *leaving your husband* to protect your children?"

"Yes." She sobbed.

I couldn't believe a mother would do that. A rare few do. Unfortunately, some brave women are heavily penalized when they go to court for a divorce. Too many times, they are not only not believed, they are accused of making up the charges of sexual abuse. Some have even lost custody of their children over this issue. Most mothers choose to believe their husbands, because to *not* believe them may mean divorce, loss of income, and shame in the family and community. It is so much easier for mothers to deny their children.

A third reason why a mother will not believe her child, is the reason why I feel my mother chose to deny me by saying, "I don't believe you." If my mother were to acknowledge what I told her, it would have shattered her image of the perfect wife, the perfect mother. Her unwillingness to acknowledge the reality of my life, and hers, kept her from ever being my mother, and caused me unbearable pain.

As we continued to hold survivor meetings, I began to share more of my story, but there were eleven words I could *never* imagine saying because I believed they would be incomprehensible to others. I had said the words to Larry and D.D. and even they, with all their love and understanding, compassion and wisdom, pondered them. They never made me feel less worthy; the words just perplexed them.

It was the fourth survivor meeting. I knew that each time I spoke, I needed to give more insights, more validation, more of myself. Those in attendance were loving and supportive, so I decided to take what D.D. calls "a leap of faith." I decided to say the unspeakable words that had been burned into my soul for so many years. Eleven incomprehensible words: "My mother hurt me far more than my father ever did." My mother never laid a hand on me. She never hit me or yelled at me or physically or sexually violated me—and yet, my mother hurt me more than my father ever did.

Please don't misunderstand; my father did devastating damage.

So how could I explain why my rage at my mother had been ten times more intense than my rage at my father? Why I would feel grief when my father died and incredible relief when my mother died? Those present knew how my mother had responded to me when I disclosed to her and that she could not, or would not, acknowledge my pain. But would that be enough justification to cause such strong feelings? I merely made the statement, "My mother hurt me far more than my father ever did," and to my astonishment, I saw a sea of heads nodding "Yes," saying, in effect, "I understand. Me, too." That night when survivors lined up to talk with me, I heard again and again, comments like:

"I've never been able to understand why I have so much anger at my mother. You validated my feelings. Thank you."

"No one can understand why I feel so betrayed by my mother when it was my father who raped me."

I realized that night that it is common for survivors to hold their mothers responsible for not protecting them. I remembered my meeting with Ken. He was a 35-year-old cardiologist, married with two children. Immediately after my presentation to Grand Rounds at University Hospital and the University of Colorado Medical School, Ken asked to speak with me privately. He came to my home the next day. When we were seated in the sunroom, his easy, casual manner turned stiff. It was as if he had lost his voice. He just sat there. Mute.

So I began, "Ken, I'm so very sorry for what someone did to you as a child. Please tell me what happened." He dropped his head, his shoulders slumped forward and his words came slowly—one at a time, "I…was…9. It was the…first time…I had ever gone…to camp. It was an…older boy. A camp …counselor." He stopped, unable to go on.

I waited. Just as D.D. had made me say the words, I knew I should not help him continue. Speaking the words is, for many, the first step in the healing process…and the most difficult.

He sat with his head down. There was total quiet. He didn't move a muscle. He sat forward, almost limp. Finally, the agonizing words came again, one at a time. "Raped…me…"

The tears flowed into my eyes. I didn't know whether to touch him or not. His head stayed down. His body was still slumped as I said the only words that came from my heart, "I'm so sorry. So sorry." We sat quietly. I hoped he would continue. He did.

"I couldn't even think that night. I lay frozen in my bed. I never went to sleep. The next day, I called my mother. I told her I didn't like camp and that I wanted to come home. She said it took time to adjust to camp. I pleaded to come home. She said I would be fine.

"I can never forgive my mother for not letting me come home from camp. I chose a college and a medical school far from my home in Texas and then I settled in Colorado. I can never forgive my mother for not hearing me."

We sat quietly for a few more minutes. Then I said, "Has your wife been supportive, Ken?" For the first time, he looked up. His look was one of surprise. He said, "I've never told anyone but you."

It was time to give him some relief from the trauma of speaking the words for the first time. I smiled and said, "You're going to be very busy tonight!" His expression didn't change. He tried to assimilate the words I had just said. When he realized what I meant, he stared at me in disbelief. It was almost as if I could see the words being typed into his brain letter by letter. "She means I have to tell Annie…"

I nodded, "It's time, Ken. It's time to let your secret go. Your wife doesn't really know you. You have kept this pivotal experience from her. Would I be right if I said this was the most traumatic experience of your life?"

"Yes," he said softly.

"Do you react to her touch or her use of certain words or gestures in ways that she doesn't understand?"

"Yes."

"You need to let her into your life now, Ken. It's time."

I knew it was incomprehensible to him—as it is to every survivor of childhood sexual abuse—to tell the person we love the most. We know they will not love us anymore. We know they will leave us. We know they will never look at us the same way again. We know they will see us as bad and dirty, unacceptable and guilty. I knew all those thoughts so well.

I also knew that he was going to tell her…that night. It would be, in both of their lives, their most significant conversation. I wanted so much to call her, to tell her how to respond, what to say and what not to say because I know the pain caused by the wrong words (my mother's words), and the incredible, life changing power of the right words (Larry's words). I also knew that priming someone is 100 percent the wrong thing to do because it is the truth—however painful it may be—that eventually sets us free.

The next morning, when I went into my office and listened to my messages, the first message was from Ken, "I told her. I told her. I told her!" With each three-word exclamation, his relief became more emphatic. "I feel as if 5,000 pounds have been lifted off me."

When, in future months, Ken disclosed publicly that he had been raped at camp, two of the five sentences he spoke were harshly devoted to his mother.

It is true with almost every survivor with whom I have spoken or corresponded; we hold our mothers responsible for not protecting us. It is grossly unfair to Ken's mother to have expected her to know what had happened to him when he asked to come home from camp because he didn't like it. He felt then—and now—that *she should have known*—heard it in his voice, intuited something was very wrong.

Many mothers have said to me, "I didn't know. How could I have known?" One of my responses was, "Your son will have anger at you for not protecting him. It is a normal part of the healing process—whether you could have known or not. Please, when he vents anger at you, don't be defensive by saying, 'How dare you be angry with me when I could never have known.' Listen. Just listen. Hear the pain. Allow the anger to pour out. It can be a time of coming together but not if you immediately become defensive. This is not about right or wrong; it is about how your son *feels*. His judgment of you may or may not be fair. You can have that conversation later; that's not what's important now. When we come to our mothers, most of us are living the memories as if they are happening to us in the present. Console. Cry with and for. Don't try to justify. During this time, you may need to find support for yourself." This advice applies to whomever the child looked to for safety and comfort.

In her book, *After All,* Mary Tyler Moore wrote about an experience she had when she was six. When her parents were having a party, it was not uncommon for her to be sent down the hall, to Mr. Archer's apartment, to sleep until the party was over. Mr. Archer was her parents' best friend. One night, she was awakened by Mr. Archer, who had climbed into bed with her. "I was awakened by his fingers between my legs. They were inside my panties, touching and probing. I was paralyzed as I remembered where I was and who was making me feel this way. It had to be bad what he was doing, really bad. But it was Gordon Archer, my parents' good friend whom I'd been taught to respectfully call Mr. Archer. But he was now not only violating everything a six-year-old knows about trust; he was also tormenting me with confusion about the flickering of sexual arousal I also felt at his hand. I was ashamed and scared because I couldn't stop him."

"I told my mother, groping for words to describe what had happened. My mother said, 'No. That's not true.' My mother said, '*It didn't happen.*'"

Mary Tyler Moore then repeated the three sentences that had been said to her—three simple sentences that changed her life forever:

"You got *The Dick Van Dyke Show*."

"Let's get married."

"*It didn't happen.*"

She continued, "I never felt the same about my mother after that. Her denial had abused me far more than her friend."

I was stunned when I read those words. They are the same words I had used. It was also fascinating to me that Mary Tyler Moore does *not* say that the sexual abuse was the event that changed her life forever. It was her *mother's response* that changed her life forever.

Sexual abuse does *not* have to hurt for a lifetime. It can be a devastating experience never to be forgotten but if, as children, we can tell someone who will hear us, believe us, empathize with us, protect and defend us, the extent of the injury is mitigated. It was *my mother's response to me*—decades after my father's violations—that engulfed and smothered me like an avalanche of snow.

Former movie star, Esther Williams, described how a boy named Buddy had been brought into her family as a foster son. When Esther was 13, Buddy raped her. He was 17. With her parents away, Buddy had pinned her to the bed, ripped away her nightgown and raped her. "I felt him forcing himself between my legs, then ramming himself into me, tearing me inside, with searing pain. It seemed unreal. This couldn't be happening to me. A voice kept echoing in my head through the pain: 'What have I done to deserve this?' Finally, he was finished. 'This is our secret,' he said. 'If you tell anyone, they won't believe you. And I'll find out.' After he left, I cried long into the night with a towel between my thighs to absorb the blood. I didn't realize that I could prove what happened with physical evidence. But even if I could, something more powerful sealed my lips: embarrassment, shame, guilt." (*The Million Dollar Mermaid*, p. 26)

Esther kept her secret until she couldn't hold it in anymore. She told her mother everything. This was her mother's response: "'But how could he?' she said, peering at me almost accusingly. 'He's so sensitive, so dear.' The words hit me like hammer blows. Was it possible that she didn't believe me, or didn't want to believe that this wonderful new son, the honor student, the hero athlete, was raping her daughter?"

Later, Esther heard her parents talking with Buddy. "He was confessing. I expected my father to rise up and beat the hell out of him. I expected my mother to order him out of the house." Instead, Esther heard her mother say, "'We love you too, but you betrayed our love.' My parents' voices weren't angry or furious. They were sad, almost sympathetic. Listening to their muffled voices through the wall, I felt abandoned, deserted. My parents—who were supposed to be my defenders, my protectors—were lost to me forever. I was alone, totally alone in the world. I was inflicted with wounds that have never healed, left scars that I carry to this day."

In her recounting of this horrific trauma, Esther writes the words that so many survivors say, in almost the same words, "Rape…hangs over a victim until she dies…" (p. 27)

It didn't have to be that way. If Esther's mother had thrown her arms around her, cried for her and with her, ordered the "son" out of the house and then into treatment, Esther would have had a mother and she could have begun the healing process immediately.

I turned to my mother when I was 48; Esther turned to her mother when she was 15; Mary Tyler Moore turned to her mother when she was six. Our mothers may have clothed us, fed us, schooled us, driven us, but they had lost the right to be our mothers. A parent's first duty is to protect and it is *never too late to be a parent.*

A young psychologist asked to meet with me. She is one of the brightest young women I know. She told me that her client is a seven-year-old boy, Bobby, who had been sexually violated by an older boy who lives down the street. The boy's parents and the violator's parents had been close friends. The psychologist said, "I don't seem to be making any progress with Bobby. He's still having night terrors. It's as if the monster is still in the room."

She told me more of the story and then she said, "The *parents* of both boys are doing fine. They're having dinner together again…" She went on talking. I could hardly breathe. I didn't hear another word she said until I finally stopped her.

"The parents are having dinner together?"

I said, "If the older boy had cut their son's face with a knife…if he had taken a knife and sliced Bobby's cheeks with deep cuts that would leave permanent ugly, purple scars and then sliced his lips open so they had to be surgically stitched, they would not be having dinner together. He sliced Bobby's *soul.* You can't see the bloody, gaping wounds. You can't see the puss and ooze because it's all inside…but it's there. This little boy isn't going to get better until the parents show him that they have some understanding of the devastation of the assault and then make it clear that they will protect him. They have done neither."

How could a parent respond? When Larry was eight, three teenage friends that he admired and looked up to, took him to a basement. Two boys held him over a washbasin while the third boy beat him unmercifully saying, "You're a Jew. You killed Christ. The Jews killed Christ." When Larry went home, his face was bloody, a tooth was chipped and one eye was swollen shut.

His dad didn't say, "Get back out there son. These things happen." His dad didn't say, "Oh, I'm so sorry. Now let's have dinner." After caring for Larry, his father stormed to one of the teenage boy's homes and raged, "You are going to *jail*. You will *never do that again*. I am calling the police *now*. You can just think about that." And he did call the police and he did prosecute the teenagers *because that's what a father does*. A parent lets everyone know, "This is my child and I'm here to protect him and don't you ever doubt it!" That's one reason why Larry is the amazing man he is.

Although it only happens rarely, a parent can go to the other extreme—expressing rage in compulsive, inappropriate ways. I remember watching a television talk show where a mother was obsessed with finding her daughter's rapist. She had been so driven, she had not been responsive to her daughter's pain or needs. Her daughter felt abandoned. In another situation, a father murdered his daughter's rapist and was sent to prison. The daughter wishes she had never told her father and now feels guilt over his incarceration.

Their responses were obviously wrong. Yes, a parent's job is difficult. There is no manual. The issue here is understanding how the child feels, connecting with him or her and doing whatever it takes to help the child feel safe, supported and heard.

When Christina Crawford wrote *Mommie Dearest*, her autobiography about her life as movie star Joan Crawford's daughter, she was *vilified*. It wasn't that people couldn't imagine Joan Crawford being that vicious and hateful. Many could. It's that a daughter should *never speak that way about her mother*. America did *not* want to hear what Christina had to say. There was no rage against what many people believed Joan Crawford probably did. The rage was directed at Christina for daring to speak ill of her mother. The message was: *You must love your mother.* What is the saying? God. Mother. Country. Those three. No matter what your mother does to you, you must love your mother.

But how can we stop the hateful treatment of children unless we know it is happening, even in the most unsuspecting homes? How can we educate judges, juries, doctors, social workers, teachers…that these things *do happen?* How do we protect children if the words are unspeakable? We are hurt so badly when those we naturally want to love and adore us, turn their backs on us or participate in harming us.

Love, protection, and respect should be the norm in our families.

Whenever I address a judges' conference, I always show pictures of my family taken at the debutante ball—four young women elegantly dressed and my parents in a tux and evening gown—so the judges will *see* what appears to be a perfect family. So that they will never again say, when presented with a vicious abuse case, "It just couldn't happen in this family." One of my main messages to judges is, "Y*es, it can.*" When a beautifully groomed, highly regarded mother says, "My daughter is in therapy, she has been hospitalized three times, she is making this up," instead of thinking, "She has a crazy daughter," please think, "I wonder what caused this young girl to have so many problems?" And consider—at least *consider*—that what the young girl is saying is true and that the perfect parents may not be so perfect after all.

"The enemy counted on the disbelief of the world."

-Elie Wiesel, Holocaust survivor

Chapter 19 – Pass It On

*"I hesitatingly went to God with a cup. If I'd known Him better,
I'd have run to Him with a bucket."*—**Unknown**

Never in my wildest dreams, could I have imagined the privilege of having men and women share the deepest part of their souls with me on a daily basis. Not only was I touched by their shame and their courage, but with each story, I had a deeper understanding of the tentacles that reach into every part of our lives when we are traumatized as children. I was about to be given an opportunity to take my story and the lessons I was learning nationwide.

Vickie Bane, a reporter from *People* magazine called to ask if she could interview me for a short article. Gently and empathetically, she asked me searching questions. I felt so at ease with her; we talked for two hours. A few days later she asked if we could meet again because the New York editors wanted more information. When we met for another three hours, she said they were considering a cover story. When she said they were sending their best photographer, I began to feel anxiety. I wasn't sure I, or my birth family, were up for a cover story!

The photographer was delightful—the session was long. He wanted serious expressions and I complied. When he felt we had finished the shoot, I asked him if he would take just a few more—this time smiling. I said, "I am not depressed or unhappy and I would like to give the editors an option of a happy picture as well as the serious ones you have taken." The smiling picture became the cover. Many survivors told me, later, that they couldn't imagine an incest survivor smiling and that the picture was very empowering for them. The article produced a flood of letters. More survivors wanting to tell their stories.

Near this time I received a phone call to appear on the network talk show, *The Sally Jessy Raphael Show*. The producer wanted Larry, Jennifer, Gwen, mother and me. I told them Mother would not be available. I did, however, call Mother and tell her that her appearance had been requested. She thought maybe she should go. I knew that Sally and the audience would rip her to shreds. I strongly discouraged her. The producer asked if she could be available by phone. I said, "No." Mother had no idea how brutal strangers could be to a mother who "allowed" incest to occur in her home for 18 years.

Larry, Jennifer, Gwen and I flew to New York. Just before going on the air, the producer asked me if there was anything I did *not* want to discuss on the show. I said, "Thank you for asking. I don't want questions asked about my mother or my other sisters." When we went on the air, Sally began pressing me about them. It is difficult for an incest survivor to trust anyone. Some experiences pulled the scabs off of wounds that had almost healed. Despite the betrayal, Sally did a superb interview.

Fortunately, the show had been taped for future airing. We were beginning to understand that there would be an outpouring of pain across the country when this show aired. I turned to John Proffitt, the president of Channel 7, the Denver ABC affiliate, to ask if we could have a phone bank so that viewers could call and have someone to talk to after the show. He said, "I'll arrange it."

The day the show aired, volunteer therapists swarmed to Channel 7 to be ready for the calls that we knew would come. We had at least 75 phones. Every phone rang instantly. Larry took calls. Jennifer took calls. She was upfront by saying her name and that she was our daughter. Her responses were heartfelt, compassionate and very appropriate.

Larry called me from his office the day after the show aired. Roseanne and Tom Arnold wanted to talk with me. This was at the height of their popularity. *Roseanne* was one of the top ten shows. Since Larry, Jennifer and I were going to Laguna Beach, California, for the month of August, we arranged to have dinner in their home soon after our arrival. When we pulled up, Tom was waiting. What a lovable man. So open, funny and warm. Roseanne was Roseanne, equally lovable, quick, funny, outspoken...until she started to tell her story.

Suddenly she changed into a vulnerable woman, searching for words, struggling with painful memories. She wanted to go public with her story. We talked about it at length. I told her what she already knew: once she spoke the words, she couldn't take them back. It is difficult to find words to describe how mind wrenching it is to make the decision to let go of the secret we have carried for so many years.

I was concerned about a media frenzy. I was also concerned that her story be told from her perspective—her words—not someone else's interpretation of her words. I told her I could give her a safe place to "speak the words" if she wanted me to pull our Denver survivor

352

community together. I recommended she think about it for a while and then let me know.

Then Tom shared his story. It happened while he was a boy, growing up in Iowa. A baby-sitter, an older boy, had molested him. He was one of the first men to share his story in person with me. I was moved by his openness and his pain.

A year or two later, Tom flew to Iowa, found the man who had molested him and confronted him at his workplace. The man, of course, denied ever having done such a thing. Around 3 a.m. the next morning, Tom and a few friends peppered the man's neighborhood with handmade posters saying he was a child molester. When this man awoke, it had to be his biggest nightmare—no matter where he looked, there was a poster nailed to a tree or hanging on a fence post exposing him. Go Tom!

Roseanne called within a few days saying she definitely wanted to address our survivors. We scheduled a date for early fall. Sharon Lions, the woman who ran our programs at SUN, went into high gear and we sent a letter to our mailing list of about 3,000 people in Colorado, telling them we would have a nationally known guest speaker at our meeting who would share her story. We did not tell them who it would be.

We were set for a Saturday night at 7 p.m. Only a select few knew Roseanne was the speaker. At least I *thought* no one knew. Early Friday morning I received a phone call. "The press knows. Everyone in the press knows. They know it's Roseanne. They know when she arrives, where she is staying and when she is scheduled to leave." I felt a sixty-pound weight form in the pit of my stomach. It was going to be a media nightmare. In 1991 I cannot think of television personalities who would have created more of a stir than Roseanne and Tom. They were superstars—"the" newsworthy couple.

I put the phone down and felt completely powerless...for about sixty seconds. Then I picked up the phone and called Roseanne. I told her the media knew and asked her if she would trust me to handle everything. She said she would. (Looking back on that, I can't imagine her not saying, "No thank you. I'll have my 52 press agents handle it!") I suggested that I felt the best thing to do would be to give the press her text—with the understanding that nothing be printed until after she spoke and that no cameras would cover the event. She agreed and immediately faxed me her text.

I called John Proffitt and asked if I gave him the text of Roseanne's talk, would he agree to not have any cameras at our survivor meeting. I said, "This is a very private meeting, John. Survivors are terrified of being identified. If survivors see a television truck, they will never even park their cars; they will go home." John said, "We aren't a newspaper. We're television. We need pictures. Not text. This is a major story."

I replied, "I'm asking for privacy, John."

John said, "If I give you my word, we may be the only station in Colorado to not carry the story live."

I said, "I'm asking you for your word, John. You are my first call. If I can get every other station and the newspapers to give me their word, can I count on you?"

He said, "Yes. You can. You have my word."

That's what I needed. One highly respected, top executive to commit. With John's commitment, I called the other stations. All agreed, although the head of one news department said, "We may not get the story but everyone in our newsroom knows it's Roseanne. Someone will sell it to a tabloid and the tabloids will be there. You can count on it." I gave my same reply, "All I ask is *your* word."

Then I called the editors of our two major newspapers. I told them I would give them the complete text of Roseanne's remarks without the few comments that she felt were too personal. They could print any part of her presentation. We asked only that they use her exact words and that they commit to no photographers.

I spent the entire day on the phone. By the end of the day I had everyone's word. A friend said, "You don't really believe no cameras are going to show up, do you?" I said, "Yes. That's exactly what I believe."

At 6:55 p.m., a long black limousine pulled up to the back door of Montview Presbyterian Church and Roseanne and Tom emerged. Alone. There wasn't a reporter or a camera in sight and, while press people did attend, there were no cameras or "live feeds."

Although the press knew, our survivors had no idea who our guest speaker would be. I opened the meeting and introduced Roseanne. She walked out in a bright yellow, smashing suit. She walked to the podium and in an almost childlike voice said, "My name is Roseanne and I'm an incest survivor." 1,100 people had been shocked by seeing Roseanne and more shocked by her simple words. They suddenly stood and burst into a long, standing ovation. I will never forget the look on Roseanne's face. It brings tears to my eyes as I write this. She had dropped her eyes in shame right after she said the words and when she looked up and saw everyone standing, she had a look of disbelief. As if "Me? You're clapping for me?" Not Roseanne the star. Not Roseanne the zany comedienne. Roseanne the incest survivor. She had the look each one of us has when we find acceptance. We can never imagine "acceptance."

Roseanne had not only found acceptance, she experienced an outpouring of love from 1,100 people. She was incredible. So was Tom. Just watching him watch her, was potent. Roseanne was warm, strong, vulnerable and vivid. If reporters were going to say they didn't believe her, they had not attended the meeting.

The next morning, Sunday, it was *the* front-page story for both papers. Old photographs were used. Roseanne's exact words were quoted. I immediately sat down and wrote letters to the editors of both papers and the heads of the television stations thanking them for keeping their word. "I give you my word" still meant exactly that in Denver, Colorado.

Requests for me to speak became more frequent. I turned down every one. Twice the newspapers had printed the text of my presentation to survivors. Word for word. There was nothing more to say.

In August, Pat Schroeder, our Congresswoman, asked me to testify before her subcommittee on family violence which was being held in Denver. I accepted. I knew exactly what to expect. Three of us sitting at a long table, facing three members of Congress. As always, I envisioned it often so that I would have been there many times before the actual day.

Each of the three of us had been allotted exactly ten minutes. Even in front of only five people, speaking the words publicly was going to be difficult. Larry was at my side as we walked into what I thought was going to be a small hearing room at the convention center. I didn't want to be early. That would just give me more time to be nervous. I wanted to arrive only a few minutes before I would speak.

The front of the room was exactly as I had envisioned it—two long tables facing one another. But *nothing* could have prepared me for who would be seated *behind* me as I testified. Nine hundred people attended the hearing, in conjunction with a national child advocacy conference. There's no question it was best that I hadn't known that before I arrived. It reminded me of the night I first spoke the words and knew only hours before that a newspaper reporter was going to be there. I just couldn't think about that. I just couldn't think about the 900 people behind me. I had to focus on the three people in front of me. Speaking before survivors had been difficult. Speaking in that public forum required every ounce of my laser concentration.

Within a week, I had at least 30 requests to address child advocacy conferences the following April during National Child Abuse Prevention month. It was during this time that I realized that I had been led to do this. It was another response to my "just-tell-me-what-to-do-and-I'll-do-it" message from my Higher Power!

When The Denver Medical Society asked me to speak at their banquet, I accepted immediately. That was a no brainer. I had *so much* to say to medical doctors. In my 53 years, no doctor had ever asked me the one question that would have explained most of my physical complaints. "Were you physically or sexually violated as a child?" That question should come right after, "Have you had mumps? Chicken pox?…"

I knew if I were given the privilege of addressing our top medical doctors, I would need to give them every bit of information I could. No holding back. I accepted as long as they could assure me that no reporter would be there. I would say things I would *not* want to go beyond the room and I began my presentation by saying that—that I was going to tell them things that were to stay in the room.

I shared with them what I had learned about the long-term physical effects of incest for me: constant, persistent body pain and chronic, tormenting, never-ending insomnia were two of the most difficult to live with. My need for control sometimes made it difficult for other people to live with me! The physical paralysis and my obsessive need for natural childbirth experiences were included at the top of the list. I also knew that my chronic constipation was caused by my trying to hold everything in. I had learned, at such a young age, how to constrict my muscles, particularly in my vaginal and anal areas, as I tried to keep everything out and not allow any feeling. I had learned it so well that I couldn't find ways to release the constriction. It had become a part of my being. Excruciating premenstrual cramping every single month. Endometriosis. Many times, we place our pain and disease where our violations occurred. Psoriasis, the causing of a skin disorder so disgusting looking no one would ever want to touch me, body rigidity, repetitive squeezing of my eyes shut, chronic blood-red eyes and on and on.

Then, I took a deep breath and told them about being raped while in the stirrups by my 5th Avenue, New York City ob/gyn ...about the psychiatrist who had urged me to smoke marijuana and about the intern who—near midnight—gave me a physical exam that was as humiliating as anything I have ever experienced.

Then I opened it up to questions, telling them I would feel comfortable with any question they would ask. A few questions were asked and then no more hands were raised. I felt anger—no, I felt *rage* starting to build inside me. I felt my breathing becoming more difficult. I could literally feel my face turning into a mask of anger. I just couldn't hold it in. I said, with anger apparent, "Isn't there *one more question* anyone would like to ask?"

My change in attitude had made them uncomfortable. I waited for what seemed like a very long time as my eyes danced from face to face, and then I said, in disbelief and anger, "Doesn't anyone care whether or not these doctors are still practicing medicine?" I made eye contact with as many in the audience as possible and then I left the podium and sat down. I couldn't believe no one *raged out loud,* "Where is the doctor who raped you?" "Who is the psychiatrist in Denver who told you to smoke marijuana?" I wanted the doctors to say, "We will put these doctors out of business." Instead nothing was said. No one was enraged. No one wanted to be sure that these doctors were not continuing to do what they had done to me—and most probably others.

Nothing is going to change when those who have the power to act do nothing. The offenders remain safe because no one cares enough to confront the perpetrators and insist they be held accountable.

Several weeks later, I received a letter from one lone doctor who wanted to know. He said, "I want to know. I am a psychiatrist and it is of the greatest concern to me that we have a top psychiatrist in Denver who is urging his patients to smoke marijuana. I not only want to know who he is, I am asking you to report him to the psychiatrist grievance committee."

I picked up the phone and thanked him for his letter, told him who the psychiatrist was, but also told him I did not want to report him. I said, "It's just a 'good ole boy' system. I really don't want to subject myself to that."

He said, "And if you are right, if it is still just a 'good ole boy' system, who is going to help change it? You are so credible, you can help change the system if it needs changing. I am urging you to report him to the committee." He gave me the name and number to call.

I thought about it for a long time. I can be very confrontational. I confronted everyone in my family...alone...while I was living in terror. But I am not a vengeful or litigious person. However, one of the important lessons I have learned, is that the people who truly brought change in our patriarchal organizations, such as the Catholic Church and the Boy Scouts, are those who took their perpetrators to court. When those courageous few went to court, other survivors were empowered to come forward and stand by their sides. By their sheer numbers, the amount of evidence they presented and the *millions of dollars* they were awarded, they *forced* organizations to change.

I really didn't want to report to the committee but after several conversations, urging me to "do what is right," I agreed to do it. I met with two psychiatrists—a man and a woman who determined that my claim warranted a hearing. I went before a panel of three male psychiatrists and faced the psychiatrist who had urged me to "go home and smoke marijuana," and his attorney. I told the head of the committee that Larry would be with me. He would verify my truth. The young man who gave me the marijuana had also agreed to come forward. The physician in charge of the hearing said that wouldn't be necessary.

So I "testified." I was not prepared for what happened, but I should have been. My psychiatrist had had four months to see the charges I had made. He had learned, during my 53 sessions with him, that there were only two things I needed to have to survive another day: Larry and sleeping pills. When I told him I was stopping therapy, he had threatened me with, "You will never get sleeping pills if you stop therapy with me."

Now he was going to go after my marriage. I found myself in a room with a man enraged by my having reported him. One of the first questions a committee member asked him was, "Did you keep notes of your sessions with Marilyn?" He said, "No." Well, of course he had—
358

unless he was doing crossword puzzles. Then, Dr. Uh-huh said, "But I do remember what most of the sessions were about. Marilyn wanted to have an affair." I almost fell off my chair. I was totally unprepared for his quiet rage and staggering accusation. But what was most appalling, is that he was allowed to continue talking about my desire to have an affair. As I looked back on it, no psychiatrist would have believed that. I had just come out of the hospital with physical paralysis. I was having spells every day. And during recovery, a sexual relationship of any kind is unthinkable for a survivor. It was absurd. Larry knew exactly what Dr. Uh-huh was trying to do. But, for days, I wondered what it must be like for a rape victim going up against a rapist, while the defense attorney asks, "Weren't you wearing a short dress?" What made me angry was that no one on the committee even attempted to stop Dr. Uh-huh from continuing.

The grievance committee found Dr. Uh-huh not guilty of anything while the psychiatrist who headed the "investigation" told me that, of course, they believed me. *Of course they believed me!* I even have a letter that said, "Marilyn's credibility was never an issue." There was never any doubt in any of their minds that what I was saying was true. The good ole' boy system was alive and well, just like it was in my father's day. If I had faced this committee when I was not empowered and filled with shame, it would have been devastating to me. Instead, it had been empowering to force psychiatrists to take a look at one of their own, knowing the truth had been exposed and that they had been cowardly for doing nothing.

Speaking had helped empower me. I soon learned speaking was empowering Jennifer, as well. One of the first speeches I gave was in Greeley, Colorado. I asked Jennifer if she would introduce me again. We were expecting two or three hundred people to attend. As always, we arrived only minutes before the meeting was to begin. There were almost 1,000 people jammed into a darkened, completely silent room. As they stared at us as we walked to the stage, I whispered to Jennifer, "Are you okay doing this?" She smiled her megawatt smile and said, "I'm fine doing this." She has very good sense. She knew we were safe with them—that they hadn't come to judge or whisper. They had come in pain, hoping they had found a family who could prove to them that peace, love, joy and committed relationships were possible. The title of my presentation was "A Story of Hope."

When I spoke in Ft. Collins, Colorado, Larry also spoke—as the support person. He was relaxed, warm, funny and loving. He talked about sexual dysfunction. Every survivor and every support person knows about sexual dysfunction. He described how impossible it was to have been exposed to traumatic, involuntary, repetitive, forced sex as a child and then suddenly fall in love and expect our intimacy to be easy, flexible and joyous. Unfortunately, most of us bring baggage weighted with lead into our relationships. There are certain places we can never be touched; certain "acts" we never can do. Certain words that shut us down completely. He talked about how we explored a sexual relationship that would be safe and comfortable for me and for us. Larry talked about patience, gentleness and having fun during intimacy, but he also let them know comfortable intimacy took time.

After the meeting, men and women lined up single file. When it was a time for a woman, about 35, to speak to me, she stood a few feet from me, shaking. I had asked survivors to tell me their names. I knew this would not be possible for her. I asked her if I could touch her. She physically drew back and vigorously shook her head, "No." I said, "Thank you for letting me know your boundaries." Finally she said, "Are you real? Are you real? Are you really real?" I said, "Yes, I'm real. And when the pain gets so bad you think you cannot get through another day, I want you to remember my face—the peace I have found. The pain ends. I promise, if you do the work of healing."

The following day, a psychiatrist called me at home and said, "Would you come over, right now, and talk with a survivor? She wants to see if you are dirty." He added, "Do you know what that means?" I wanted to say, "If *you* don't know what that means, you need to get another job!" However, I said, "Yes. I know what that means. I'm leaving now." I walked into his office and he introduced Janice to me. She had graduated summa cum laude from Stanford.

She had dissolved into a crumpled heap of dysfunction and despair as my very public story had bored into her childhood memories of barbaric sexual abuse. Every part of her was trembling. She was thin as a rail. I pulled up a chair and sat across from her—not too close. She stared at my shoes and slowly examined every part of my body. She especially focused on my arms, neck and face. I knew she was not going to speak one word to me. Her fragility was frightening. I thought, at any second, her final breath might exude from her body and she would be left with nothing inside. Nothing at all. She had been emotionally eviscerated. The depth of her despair filled the small room, sucking out the oxygen. She was too deep in pain to respond in any way to me. I knew that. The tears flowed freely from my eyes as we sat in silence. Finally, I said so slowly and quietly, "Is there anything you want to ask me?" She didn't even have the energy to shake her head. She just dropped her eyes. I said, "I'm so sorry, Janice. So very sorry that someone hurt you so badly."

Two days later, I received a letter from her. "How did you get clean?…Thank you for crying for me. No one has ever cried for me."

In the following weeks, she would come over and ask me to hold her. She didn't want words; she just wanted to be held, gently but firmly. For a long time. When she told me it was the only time she felt safe, I remembered the feeling of safety I had when Gregg gently held me during the self-defense class. Janice's journey had been inexpressibly agonizing.

I have wondered hundreds of times how it is possible for an adult to so torment a small child. Hundreds of nights I would go into Jennifer's room and watch her sleep, wondering how a father could pry open a child and violate her young body, forcing her to separate her mind in two parts in order to just survive.

When Liz Lafferty read my story in her local southern California newspaper, she got in her car and started driving to Denver. She had to talk with me. She had to tell me "her story." When she arrived, she was told I had flown to Atlanta and then, the next day, I would be arriving in West Palm Beach. She got back into her car and drove to Florida.

I had been told she was coming and immediately after my presentation, we spent several hours together. I knew when she agreed to have a picture of us in the local paper, along with her name, she was ripping off the psychic chains that had bound her.

Later that fall, a reporter from *The Rocky Mountain News* called. She said I had been named one of the 10 Best-Dressed Women in Denver. I started laughing. "Me? Best dressed? Have you ever met me?" As the words left my mouth, I suddenly remembered Janice. I stopped myself right in the middle of laughing at such a thought when I remembered Janice asking me how I got clean. Survivors would write to tell me they couldn't figure out how an incest survivor could be honored. How was that possible? With each letter, I would be more open to accepting any and every honor, giving survivors hope as they watched me "speak the words," knowing that one day, they would want to do the same in their worlds. Maybe they wouldn't be honored but maybe they would be accepted. That would be enough. That would be beyond their comprehension. My experience was beginning to challenge their negative beliefs with positive possibilities.

Each time I opened my mail, I was allowed into more people's secret worlds. Sometimes I would literally cry out, "No. No." I cried out the day I received Anthony's letter. Was nothing sacred? Was there no safe place?

Anthony Smith, 42, was having flashbacks. He had grown up in Boys Town. I didn't want to read another word. I had grown up knowing about this as a safe place for troubled boys or orphans. Bing Crosby had starred in a movie about it; a warm, loving movie. Anthony had been gang raped, with a broomstick, while living at Boys Town. He wanted to know if I had heard from other boys who had grown up there. I hadn't but there were other young men who had had somewhat similar experiences. I offered to contact these other men if Anthony thought it would be helpful to be in touch with them.

Anthony began attending our survivor meetings. I felt an immediate bond with him and quickly grew to love him dearly. He is a gentle, kind, loving man who found a safe relationship with his precious wife, Robin. They have two adorable children. Anthony fought hard—as we all do—for his life.

I asked Anthony if he would like to participate in a video I had been asked to produce that would help doctors and nurses—all health care providers—to better understand the long-term effects of childhood sexual abuse on our bodies, not just our minds. I asked Anthony if he would tell his story. I was moved to tears, as was the camera man, when he told about how—finally—in his late 30's, a doctor examined his rectum and said, "You got torn up pretty bad, didn't you?" He looked into the camera and said, "He is the only person who ever validated my pain."

The following year, Montel Williams asked if I would be a guest on his show. The topic was the long-term impact of childhood sexual abuse. Montel has been a leader in this area by continuously doing shows that educate. I asked his dynamite, compassionate producer, Liz Frillici, if I could bring Anthony with me. She said, "Of course." Anthony touched everyone's hearts with his story. As we flew home, Anthony made me smile when he said, "I can do the next show alone." His message to me was very clear. "I am empowered enough now to walk into the light and educate by myself."

I was beginning to understand that survivor meetings could have a dynamic, healing impact. I knew what had finally set me free…letting go of my secret, going public.

Letting go of shame comes when we let ourselves be known in our communities. It doesn't mean, "telling the world," it does mean letting close friends know who we are and then seeing how they accept or reject us after we disclose our secrets. Beginning the process by standing with other survivors, knowing we aren't alone, has a power difficult to describe in words.

My mission became giving survivors every opportunity to take huge leaps in their recovery process by overcoming shame. My first major step of public disclosure had been *showing up* at the support group meeting, consisting of six women, including me. So, having survivors "show up" at a community survivor meeting would be a first step…just walking through the door, believing they had huge signs on their foreheads saying, "Survivor," or more accurately, "Victim."

Standing publicly as an incest survivor was what had been life-changing for me. I suddenly knew exactly what I was going to do at the next big meeting. Ask survivors to stand. Everyone was still trying to be invisible. Men and women walked in with their heads down. No one spoke to anyone else. As I began to close the meeting, I said, "In a minute, I'm going to ask survivors to stand." As I looked at individual faces, I saw expressions frozen in disbelief. Others had looks that said, "Are you serious?" "You don't really think anybody is going to stand do you, in front of 800 to 1,000 people?" No one budged as I continued, "Standing is one of the ways I freed myself from shame. For those of you who do not feel comfortable standing, please keep your boundaries. But for those of you who do feel comfortable or for those of you who are feeling fear but wanting to take a first step in letting go of your shame, please stand now."

A courageous few (maybe 15), stood almost immediately. I decided to not say anything—just wait. Very slowly, another 30 or so stood. Then another 40, but now they were beginning to stand one by one, not as a group. As I watched the rows, I saw one trying to stand, wanting to stand, as someone in front of her rose, giving her the courage to rise. Perhaps a third of the room finally stood the first time I asked. It wasn't until after the meeting, as survivors lined up to talk with me, that I began to understand the power of asking survivors to stand. Those who stood felt enormously proud that they had had the courage to stand. The power of that moment was transforming to everyone there.

Many of those who did not stand told me that if I asked again, they would try to be ready. Others found even the thought of standing beyond comprehension. I knew that, in time, we could empower even the least powerful to find, if not their voices, then at least their legs! Standing would precede speaking. Standing would be the first step.

Most of the survivors who came to the church sanctuary had been there at our first SUN meeting when I first said the words, "My name is Marilyn Van Derbur Atler. I am an incest survivor from age 5 to age 18 and I feel no shame." The second I finished my opening sentence, the entire sanctuary rose to give me a standing ovation.

Similarly, when Roseanne said, "My name is Roseanne and I am an incest survivor," survivors stood and gave her long, rousing standing ovation. They interrupted her presentation twenty times with applause.

I knew hundreds wanted to stand at the same podium, speak the words that had been held within them for so many decades, and be affirmed by a standing ovation. Speaking before a thousand people was like crossing the deepest, darkest wasteland. Many who had the courage to do so would later say it had been a life changing experience.

We began scheduling twelve survivors to speak at each of our four meetings per year. I began to understand the healing process that would take place, as we asked who would like to speak at the next meeting.

Many found the initial decision the most difficult—saying, "I would like to speak." Then, survivors would agonize over what they wanted to say. We tried to limit each speaker to five minutes, but that never worked, so we limited speakers to five sentences. (Their sentences would be very long.) What did they want to say? It became necessary to cull the very heart of what they wanted others to know. Deciding on the exact wording and then going over and over and over their words became, for many, the most healing part of the process. Then they needed to show up at the church, which included deciding what they would wear, whether or not to ask friends or family members to attend, getting in the car, starting the engine…The last big step, of course, was actually getting up, walking to the podium and speaking. I would always tell survivors that they could decide at the very last second to not go to the podium. It was astonishing to me that *every* man and woman who asked to speak ended up at the podium.

A major reason why survivors were able to take this huge step was because Sharon Lions, who ran our programs at SUN, worked with each person for several weeks before each meeting. She would give support, go over what they wanted to say, encourage them to work with their therapists and have their own support people in attendance. She also had up to 30 trained volunteer support people (most were therapists) at our meetings, with referral lists and emergency support agencies—although, amazingly, we never had an emotional crisis that Sharon, D.D. and others at SUN could not handle. Every survivor who came to SUN was strongly encouraged to be in individual therapy.

Although all survivors, who had asked to speak, walked to the podium, some came close to not being able to read their five sentences. One of my most precious friends, Catherine Joy walked up to the podium but could not speak. She just stood there, terrorized. It was uncomfortably quiet in the sanctuary as we waited and waited. I decided to give her another 30 seconds and then I was going to go up and stand next to her. Her shame would be intensified if she didn't follow through once she was standing there. Just as I was getting ready to move, she started. She beamed her beautiful smile when she finished. She was so proud of herself for having done it. The applause was thunderous and heartfelt. Everyone knew the feelings of not being able to speak the words…and understood the pride of doing it anyway.

After three or four survivor meetings, a problem had developed—a major problem. Most who attended had written me personal letters, telling me (usually for the first time) "their stories." Secret, shaming, intimate stories about their lives. I knew that even writing the words had been agonizing for most, if not all. Now I was meeting them again and again and not recognizing their faces. It is a huge handicap I have lived with all my life. I can see people over and over and still do not recognize their faces.

I was stunned when one of my father's key executives told me (years after my father's death) that one of his "jobs" was to stand next to my father at national conferences and quickly say the name of someone approaching, someone my father had met numerous times. The executive said, "I couldn't understand how a man as intelligent as your father could not remember faces." As he related this to me, I remembered thinking, "Is it genetic?"

My eyes lit up as I read Jane Goodall's book, *Reason for Hope,* and found that my "disorder" even has a *name.* She writes, "In the course of my travels, one thing detracts from my enjoyment of meeting people. I suffer from an embarrassing, curiously humbling neurological condition called "prosopagnosia." I use to think it was due to some mental laziness and I tried desperately to memorize the faces of people I met so that, if I saw them the next day, I would recognize them but I failed, miserably…" She writes that, as she began to talk about it, others told her that they, too, had the disorder. When she learned that a well known neurologist also suffered from it, it gave her comfort. (p. xiv)

I knew it was devastating to survivors who had shared their most personal stories with me, when I didn't recognize them, so I decided to address it head on. At the beginning of every meeting I would say, "It is embarrassing to me and hurtful to you when I do not recognize your faces. If you will just say, 'my name is Susan Mary,' I will instantly know you and remember what you have written or said to me." Following the meeting, each would say, "I'm Janice" or "I'm Linda." The truth works so well!

Several weeks later, Roseanne and Tom returned to Denver to do a fundraiser for us. They were fabulous, funny and warm. Immediately following the show, there was a cocktail reception for those who purchased higher priced tickets. Just before we went in, I said to Roseanne, "Let's go work the room." I will never forget the look on her face or her response. She said, "What do you mean, 'work the room?'" Her face had a childlike quality. Her look was a mixture of fear and trepidation. There wasn't time to think about or question her reaction. I just knew she was frightened, so I said, "I'll get you out of here as fast as I can."

Until then, I had never, knowingly, met someone who suffered from multiple personality disorder (MPD), which is now called dissociative identity disorder or DID. Nor did I know Roseanne had DID. Only a year or two later, when I read interviews Roseanne was giving, did I realize she had split into an alter that night. We talked about it later. Roseanne was not responding to the "work the room," a child alter had responded.

For anyone who is not sure DID is real, I can tell you, it is. I have personally met many—perhaps as many as 50 adults who have been so traumatized by childhood sexual abuse that they split into different alters. I have corresponded with many women who have alters (different personalities). Becky is one woman who has written to me for years. She attended every survivor meeting. Her handwriting can change, totally and completely, six times in a single long letter. (You might find it interesting to sit down and try to write in six totally different handwritings.)

Men can also develop DID, although I can only recall talking personally with one man who did. I also received a letter from a man who wrote, "...I have not yet determined if I will survive the journey. I keep running away into the oblivion of death and self destruction rather than confront something which seems worse: the truth of what happened to me so long ago...I am a 40-year-old man...I truly believe I am losing my mind and have appreciated hearing that you once felt that way too...One of the ways I survived was to fragment into alternate personalities. Their containment of traumatic memory allowed a part of me to complete college, have a career and enjoy a few years of successful living..."

After we convened our survivor community together about eight times, we were feeling safe and comfortable with one another and I began asking questions that could never have been asked under other circumstances. One night, before closing a meeting, I mentioned how many people with MPD had talked with or written to me and how much shame each had. Each believed he or she was the "only one." I asked if those with MPD, who would feel safe and comfortable, would stand so others would see they are not alone. At least 15 stood. Becky watched as others stood one by one. Slowly, Becky began to rise. It was a major step in her healing process and in her acceptance of her "selves."

When I was asked to address physicians at University Hospital and University of Colorado Medical School, the small hospital auditorium was packed when I arrived. Larry's and my doctors were there—our internist, cardiologist, my ob/gyn. Every seat was taken. Men and women were standing against the back wall or sitting on the steps.

As I began my presentation, I noticed a woman in the third row crying softly. She cried through my entire presentation—55 minutes! I had been told I had exactly 60 minutes. When I finished and looked at the clock, I decided to take a risk. I decided to ask survivors to stand. It's one thing to stand at a survivor meeting. It is a far different challenge to stand in front of your peers. I knew it was possible, or more accurately probable, that no one would stand. I wasn't sure what I would do if that happened. The climax of my speech would dissolve into a huge letdown, but I decided to risk it. When I ended the last sentence with, "would you stand, now," I held my breath and waited. From the looks on their faces, it was obvious that they were stunned by my request. It looked as if someone had taken a snapshot and that the audience had been freeze-framed. No one moved, not even their eyes. Nor did I move. I stood quietly and continued to wait.

I was somewhat surprised that the woman who had been crying did not stand but my attention was instantly diverted by a man, well over six feet tall, probably in his early 60's who had been sitting front and center. Very slowly, he had begun to stand, unfolding as a tall, statuesque man. Alone. Looking straight ahead. I felt the breath leave my body. I was stunned by his dignity and his courage. It is a moment I will never forget—nor will anyone else who was there that day. He had no way of knowing that, after he stood, at least ten women stood in various rows behind him. By his example, he had inspired others.

I don't remember how I ended the meeting. Everything was a blur to me after he stood. His standing—so tall and alone was incredibly powerful for everyone in the room. After the meeting, I went over to talk with him. I said, "How did you have the courage to stand?" He said, "Because you have been standing and standing and standing." I asked, "Who was your violator?" His eyes dropped as he said, in a whisper, "My mother." I said, "I'm so sorry. So very sorry."

I realized the entire experience had been overwhelming for him and that he needed time to internalize what he had just done. I gave him my unlisted phone number and asked him to call me.

Within a few hours, he called. His name was Fred, Fred Mimmack, M.D. We talked for a long time and then I asked if he would speak before our next large survivor meeting. I warned him that there would be 600 to 1,000 people there. When he responded, he was not the commanding, knowledgeable doctor he was known to be. He was a survivor of horrific sexual abuse. He said, "Would you help me?" "Of course I will," I replied.

The meeting was only two weeks away. We spoke often on the phone. During a conversation just prior to the meeting, I said, "Will your sons be there?" He said, "I've never told them. I've never told anyone but my wife, my therapist, and you."

368

"You need to tell them now. You know that. You're going to be speaking before a large audience. Your sons need to know."

He told them, one by one, over a period of two weeks. The night of the meeting, one of his sons attended. He was easily 6' 5" and very handsome. Family members or support people were always seated in the first two rows. Fred's son was seated about twelve people in from the aisle in the second row. Fred spoke eloquently. He talked about how his ability to father had been impaired by incest at the hands of his mother. He knew he had not been emotionally available to his sons. There wasn't a dry eye in the room.

When he finished, I saw his son stand and climb over twelve people to meet his father in the center aisle. As they held each other, it was obvious that neither was comfortable with the physical expression of love and respect. It was a language they would learn because of Fred's incredible courage. It is never too late to be a father. We can never undo what has been done but we can speak words now, from the heart. His son would begin to put a puzzle together as they began to touch one another's souls for the first time. It is never too late to begin.

While survivors like Fred were becoming empowered, perpetrators were being forced out of the comfort of the shadows of anonymity and a backlash was brewing. One night as I was preparing dinner, I was listening to the local news on television. I heard our local reporter introduce the head of the Colorado False Memory Syndrome Foundation, Roy Mattson. In her introduction of him, the reporter stated that Roy's five daughters had accused him of incest. *Five daughters!*

By this time, I had spoken to or corresponded with thousands of survivors. Women who had been violated by fathers or stepfathers had told me by the hundreds that, almost always, all of their sisters had also been violated. In most families, siblings had different responses— one sister may live in denial that it ever happened, another may say, "It wasn't a big deal," another may be locked in rage or shame, unable to speak about it, another might have been hospitalized because of a suicide attempt or severe eating disorder. I had never known all siblings to come forward *together* to press charges against a father. I found it profound that these five sisters had been able to come together and support one another.

I listened to Mattson talk about how he had been falsely accused. I couldn't wait to hear from the daughters. Instead, the interview ended.

I was furious. How could this local reporter have given this man air-time without allowing his daughters to speak?

Early the next morning, I called the reporter, "I was very upset that you did not interview even one of the daughters. Do you know where they are?" Her response fueled my anger, "Oh, yes. I know where they are. I guess I should have interviewed them, as well."

"May I have a phone number or address for one of the daughters?" "Yes. One of the daughters is an M.D., now living in Tucson. Her name is Dr. Kristi Mattson."

I called Kristi immediately. Yes. All five sisters had signed a legal document charging their father with incest. Yes, she knew that her father was saying that they were making it up. Yes, she would have been interviewed if the reporter had asked.

When the False Memory Syndrome Foundation (FMSF) began deluging the press with its idea that therapists were implanting false memories of childhood sexual abuse in adults, I was dumbfounded to find that so many people were believing it.

When Holly Ramona was a college student, she entered therapy because of bulimia and severe depression. She began to recover fragmentary images of her father, Gary Ramona, raping her. With her therapist and her mother present, she confronted her father who, of course, denied everything. (I believe all perpetrators will deny everything if there is any third party present.) Her father initiated a lawsuit, not against his daughter, but against her therapists, claiming they had implanted "fantasies of incest in his daughter's mind." [2] The jury found that the therapists had not implanted false memories but that their treatment had been negligent and too aggressive. Gary Ramona immediately claimed his name had been cleared and that he had been found not guilty.

The jury foreman was so angry at Gary Ramona's comments that he spoke publicly, saying, "...the jury did not find him not guilty...that's certainly not what we said...the only reason that I feel compelled to talk about it is because I don't want it to look like we said, ' He never did anything...he's innocent...' I think there's a possibility that he *did it*." [3] Ramona's lawsuit was the beginning of a spate of lawsuits by

---

[2] *Dateline,* May 17, 1994

[3] *Dateline,* May 17, 1994

alleged perpetrators against their victims' therapists. In light of the vast research, it is difficult for me to understand how anyone, other than an uneducated person, could not know that some traumatic experiences are repressed.

With FMSF leading the charge, a backlash developed that was so effective and powerful, survivors began to retreat into historical muteness. Margot Forrest, founder of the amazingly successful *Healing Woman* newsletter wrote, "Our subscriber numbers began to drop. Fewer women were 'coming out of the closet.' Fewer therapists were willing to see survivors, due to the lawsuits that could ensue. The 'false memory' proponents were having a field day. Backed by the pro bono services of a prestigious public relations firm, they had captured the media's attention. 'There's no such thing as repressed memories,' they said. And they encouraged accused parents to sue their daughters' therapists. This gave our nation permission to slide back into denial of how bad and how prevalent child sexual abuse is. And slide it did." [4]

While I should have known that there would be a backlash from the accused, I never anticipated being stifled by those whose mission was to help children. I am always surprised by those who try to muffle my work. I addressed 800 people attending a fundraiser banquet for the Colorado Christian Home (CCH), a highly regarded organization that lovingly cares for many of Colorado's children who have nowhere else to go. When I asked survivors to stand, even the waiters stopped as if frozen in time, as men and women at almost every table began to rise. It was mind numbing to all present, not only to see how many stood, but to witness the timidness and the shame with which they stood.

But my attention was instantly focused on Don Brewer, a CCH executive, seated at my table, front and center. He stood almost robotically. Looking neither right nor left, unaware of whether or not he was the only one standing in that large ballroom. A 65 year-old man who had dedicated his life to troubled children at the CCH.

For many, I have learned, standing is a life changing moment. I would have no way of knowing how life changing it would be for Don. Weeks later, I would learn that the impact of standing had been so potent and yet so disturbing to him that he made the decision to attempt to find, and confront, the minister who had sexually violated him 50 years earlier.

---

[4] *The Healing Woman,* November 24, 2000

He told me his hand was trembling as he lifted the phone to call the church in Oklahoma where he had attended youth services as a boy. The words would ring in his ears long after the phone conversation ended. The sexual predator was still a minister there. How could that be? How many other boys' lives had he devastated? Hundreds? Don flew to Oklahoma and met with the board of directors. The minister resigned immediately. Although Don did not confront the minister, he knew his perpetrator had finally been confronted by church elders.

In a letter to me he wrote, "I knew when you first mentioned that you would be asking people to stand, that I would stand. That evening changed my life. First, three people came up to me after the banquet to say that they knew they *should* stand but that they had decided not to—until they saw me standing." There is something affirming and powerful about knowing that your courage touched and inspired others. Having a top executive stand tall at the front table before 800 people at a black tie dinner, moved many to tears and to action. He also wrote, "There is too little attention to the life-changing devastation which survivors experience. It is *not* something one can get over."

I had been pleased to also receive a letter from the Executive Director saying, "Many, many people told me you were the best speaker we have ever had. Your message of courage and leadership…is so powerful, so effective…We raised more money for the CCH than we ever have…"

So I was caught off guard by the phone call I received a year later. A woman from CCH called to invite me to speak in Ft. Collins and Greeley, two smaller Colorado cities. She anticipated 300 people would attend each dinner. I hadn't recognized her name so I was not surprised when she told me she had just been hired but I was unprepared for her next words, "I'm going to ask you to *not* ask survivors to stand." Her words stopped our conversation cold. Finally I said, "May I ask why?" She said, "I am told you made many people uncomfortable." I was stunned by her comment. Only once, in the hundreds of times I had asked survivors to stand, had I ever had anything but a very positive response. I wasn't sure where to go with the conversation. I said, "Who was uncomfortable? Survivors?" She said, "No. Not survivors, some of the attendees were uncomfortable when survivors stood."

Now, I *did* know what to say, I just wasn't sure how to phrase it. I said, "I'm having trouble finding the right words to respond to that so I'm going to be straightforward. Good! I hope they were uncomfortable. Everyone should be uncomfortable to see men and women struggling to rise. The pain and hesitation with which they stand makes a stronger statement than I could ever make about what happens to children when they are sexually violated. What surprises me about your request is that this is what the Colorado Children's Home is about. The quote on your stationery says, 'Changing Lives, Giving Hope.' There is no doubt in my mind that many, if not most, of the children living in your facility are there because they were sexually traumatized. One way to help free them is to take away the stigma and the shame." I continued, "Let's leave the decision up to Don Brewer. Please ask him whether or not I should ask survivors to stand. If he says I shouldn't, then I won't." She called me back later that morning to say, "It's fine if you ask survivors to stand."

In Ft. Collins and Greeley, as I rose to speak, the ballrooms were dark except for the lights on the dais. Standing, publicly, takes incredible courage. "Will I be the only one standing?" is one of the greatest fears. "Will I be acceptable to others if I stand?" Some have told me they thought they might lose their jobs if they stood; instead, most saw for the first time that they are not alone. There are others. So many others. Standing can transform a life but it is also a potent experience for those who are not survivors, to see men and women stand, especially when it is someone whom you have known for years. It is, without question, the most dramatic part of my presentation because everyone present has to confront that this is happening in our community, to people within our organization, to our close friends. Until I was 53, I believed I was shamed. To see that others are uncomfortable around us in the 21st century makes me deeply sad. I felt the message of the lights off in the ballroom was, "We don't want to see it." If they, who devote their lives to children in crisis, don't want to see it, what hope do we have that floodlights will ever eliminate the darkest secrets?

Similarly, I was surprised that a woman who had dedicated her life to empowering young women would also want me to stay in the shadows. After a speech in Phoenix, I stopped to see Lenora Slaughter, the former executive director of The Miss America Pageant. We had had a very close relationship for over thirty years. Not because we were best friends but because we had so much respect for one another. She knew how hard I had worked during my year to build and support the scholarship organization she had founded. I was not prepared for her greeting. She had always been candid, even blunt in her comments but never more than that day.

After a brief "hello," she said almost angrily, "I don't like what you're doing and I want you to stop. I want you to stop talking about it." I'm sure there was more to the visit than those sentences but that's all I remember. On the way home, I began thinking about writing her a letter, explaining how similar our goals were. She wanted to empower young women and that's what I was doing. Our ways couldn't be more different but our results were stunning. Once she understood the impact I was privileged to have on people's lives, I knew she would understand. The second I began writing, I knew the truth. She was never going to understand. She was from the "old school." "Don't talk about it."

My letter turned out to be very different from the one I had planned. I told her how much I loved and respected her and what a strong impact she had had on my life. Then I wrote, "I was ashamed of myself for 53 years. I felt bad, dirty and ugly. Today, I am filled with pride for who I am and for what I am doing. I fought so hard for my self-acceptance. I now choose to never be with anyone who doesn't approve of me. I will always love you but I wanted you to know why I will not be in touch with you again. I will carry you in my heart always. My love to you…" and I mailed it.

While CCH and Lenora had disappointed me, *nothing* could have prepared me for a letter I received later that year. I couldn't imagine anything a survivor could write that would impact me in such an overwhelming, life changing way.

"About twenty times in 1983." That's what she wrote…that my father had sexually violated her about twenty times in 1983. He would have been 75. I stared at those words. The impact of that sentence would forever change the beliefs I had clung to. How could it be? How could he have violated until he died at age 76. When I looked at his hands in the casket, I had been forced to contemplate that he hadn't stopped but I had held it in my mind for only a split second. Who else could there have been? What access would he have had to others? But she gave details that were irrefutable. Her only reason for contacting me was to be known and to share this devastating connection.

He never stopped. He hadn't meant one word he said to me when I confronted him at age 40, "If I had known what it would do to you, I

374

never would have done it." It was an egregious lie. He used her as he had used me. I couldn't seem to absorb the truth. He didn't give a damn what the consequences were for us. He would continue to gorge his insatiable appetite for power and perversion until a fatal heart attack stopped him cold. That was the truth.

The truth can be so excruciatingly painful. I had clung to that one last hope that if he *had known* what it would do to me, he wouldn't have done it. Now all hope was gone. It was over. It wasn't anger that I felt nearly as much as a deep sadness. What the psychiatrist had said was the truth, "He didn't care very much about you, did he?" I didn't think it was possible to be more galvanized in my mission, but my work seemed to have even more focus after her letter. She forced me to face head-on how relentless and vicious child rapists are. The only hope we have of stemming the tide is to mobilize and free the adult survivors whose voices have been muted by shame for decades. Nothing is really going to change until society understands how many of us there are and how devastating the long-term effects are for us.

I learned about one of the most troubling long-term effects of childhood sexual abuse when Gwen and I visited the Giorretto Institute when I was allowed to sit in on a therapy session with five 9- and 10-year-old girls. After the girls were settled and focused, the therapist said, "Mari, a counselor told me that you have been cutting again." Mari dropped her head. The counselor continued, "May I see where you cut?" Hesitatingly, Mari pulled up the long sleeve of her sweater. There were old scars that had healed, newer scars that were purple and freshly cut slits. It was obvious she had taken a knife or a razor blade and sliced her arm many, many times. The counselor said, "Why do you cut on yourself, Mari?" And in an innocent, sweet, soft voice, she answered, "To let the pain out." In future years, I would learn how common "cutting" is among survivors of sexual abuse.

After speaking in Boston, three college girls stood in line to talk with me. Although it was oppressively hot in the auditorium, one of the girls had on a baggy, long sleeved sweatshirt with college initials on it. She stayed back as her friends stepped up to speak with me. After we talked for a few minutes, I asked if I might speak privately with their shy friend. As I took a few steps towards her, she put her head down. I stopped a few steps away from her, knowing that she did not want me close. I stayed quiet and motionless. Without lifting her head, she pulled up the sleeve of her heavy sweatshirt. I had seen it before but never like this. Like Mari, she had sliced her arm time after time. Some slices had left ugly scars, other were more recent, purple. Other slashes were very fresh.

Very slowly and gently, I touched my hands to her scars. "I'm so very, very sorry for your pain. Cutting is common for survivors. I think I can help you find other ways to let the pain out. Will you write to me?" Her letter came immediately, "I'm sure you don't remember me…" I would never forget her. If I could keep her responding to my letters, perhaps we could find other ways together. As our letters continued, I would learn whether or not she was in therapy, whether she had told anyone else…Our scars rarely show. Most are inside. Cut up hearts. Battered and blackened souls. Emptiness. Her scars will show for a lifetime and they will be but a glimpse of her pain.

After speaking in Frankfort, Kentucky, Andrea stood in line for over an hour to talk with me. She told me that just as she was leaving her home, her phone rang. It was a friend who was getting ready to graduate from nursing school.

Andrea said, "I'll call you tomorrow. I'm just running out the door."

"Where are you going?"

"To hear Marilyn Van Derbur. Do you know who she is?"

Andrea said there was a long pause before her young friend answered in a completely different voice, "Yes. I know who she is."

"I knew by the way she answered me that she had been sexually abused." The nursing student disclosed that her father had sexually violated her as a child and teenager, at night, after everyone had gone to bed. "So I chose nursing so I could help other people and so that I could work night shifts. I can't sleep at night. The only time I can sleep is during the day."

How many times have I heard those words, "I can't sleep at night." I had just finished reading *Power Sleep* by Dr. Maas, a sleep expert at Columbia University. Never once in 294 pages, did he mention childhood sexual abuse as a reason for being unable to sleep as an adult. Never once did he mention the *fact* that childhood trauma changes brain chemistry. How can someone so educated be so uninformed. My letter to him began, "Dear Dr. Maas…"

While it was healing for the student in Boston to know cutting was not uncommon and for the nurse to know that insomnia is almost a given, the most powerful moments of healing came when survivors stood publicly and learned that they were not alone.

When I arrived in a large mid-western city, Sherry met my flight. We had met two years earlier when she had invited me to speak to a survivor meeting. I had returned to address a formal banquet, to help raise funds for a Children's Advocacy Center. Six hundred people, including a large number of corporate executives, would be attending. That night, as we were walking into the large hotel ballroom, I said to Sherry, "I may ask survivors to stand tonight. I have begun to ask survivors to stand even when it is a corporate banquet. It's risky because if no one stands, I have nowhere to go with the close of my presentation. I make the decision at the last minute..." Sherry broke in, "I can't stand tonight. I'm in a new job and my boss is sitting with me. He is a 65-year-old ex-sheriff. I could never stand in front of him." I said, "I'm so glad we talked about it. The reason I was telling you, was to assure you that I would not be looking for you to stand, if you didn't feel comfortable doing it." As people approached us, she closed our conversation with, "No way." With that, we turned to greet people.

As I approached the end of my talk, I made the decision to ask survivors to stand although. I didn't have a plan B if no one stood. I said I knew there were survivors in the room and that I was going to ask if there were any survivors who would feel safe and comfortable in standing. I wanted people in the room to understand that survivors were not "those other people," but a friend seated next to them or a co-worker at the next table. I also wanted to give survivors an opportunity to stand for children who had no voices. How can we turn to children and ask them to speak of it when we remain shamed and silent? I then said, "Would those of you who would feel safe and comfortable in standing, please stand...Now!"

I looked out over the 600 people and not one person was standing. I didn't move a muscle. I stood still and I waited...and waited.

Finally, a woman at my VIP table, the wife of the medical director of the hospital, stood. All alone. She had a regal appearance and she didn't flinch. She did not look left or right. She looked straight ahead. Suddenly, three women stood, then four more near the back, then five over to my left. Another three, maybe six more stood in the center. I quickly glanced at Sherry's table and stared, transfixed. Her boss was standing and she was just starting to rise, with tears pouring down her face. He was the only man who had stood. After the banquet I went quickly to his table and said, "I'm so sorry this has happened to you. Who was your violator?" "My Boy Scout leader." I said, "Have you had support?" Even with as many experiences like this as I had had, his answer surprised me, "I've never told anyone." As many times as I had heard his answer, it still caught me by surprise. "And you chose to stand at a public, formal banquet?"

"Yes."

"How did it feel for you to stand publicly?"

He answered with a word I had chosen as well. "Free. I felt free." I left that night remembering how common it has been for me to have men and women speak the words (or stand) for the first time in their 60's and 70's.

Sherry was shocked that her macho boss, the former sheriff, was a survivor but I wasn't surprised because everywhere I went and everywhere I continue to go, men and women stop me to share their stories. My most unexpected encounter came at New York's LaGuardia airport as I was rushing to catch a flight. I had less than five minutes before they would be closing the doors. The fact that people were staring at me as I ran madly mattered not at all. As I caught sight of the x-ray machine, I was grateful there was only one person in front of me, a young man, probably in his early 20's. He was just taking off his backpack to put it on the rolling belt.

When he heard my commotion, he turned to look at me and while he was hesitating, I dashed by him and said, "Would you mind if I put my bag on first?" He looked at me as if I were an apparition. As I laid my dress bag on the belt, he said, "You're Marilyn!" Of all the times in my life when I didn't want a conversation, this was one of them!

"Yes."

"You're Marilyn Van Derbur!"

"Yes."

His next comment caused me to put aside the flight, my luggage, my rush. "I've written you a letter. I didn't know where to find you." And with that he opened his backpack and pulled out a letter, in an envelope that said, "Marilyn Van Derbur." He handed it to me.

I said, "Is your name and address inside?" He said, "Not my address." I said, "Would you put your address down so I can write to you? I'm going right over there to see if I can get on that plane. I will wait for you."

He came to the boarding area, gave me the letter, assured me his address was inside. I put my arms out, gave him a long hug and said, "I'm so sorry. I can help you. I'll get right back to you."

He had written a long letter about having been violated by an older boy. He knew he must be gay or an older boy would not have chosen him. He felt so confused. He didn't know whom to talk to. Could I help him? I had already learned that homosexuality has nothing to do with childhood sexual abuse but abuse can cause victims to become confused about their sexuality. I called him and asked if he would like to talk with another man who had had a similar experience. He said he would appreciate it so much. I called Anthony Smith. Of course, Anthony would call him and stay in touch with him and help him in any way he could.

I would never have chosen the path I was given these past twelve years but I have had hundreds of mountaintop experiences, as adults and children have allowed me into their lives.

As one is empowered, he reaches out his hand to help another. And the work goes on...

Whether you are a parent, survivor, friend, therapist, judge or support person, the following chapters will give you new information and strategies for keeping your family safe, and helping victims through the recovery process.

As a speaker in the 1960s.

Relishing my chosen career—
motivational speaking—finally freed
me from anxiety and panic attacks.

Diana's rival: Charles is lured by an old flame

JUNE 10, 1991 $1.95

People
weekly

A STORY
OF INCEST

MISS
AMERICA'S
TRIUMPH
OVER
SHAME

It began at age 5.
Now Marilyn Van
Derbur tells of her
shocking 13-year
ordeal of sexual
abuse by her
millionaire father.

Marilyn Van Derbur as
Miss America 1958

Jennifer, during her first year of college.

Larry, Jennifer, and I return
from climbing a mountain.

Chapter 20 – How Common Is Forgetting?

I had never thought very much about the many different ways we forget things until I was told that some people didn't believe I had dissociated the memories of the night child…that my memories of incest had been *involuntarily* severed from my conscious awareness. "You *forgot?*" "*Until you were twenty-four, you forgot?*"

What does it mean to "forget?"

In his autobiography, *A Good Life,* Ben Bradlee, who was then the executive editor of *The Washington Post*, recounts his experience of forgetting the day President Kennedy was assassinated. He received an emergency phone call asking him to join members of the Kennedy family at Bethesda Naval Hospital, where Jackie Kennedy and President Kennedy's body had been brought immediately upon their arrival from Dallas.

He wrote, "There is no more haunting sight in all the history I've observed than Jackie Kennedy, walking slowly, unsteadily into those hospital rooms, her pink suit stained with her husband's blood. Her eyes still stared wide open in horror. She fell into our arms, in silence, then asked if we wanted to hear what happened. But the question was barely out of her lips, when she felt she had to remind me that this was not for publication. My heart sank to realize that even in her grief she felt that I could not be trusted, that I was friend *and* stranger. Perhaps because of her warning, I remember almost nothing of what she said." He "forgot." He, a journalist, forgot the historically significant words Jackie Kennedy spoke during perhaps the most memorable experience of his life.

But he remembers that he forgot. He remembers the fact that Jackie Kennedy told him something he can't remember. That is far different from never having remembered the phone call, his arrival at the hospital, seeing Jackie Kennedy, or her words of warning.

Everyone has had the experience of forgetting where they put their car keys. However, they know they have car keys and they know that they misplaced them.

When I am asked if I "forgot" my father coming into my room at night, and I say, "Yes," I am not talking about the kind of forgetting Ben Bradlee recounted or the kind of forgetting we experience when we misplace our car keys. Although the words "forgot," "repressed," "split my mind," and "dissociated," are sometimes used synonymously in this book, I am writing about having no memory whatsoever of the experiences. That would mean Ben Bradlee would have had no memory of even being with Jackie Kennedy on that fateful day.

Some memory experts, in an effort to discredit adults who suddenly remember repressed childhood memories of sexual abuse, will do experiments where they test people's memories by showing them a videotape of a car accident. They will then ask them questions about it. Was the car that was hit blue or black? How many people were in that car? One or two? Then, to prove the point that memory is not reliable, they will tell us that some people remembered that there were two people while others remember there was only one. Their memories of the details may differ *but all of them remembered there was a car accident.* Ben Bradlee remembers Jackie Kennedy telling him something. That is very different from an adult, sexually abused as a child, not remembering anything about the sexual trauma.

"When neither resistance nor escape is possible the human system of self-defense becomes overwhelmed and disorganized…Traumatic events produce profound and lasting changes in physiological arousal, emotion, cognition, and memory…Traumatic symptoms tend to become disconnected from their source and to take on a life of their own…A century ago, Janet called it 'dissociation.'" (Herman, *Trauma and Recovery,* p. 34)

How common is it for children to repress or dissociate, thereby having no memory of the trauma? Research by Linda Meyer Williams, reported in the *Journal of Traumatic Stress,* is compelling. 129 children were examined and treated in a hospital emergency room after having been sexually abused. Seventeen years later, as adults, they were located and interviewed; 38% had "forgotten" the sexual abuse. Williams notes that these women would be most likely to *remember* the abuse because the abuse *had been reported* to authorities. (Williams, *Journal of Traumatic Stress,* pp. 649–673)

When hundreds of survivors came forward for help and support after we started SUN, research was done with 228 women. Twenty eight percent had repressed memories of the abuse. (Roseler and Wind, *Telling the Secret)*

Dr. Judith Herman and Emily Schatzow studied 53 women who, as adults, remembered being sexually abused. "Seventy four percent of the women found independent corroboration of the abuse." (Herman and Schatzow, *Psychoanalytic Psychology,* pp. 1–14)

Many do not remember for decades. Memories which have been buried can be suddenly disinterred and dominate our conscious reality, like a dam breaking and overwhelming everything in its path. The trigger could be major surgery, a divorce, a sexual experience, seeing a child playing in the park or a smell of cologne.

Lois Spacapan, a retired middle school teacher in Idaho, wrote about when her repressed memories returned. One day she found herself enraged and sobbing, wondering why her feelings were so intense. She wrote, "Without warning, the face of the doctor I had visited the day before swam in front of me. Almost 50 years of pain began to spew out of me as I wailed and gasped for breath. My arms and legs went numb. I felt on the verge of fainting. I lost all sense of where I was or what sounds were coming from my mouth…The day before, I had had my eyes examined by a doctor who was new to me. Although the exam was routine, like dozens of others I have had, I was uncomfortable when he shone his light into my eyes; his face was so close to mine that it blocked my view of the room…I never gave my uncomfortable feelings another thought.

"But someplace deep inside, I remembered another encounter, a feeling memory sparked by the similarity of circumstances, a memory almost 50 years old, buried by time and shame. One of those repressed memories bubbled up through layers of mental silt, finally exposed as the sick behavior of my alcoholic father directed at my four-year-old self." Her memories of being incested by her father were traumatically returning. (*The Healing Woman*, November 1995)

Two years ago, when I flew into Maine for a speaking engagement, I was met by Cyndi Yerrick. As we drove to my hotel, she told me her story. When feelings of rage began to overwhelm her life, she had no idea what was causing those feelings. She decided to go into therapy. She and the therapist explored different avenues that might have been causing her anger, all to no avail. One day her therapist said, "Cyndi please take a crayon and draw your anger." Cyndi said she was surprised by this assignment. She just sat there without one idea in her head. Suddenly, she found herself reaching for a black crayon. She began drawing bold, thick black lines. With each line, she drew more obsessively. After quickly drawing eight lines, she stopped to stare at what she had drawn. Fear gripped her as sobs began erupting. She had drawn a church. Flashbacks began of being sexually violated by her priest when she was six; the priest forcing her to do things no six-year-old could comprehend. Her memories had surfaced in 1993. When she tracked Father Robert Kelly down, she learned that, in 1990, he had been convicted of raping a child and had been sentenced to five to seven years in the state prison.

There is a great deal of research being conducted on the effects of trauma and how the brain stores and retrieves traumatic memories. "…Extensive childhood abuse prior to adolescence frequently results in either partial or complete amnesia for the abusive events."[5] .

Not all children who have been sexually abused dissociate or repress the abuse, but many do. Whether one always remembers what occurred or in how much detail has nothing to do with the validity of the trauma.

As a child, my psyche could not accommodate the magnitude and intensity of what was happening to me and so, in my words, my mind split. Without this involuntary defense mechanism, I believe I would have psychologically imploded. Forgetting childhood sexual abuse is common, and we bless the power of the mind for finding ways to help us to survive.

---

[5] James A. Chu, M.D. writes (Briere & Conte, 1993; Herman & Schatzhow, 1987; Loftus, Polonsky, & Fullilove 1994; Meyer-Williams, 1994; Terr, 1988

Chapter 21 – Do Babies and Toddlers Remember?

Recently, on local television, a reporter was "live" at the scene where a crazed man was holding his 2-year-old son by his ankles over the third floor balcony. A SWAT team had guns aimed directly at the man who was shouting as he dangled his son, "I'll drop him if you come any closer. Did you hear me? I'll drop him!" As the stand-off continued, the reporter concluded his report by saying, "I only hope this little boy is too young to remember this."

The toddler being dangled by his ankles over a balcony while his father screamed, is *not* too young to remember but he is too young to verbalize and process the experience, which may change his brain chemistry and cause violent behavior later in life.

Since, as adults, we don't remember events that happened before we were two or three years old, it is assumed that what happened during those years is not particularly significant to our adult lives. That assumption is wrong. Toddlers are not too young to remember. Babies are not too young to remember.

I have often wondered if some of the overwhelming feelings of terror and despair I felt were brought on by experiences I had as a baby or toddler—before I was able to form words that would have given my feelings context and a voice. Terrors that occur before we are verbal will come up as very intense feelings with no pictures…feelings without verbal memories.

"For children of any age, long-term damage can occur from a single searing trauma or prolonged exposure to chronic stress or fear…when serious trauma occurs to babies and toddlers during their most explosive phase of brain development, *the injury reverberates beyond anything we have ever imagined possible*." (*Ghosts From the Nursery*, p. 156)

The first time I read that, I recalled one of the most disturbing film clips I have ever seen. It was shown repeatedly on network telecasts. Parents had been concerned about the baby-sitter they had hired to care for their toddler, who appeared in the video to be about a year and a half old. They set up a hidden video camera to record what happened when they were away.

What they saw on the video was devastating. They watched the baby-sitter put the infant into a high chair to be fed. When the child turned away from the food, the adult baby-sitter hit the baby so hard across the face that it whipped the child's head around. The child began screaming. The baby-sitter, while yelling at the child to "shut up," took a full swing at the baby's face again and again, hitting the child with tremendous force. This continued on and on. I couldn't watch anymore.

Let's assume this child grew up to be an angry, aggressive, violent person. The parents would have searched their minds for what might have happened to cause such anger in a child that was reared in a calm and loving environment. They would never have known what was happening as they went to work day after day, nor would their toddler have been able to tell them, because the toddler was preverbal when it happened.

Children may not be able to "tell," but they will act out in ways neither they nor their parents will understand. Twenty children with documented histories of trauma between the ages of birth and 2 ½ could not put the trauma they had experienced into words but the experiences had been encoded in their memories. Eighteen of the children replicated specific traumas they had endured in their play. (*Ghosts From the Nursery,* p. 42)

We now know that even the earliest experiences can and do impact our lives. Studies done by Dr. Joseph LeDoux concluded that early, precognitive emotions continue to play out in later life even though the person may have no conscious memory of the event. (*Ghosts From the Nursery,* p. 40)

A cousin of mine, Cindy Friedland, adopted an adorable 14-month-old girl from China a year and a half ago. The child, whom they call Allie, had been so traumatized that she would not look at anyone—even Cindy. When Allie would wake up in the morning and Cindy would go into her room, Allie would face the wall. It was many weeks before Allie made eye contact with her mother. Cindy literally stopped her life and focused on Allie—never urging or pushing her, allowing the child to begin to trust at her own pace. If anyone came into their home, Allie would be extremely upset so Cindy, her husband George, and Allie spent months alone together.

After more than a year of Cindy and George's devotion to their child, Allie is now smiling and laughing. She goes to preschool two mornings a week and enjoys playing with other children. A few weeks ago, there was a reunion of children who had been adopted from China. When Cindy arrived at City Park, there was much excitement as mothers greeted one another. As Allie approached the other children, she began screaming. Not crying. Screaming. Cindy could not console her. They left immediately. There is no doubt in Cindy's mind that although Allie was preverbal when she left China, being surrounded by Chinese children triggered the feelings of horror Allie experienced in the orphanage.

Sexual stimulation of a baby can cause long-term trauma. Last year, when I spoke in Plano, an affluent suburb of Dallas, my host told me that the youngest victim they had at the Rape Crisis Center was six months old. *Babies* are sexually violated and they don't forget. Perhaps I hadn't thought about it because it is so abhorrent. What is so disturbing is that babies and toddlers can't tell us when they are being traumatized. But they will remember. Babies and toddlers remember.

"Infants have preverbal memories that are stored in their bodies. These body memories may resurface throughout an adult's life, causing unexplainable, uncomfortable, physical sensations. They may be in the form of chronic genital arousal, stomachaches, painful intercourse, uterine pain, etc. A certain smell, sound, time of year, or touch can stimulate these preverbal memories.... Infants under the age of two are at the highest risk for sexual abuse because they can't tell anyone what has happened to them. Adolescents who baby-sit infants may be in the stage of sexual experimentation and believe that the sexual exploration of a baby's genitals will not harm the child because the child won't remember, but that's not true...A baby or infant who is stimulated sexually will be aroused far beyond what is normal for the child and therefore, the sexual drive will prematurely 'kick in' and cause the infant distress, discomfort and overwhelming physiological sensations. Early sexual stimulation causes a release of certain hormones and may activate the sexual organs to prematurely develop." [6]

Dr. Judith Herman reports that a child who had been sexually molested by a baby-sitter before he was two years old, didn't remember the abuse or the baby-sitter but during his play, "he enacted

---

[6] December 14, 2002, personal correspondence with Dr. Leigh Baker, author of *Protecting Your Children*

scenes that exactly replicated a pornographic movie made by the baby-sitter." (Herman, *Trauma and Recovery*, p. 38)

In a child's earliest years, "every neuron in the brain is waiting for stimulation…Trauma and cuddling call different neurons into action. Once these neurons are called on to do certain jobs, they can be called again with less intense stimulation. Hypersensitivity can become wired into basic brain chemistry…brain capacities that were available for learning other skills may be deflected to help defend against future trauma…When stress is especially severe…*permanent changes* may occur…that alter the brain's chemical profile."(Karr-Morse and Wiley, *Ghosts From the Nursery*, p. 159) "…The impact of trauma can shape the entire organization of key brain functions." (p. 168)

Dr. Bruce Perry, one of the nation's leading authorities on how trauma impacts brain development, has concluded from his research that even *one intense exposure* to fear or trauma can dramatically impact a child's ability to modulate stress. "If trauma continues, the neural thermostat becomes stuck on high."

One of the most crucial jobs a parent has is helping to soothe a child who becomes over stimulated. The infant can then learn, in time, how to self-soothe. Doing the opposite, causing extreme hyper arousal, will have severe long-term consequences. The sensory and emotional experiences of an infant or toddler lay the foundation for whether or not the child perceives the world as a safe and loving place or an unsafe, frightening environment.

Chapter 22 – Conversations With Children

This chapter addresses startling statistics about sexual abuse and urgently important conversations you need to have with your children—and gives you actual verbiage to guide you in communicating.

When I talk with parents or caregivers about sexually inappropriate touch, some become uncomfortable and worried that any physical contact with or among children can be considered abusive. This could not be farther from the truth, nor is it my message. Children need nurturing, hugging, touching, bathing and holding. Appropriate physical contact is vital, pleasurable and contributes to healthy growth and development. At issue in this book are the unhealthy expression of adult sexual urges, inappropriate behaviors and the exploitation of children.

It is never acceptable to satisfy one's needs for power, comfort or sexual pleasure from a child or anyone who is incapable of understanding or freely choosing to participate. Adults and children must learn to recognize their feelings and be able to express their needs in ways that are not exploitive of others who are vulnerable.

A very important conversation that has probably never occurred to you.

If, at a neighborhood meeting, a police officer told you that, based on recent research, one-third of the homes on your block were going to be burglarized, would it get your attention? If he went on to say that most homes are broken into by getting in through the glass sliding doors many houses have—and that he had a special "sliding door stop" that kept most burglars out, would you ask for one and go home and immediately put it on your door?

If you didn't, you would be irresponsible to your family. You *didn't know* that so many homes in your area were being broken into—you were startled to find out—but now that you knew, wouldn't you immediately take the *one step* that the police officer said would be the most effective way of protecting your family? Of course you would.

One of the most startling facts I have learned during the past twelve years of speaking, traveling and reading thousands of survivor letters is—without question—how many older siblings are sexually violating younger siblings.

Research educates us that one out of three to four girls and one out of six boys will be sexually violated before the age of 18 and that the highest percentage, by far, are violated in their homes. Sibling incest is a serious issue that most of us have been unaware of. Just as a lock on a sliding door can help bring safety, there is something specific we can do to help keep our children safe from sibling abuse, but first we must understand the issue.

We cannot prevent what we do not know and understand.

The first exposure I had to the rampant numbers of siblings inappropriately touching or forcibly raping younger sisters or brothers was when I attended group support meetings while in my late 40's—at the lowest time of my life.

There were six women who attended the first night. Three of the six had been violated by older brothers. I had assumed that being forcibly penetrated by a father was the worst thing that could happen to a child. I was wrong. Their shame, feelings of helplessness, and need for years of therapy was no different from those of us who had been violated by parents or stepparents.

My own recovery was so overwhelming that I didn't think more about sibling incest until my story became public years later. Suddenly, I was stopped everywhere I went, and I do mean everywhere I went, by women who said to me, "When I was eight and my brother was 14…" These harmful experiences are not limited to girls and are not committed only by boys, although there has been more research done on female victims of male siblings.

Recently, as I was coming out of a store, another woman was coming in. As we quickly passed one another, I saw the "look." She had recognized me, and her look told me instantly that she was a survivor. My momentum took me out the door but I immediately went back in. I knew she would be waiting. "When you came forward, I felt the strength to finally confront my brother and to tell my parents. My brother denied it. My parents didn't believe me and I have been ostracized from the family. "

How common is inappropriate sexual behavior between siblings, or more accurately, sibling incest? If men and women hadn't stopped me literally hundreds of times to say their violators were their brothers or sisters, I would not have believed the research. Now I do.

"The term incest is generally thought of as referring to sexual relations between fathers and daughters…even though many researchers feel sibling incest is more common." [7]

"The estimates are that incest between siblings may be *five times* more common than paternal incest." (Wiehe, *Sibling Abuse,* p. 59)

Too many times I am told that parents did nothing because they said the abuse was "just typical childhood behavior" or they simply felt it was no big deal. Sometimes I hear, "boys will be boys," as if boys can't be expected or taught to express their aggression or sexual feelings in a healthy, appropriate manner.

At what age do you believe most offenders sexually abuse? When they are 40 years old? 25 years old? The answer is 14 years old. [8] *14 year-olds comprise the largest number of sex offenders of any age group.* I will repeat this statistic later in the book because it is one fact that I want you to remember. Here's another source: "The modal [most commonly reported] age of the violator was 14 years." [9]

What can be done to keep your children safe?

The first thing may be the most difficult: Believing that it's true. How can you, as a parent, even consider sexual behavior between your children as a possibility? We can only begin to stem the tide when you begin to know this *could* happen *in your* family and that it is a serious issue. At least as serious as playing with loaded guns or matches.

Alerting and educating parents as to the rampant sexual activity between siblings is one of the major reasons I am writing this book. I don't know how to stop a man like my father but I do know how to dramatically reduce sibling sexual activity. Since we now *know* how prevalent it is, it is our parental duty to do the *things* we *know* can help prevent this behavior.

One of the most effective ways of preventing sexual abuse among siblings is to *talk about it*. My urgent plea is that you sit down with all your children as soon as possible and talk to them about what is and is

---

[7] Wiehe, *Sibling Abuse,* p. 57; Justice & Justice, 1979; Meiselman, 1978

[8] Criminal Justice Source Statistics, 2000, Table 4.7 p. 362

[9] *Child Adolescent Psychiatry,* 35:1, January 1996

not appropriate behavior, as they grow into their sexuality.

A mother in Ohio told me that she couldn't talk to her daughter because she was only 8 years old. I told her that the average age a sibling is violated is 8.2 years. The most frequently reported age when the abuse began was 5 years old." (*Sibling Abuse,* p. 62)

"A recent *Seventeen Magazine* survey found that 21% of teens who had never talked about sexuality with their parents were more likely to have sex at a young age." [10] And this could certainly occur with a sibling.

I hope I can convince you that this can happen in *your* family. Three daughters of friends of mine, from three different families, have disclosed to me that years ago they were violated by older brothers. The men who are now in their 40's are successful and highly regarded. I suspect these men have no idea how severely they traumatized their younger sisters when the brothers were 13, 14 and 16 and their sisters were 6, 10 and 14. If asked, they might say, "It was just a part of growing up." But it isn't.

Currently, one of the women cannot face the "work" she needs to do for her own recovery. She is a social worker and her supervisor has told her that she needs to "get a grip." She often breaks down and sobs at work when confronted with a sexual abuse case. I know her brother. He lives only blocks from her. I am sure he has no idea of the pain he caused or the shame she feels. I want to tell him to, "Pick up the phone, call your sister and say, 'We need to talk.' Don't pretend this never happened. Help her through this. Take responsibility for what you did when you were 14 and she was 10. There could be healing for both of you if you talked about it." However, it is not my place to tell her story.

Several months ago, I was talking with Rachel. She was born into an affluent family. As a child, she had been violated by an older brother who was put in charge when their parents went out for the evening. He forcibly held her down countless times and raped her. As a young woman, she was hospitalized twice in a psychiatric ward. During the past twelve years, she has made a remarkable recovery from her shame. When the subject of brothers baby-sitting younger siblings came up in our conversation, she became enraged. "How

---

[10] *The Rocky Mountain News,* March 12, 2001, p. 8D

could parents ever allow a teenager to baby-sit a younger sibling? How could they do that? Don't they know that adolescent hormones are off the chart during that time? Don't they know that the 'nicest kids from the nicest families' can, and do, sexually violate younger sisters and brothers?"

If you, as a parent, knew you could do something that might keep your children from being sexual with one another how could you *not* do it? You must educate your older children, and empower your younger children. Please don't think this issue will never affect you because of race, religion, wealth or culture. No one is immune. Your family is at risk, my family is at risk, and all of our children need protection and guidance.

If it is necessary for you to have an older teenager, including a sibling, baby-sit a younger child please *never say*, "Your brother (remember that sisters violate, as well) is in charge tonight. We won't be home until after you are asleep. You need to mind your brother and do everything he tells you to do." Those instructions need to be reworded. Instead, say: "Your brother will baby-sit tonight. You know the rules: Lights out at 8:30 p.m. Only the television shows we have okayed. Don't do anything you wouldn't do if we were in the room with you. Anything that would be a secret is not okay. Have fun. We love you. See you in the morning."

Then talk with each child separately the next day about how their evening went, what they did and how they all got along. Let them know they can come to you if something troubling is happening.

This research deserves to be repeated more than once…"The most frequently reported age when sibling abuse began was 5 years old…" (*Sibling Abuse,* p. 62)

Why you need to rethink your decision to have your teenager baby-sit.

Fascinating new research is coming out that gives us another reason for talking to our teenagers. For the first time in history, it is possible to actually see what goes on in a teenager's brain as he or she nears puberty. Within the past few years, through the new technology, magnetic resonance imager (MRI), long held beliefs have been changing.

Dr. Charles Nelson said on a recent *Frontline* show on PBS, "Many people mistakenly believed that most of the changes in the brain occurred in the first few years of life, and then after a child was about 3, there was actually little change occurring. W*e know now* that's absolutely incorrect. We have found an unexpected growth spurt, an overproduction of cells just before puberty." Dr. Nelson continues, "…it's the changes going on in the frontal cortex that gradually give the child the ability to regulate those powerful emotions, to solve problems effectively, to be more planful in their behavior." We now know that teenagers "often do not make the most responsible, reasoned decisions because this part of their brain is still developing." [11]

"The basic part of the brain that gives teenagers strategies and perhaps *warns them of potential consequences* isn't fully on board yet." [12]

This research reaffirms the importance of telling our children, in simple language, what is and is not acceptable behavior between siblings.

There is one very significant criterion in the professional literature on sibling incest with which I *strongly disagree.* Some authorities believe that if there is not a significant age difference (most stipulate five years) then sexual contact between siblings will not be harmful. This is not true. When talking to your children don't focus on age or even gender. Consider psychological advantage, physical size, strength and experience. I have yet to meet a sibling who told me she or he had had consensual sex with a brother or sister and that the long-term effects had been positive or even neutral. The message for children is that their bodies and their sexual curiosity or feelings are normal but that it is never acceptable to coerce, force, bribe or manipulate another person into sexual activity. Just as we teach that stealing and lying are not acceptable behaviors, any sexual behavior among siblings is not okay.

"Fifty-nine percent of child molesters developed deviant sexual interest during adolescence." (Handbook of Family Violence: Becker & Coleman reported by Greig Veeder) Clearly, there are a lot of children in desperate need of parental guidance.

---

[11] *Frontline* PBS, January 31, 2002

[12] Dr. Jay Giedd, National Institute of Mental Health, *Frontline* PBS, "Inside the Teenage Brain," January 31, 2002

If you hear yourself going into denial, "This could never happen to my son or daughter," please stop and say, "Yes, It could! I know now that it can happen in any family because most 13- and 14-year-old children do not comprehend the long-term consequences of acting out with children who are vulnerable." Many children are troubled by their sexual impulses and drives and need to be able to talk with safe adults about how to handle these strong feelings. It is up to us to *teach our children—totalk about it.*

This conversation should be given importance by turning the phones and television off and calling your kids together in a way that they know this is a significant discussion.

Larry will never forget what his father said to him on the day of his Bar Mitzvah. Papa asked the family to gather in the living room, which established the importance of his remarks. Then his father said, "In our tradition, today you are a man. If something happens to me, you are the man of the family. I count on you to look after your mother and your sisters." Larry told me recently that those few words were far more significant than anything else that happened on that memorable day.

Suggestions for how to talk to children.

After speaking in Binghamton, New York, at a black tie fundraising dinner for a Children's Advocacy Center, a patrician looking man came up to me and said, "Okay. You've convinced me that I should talk to my kids but you're going to have to help me with what I say."

I said, "Well, let me try one idea. We'll write on an imaginary blackboard knowing that we may want to erase everything and start again. The truth is always a good place to start:

'Last night at the banquet, a former Miss America talked about her childhood. She was sexually abused (choose wording that is age appropriate, e.g. touched in ways that made her feel very badly) by her father and she was so ashamed, she didn't tell anyone for a very long time. My heart just broke for her and I thought about how heart broken I would be if any of you were ever touched in an uncomfortable way and you couldn't talk to me about it.

'Then she told us that the most surprising thing she had learned is that uncomfortable or scary sexual activity sometimes happens between sisters and brothers and that one thing all parents should do is to talk to their children—together—and tell them that there should be no sexual contact between siblings. Ever.

'She said that children are naturally curious about their bodies and others' bodies, especially their private areas. Some kids may think it is okay to touch or force or tease a sister or brother because no one ever told them that this is wrong. But it can be very harmful to the younger or less powerful child. Even if you don't understand right now how this can be true and you think it's just playing around, you need to believe me that it is not okay for you to do these things. She said there are good touches between brothers and sisters and secret touches. There should never be secret touches with anyone. She said that siblings should never touch a part of the body that a bathing suit covers and went on to say that if anyone touches you in a way that doesn't feel right, you should say, "No" and then come to your mother or me and we can talk about it. We are here not only to love you but also to protect you. I always want you to come to me any time you have questions or if there is anything you want to talk about.'"

If you start to put this conversation off, please let these facts ring in your mind; most often, when the abuse began, the younger sibling was 5 years old, and the largest number of sex offenders in *any age group* is 14 year-olds.

I didn't know sibling sexual activity was rampant, nor I'm sure, did you. But now we *do* know and with that knowledge comes responsibility.

Is incest passed from one generation to the next?

The research on families where sibling incest occurred is *profoundly* thought provoking:

• The average age of the parents was 34.6 years old when their children had sexual experiences with one another.
• 76% of the families were two-parent families.
• 24% had only one parent in the home.
• 56% were stepfamilies.
• 48% of the sibling perpetrators had observed sexual activity between their parents or one parent and another party. One sibling pair hid in their parents' closet to watch them make love.
• 52% of the offenders were child victims of sexual abuse.
• 32% of the victims had been incested by their fathers before their brothers incested them.
• 40% of the mothers qualified as seductive.

• 32% of the mothers had extremely devout religious backgrounds and were not open to conversations regarding sex of any kind.

• In 76% of sibling incest families, extramarital affairs were occurring.

This is the *most startling statistic* to me:

• In the 20% of cases where girls were the offenders, *all the mothers* were involved in extramarital affairs at the exact same times their daughters were initiating sibling inappropriate contact. There wasn't even one exception. *(Sibling Abuse*, pp. 101–108)

Yes, I believe sexual abuse is generational. Incest doesn't happen in a vacuum. The family environment is often polluted with pornography, abusive language and inappropriate sexual behavior. For example, my father relished dirty jokes and told them often. He commented on beautiful women, many times, in a flirtatious, almost lascivious way. After my father died, Gwen found extensive pornography in his office.

I remembered highly successful men I had worked with, whose sons have acted out sexually in inappropriate ways. The sons may or may not have known that their fathers had numerous affairs...but these fathers conveyed to their sons through their everyday behavior and comments, what their values were. It wasn't, in my opinion, only what they had or hadn't *seen* their fathers *do*, it was the complete environment they had grown up in. The daughters received equally strong messages about relationships, trust and valuing themselves and others.

When I was talking with Larry about this, I saw him drift away, and then he said, as if he had never thought about it before, "I can never remember my father *even commenting* on another woman. I can never remember him saying, 'Isn't she beautiful?' or 'Wow, look at her.'" He went on to say, "I never heard my father tell a dirty joke, nor did he want to listen to one."

We begin with our own families. If your family is like ours, there are strong connections between aunts, uncles, nieces and nephews. Close, strongly connected family members can also have these conversations with children. Although most children who have been sexually violated do not go on to violate other children, a high percentage will find themselves in abusive relationships. This leaves *their* children vulnerable to abuse. This can change if behavior is confronted, victims become empowered, and perpetrators are held responsible.

Many times children learn from a few spoken words. What we say on a daily basis reinforces our messages to children. "What President Clinton did in his personal life is his own business." The message we send to our children is, "So, as long as I am involved in school activities and get good grades, even if I hurt someone else, what I do in my personal life shouldn't be anyone else's business. Cheating, lying and never taking full responsibility for your actions are acceptable."

While watching a sitcom on television, there are ample opportunities to make comments. "She should never allow anyone to speak to her that way." "That kind of sexual behavior is not acceptable. It's demeaning." "There is nothing about that that is funny." When it is reported that a high paid athlete is convicted of rape and then given probation just before an important game, your comments (or lack thereof) will reflect your values. It's important for us to *talk back* to the television.

Woody Allen took pornographic photographs of his stepdaughter, Soon-Yi. She was nude and posing in a reclining position with her legs spread wide open. Soon-Yi had never been on a date. No boy had even called her on the phone. Woody had been her father-figure since she was ten years old. In her book, *What Falls Away*, Mia Farrow writes (after confronting Allen about the pornographic pictures and sleeping with Soon-Yi), "What am I supposed to tell the kids? That their father wants to marry their sister?"

When Woody said, "Let's put this behind us," Mia answered, "How do we do that? She's the sister of your children." She continued, "You're not supposed to f... the kids." (p. 276)

Woody ended up marrying Soon-Yi. It was, of course, a major news story. What you, as a parent, said, as the story unfolded, communicated volumes to your children. If you said, "It's none of our business," that sentence, in and of itself, made a very strong statement.

I, and many adults I know, will never see another Woody Allen film and any time anyone is "surfing" the television channels and one of his movies is on, I say, "Move on. I will not watch him. Ever." I believe he has violated the trust and innocence of the children in his care. Anyone in the room will know exactly how much I believe it is our business, and that I will shun him and let others know that I believe he is a perpetrator who must be held accountable.

Ask your children questions.

Do you know how your children feel about rape? For example, does your son believe there are certain circumstances in which rape is okay? Does your daughter think it is acceptable for a boy to rape her under certain circumstances? You may be stunned by your children's responses, as thousands of other parents were, after reading their children's replies to a survey that they took regarding sexual relationships.

In research made available through the American Medical Association, a survey of 1,700 eleven to fourteen year-old boys and girls found that:

• 51% of boys and girls said forced sex was acceptable if the boy spent a lot of money on the girl.

• 31% of boys and 32% of girls said it was acceptable for a man to rape a woman with past sexual experience.

• 87% of boys and 79% of girls said sexual assault was acceptable if the man and woman were married.

• 65% of boys and 47% of girls said it was acceptable for a boy to rape a girl if they had been dating for more than six months.

• One third of acquaintance sexual assaults occur when the victim is between the ages of 11 and 17. [13]

Many parents tell me that it is very difficult to start a conversation about sex. One of the best ways is to get them involved in a conversation that can lead, in a very natural way, to their own personal beliefs or any unanswered questions they might have. We don't really know our children unless we take the time to engage them in meaningful discussions.

How to begin the conversation:

This is how I might begin a conversation if Jennifer were 11 or 12 today. "Jennifer, I read something today that I could not believe. I had to read it again just to be sure I had read it correctly. It's about a survey of what children between the ages of 11 and 14 believe about sex. It's short. May I read it to you?"

I would read each statistic and then ask, "How do you think your

---

[13] *Strategies for the treatment and prevention of sexual assault.* Chicago: American Medical Association, 1995.

friends would answer that?" (Wait for an answer.) "What are your thoughts?"

• "Do you believe it is okay for a boy or a man to rape a girl or a woman if she has been sexually active with other boys or men?"

• "Do you believe it is okay for a husband to sexually assault his wife?"

• "Do you believe it's okay for a boy to rape a girl if they have been dating for more than six months?"

• "Do you believe that a boy or man can be raped? How do you think it would affect him if he were raped?"

This survey is an excellent introduction into how your children think about these subjects. You might be making assumptions about their beliefs that are not true. What better way to plunge right into it than by using this survey? (20% of the girls and 6% of the boys taking the survey said they had been sexually abused.)

Sometimes listening to the network news forces us to address issues with our children. We need to have conversations with our youngsters today, that would have been unthinkable even 15 years ago.

Recently, Oprah opened her show by saying, "There's an oral sex epidemic going on in junior high schools across the country. Children are getting caught doing it in bathrooms, on buses, on the playground, and it's not just the fast kids having oral sex. It's the clean-cut ones too—the athletes, the cheerleaders, even the honor students." A 14-year-old said she believes 75% of the kids in her school are having oral sex. None of the teens knew that sexually transmitted diseases could be transmitted through oral sex.

Jeff said, "I didn't even know what oral sex was until 6th grade when everyone was talking about President Clinton and Monica Lewinsky. When President Clinton said oral sex wasn't sex, I think he kind of opened the door for us to say, 'Well, it's okay. You know if the President does it and it's not sex, why can't I do it?'" Other teenagers said, "Oral sex is not considered sex in my school," and "I don't think oral sex is as big a deal as a goodnight kiss." [14]

On a similar show, there was *good news*. Teenagers said they *wanted their parents to talk to them* about sex. Three adolescent boys said, "We listen to our parents, we do listen to them sometimes. Maybe

_____

[14] *Oprah*, May 7, 2002

they don't believe it, but we actually hear them."

"Out of any kind of punishment I could receive, the worst thing is seeing disappointment in my parent's eyes." "Kids look up to their parents a lot."

Parents were asked if they had talked with their kids about sex. All said, "Yes." When their teenagers were asked if their parents had talked with them, a number of them said, "No." [15]

We are living in a world different from the one in which we grew up. We need to talk to our children at earlier ages than most of us would ever have anticipated.

Parents know that kids need to hear the same messages over and over again. We have to tell them many times to put their dirty clothes in the hamper, not on the floor. Corporations know that the way to motivate customers to buy their products is to repeatedly capture their attention in order to *sell them* on why they want a particular product. And what are they willing to pay to do that?

A 30-*second* commercial during the 2010 Super Bowl was $2.2 million. That was for air time only. It can easily cost an additional million dollars to produce the commercial.

If a corporate sponsor is willing to spend $2.2 million to have you hear the 30-second message they want to send, they must have validated how important words are. Most corporations will run the same ad over and over again until we say, "It just keeps going and going and going," (Energizer Bunny) or "Just do it." (Nike). No advertiser thinks you are going to remember their message if you hear it only once.

Talking with children means sharing your values and involves *continuous* discussions as different opportunities arise.

Many times, we think our children understand what we're doing, and many times we are wrong in our conclusions.

When Jennifer was six or seven, we were finishing a sensational dinner at a restaurant when the waiter asked me, "Would you like our homemade chocolate cake with mouth-watering chocolate sauce on it?" I said, "No. Thank you." Later, I found out that Jennifer thought I

---

[15] *MSNBC Weekend Magazine,* "Sex and Sensibility, November 3, 2001

didn't *want* mouth-watering chocolate cake. That's what I said!

The next time we were out for dinner and the waiter said, "Would you like our premium chocolate ice cream, covered with coconut and fudge sauce," I replied, "Yes I would! I certainly would! But I'm not having dessert tonight, thank you." Sometimes we think children understand when they don't. Often they need more conversation because what may seem obvious to us is not to them. Ask them how they think a situation ought to be handled and then listen to their answers. Talk *with* your children and teens, not at them.

One question changed my life forever. It is a question every parent should ask every child. Whereas sibling abuse should be discussed with all children together, this conversation is a one-on-one.

Last year, I received a letter from a doctor in Cherry Hills Village, an affluent suburb of Denver. She said, "I read an interview you had given and you said a parent should ask her children if anyone had ever touched them in an uncomfortable way. I thought, 'pfft! Not *my* two little boys.' But then you said, 'It is an important part of parenting,' so that night when I was bathing my youngest boy, I said, 'Has anyone ever touched you in an uncomfortable way?' He said, 'Yes.' I could barely breathe. My heart stopped. My world stopped. All I could think about was asking my other son. He said, 'Yes.' They told me that their teenage baby-sitter (from what I thought was an excellent family) had used them sexually. I later learned that he was violating young boys throughout our neighborhood. I have been bewildered, heartbroken, enraged. It has taken me one year to write this letter to you. My boys have been in therapy for a year and they're doing fine."

When I ran across her letter recently, I realized I didn't know how old the boys were so I wrote her and asked her if she would share their ages.

She wrote a long letter. Her sons were five and seven when the sexual abuse occurred. And they weren't "doing fine." She said last week, she was driving her son somewhere and he just flipped into rage, screaming, "I'm going to kill you. I'm going to kill everyone. I hate you." She wrote, "If I hadn't known about the abuse, I would not have known where this was coming from."

She continued, "I broke into uncontrollable sobs recently when I wrote in my journal that this has become a part of the fabric of our lives. Not an event. Not something we can just 'get over.' But a part of the fabric of our lives forever. That's what is so hard, realizing the damage that was done. I would never have believed sexual abuse of boys so young could impact them so strongly."

These two boys have a very good likelihood of being able to work through these issues because they have: 1) a parent who knew how important it was to ask, 2) a parent whom they could trust with the truth, 3) a parent who acknowledged the seriousness of the abuse and acted immediately, 4) a parent who sought even more help from specialists when she felt it was needed, 5) a parent who did what she could to find out who the offender was and took steps to ensure that her boys would now be safe from the offender, and 6) a parent who felt and had compassion for her sons' pain and acting out.

If you know this conversation is going to be a white knuckle, grit your teeth, "Let's-get-this-over-with-as-quickly-as-possible," conversation, be truthful. Say, "I grew up in a family where everyone was uncomfortable discussing anything to do with sex. I can't believe that I am uncomfortable right now. I hope that by talking with you today, you will be more comfortable talking with your own children. I'm reading a book about a woman who could never tell anyone that someone had sexually abused her because she felt so much shame. Then, when she was in her 20's, someone asked her if anyone had ever touched her in an uncomfortable way and it was a life changing moment for her. She said, 'Yes.' With that one question and her one word answer, she could begin to let go of a secret she had kept for years."

You could continue, "Most children are violated by someone they know—someone they trust. Like a family member, coach or baby-sitter. It's usually not a stranger, but that *could* happen too. Most children feel that they are to blame or that no one will believe them or love them if they tell. But it is never the child's fault. You know that there isn't anything you could ever do or say that would change my love for you. Has anyone ever touched you in an uncomfortable way?"

I know that only a rare few children will answer, "Yes" to this question. *Most will say "No."* No doesn't always mean no even when children are asked a direct question. If, when your child says, "No," you give a huge sigh of relief and say by word or gesture, "Oh, I am so glad. So glad," your child may have just been testing how you would respond. If you express ineffable relief, they will be unlikely to ever tell you if something happens. If, on the other hand, you respond by saying, "If you ever do want to come and tell me something just remember that we can always work things through together. Most kids don't tell because they feel ashamed. There is never anything to be ashamed of. I love you so much. There is nothing that could ever change that."

It's like so many other problems in our world. We begin by addressing it in our own homes. I didn't know childhood sexual abuse was rampant, nor I'm sure, did you. But now we *do* know and with that knowledge comes responsibility.

Whether your child is 5, 15, 25, 35 or 45 (I was 48 when I told my mother), initiate the conversation: "Has anyone ever touched you in an uncomfortable way?" By asking that question, you may open a door for a conversation now or in the future. You have to ask because children don't tell.

Please talk with your children tonight. You will find your own way to express the thoughts. What is important is that you do it.

Chapter 23 – Seven Things You Should Never Say

Oh, how often do we unknowingly say something that hurts someone? There are no social situations more sensitive than when dealing with a person who has endured a sexual violation. What is said, and how it is said, are critically important.

1. *"Did he rape you?"*

Just by asking that question, you have sent a painful and damaging message. If she says, "No," then you have already as much as said that if there was not penetration with his penis, then—"whew!—we need to be grateful. It's not such a big deal." It isn't what sexual act was *done;* it's how the act made the victim *feel.*

"Numerous studies confirm that any sexual act (such as fondling) *is frequently as traumatic* for victims as molestation involving penetration. The magnitude of trust betrayed, the violence involved and the victim's perception of complicity can be more important factors." [16]

In his book, *Sibling Abuse,* Vernon Wiehe observes, "Fondling can no longer be labeled as less harmful than sexual intercourse because the consequences are essentially the same." (p. 73)

That opinion has been codified by the U. S. Department of Justice, which has expanded the definition of rape to be, "an event that occurred without the victim's consent, that involved the use or threat of force to penetrate the victim's vagina or anus by penis, tongue, fingers, or object, or the victim's mouth by penis." [17]

Oprah said, "What really upsets me and what you don't seem to get, America, is there aren't varying degrees of abuse. It's about the abuse of power and trust. So whether you physically penetrate a child with your penis or your finger or an object, whether you just touch their breasts, whether you *just* fondle them or you *just* kiss them, it doesn't matter. It's an issue of trust and power. I'm so sick of people not getting that! I do 'abuse shows' and they say, 'Was there actual sex

---

[16] Dr. David Finkelhor San Francisco Chronicle, 1994 p F7

[17] National Institute of Justice, U.S. Dept of Justice, November 1998

involved or was there *just* touching?' America doesn't understand that it is the raping of the spirit and the soul."

Later in the show she said, "I don't think people understand the ramifications of the problem. The permanent scars that you leave on your children. It's not something that's even tangible, that you can say, 'Oh, I abused and therefore the kid turned out this way.' It just permeates every area of your life. That's what people don't understand." [18]

I addressed a judges conference in New Jersey. After an hour presentation and a thirty-minute question and answer period, I stayed to talk with individual judges. As I was leaving the hotel ballroom, a judge said, "May I stop you for one more question? You said something about how fondling could have as severe a long-term effect as penetration. Did I hear you correctly?"

I said, "Yes, you did. It's something I've learned that I didn't know before talking with thousands of survivors and reading thousands of letters, having men and women tell me experiences they had never told anyone. Whether an offender has intercourse with a child or fondles her or him, isn't the issue. It's whether or not that boundary of trust has been crossed and how the violation makes the person *feel*. If the offender is sexualizing the child, trying to dominate, control, manipulate or coerce the child, then it is also a psychological and spiritual assault that goes to the core of a child's being."

"What do you think was one of the worst things my father did to me?" I asked the judge. I knew he would not venture an answer but I wanted him to think for a minute before I told him because I knew it would be a foreign concept for him and one that would be very difficult for him to accept. I said, "I never talk about this in my presentations because it takes a long time to put it into context, and if anyone went away saying this was one of the worst things my father did to me, they would say, 'So? What's the big deal?'"

I said, "My father penetrated every part of my body, but one of the worst acts he did was to French kiss me." The judge stared at me in bewilderment. I told him how I had always tried to mentally separate my head from my body. I tried to cut off my awareness of my body and "not be there" by focusing on going into "nothingness," but when

---

[18] *Oprah*, October 23, 1995

he invaded my face, I had nowhere to go in my mind to escape. For children with similar experiences, other aspects of their assaults may be more traumatic. Each child's reaction will be different. For many, I have learned, fondling *can* (I did not say will) have the same shame and long-term trauma as penetration. An example of how this could happen, might involve *how others responded* when victims disclosed the sexual trauma.

After a presentation in Omaha, a 35-year-old woman told me that when she was 14 and 15 years old, she was repeatedly held down and fondled by her older brother. She was humiliated and enraged that her brother would fondle and kiss her breasts. She finally had the courage to tell her parents. They said, "You're just making that up. We don't believe you."

Tamara Brooks, 16, and Jacqueline Marris, 17, were kidnapped and raped at gunpoint. In less than 24 hours, the rapist had been killed and the girls were freed. They immediately came forward to tell their stories. As they spoke publicly, they were honored and called "heroes" for their bravery. Because it is the secret and the shame that keep most of us tethered to our rapes, I believe we will find that their recovery has less long-term trauma than the woman who was "just fondled" by her brother and not believed by her parents.

"Acceptance and validation are crucial to the psychological survival of the victim. A child molested by one parent and rejected by the other parent is psychologically orphaned and almost defenseless against multiple harmful consequences. On the other hand, a parent who can advocate for the child and protect against the abuse seems to instill in the child the power to be self-confident and to recover with minimum psychological injuries." (Summit, *Child Abuse and Neglect,* p 179)

It isn't what is done to us, it's how it makes us feel and if we have the courage to "tell," it's how people react to us. To say, "I'm so grateful you weren't *raped"* is to misunderstand the now accepted meaning of the word rape and to diminish and demean the sexual experience(s) the child/teen/adult endured. What you are really saying is, "I don't think this was such a big deal."

What could you say? Sometimes a few words will make a difference. "I'm deeply sorry. If you ever want to talk, I'm here to listen."

If you aren't comfortable saying words, then write a short note.

"You're in my thoughts." A survivor who has emailed to me for years wrote five words to me recently:

"I'm falling. Please hold me." It was a particularly demanding day—but her email didn't need a lengthy response. I quickly wrote eight words and immediately emailed her back. "I'm holding you. I won't let you fall."

If you don't know what to say, communicate how sorry you are and acknowledge the seriousness of what has been shared with you.

"It is in the shelter of each other that people live." says an Irish proverb.

2. *"You need to forgive."*

"Have you forgiven your father?" I've been asked that question countless times. No one has ever asked me if I have forgiven myself. Forgiving myself was, without question, the most difficult issue of my recovery. I now realize that I didn't have anything to forgive myself for, but it took me 53 years to expunge the shame that filled every pore of my being.

During my recovery in my late 40's, when the memories and the feelings came back as if the nights of horror were happening to me in real time, my shame was so overwhelming; there were many days when I felt I would have to die. Until I could comprehend in the marrow of my bones that the guilt and shame belonged to my father, how could I even contemplate forgiving him? Until we work through these feelings, we can't try to resolve what someone we loved, admired and obeyed did to us.

Sexually abused children often believe they deserve this, or that God is punishing them or that they caused it to happen. It is a natural tendency for children to blame themselves. They may have been told things by the offender that are intended to make them believe it *is* their fault. The most confusing thing that happens for many children who are sexually used to satisfy another person's sexual desires, is that their bodies will become aroused and they will have a physical response to the stimulation. There is overwhelming shame associated with this. Does this mean they participated, asked for it, liked it? No, but we are plagued with that shame… *"I am a bad person."* It is not the same as guilt, which can be described as regret about a behavior. It is a complex collage of extreme emotions. It's about who we are as human beings. Some of the words survivors have used to describe the deep

414

excruciating shame they feel as a result of the abuse are, "I am bad, revolting, unlovable, unworthy, disgusting, pathetic, dirty and loathsome."

Two years after my story became public, when I was 55, Mother and I were driving somewhere together. We never talked about "it," not even if I had recently been interviewed on a major television show or shared additional information in a newspaper article. Well, almost never. We had been talking about the beautiful flowers in the park when she said, as casually as she could, "I received your newsletter about your next (survivor) meeting." She kept going without taking a breath as if she needed to get the words out as quickly as possible. "You mentioned that you were going to talk about forgiveness." She took a breath but kept looking straight ahead as she said, "Have you forgiven your father?" She had caught me off guard. For most survivors, the word "forgiveness" conjures up overwhelming, unresolved, conflicted feelings so I knew it needed to be addressed, but I hadn't yet figured out what I was going to say!

My response to my mother came straight from my gut, "He never *asked* for my forgiveness." Still looking straight ahead, she immediately returned to our previous conversation. I had *no idea* that forgiveness would be *the most combustible word* I would ever say at a survivor meeting or professional conference.

What was most disconcerting to me was how many survivors were coming up to me to tell me that their therapist or religious leader had repeatedly told them that they had to forgive. That, in essence, they were "bad people," and that healing would not be possible unless they forgave.

I was very disturbed by what this demand was doing to survivors already consumed by their unworthiness. It didn't seem to matter what the circumstances were. Whether or not the survivor *wanted* to forgive or whether or not the perpetrator had taken responsibility. We cannot command someone to feel love, hate, respect or forgiveness. These are emotions that come to us over time and through a process.

In the following months, I would learn that for some, there was only one right answer to the question, "Have you forgiven your father?" If I simply said, "Yes, I have forgiven my father," I knew the audience would fervently applaud and then people would stand in line to say, "You are so wonderful."

But that was never my answer. At the meeting two weeks later, I began by relating the question my mother had asked and my gut response: "He never asked for my forgiveness."

Two therapists wrote to me immediately saying, "The only way survivors can let go of the anger, is to forgive." I couldn't disagree with them more. One can let go of anger without forgiving. I know because I've done it. When my suppressed anger came up it was *blood-red rage.* I wanted to blow up my father's crypt and slash the oil portrait of him that hung in my mother's bedroom. I had anger for many, many months, but I moved *through* it. My father no longer had power over me as he had when I was tethered to him by my rage. Even now, nine years after I learned he had never stopped violating innocent people, even now, almost twenty years after his death, I do not forgive him. I am completely peaceful about that. There is no unfinished business.

In the book, *The Courage to Heal*, Laura Davis and Ellen Bass wrote: "Healing depends on being able to forgive yourself, not on being able to forgive your molester…You don't try to forgive Hitler. You don't sit around and work on that. You cannot absolve someone else for what they have done. If abusers are to heal, it will only be because they've acknowledged what they've done, made reparations, worked through their own pain and forgiven *themselves.*" (p. 152) "You are not more moral or courageous if you forgive." (p. 149)

To the person who might say, "You forgive him for yourself, not for him," I reply, "No, it would violate my sense of honor and integrity to forgive this lifelong behavior, but if *your* father sexually violated *you*, you may want to forgive him, for yourself, and *I honor that decision*. All I ask is that you not judge others because we may have different resolutions to our betrayal and pain."

Bill and Camille Cosby's only son, Ennis, was murdered when he was only 27. Three years later, Oprah asked Camille, "Will you ever be able to say 'I forgive this person' and is it even important to forgive?'" Camille said, "I don't think forgiving the murderer is a condition for healing because what he did was so egregious, so outrageous, so evil."

Forgiveness was a key issue for so many survivors who wrote to me. Mary first wrote to me six years ago. She had been sexually violated by a neighborhood teenage boy when she was six. I have spoken three times in her Florida community. We have emailed to one

416

another at least once a week for six years. Mary has earned a graduate degree in computer graphics and now works full time for a software development company. She appears very social and competent on the outside but still struggles intensely on the inside.

One of the ways she copes with the feelings she has unearthed is to cut on herself. She takes a knife or a razor blade and slices into her breasts and pubic area, the same areas that the boy fondled. ("Cutting" is a way many survivors cope with their emotional pain.) She is progressing in therapy but when the pain of the memories is overwhelming, she still cuts. I have asked her to write in her journal when she has the compulsion to cut, hoping she can learn to take her pain out on paper rather than on herself. Yesterday, I received a copy of a page in her journal. "I have to cut on myself. Badbadbadbadbadbadbad. Hurt the body. Punish the body. I have to cut it and hurt it. My God, please help me. I am so afraid. Bad sexual feelings. Must die."

Ask Mary to forgive her violator? Her first major step will be forgiving herself. If she continues to do the work of healing, it will be months (at least) before she can even begin to address her feelings about him.

Forgiveness is not a quick solution. Asking people to forgive, without allowing them to go through a process that would perhaps lead them to forgiving, is to not understand how complicated violence, violations and betrayal are and how deeply traumatized we are at our very cores.

The theme of a recent television show was forgiveness. A woman had forgiven the young man who had murdered her son. Astonishing! Under what circumstances could a mother forgive her son's murderer? The teenage boys had been best friends. They had been drinking heavily, began arguing and it happened. A moment of drunken insanity. The teenager immediately pled guilty. The complicated, agonizing, overwhelming feelings a mother would have over her son's senseless murder are incomprehensible. She couldn't acknowledge the young man's remorse, grief, or his prayer for forgiveness. It was months before she saw him at the trial. She realized he was all alone. No one was there to support him. He was overcome with grief over what he had done.

It was many more months before she responded to a letter he had written, expressing his anguish and guilt. In future months, as she worked through her process of grieving and accepting the death of her son, she was finally able to make a connection with the young man in prison and then begin to acknowledge his feelings. In time, she was able to forgive, due in great part to his repentance, but that required a process over a long period of time.

What is repentance? "Repentance, if it is real, will be painful. Like a plow, repentance tears up the ground, breaks up the clods, uproots weeds, and prepares the soil for new planting..." (Arnold, *Seeking Peace,* p. 150)

Many times, during a question and answer period, someone will say, "In the Bible it says you should forgive 70 times 7." When this happened in Seattle, a very shy, young woman stood and, without any introductory remarks, she said, "Luke 17:2—But who so shall offend one of these little ones who believeth in me, it would be better for him if a millstone were hanged about his neck and that he were drowned in the depth of the sea." And she sat down. I tried not to smile. When I looked up the first verse in the Bible, I found Luke 17:4, "If your brother sins, rebuke him *and if he repents* forgive him."

In the Gospel of Matthew, Peter shows true repentance after he had denied Jesus three times the night before the crucifixion. When he fully realized his betrayal of Jesus, he went out and "wept bitterly."

I could have forgiven my father if he had wept bitterly. That means from the depths of his being. Not a cursory, "I'm sorry," although he never even said that. Some perpetrators can roll those two words off their tongues, but there is no repentance.

The same healing could have happened with my mother. She once said to me, "I love your father, but I hate what he did to you." She could have been saying, "Are your tulips blossoming?" There was no feeling at all behind her words. My sister, Gwen, had told me many times that she had pounded that sentence into my mother's head. She had told her that she *must* say those words to me and so she did. As she recited the words like a robot, I felt pain and rage. Not one ounce of despair or repentance accompanied those empty words.

Dr. Judith Herman writes, "Folk wisdom recognizes that to forgive is divine. And even divine forgiveness, in most religious systems, is not unconditional. True forgiveness cannot be granted until the perpetrator *has sought and* earned it *through confession, repentance, and restitution."* She continues, "Genuine contrition in a perpetrator is a rare miracle." (Herman, *Trauma and Recovery,* p. 190)

As I was confronted again and again by people urging others to forgive, no matter how the perpetrators had responded, I kept turning to Nelson Mandela. He became the stumbling block to my belief system. He is one of the men I most admire. Jailed in South Africa for 27 years for his political beliefs, he should have been filled with bitterness and an uncontrollable need for revenge. Yet, he forgave. But was it as simple as that? Did Nelson Mandela just walk out of prison and say, "I forgive?" No. He said, "…before perpetrators can be forgiven, there first needs to be an honest accounting and a restoration of honor and dignity to victims; the facts need to be fully acknowledged in order to heal the wounds of the past. Only then can there be genuine forgiveness." (van der Kolk et al, *Traumatic Stress,* p. xxi)

Two thousand years ago, Jesus proclaimed he was the Son of God. He performed miracles. He forgave people, "Go and sin no more." But when Jesus was dying on the cross, he didn't say, "I forgive you." He said, *"Father,* forgive them…" Perhaps some crimes are so heinous we leave judgment or forgiveness to God. *Thy* will be done.

If you are a well-intentioned religious leader, therapist, loving family member or friend, please do not judge us on whether or not we forgive our perpetrators. It is not anyone's right to ask us to forgive. Forgiveness is a personal decision that might be made soon, in the future, or never. Please consider the *further damage* you inflict by telling us we must forgive in order to find peace of mind or to be a "good person." *At our most vulnerable time,* when we are feeling so guilty and bad, *you may exacerbate those negative feelings* by asking us to do something most of us are incapable of doing, at that time. Forgiveness is a process. It is as individual and as personal a decision as we may make in our lives.

3. *"Why didn't you tell me?"*

Please never ask, "Why didn't you tell me?" It's important that you know the answer so you will never ask that question. The answer is: because children don't tell. Most children don't tell. Most adults don't tell.

Last year, I flew in a small plane, during a scary thunderstorm, from Chicago to a city in Indiana. The presentation went well and after a 45-minute question and answer period, people lined up to talk with me for over two hours. After I spoke to the last survivor, who had been sitting on the far right just watching for almost two hours, it was after 11:00 p.m.

As I walked into the foyer, Sandy, the woman who had booked me, was extremely rude. I wasn't prepared for her rudeness. I couldn't imagine what I might have done to cause it. I learned why from Paula (who worked with Sandy), when she drove me to the airport at dawn the next morning. The second I got into the car, Paula said, "I need to explain what happened last night. Sandy has been a therapist for 25 years. When you asked survivors to stand, her husband stood. She was dumbfounded. He had never said a word to her. She was humiliated, crushed and angry that he would stand, publicly, when he had never even told her. She was misdirecting her anger at you."

Several months and many presentations later, I addressed a professional conference in New Jersey. As I was leaving the ballroom, a woman ran out of a breakout session and said, "My husband stood today. I never knew. He had never been able to tell anyone." I immediately began to try to help her understand the dynamics. I said, "You know that the person he is most terrified to tell, is the person he loves the most. Our greatest fear is that the person we love will reject us." I wanted to put his public standing (after decades of keeping a secret) into some context that would not make her feel he hadn't trusted or loved her enough to tell. But she interrupted and said, "I know all that. I really do. I'm just so grateful that he has finally been able to let go of this secret."

Recently, I received a letter from a program chairperson in a large mid-western city where I had spoken. She told me that one of the women in attendance finally felt the courage to disclose to her husband of 38 years. "Unfortunately his response was one of disbelief." My heart aches for her. This is why so many survivors are afraid to tell. Her worst fear had come true. Her husband did not believe her. Even if he should come to believe her in the weeks and months to come, his initial response was devastating and something she may forgive, but never forget.

Questions to *not* ask are: "Why didn't you tell me?" or "Why did you tell her and not me?" Most of us need a great deal of encouragement and huge amounts of internal courage to disclose. Many survivors feel a strong motivation to stand when I ask them to, during a presentation. It is an unexpected moment where they are encouraged and supported to let go of the secret. I then ask those seated next to a person who has just stood to turn and say something to them. I suggest that if they can't think of anything to say, "I'm so very sorry" would be appropriate.

What would be another response? Recently, while getting my hair cut, my hairdresser, Kathy Hallinan, told me something very healing her surrogate aunt Loretta had said to her. Kathy was one of 1,100 people in the greater Denver area who came forward for help and support immediately after my story became public. The following year the Miss America Pageant called to say that NBC was going to do a special on five former Miss Americas. The focus of the special would be what we are currently doing with our lives. They asked if I would I like to be one of the five. I naturally said, "Yes." I told NBC I would talk about the impact of childhood sexual abuse and, during my segment, I wanted to have three survivors tell their stories. I knew it would be an incredible opportunity to give them a chance to "go public." I called Kathy. (She had told me that she had been sexually violated by more than one male family member.) When she said, "Yes," we both knew what a scary experience that would be for her— to say on national television that she was an incest survivor.

The program was aired during prime time. Recently, when Kathy was at a large family gathering, Loretta said, "I wish I had known, Kathy, I could have helped you." Loretta was not angry or hurt that she hadn't been told, she was merely sharing her sadness that she hadn't been able to help. Kathy told me that those words had held such power for her. Even though she was 40 years old when her aunt said this, they were incredibly healing words. There is a major difference between, "Why didn't you tell me?" and "Oh, how I wish I had known…"

4. "Why didn't you say 'no'? Why didn't you cry out?"

Please never ask those questions because *we don't fight back* when it is someone we know, respect, love or fear. We stay silent and as adults and most of us blame ourselves because we *didn't* fight and scream. Millions of us stay silent and shamed. Millions of us still have that primal scream inside of us—a scream buried so deeply in our core that it is inaccessible…but we know what it sounds like…we know what it looks like…and it's always there.

"Children often describe their first experiences as waking up to find an adult or sibling exploring their bodies with hands or mouth…Society allows the child one acceptable set of reactions to such an experience. The child victim is expected to forcibly resist, cry for help and attempt to escape the intrusion. By that standard, almost every child fails. The frequent reaction is to feign sleep. Most often children will quickly go into a shock state and be frozen. Most children are so shamed that they have no choice but to try to hide, even if the only place to hide is somewhere deep inside their minds. Children often learn to cope silently with terrors. It is necessary to recognize that no matter what the circumstances, the child most often feels no choice but to submit quietly and keep the secret. People who seek to use children quickly discover that: needy and dependent children are even more helpless to resist or to complain." (Summit, *Child Abuse and Neglect,* p. 183)

What is true for girls is also true for boys; "Male victims are just as helpless and even more secretive than females." (ibid.p. 180)

I was one of many survivors who went to see Barbra Streisand in the movie, *Prince of Tides*. I was in the throes of recovery and when I realized childhood rape was at the heart of the story, it became difficult for me to breathe. When the young boy was raped, I could barely contain the pain I felt. When he screamed the primal scream, I could feel the emotion in the core of my being. This is an example of how a child who is terrorized by an unknown intruder might react *but* a child who violated by a loved one or trusted adult almost always stays silent, internalizing the screams. As adults, in recovery, we try to unearth them. One artist, Ariel Orr Jordan, has been able to capture the primal scream that lived within me.

5. *"Why are you talking about this now? This happened decades ago. Let it go. Move on."*

Charles Rangel, the Democratic U.S. Representative from Harlem, went into the Army at age 18. When he was sent to Korea, he said, "We saw people dying. We saw bodies all around…before we got to the front lines, trucks were going by and we saw GI's in the same uniform that we were wearing stacked up just like you stack wood. We cried. For the first time, death looked like we did." Ninety percent of the men in his unit were killed.

50 years later, President Clinton selected Representative Rangel to go back to Korea to commemorate the 50th anniversary of the war. He said, "…until I went back to Korea, I realized *God had allowed me to*

block it all out. True, I would have some nightmares but not that often. There weren't that many people I would see who would remind me of the war and *I wanted to forget the pain* and the mistakes that my country made in sending so many untrained reservists into harm's way. People who were never trained for military maneuvers were sent to the front line. It was called 'the forgotten war.' But when, 50 years later, they said we had to *celebrate that, then all of the bitterness came up just as though it were yesterday."* [19]

The Girl Scouts of Denver recently honored outstanding women. I was complimented to be among them. When Carlotta LeNier, one of the nine Black students who integrated Central High School in Little Rock, Arkansas, was also selected, I was thrilled to meet her at the awards event. She is an elegant, proud, dynamic, successful woman. She *is* the definition of heroine. She confronted terror each day knowing that enraged, irrational people were going to scream at her, spit on her and threaten to kill her. She endured this the same year I won Miss America.

I asked her how she survived the terror of knowing she could be murdered. She said the impact didn't really hit her until many years later when she was in her *40's. S*he was telling students about a white policeman who would call her family at night and warn them about where the danger would be the next day. She said, "When I told the class what had happened to him, that he was shot to death, I was thrown back into the terror of that time. I found myself overwhelmed with flashbacks and emotions I hadn't fully acknowledged as a young teenager."

People can be very judgmental about how long it should take one to "get over it."

Susan Smith strapped her two little boys into their car seats and rolled the car into a lake and drowned them. Her former husband, David, was left to grieve for his precious boys. In a recent interview, he said that the 5th anniversary of their death was the most difficult. [20] Would anyone question why he couldn't just "get over" the murders of his sons or would one honor his strength in going on with his life. Why was the 5th anniversary more difficult than the 1st or the 3rd? We

---

[19] Tim Russert, April 2001

[20] *Oprah,* May 22, 2002

grieve and heal in different ways. There is no timetable for healing and there should be no judgment of how and when people grieve.

"Most people are in their 30's or 40's before they go into therapy to try to understand their dysfunctional behavior and/or relationships. As children, most of their energy was consumed by trying to cover up the abuse and look good. Until people feel safe and capable of handling the intense feelings of shame, anger, betrayal, and pain, their energy will go into defenses to keep it buried. It is only when they can no longer hide the symptoms that are seeping out into their current life or when their lives are more settled that they go into therapy." [21] Of the more than 8,000 letters and tens of thousands of emails I have received and answered, most are from women between the ages of 35 and 50.

Why do the feelings come back decades later to invade and, too often, shut down our lives? A long time Denver columnist wrote accusingly, soon after my story became public, "One can only wonder why she is making these allegations *now!*" If my family and friends didn't say it, they also wondered it, *"Why are you talking about this now?This happened decades ago. Just let it go."* These comments exacerbate our pain. Please know that our time frame is "normal." When we are forced to bury our memories and feelings as children, they usually erupt during mid-life, and we go through a stage of needing to talk about it over and over again. I know this was one of the most difficult parts for Larry. I don't know why he didn't cry out, "I just cannot listen to this one more time." When survivors ask me how long it will take, I always have the same answer, "It takes as long as it takes."

When we were neither heard nor known as children, healing involves finding a lost connection to our "selves." We need to feel empathy and compassion from loved ones. If we disclose to you, please don't start any sentence with the word, "why."

6. *"We think it would be better if you didn't discuss this with anyone else."*

If these words are said, this is what we, survivors, hear: "We are ashamed of you. Don't tell anyone." How significant people in our lives respond to the sexual violations we endured plays a major role in our recovery process.

---

[21] Personal conversation with Sharon Lions, psychotherapist, 2002

When I was asked to be the banquet speaker at a fundraiser for a Children's Advocacy Center in a mid-western city, I accepted immediately. Significant money can be raised when corporations purchase tables. Significant education can occur when executives from the business communities attend. It was also the city where Alicia, a survivor I had been corresponding with for five years, lived. She was in her late 30's. She had been violated when she was seven by a 16-year-old boy who lived nearby and she was still overwhelmed by shame.

I knew there would be local newspaper coverage and that would give me an opportunity to bring Alicia to another level in her healing process. Once there is enough internal and external support established, sometimes the best way to address terror is confront it directly. Alicia's secret and shame were keeping her trapped in dysfunction. She had been doing her individual therapy and corresponding with me, but she still felt she was carrying a shameful secret.

Remembering that it was the front-page newspaper articles that finally freed me from shame—by having everyone know "my secret"—I hoped Alicia would agree to be in a picture with me. I believed she was ready and her therapist and I would be there to support her. The next morning the two of us would be in her local paper together and she would no longer have a secret. How supportive the community would be of her would help determine whether or not she could begin to let go of her shame and realize, in every cell of her being, that it was not her fault.

When I called and asked her if she would come to the press conference before the banquet and be in a picture with me, she responded immediately with one word, "Yes." I felt such joy inside. She was going to walk right into her terror.

She called me back the next day. "I called my parents. My mother said, 'I really don't think you should do this, Alicia, and your father agrees with me. There is no reason to bring attention to this.'" Her parents had sent her a very clear message, "We are ashamed of what happened to you." Which means, to her, "We are ashamed of you." I was holding my breath as I responded, "What have you decided to do?" I exhaled as she said, "I would like to be in the picture with you."

When Alicia joined me at the press conference, I asked her if she would want to share her story, if a reporter asked. I wanted to be sure she was ready to do this. She was ready.

The following morning, there was a picture of the two of us and two separate articles—one centered on "my story" and why the Children's Advocacy Center was so important to the community and the other story was on what had happened to Alicia. It turned out to be an incredibly healing experience for her. Friends of hers even disclosed to her that they, too, had been sexually violated and had never told anyone. Some went on to tell her how courageous they thought she was by coming forward. Her shame began to melt.

Another of the many examples survivors have shared with me involved a young woman who, after working with her therapist, decided she was ready to have a meeting with her parents and her adult siblings to confront the family secret. The eldest brother had molested her and her younger siblings many times during their childhoods. She wanted to talk about the wall that existed between all of them and why she and her brothers were struggling in their adult relationships.

She knew the conversation would be difficult for all of them but she also knew how much healing could occur if the family finally confronted the truth. She had prepared and was ready for her parents' initial disbelief and denial. She was not prepared for their question, "You haven't told the Weavers, have you?" (The Weavers were long time friends of the family.) She was stunned that her parents were more concerned about what their friends would think than what had happened to their children.

When Jennifer was thirteen, I came home one afternoon with one of the few books then available on incest. I told her how much anxiety I had had when I paid for the book. How embarrassed I felt. Jennifer responded, "Why, Mom? You didn't do anything wrong."

One day Jennifer and I were in the car together, driving to the Denver jail to bail out Mike, one of the street kids I was working with. Jennifer said, "Mom, why don't you tell Mark and Mike about what happened to you? They think your life has always been easy—that you've never had to overcome anything." I said, "Because, if I told Mark and Mike, then maybe they would tell their friends and then maybe the boy you are dating would find out and then his parents would find out and they wouldn't want him to keep dating you." Jennifer said, "Well, then, Mom, I wouldn't want to go out with him."

I know, now, that this would have been remote but it's another example of how terrorized I was about anyone knowing. Jennifer's complete acceptance of me—especially at an age when teenagers are struggling for their own identities and so want their parents to be "cool," played a major role in my healing process.

Please never send the message to a survivor that "It would be best to not talk about this to other people," because we hear your words very clearly: "We are ashamed of you."

7. "Why did you do this to your/our family?"

When my story became public, a good friend called and said, "Why did you want to ruin your father's reputation?" My first thoughts were ones of guilt and then I thought, "Wait a minute, who did this to the family? Who brought this shame to the family? My father did. My mother didn't protect us. She didn't keep us safe. It is not my job to quietly carry that shame or to protect the ones who are responsible."

A reporter asked, "Did your mother know this was happening?" I responded, "It went on in our home for 18 years." The reporter asked again, "But did your mother know it was happening?" And I responded again, "It went on in our home for 18 years." Finally, I said, "If incest had gone on in your home for 18 years, do you think you would have known about it?"

I can never remember a friend or stranger saying, "You must feel so betrayed by your mother because she did not protect you for 13 years. How could she not protect you for such a long period of time?" Unfortunately, the sentence I heard time and time again was, "This must be so difficult for your mother." The message I heard was, "Look what you are doing to your mother." Please don't fill our buckets with one more drop of guilt. Our buckets have overflowed for too many years.

Many children recant because they are told, "Look what *you have done* to your family" or "Why did you have to tell; now your whole family is shamed." The truth is, someone should be ashamed and it isn't the child. How can we ask children to carry this burden *and* protect the family? This is not a child's responsibility nor is it the responsibility of the adult survivor to keep this secret. The *only* way to stop abuse from continuing and the *only* way to heal is to speak the truth.

In her book, *Must I Turn the Other Cheek?*, Dr. Ducharme wrote, "Recently, after a high ranking member of the clergy acknowledged molesting several boys, many people were *angry at the victims* for bringing up the past and destroying this religious man's career! Incredible? Not at all. This type of thinking is common. Many people want to believe the person in 'power.'" (p. 20)

Then how do we stop domestic violence, sexual assaults and incest? How do we change something if we don't even know that it is happening? We will never stop the sexual violations of children until society understands how pervasive and life changing it is. Should I have denied the newspaper report and said, only, that my father was the outstanding business and civic leader that most people believed him to be? That I'm sure incest only happens in "those" families? That my mother protected me and kept me safe? We can't change what we don't believe to be true and I never, ever want any child to go through the nights I did.

There was a front-page editorial commentary in one of our Denver newspapers recently. The article made one simple statement, which was, in essence: "Honor thy father and thy mother—no matter what." I picked up the phone to talk with the religious leader who had written the article. He was in a meeting so I sent a short fax. A very short fax. A one sentence fax: "Would you ask me to honor my father?" He faxed me back, "That is a compelling question. Please call me." I called. He was in another meeting and I was leaving town. I faxed him again. "Your response requires a simple yes or no." He never responded.

When I testified before a Family Violence Congressional subcommittee, I closed my remarks by saying, "The Commandment should read: 'Honor thy children and they, in turn, will honor you.'"

Chapter 24 – Why Don't Children Tell?

Most children don't tell. Most adults don't tell. It's usually because of overwhelming shame. It is not until mid-life that most people disclose. Many survivors carry their secrets for decades.

A woman, 73, wrote, "This morning, I read your story in my Santa Barbara newspaper. I picked up the phone and called my best friend. It was the first time I had ever told anyone. I have cried all day. Tonight, I have never felt as emotionally exhausted…or as peaceful."

It is also excruciatingly difficult for men to disclose because, too often, boys abused by men are afraid they will be called gay or questioned as to why they weren't able to defend themselves.

As a young boy, Carlos Santana, the Grammy winning guitarist, was taken over the border from Tijuana, Mexico, by an American called "Cowboy." For two years, Cowboy bought him presents and molested him several times a week. Carlos was 48 years old before he entered therapy. "After years of inner torment, Carlos, now often in tears during his sessions, was finally able to deal with the embarrassment and guilt. With his long-buried secret finally out in the open, Carlos began the long, painful process of coming to grips with how his childhood horror had impacted every aspect of the rest of his life." (Shapiro, *Back on Top,* p. 206–207)

Another man told me, "I was in my late 30's before I finally had the courage to tell my best friend. He laughed and said, 'Hey, you were just getting it early; you lucky guy.' Until now, I never spoke of it again."

This message was brought home to me again when I was working out recently. While I was lifting weights, I saw a muscular, handsome man, who looked to be in his 40's, looking at me. As I turned toward him, he said, "I've seen you here many times and I've always wanted to say something to you. I'm going to say it today. You're my hero." I'm sure he expected me to just say, Thank you, but he had opened the door to conversation and I walked in. "Thank you." Short pause…"May I assume it is your wife or daughter?" The look on his face made it clear that he had not anticipated a conversation. He struggled to say just two words, "No, me." How could I not have known? I said, "I'm so sorry. So very sorry." Slowly, I continued, "Who was your violator?" He was stunned by my question. He instantly backed up a step and said, "Whoa," which I interpreted as meaning, "How could you possibly ask me that question?" I said, "Please forgive me for asking. I didn't mean to intrude. I ask the question because that was the question that changed my life."

He didn't answer and I didn't press him. I respected his right to set that limit but I didn't want to let him go. His shame was so overwhelming, I had to try to bring him another step in his healing. "Have you told your wife?"

"We're getting divorced."

"Do you think this played a role in your divorce?"

"I'm angry and depressed. I'm a black belt in karate. I want to fight all the time."

I said, "You don't have to live this way. You fight because you couldn't fight when he or she…"

He interrupted me, "They."

I tried not to look horrified but I always am by what is done to children. I continued, "When *they* assaulted you?"

I knew it was risky to ask another question because he was not liking this conversation, but it seemed obvious he had never told anyone. My resolve to keep him "speaking the words" was heightened. "And you thought you should have fought back? How old were you?"

"Ten."

I said, "Please, drive by an elementary school and see how big a ten year old is. Then ask yourself if that little boy—and he will be *a little boy*—could have fought them off. There was nothing you could do. You were a little boy. It was not your fault." And then I said once again, "You don't have to live this way." If he only remembered one sentence from our conversation, I wanted it to be *that* sentence.

He said, "I really didn't think you would ask me so many questions." I said, "I'm sorry but I ask because I know you don't have to live in anger and depression. You can work through it."

He said, "Thank you" and turned to walk away. I said, "One more thing…I have a problem recognizing faces. There's even a name for this disorder. (I smiled.) If I see you again, I may not recognize you. All you have to do is say, 'We spoke a few days ago' and I'll know you."

The following Sunday, I went at exactly the same time, hoping to find him again. I didn't even know his name. All I knew was that he was sexually assaulted by "them" when he was 10; that he was consumed with anger and that he was getting a divorce. I searched the large facility several times during the hour Larry and I were there. Each successive day, I looked for him. Finally, one day when I reached the top step leading to the weight room, I saw him directly in front of me, working out on a weight machine.

I walked over and said, "Hello." He said, "I thought you weren't going to remember my face." I said, with a smile, "You *wish!*" I continued, "I produced a video I'd like to have you see. I live four blocks away. May I put it outside our back door tomorrow for you to pick up if you're going to be working out again?" He said, "Yes, thank you."

Several minutes later he found me in a different room and said, "I could pick it up today." I said, "I'll have it there in thirty minutes."

On the video, *Once Can Hurt a Lifetime*, men and women look directly into the camera, without shame, and share how they, too, were violated as children. I especially wanted him to know about Anthony Smith who had been raped with a broomstick, by five boys, while he was living at Boys Town. Because he had done so much of the work of healing, he could stand before the camera, finally, without shame. I knew Anthony and others on the video would help my new acquaintance know that he was not alone and that it was possible to let go of the shame and find peace. I put a note with the video, telling him that I had produced *another* video that might be important to him. I gave him my unlisted phone number, hoping to at least learn his name and perhaps even have another conversation.

He picked up the video but he didn't call. A week later, he came into the workout room Larry and I use most often, where the treadmills are located. In the years we've been working out, I had never seen him jogging on a treadmill. I wanted him to know that he could be in the same room with me without my trying to engage him in conversation. He would know that the next move would be his. There were machines available on both sides of him. I merely said, "Hello! It's nice to see you again," and I walked by him to a machine farther away.

The next day, we left for our summer vacation. I knew he would look for me every time he entered the workout facility because I was the one person he did *not* want to see and, yet, I was the one person he did want to see. My hope was that he would hear the words, "You don't have to live this way," again and again. Six weeks later, when we returned, he said to me, "It's good to see you again. I'm in therapy and I would love to see the other video."

The good news is that the pain can end. The bad news is that recovery is an indescribably agonizing process. Most people do not choose recovery until they hit the wall. That was true for me.

Knowing how difficult it is for adult men to disclose, one can only imagine how difficult it is for adolescents. Research showed that, of those studied, "None of the abused adolescent boys had ever told their primary care providers and *only 15%had ever told anyone."*(Holmes and Slap, *Journal of the American Medical Association,* p. 1859) Most other studies report similarly low rates of disclosure.

For a teenage boy to come forward and report sexual abuse by other boys takes incredible courage. ABC news reported that Zeke Hawkins, a 16-year-old student at the elite Massachusetts private school, Groton, had come forward because he had been sexually assaulted by other students. While several boys restrained him, others "ripped off some of his clothes, licked him, grabbed his genitals, and digitally penetrated him…He said he was attacked 10 to 15 times." Two years later, he told his parents and then school administrators. His mother said, "Instead of applauding our son for his moral courage in the face of such pain and embarrassment, the school questioned his credibility and downplayed his allegations."

At least three other students came forward to say that they, too, were sexually assaulted by other students. A spokesperson for Groton said that "despite the allegations, the accused students were 'good kids' and were not a threat to anyone's safety. They said the accused boys were disciplined, but because of privacy laws, they could not give specifics."

What is astonishing to survivors is not that it took Zeke two years to come forward but that he was able to come forward at all. Many of us are in our late 30's to 40's before we disclose our secrets.

When Zeke saw that nothing was being done and that the boys were still going to school, he stood up at a school assembly and told what had happened. His explosive story threw the school into a crisis and Zeke became "the enemy of the state." Many teachers and students were furious at him for embarrassing the revered institution. Feeling lonely and isolated, he left Groton and graduated from a public high school.

And we wonder why children don't tell.

"In a study of 1,200 college students, 26% acknowledged being sexually abused *before the age of 13* and yet only 6% reported it. Most children do not tell until many years later." (Ronai, *Journal of Contemporary Ethnography*, p. 406)

In my communication with thousands of survivors, I have found that the major reason children and adults don't tell is because of the shame they feel but, of course, there are other reasons. Some survivors have an experience that triggers a compulsion to disclose. One of the most intriguing personal experiences I've had with this was with Carey Davis. Carey is Jennifer's best friend. When they were 13 years old, Jennifer asked me if she could tell Carey about my childhood. Recently, Carey told me she went home that same day and told her mother, Mary Ellen Anderson. She and her mother have always had a close and loving relationship and they talked for hours. Six years later, my story of incest was reported on the front pages of our Denver papers over many days. Once again, Carey and her mother discussed the impact of sexual abuse. Several years later, Carey married and gave birth to a son, Quin.

When Quin was nine months old, Mary Ellen told Carey what had happened to her. A man broke into Mary Ellen's home and raped her. Terrorized her. Devastated her. He emotionally crushed her while Carey, *then nine months old*, was sleeping in her room.

As close as Mary Ellen and Carey had always been, and as many opportunities as Mary Ellen had to share this devastating experience with Carey, she, I'm sure subconsciously, chose the same exact time in Carey's life, when *her son* was nine months old, to finally disclose the rape.

Recently, when I asked Mary Ellen if I could use her name in this book, she said, "Please use my name and my story, if only to give another woman her voice. Carey and I agree that using our names gives another layer of integrity about feeling no guilt, no shame."

Most children will stay shamed and silent until millions of us tell four or five loved ones or friends that we, too, were sexually assaulted as children. Only then will America begin to understand how pervasive childhood violations are, how the assaults have devastated our lives, and why we hold on to the secrets for as long as we do.

It is my fervent hope that children and adults will begin to let go of their secrets, but we can't expect them to unless it's safe to tell.

Chapter 25 – Is It Safe to Tell?

Is it safe for children to tell? Only if you and I make it safe.

Recently, on a network talk show, I was asked to look into the television camera and say, "If you are a child being sexually violated, tell someone now." I couldn't do it. I just couldn't say the words because for too many children, it is not safe to tell.

A group of adult survivors were interviewed. The average age of the first sexual violation was six years old (Roesler and Wind, *Telling the Secret)*. Those who told a parent before age 18 encountered the following parental reactions. (Some experienced more than one of the listed responses.) Their parent was:

Angry with them (42%)

Blamed them (49%)

Ignored the disclosure (50%)

Became hysterical (30%)

Children have to feel safe to tell the truth. A child who faces rejection, shaming, guilt, anger, ridicule or disbelief will deny or rarely tell, especially if the parents act as if this is a horrific problem in *their lives* rather than responding to their child who is in need of help and protection.

"The average child *never tells*….the majority fear they would be blamed or that a parent would not be able to protect them from retaliation. Many children who sought help reported that parents *became hysterical or punishing or pretended that nothing had happened."*(Summit, *Child Abuse and Neglect,* p. 181)

"Adolescent boys who disclosed sexual abuse felt pressured, threatened, or rejected after the disclosure. They also experienced *parental blame and punishment and regretted having disclosed."*(Holmes and Slap, *Journal of the American Medical Association,* p. 1859)

On the news recently, a man said that when his cousin told his mother that he'd been sexually abused by their priest, she hit him across the face and said, "Don't you dare say anything like that again." He said, "I had been abused by the same priest but after seeing what happened to my cousin, I knew I would never tell…and I didn't until I was in my 40's."

Many children who tell, when their violator is a family member, later recant and say it never happened because the family will not believe or accept what the child has said. When the caseworker asked these children if they would report again, "*Almost 100%* said "No." The outcome almost always ended up being more devastating to the *child* than to the perpetrator." [22]

In one study, "Those who told immediately or very shortly after the abuse occurred *and were believed and supported* showed relatively few long-term traumatic symptoms. Those who either did not tell (typically due to fear or shame) or who told and then encountered a negative, blaming, disbelieving or ridiculing response were classified as extremely traumatized." (Hindman, *Just Before Dawn,* p. 87)

On *60 Minutes*, the mother of a boy who had been sexually molested by his priest "25 or 30 times," said, "Tom didn't tell me until he was 29 years old. I thought I'd fall out of my chair. He said, 'The nuns taught us in catechism that we musn't say anything bad about priests. If we did, we'd go to hell because they represented God.' That's what makes this crime so despicable." [23]

Unfortunately, for most children, it is still not safe to tell. If that's true, then is it in the best interest of the child for you to report suspected child abuse to the authorities? I wish I could give a simple "Yes" answer to that question but it wouldn't be true.

Molly, an eight-year-old girl I dearly love, asked her teacher to listen to a cassette she had brought to school. After school, when the teacher listened, all she heard was a child screaming and screaming. The next day, Molly told the teacher she recorded her father beating her younger brother. Without telling Molly, the teacher called social services. When Molly went home, she found that social services personnel were taking her parents to an emergency crisis center to be interviewed. The children were taken, as well. Within a short period of time, the parents were released. The first words Molly heard were from her mother, "Look what *you* have done to this family!"

Three examples from the most recent report from The United States

---

[22] Personal conversation February 19, 2003, with William Marshall, MD, professor emeritus of psychology and psychiatry at Queens College, Canada

[23] *60 Minutes* -April 21, 2002

Department of Health and Human Services show that the system *does not work for most children:*

• Only 25% of the children who were *seriously harmed* had their abuse investigated by Child Protective Services. (pp. 7–19)

• Less than *19%* of the child abuse reports submitted by hospital and mental health agencies *were investigated.* (pp. 7–23)

• Only 4% of suspected abuse cases, reported by childcare workers, were investigated. (pp. 7–25)

By whatever standard you use, the conclusion of this report is simple:The current system is not working. [24]

What happens to too many children whose reports *are* investigated? Molly's teacher never warned her that she was going to tell the authorities. How did Molly feel when she arrived home only to find the authorities were there. How could Molly not have felt violated...again? No wonder, two years later, she had no words after being raped at age ten.

Perhaps the following poem, written by a 12-year-old girl, best describes how too many children feel after they tell.

Promises, Promises

**I asked you for help
and you told me you would
if I told you the things
my dad did to me.
It was really hard for me
to say all those things,
but you told me to trust you—
then you made me repeat them
to fourteen different strangers.**

**I asked you for privacy and you
sent two policemen to my school,
in front of everyone,
like I was the one being busted...**

[24] U.S. Department of Health and Human Services, 1996

I asked you for confidentiality
and you let the newspapers
get my story.

I asked for protection,
you gave me a social worker
who patted my head
and called me *Honey*.

She sent me to live with strangers
in another place,
with a different school.

I asked you for help
and you forced my Mom
to choose between us
She chose him, of course.
She was scared
and had a lot to lose.
I had a lot to lose too,
the difference was,
you never told me how much.

I asked you to put an end
to the abuse
you put an end to my whole family.
You took away my nights of hell
and gave me days of hell instead.
You've exchanged
my private nightmare
for a very public one.

Credit: Hindman, Jan, *Just Before Dawn*,
Excerpts from a poem by Cindy,
Edited by Kee MacFarland, p. 18

If children entrust us with their secrets, don't we at least owe them
honesty? If we don't tell them we are calling the authorities, we betray
their trust and become complicit in their continuing betrayal.

After addressing a national conference for the Department of the Army, a pediatrician said, during a question and answer period, "I always report." I responded, "Please make that your *first* call. Two weeks later, you need to call and ascertain what happened to that child because the system isn't working very well. Each of us needs to follow up to help make the system more accountable."

In most instances, I'm sure social workers are committed to doing the best job they possibly can. Too often, they have far too many cases to even begin to handle them efficiently and compassionately.

Children's Advocacy Centers give me hope. They are being established in communities throughout America. Now, rather than taking children to a hospital emergency room or police station, they are taken to a center where they are physically examined only once by a physician who is an expert in the field of childhood sexual abuse. In addition, the child is interviewed by one qualified professional, who is trained and accepted as a child abuse expert, rather than being questioned multiple times by a social worker, policeman and psychologist. The interview is videotaped so that a judge or attorney can witness the original, and only, interview. The center's goal is to be sure the child feels as safe and secure as possible under the circumstances. This is an important first step toward making it safe for children to tell...but there is still much work to be done.

Is it safe for adults to tell?

Unfortunately, in too many instances, disclosing, even as an adult, compounds the original trauma. Too many of us learn the devastating truth: it is not safe to tell.

For example, when Oprah was nine, she was raped by her 19 year-old cousin. She didn't tell until she was 39. Sadly, the person she told, blamed her. [25]

No matter what reactions adult survivors receive, they are making it safer for children to tell by coming forward with their stories of childhood sexual abuse, educating communities that if one in three to four girls and one in six boys are being violated, it is happening in their community, their block or even, perhaps, their home. As adults disclose long held secrets without shame, children will begin to know that perhaps they, too, can come forward and be believed and

---

[25] *Oprah*, August 11, 1999

supported in their healing process.

Chapter 26 – Do Children Lie?

"Is the child lying?" This is the question that is always asked. Why don't we ask the other equally important question, "Is the perpetrator lying?" Does anyone believe a father, an older sister or a Boy Scout leader would really answer, "Yes, I have raped my daughter for years," or "Yes, I violated my younger brother for five years," or "Yes, I have molested over 100 Scouts."

Do Presidents of the United States, U.S. Congressmen or Bishops lie?

1. "I am not a crook." (President Nixon)

2. "I did not have sexual relations with that woman…Miss Lewinsky." (President Clinton)

3. "I did not pay hush money to keep a survivor quiet." (Bishop of Brooklyn)

4. "I did not have a sexual relationship with Chandra Levy." (Congressman Condit)

Why did these men in prestigious positions finally admit to the truth? Because there was *proof,* and for no other reason.

1. Nixon: Tape recorded conversations from the Oval Office. Nixon denied again and again any involvement in Watergate and most people believed him. When his most intimate conversations were heard, there was indisputable proof that he had lied.

2. Clinton: A semen stain on Monica Lewinsky's dress. After her reputation had been trashed, without the stain on her dress and the DNA testing, who would have believed her? But it was Clinton who had lied.

3. Bishop: An article in the *New York Post* caused the Bishop to finally admit that he *had* approved paying hush money to a survivor in return for a signed agreement stating the survivor would never talk about the sexual abuse by his priest. [26]

4. Congressman Condit: The truth surfaced during a three-hour FBI interview of Condit's former bodyguard.

---

[26] *New York Post,* March 15, 2000

"Hell hath no fury like a man exposed."—Catharine MacKinnon

Who is more believable—a child or an adult? "Rather than being calculating or practiced, the child is most often fearful, tentative. If a respectable, reasonable adult is accused of perverse, assaultive behavior by an uncertain, emotionally distraught child, most adults will fault the child. Disbelief and rejection by adult caretakers increases the helplessness, hopelessness, isolation and self-blame that make up the most damaging aspects of child sexual victimization." (Summit, *Child Abuse and Neglect,* p. 178)

Do children lie? Of course children lie, but it is extremely rare for a child to lie *about sexual abuse*. It is far more likely that a child *will deny* having been sexually violated because of shame, fear or other reasons. If they do disclose, they will almost always *tell just a little bit at a time*. They will test the water, watching and listening for subtle clues as to how their potential listeners will respond. Then they decide whether or not it is safe to tell the full story. If they take the risk and tell, and then receive a negative response to their disclosure, many will recant.

A study was done with 116 *confirmed cases* of childhood sexual abuse. Of those cases:

Only 11% of the children disclosed *without minimization or denial.*

72% displayed a pattern of initial denial of the abuse followed by "tentative" disclosure.

22% of the children retracted their reports. *92% of these reaffirmed the complaint, later.*

Disclosure appears to be a *gradual process* involving denial and minimization followed by "tentative" disclosure in most cases.

(Sorenson and Snow, *Child Welfare,* pp. 3–15)

"...*Denial is predictable* and does not mean that the sexual assault did not occur. Once a child has disclosed, *denials almost inevitably follow*...." (Dziech and Schudson, *On Trial,* pp. 56–57)

I know that for myself, if I had told, I would have run back to the lawyer or the judge and said, "I lied. I lied. I made it up," so terrorized would I have been by my father and so unprotected would I have been by my mother.

Some children feel so ashamed and scared that, when asked, they will reject any accusations. They are simply too fearful of retribution by the perpetrator or family members, as seen in the following quotes:

"Most victims not only do not disclose, they strongly deny it happened when confronted," said the FBI agency's expert on child molestation, Kenneth Lanning. "Fear, guilt, and embarrassment keep children quiet." (Boyle, *Scout's Honor*, p. 101)

"A Boy Scout who was molested by his Scoutmaster first told police nothing happened, and later took the witness stand to explain that he lied 'because I was embarrassed and because I thought it was my fault.'" (Boyle, *Scout's Honor*, p. 101)

If a child does disclose to you, take the disclosure seriously and investigate further, because research has shown that false accusations are extremely rare. A study by Jonathan Horowitz, a professor of clinical psychiatry at Boston University Medical School, found 5% of the reports could not be validated.

Two different studies reported the fabrication rate to be 2% or less. (Kempe Center and CPS in North Carolina) Further, "most children who did misrepresent their complaints had *understated* the frequency or duration of sexual experiences...Very few children, no more than 2 or 3 per thousand have ever been found to exaggerate or to invent claims of sexual molestation." (Finkelhor, *Sexually Victimized Children*)

If a child does fabricate the accusation, it is important to discern why. *Something* has caused this child to say this to you. What would the motivation be to make such an accusation? Are there any other signs in the child's mood, behavior, statements, or physical appearance? What kinds of experiences would a child have had, to make up a story involving activities he or she had never been a part of or had any exposure to?

Too often, when a child "tells," her mother does not believe her and blames her for lying and for causing such trauma within the family. If charges are pressed against her father, the child is often blamed for causing him to go to jail, their loss of income and the shame that will be brought on all of them. Her father rages at her for lying and other siblings side with their parents and blame her. What child would not recant?

I understand why even adults recant. My mother said, "I don't believe you." I was 53 when my story became public. A friend said,

443

"Your poor mother. This must be so difficult for her." Another said, "Why did you want to ruin your father's reputation?" A columnist wrote, "What this really boils down to is one person's word against another's, or in Marilyn's case, her word against her father who is dead and cannot respond." For many people, I needed a sister to validate me. That stunned me. It still does. I understand why children and adults recant.

Ross Cheit, an associate professor of political science at Brown University, was sexually violated as a boy, by William Farmer, the administrator of a summer camp he attended. When he was 36, he wanted to find out if there had been others who had also been sexually violated. He located 55 people who had attended the same camp during the same time period. Within a month, he found a man who completely verified his experience.

Another man said that Farmer tried to get him into his sleeping bag once but he didn't get in because he realized the man was naked. Cheit said that a few days later, he received a letter from the man saying, "I feel really sheepish. What I told you the other night wasn't true. I did get into the sleeping bag. I just wish that the other story were the true one." (Freyd, *Betrayal Trauma,* p. 184) If he was so ashamed as an adult that he had to lie, it's not surprising that he didn't tell as a child.

A few weeks ago, a young man stopped me in my neighborhood supermarket. He had heard me speak at his university nine years ago. After having been sexually violated by his grandfather from age five to twelve, he was placed with a foster mother, who had been told about the boy's abuse. She began sexually violating him when he was 13. When he turned 15, the foster mother and the boy began having arguments and the foster mother began to worry that he would reveal the sexual abuse, so she planted a rumor throughout the neighborhood that the boy had raped her. With his head down, this young man, now in his late 20's, said to me, "I was bigger than she was. Who would have believed me?" I responded, "I would have."

Our bumper stickers say, "Believe the Children," and research validates the same compelling message.

Do perpetrators lie?

Almost always. 36 convicted sex offenders admitted to, on average, two sexual assaults each. After a polygraph test, inmates disclosed an average of 165 victims *per offender*. (Ahlmeyer et al, *Sexual Abuse,* pp. 123–138)

At age 11, Anna Dalton thought that if she reported her father, the police might talk to him and he would stop. She wrote, "At the trial, my love for my father was so strong, I said I lied so they would let him go. I just knew we would go home and be happy. Instead, I was told I was going to be sent to a mental hospital. My father stood up in the courtroom and said the court was doing the right thing by putting me in a mental hospital after the terrible lies I had told about him." Her father later admitted the incest. [27]

Research was done with 23 rapists involved in a sex offender program. "Arrest records indicated the rapists had an average of 1.9 offenses. During the program, the 23 rapists admitted to committing: *319 child molestations* and *178 rapes.*" [28]

When I asked two friends to read this book when it was in rough draft form, both cautioned me to not use statistics so outrageous that I would lose credibility. I, too, found the numbers above so difficult to believe, I did more research and found corroboration. It is important to note that when it comes to people's experiences, no two studies will come out exactly the same. If you asked three groups of 50 people, "Do you smoke cigarettes?" each of the three groups would have different numbers of people responding, "Yes." What is absolutely clear, however, is that perpetrators vastly underreport their victims.

I continue to be astonished that many people tend to believe adults, rather than children. In all my experience, I can only think of a handful of violators who admitted their guilt. Without proof, how many perpetrators are going to say, "Yes. I did that." What proof can be found in a child's small bedroom with a mother who has turned away?

Before questioning whether or not a child is lying, stand back and wonder why a child would say something like this. And then wonder if the adult is lying…"I did not have sexual relations with *that woman*— Miss Lewinsky."

---

[27] *The Healing Woman,* October 1993, p. 3

[28] *Sexual Abuse in America* by Freeman-Longo & Blanchard, 1998

Chapter 27 – Three Simple Gifts Every Child Should Be Given

One

"Every child needs someone who would die for him." That sentence underscores our most basic need. Richard Wexler, head of the National Coalition for Child Protection Reform, went on to say, "A shift worker at an orphanage does not fill that role." [29]

A guest on a recent *Oprah* show stated it this way, "A child needs someone whose eyes light up the second he walks into the room."

Two of the most agonizing realizations I had during my recovery process were that my father never loved me—that he only used me—and that my mother was incapable of acknowledging, let alone empathizing with, my pain. Prior to those realizations, I believed I could earn my father's love. I knew he would love me if I had the lead in the high school play. I knew he would love me if I graduated from college with Phi Beta Kappa honors, skied on my high school and college ski teams, played the piano at my graduation, cooked his favorite soup, walked his dog, rode wild horses and became as fine a speaker as he was. I just knew, with each accomplishment, it would be "the one" that would win his love. It was heart-stopping to finally grasp the fact that you can't *make* someone love you. How devastating it is to finally accept the fact that you can't *earn* someone's love…not even your mother's love…not even your father's love. It cannot be bought or earned. Love is a gift.

On a recent *Oprah* show, David Pelzer talked about how much he yearned for his mother's love. His mother beat, tortured and nearly killed him in one of the most severe cases of child abuse in California history. When, at age 12, he was mercifully put into foster care, he said of his mother, "What is it going to take to get her attention and have her wake up and love me? It took me many, many, many years to discover that no matter what I say or do, she will never love me." [30]

What child or adult doesn't want to hear the words, "I love you," from a parent. Peter Fonda, son of Henry and sister of Jane, wrote in

---

[29] Iimse, *Rocky Mountain News*, 2001

[30] *Oprah*, January 30, 2002

his autobiography, "My Dad could sit on a bus and talk to strangers for hours but for Jane and me, he never knew how to fill the space. The more we demanded, the further he withdrew. And we misinterpreted that as anger." It was devastating to Peter that his father had never told him that he loved him. Peter wrote, "One day I called my father up and said, 'If I had enough ego, I would write a scene for Henry Fonda and I would direct it. The name of it would be 'I Love You Very Much, Son.'" His father said, "Uggggh!" and hung up the phone but it was the beginning. Peter kept trying different approaches and before long, his father was saying, "I love you" at the end of every phone conversation.

Months before his father's death, Peter flew home to see him. His father was weak and frail. When Peter was ready to leave, his father "Grabbed me by my shoulders and said, 'I love you so very much, son.' He hugged me so hard I could feel his pacemaker. I said, 'I love you, Dad.' Then I got into my car and wept like a baby." (Fonda, *Don't Tell Dad,* pp. 441–443)

Larry had a similar experience with his father. His father is one of the great men I have known, but it was difficult for him to articulate affection. He had never told Larry that he loved him. It was not unusual for men of his generation to find those words difficult to speak. Larry began ending every telephone conversation by saying, "I love you, Dad." His father would not respond with those longed for words. Finally, when Papa was in his early 80's, Larry made a passing remark about it to his father. After their next telephone conversation, when Larry said, "I love you, Dad," his father responded, "I love you too, son." When Larry put the phone down, he was unable to speak. He had huge tears in his eyes. After that, his Dad couldn't stop saying it. Whenever Larry would say, "I love you, Dad," his father would say, "I love you too, my son. I love you too, my son."

I will always be grateful to Larry that he didn't constantly say, "How could you love your father?" It would be years before I would understand that to not believe I loved him and he loved me, would be to open the floodgates to the feelings of having no love as a child…from anyone.

Most children will do almost anything to hold onto the belief that their parents love them and, with rare exception, young children want to stay with their parents, no matter what the circumstances are. I was moved by a story in *USA Today*. A couple was going to adopt 10 children from the same family. Their mother was an alcoholic and would disappear for days. The children had four different fathers. When the children were discovered, they had lice. The youngest child was dehydrated and running a fever. An older child was stealing food to feed his siblings. The authorities split the children up and sent them to different shelters and foster homes. When one couple agreed to adopt all ten children, they knew the children would be overjoyed. They decided to give a pizza party. When they told the children they were going to adopt all of them, "Everyone was excited, but Juan had a question, 'What's adoption?' When this little boy, who was forced to take food out of garbage cans, realized he would never go back to his birth mother, he left the table. 'I found him in the hallway, crying so hard he was hyperventilating. He was grieving, and my heart broke for him…'" (Hellmich, *USA Today,* p. 1D) He couldn't believe that his mother loved alcohol more than she loved him. No matter what she had done to him, he wanted to go back to her, because she was his *mother.*

Most children, if given the choice, want to stay with their parents. Children want and need to be loved by a mother and a father. Loved by someone who would be willing to die for them. If the love exists, children know it; if it doesn't, they feel it.

Two

They want their parents (particularly their fathers) to be proud of them. One of the most memorable movies I have ever seen is *Spartacus*. I was a teenager when I first saw it. Kirk Douglas (the star who played *Spartacus*) was not just a movie star, he was a superstar. Years later, when I learned he was writing his autobiography, I expected the title to be, *Spartacus!*

The title he chose set the tone for his book, *The Ragman's Son.* Although he wrote about his life experiences, the central theme was that his father (who had sold rags for a living), had never told his son that he was proud of him. His father never said, "Good job." Not even after he became a major film star. He yearned, ached, longed for his father to give him even a crumb of approval. It never happened.

Barbara Walters interviewed Douglas just prior to the book being released. She asked him, if he could say just one thing to his four sons, what it would be. Douglas, charming and engaging, responded immediately with warm, loving comments. She then asked if he could say just one thing to his then deceased father, what it would be. The camera moved in for a close up of his face. His expression instantly changed from confidence and composure to tears flooding his eyes. He was visibly shaken and unable to speak. He could not answer. Having achieved superstar status, Douglas still had a huge hole in his heart because he had never felt his father was proud of him. (Douglas, *The Ragman's Son)*

Three

Children need the truth. Too often, it's easier to lie to our children because we believe it is in their, or our, best interest. We are usually wrong when we come to that conclusion. Until Jennifer was 13, I believed the truth would end our relationship. Fortunately, I realized how wrong I was to not include her in my life. It was one of the biggest risks I have ever taken but she had a right to know the truth.

Judy Lewis grew up knowing she was the adopted daughter of Loretta Young—one of the most beautiful and famous movie and television stars of the '30s, '40s and '50s. Judy knew that after her birth, she was placed in a group home for a year and then she was adopted by Loretta Young. But Judy kept hearing rumors that she was really the child of Loretta Young and Clark Gable. Finally, in her 30's, she confronted her mother. Her mother told her the rumors were true but she made Judy swear she would never tell anyone.

Judy had longed for her mother to legitimize her parentage by publicly telling the truth. Just before her death, when Judy was 65, her mother acknowledged that Clark Gable was Judy's father. Even though Clark Gable died before Judy could have her wish of hearing him say, "I love you," she said all the years of pain were suddenly washed away. The truth had set her free.

The famous 1970's comedian, Freddie Prinze, committed suicide soon after his son, Freddie Prinze, Jr., was born. Freddie, Jr. said, "I had a happy childhood until one day I realized I didn't have a regular family. About age eight, I started getting really angry because everybody else knew what happened to my dad and nobody wanted to tell me. One day, this kid got mad at me and said, 'My dad told me your dad was a junkie and shot himself.'" When he went to talk to his mom, she started crying. Finally, a friend of his father's told him the truth. Thereafter, Freddie said, "For years, I didn't trust anybody. It seemed to me that my whole life had been lies." (Rader, *Parade,* pp. 4–5) Family lies are destructive. Children want and need to know the truth.

Recently, President George W. Bush talked about his feelings when he was six years old and his younger 3-year-old sister was very sick. He said his parents were often away, taking his sister to different hospitals for treatment. Although he knew his younger sister, whom he adored, was very sick, he was never told how serious her illness was. When his parents came home one day without her and told him that she had died, he was inconsolable. He said he knew his parents kept the truth from him to protect him but he wished they had told him the truth, that she was dying. He wanted the truth even though he was only six at the time.

A dear college friend of mine told me that in her late 20's, while living in the South, her mother was diagnosed with cancer. Her family decided not to tell her how near death her mother was because my friend had young children and they thought it would be difficult for her to fly to New York to be with her mother. They decided to wait.

As she related this story, forty years later, every word my precious friend shared was agonizing but her next comment was almost unspeakable. I had never seen her cry. She said, "When they called, I flew immediately. I was too late. Mom died before I reached her bedside. I never got to say goodbye." The pain of that memory was not the pain of a wound that had healed. It was the pain of a wound that was as fresh as if it had been yesterday. The truth. We deserve to be told the truth.

Shortly after my story was in the Denver newspapers, I received a letter from a woman in her early 40's. The letter was filled with rage—rage at a trusted person who had raped her when she was only fourteen. She had never told anyone. I picked up the phone and called her immediately. She did not pick up. Her answering machine took my message.

I wrote to her and said I would like to pick her up and bring her to one of our large survivor meetings. I knew it would be huge first step for her to take. I also knew she would be shocked to see how many men and women were finally free of shame. With Larry meeting and greeting people at the door, calling many by name, it was truly unbelievable to survivors who carried the same shame all of us had only months earlier.

She left a message on my answering machine that she would attend the meeting. A friend would bring her. She didn't come. I called her the next morning and left a message. She did not respond. I wrote her.

She did not respond. Two weeks before the next survivor meeting, I left a message, asking if I could pick her up. She left a message that she would attend. A neighbor would bring her. She didn't come.

Days later, a neighbor became concerned when newspapers began to accumulate and no lights were on at night. The neighbor called the police. They found the woman dead. The police report stated that she died from a mixture of alcohol and drugs. That's what the police report said. What the police report did not say is that a trusted man had murdered her soul when he raped her as a child. It took a number of years for her to physically die but the cause was premeditated, first-degree murder of the soul.

She left three young, beautiful daughters. Now, almost ten years later, all of them are teenagers. They still do not know why their mother took her own life. No one in the family has chosen to tell them what I believe they need to know. The truth. It is very possible that the truth—that her soul had been murdered—would not assuage the teenagers' anger, believing as they surely do, that their mother had not cared enough about them to stop drinking. That doesn't justify why they should not be told. They should be told because it's the truth and it is their right to decide how to integrate truth.

To be loved; to know our parents are proud of us; to be told the truth. Three simple wishes. Three simple gifts every child should be given.

I have never been able to describe in words the scream I held inside for so many years.

An artist, Ariel Orr Jordan, captured the scream he knows all to well. Ariel was raped by his father from age three to age fourteen.

Chapter 28 – 11 Simple Ways to Keep Your Child Safe

Does it really matter if one research report tells us that one in three girls and one in five to seven boys will be sexually violated before the age of eighteen—or if another reputable study tells us it is one in four girls and one in six to eight boys?

What *is* important is that we *know* that millions of our children are being sexually violated *today* by fathers, grandfathers, sisters, brothers, step-parents, aunts, neighbors, baby-sitters, boy scout leaders, priests, coaches, strangers, and yes, even mothers and grandmothers.

Since we cannot always be with our children to protect them, what are *specific things we can do to help ensure their safety?*

1. Teach your children at every available opportunity that they can decide if and when they want to be kissed or touched by a friend or family member.

We should teach our children before they even learn to walk and talk how to have their own power and create their own boundaries. Your daughter, Becky, is ten months old. You are going to a large family dinner. This is the first time many family members have seen Becky and you want them to see how adorable she is. As you enter the house holding Becky in your arms, Uncle Bill comes running over and reaches out to Becky saying "Give Uncle Bill a kiss." You feel Becky pull back. You immediately say, "Bill, I don't think Becky feels like kissing anyone right now, but I'll plant a big kiss on your cheek!"

Becky has learned that she doesn't have to kiss someone she doesn't feel like kissing. This has *nothing* to do with Bill. He may be the kindest, most moral man in the family. This is only about Becky learning that she has power to decide whom she kisses.

You return to the same family event the next year. Becky is almost two. She dashes in and Grandma says, "Becky, come sit on Grandma's lap," and Becky says shyly, "I don't wanna." You chime in quickly and say, "I bet Grandma would love it if we sang the new song we learned the other day, I'll start and you join in if you want to." And you smile and sing the song. After a little time with Grandma, Becky might decide that she would like to sit in Grandma's lap. You let her wait until she feels comfortable and ready.

Later, when you are alone with Becky, you say, "You never have to sit on anyone's lap if you don't want to. You never have to kiss anyone you don't want to. I'm sure Grandma understood." Then you could say, "Let's sing the song again. Want to?"

You are not teaching your child to be disrespectful. You are teaching your child that she has control over her body, whom she kisses, whom she touches and who touches her. She has the right, even as a toddler, to say, "No!" This is equally important for your sons. If your sons also learn at an early age that they don't have to sit on anyone's lap—not even grandma's—until they feel comfortable to do so, they will be more empowered if a coach or priest or anyone in a position of trust tries to violate them. Moreover, because they learn that they can expect to have their boundaries respected, they may be more respectful with how they treat others' boundaries as teens.

Some of you may worry that I am suggesting that you teach your child to be fearful, stand-offish, or uncomfortable with affection. This is not what I am suggesting. Children need all the cuddling and affection we can give them. This is about letting them learn to trust their instincts and set their own physical boundaries with others.

2. Listen carefully to what your children say. Listen very carefully.

Adults have told me how they *tried to tell* their parents when they were children that they were being violated. I was especially struck by Ken, age nine, who told his mother that he didn't like camp and wanted to come home. At age 35, he still cannot understand why his mother didn't hear what he was trying to say i.e., that a camp counselor was violating him. I know that is illogical thinking but that's the way many children try to tell.

I am not recommending that you jump to any conclusion. I *am* strongly suggesting that if your son says, "Please don't ask John to baby-sit me anymore. I don't like him," you don't reply, "But he's your cousin. He loves you." Before you say those words, listen, really listen to what your son *might* be saying. It is very possible that John won't let him watch his favorite television shows because he feels they are inappropriate or that he makes him go to bed on time. It is also possible that there is something inappropriate going on that makes your son uncomfortable. Listen, carefully.

If you have the slightest concern, change the plan. Be sure you give your children the message in your words and actions that they can tell you anything and you will listen and help problem solve with them.

My sister, Gwen, asked for a lock on her bedroom door. It was Gwen's way of trying to tell Mother what was happening at night but Mother either didn't "hear" her or she ignored the plea. My father heard. He replied that there could be no locks on the doors because of fire danger.

If your child doesn't want to spend the night at a friend's house, listen. She may have a very valid reason for not wanting to spend the night in that house ever again.

Remember what Mary Tyler Moore (sexually abused by a close friend of her father) and Esther Williams (sexually assaulted by a young man who was an older brother figure) suffered. Oprah was raped when she was only nine by an older cousin and again at age 14 by an uncle. Drew Carey and Carlos Santana, Tab Hunter and Tatum O'Neal were molested as children. Natalie Cole (daughter of Nat King Cole) wrote in her recent autobiography that she had been sexually violated by "a male family member,"…as did Marie Osmond, Rosie O'Donnell and Muhammad Ali's daughter, Laila Ali. Deloris Jordan, Michael Jordan's sister, recently disclosed that she was raped by her father. Melissa Ethridge has said publicly that she was sexually molested by her sister.

Don't expect your child—ever—to come and say to you, "I don't want Sally to baby-sit because she is molesting me." You are not going to hear that. In the thousands and thousands of stories I have been told, I can think of only three times when children explicitly told their parents.

I *thought* that's what a woman on the plane, seated next to me, had said. A flight attendant came to talk with me after the meals had been served. She told me that her brother had violated her. The woman seated next to me overheard the conversation. After the flight attendant left, she said, "My daughter was molested when she was seven. She told me." "Really," I responded, extremely surprised. "I'm so sorry you have had that experience and I'm so grateful your daughter could immediately tell you."

She is one of the rare people who didn't seem to want to talk further so I went back to answering letters. As we were pulling into the gate, I had packed everything up and was ready to deplane. We were told there was a problem with the jet way and that it would be at least a fifteen minute wait, so I continued our conversation. "Would you tell me what she said to you?"

"Well, actually, I'm not the one she told. She began acting differently. She was angry and defiant. Her disposition changed so drastically, I had her see a therapist. *After about nine months in therapy*, she told the therapist that an older boy had molested her." Now it made sense. I'm grateful the jet way had problems. I would have gone on my way believing this child had done the unexpected.

When I spoke in Portland, Oregon, a young woman cried when she told me, "I begged my mom to not make me to go my uncle's house but I had to go anyway." Another said, "I cried every time I knew Meagan was going to baby-sit me." Parents ask me, "Why didn't my daughter/son *tell* me?" Children may try to tell in indirect ways. Listen…carefully.

3. Talk to every baby-sitter.

The first time I became aware of sexual abuse by baby-sitters was when I learned that a woman I know had been violated when she was seven, by a male, teenage baby-sitter. Although she is now in her 40's, the shame is like a huge cement wall that surrounds her.

Then Tom Arnold publicly spoke for the first time about having been sexually violated by a male, teenage baby-sitter.

Since then, hundreds of men and women have stood in line, after speeches I have given, to disclose to me that they too were violated by baby-sitters. I had no idea what a huge problem this was and continues to be. My mail confirmed the same heartbreaking, unimaginable information.

Research states how prevalent the problem is: "Although most perpetrators are boys or men, up to half of female perpetrators are teenage baby-sitters." (Holmes and Slap, *Journal of the American Medical Association,* p. 1859)

"30-50% of abusers are under the age of 18 years." [31]

In a study of female adolescent sex offenders, ages 10 to 18 years, approximately 70% of their sexual offenses took place while they were

---

[31] STOP IT NOW, Do Children Sexually Abuse Other Children? 1999

baby-sitting. The average age of the victims was *5.2* years. [32]

"An adolescent who wishes to engage in sexual experimentation may assume that fondling an infant will do no harm because the infant will not remember what has happened. This is not true. Infants can be traumatized, and they will manifest this through observable changes in their behaviors. Listlessness, prolonged crying, inability to be soothed, a refusal to drink or eat, and a lack of eye contact are classic symptoms of infant trauma." (*Protecting Your Children,* p. 154)

There is no question in my mind that a responsible parent must address this issue. It's one thing to believe it is important to do but it's almost unfathomable to contemplate what you would say to a teenager you trust implicitly. How do you say to a precious 16- year-old neighbor, "Please, don't molest my child." We would never say it that way but it is critical that we address it. So, what words could you use?

"We are so pleased to have you in our home. We have asked you to baby-sit because we know you will take good care of Amy and Charlie. We choose baby-sitters very carefully because our children are the most important people in our lives."

By opening the conversation with remarks similar to these, you have set the stage that this is an important talk—not something you quickly go over while putting on your coat and walking out the door. And this is an important talk! If you hesitate, ask yourself if you plan to have an important talk with your teenager when he or she begins to drive. I hope, as you approach this first conversation with a baby-sitter, my words will ring in your ears, "Even one sexually inappropriate experience can hurt for a lifetime."

I can promise you, there aren't 2% of all teenagers who know this. We cannot just hope their parents have taught them to never touch a younger child in an inappropriate way. We have to make sure they know the values and expectations in our homes.

As you ease your way into "the conversation," you might say, "There are a couple of things I'd like to go over with you." Talk about bedtime, television shows, emergency phone numbers, who is and is not allowed in the house, keeping the doors locked and...then, "We have talked with Amy and Charlie about 'good touches and secret

---

[32] Fehrenbach and Monstersky 1988, *Journal of American Academy of Child and Adolescent Psychiatry*, Decembers 1999

touches.' They know that any touching in areas their bathing suits cover, is not okay. And that 'secret touches' are not okay. We've asked them to tell us if anyone ever touches them in a way that is uncomfortable for them. It's very possible they would confide in you. Please tell us if they say anything that causes you concern or that we should know about. Here's a phone number where we can be reached. Don't hesitate to call us. Do you have any questions? Thanks again. Amy and Charlie are very excited you are going to be with them tonight."

If this is a person who has sexual behavior problems, we have put them on alert that our home is not a place to violate and if they do not have sexual behavior problems, we have helped them look out for our kids.

This conversation also applies to adult baby-sitters, daycare workers, preschool teachers, etc. We need them to know that we talk about what goes on with our children when we are not there; we also need them *to work with us* to enforce our personal and family rules.

My purpose is not to terrify you. My purpose is to urge parents to give at least the same concern to their children's sexual safety as they give their teenagers when they are learning how to drive. A car can irreparably injure a body; a sexual violation can irreparably harm a soul.

4. Be aware of what your child is doing on the Internet.

Many ten year olds have as much, if not more, knowledge about the computers and Internet than their parents have. If you know nothing about the Internet, ask a friend. Become knowledgeable and aware. Children are curious. Most pedophiles are very good at what they do and how they do it. They know how and where to find vulnerable children.

When I was in the post office last week, I saw a huge poster that said, "*One in five* children received a sexual solicitation or were approached over the Internet in the past year." (National Center for Missing and Exploited Children) Your child could be that one.

Will your child immediately move on? Keep reading? Respond out of curiosity? A recent survey may keep your inner dialogue from saying, "Not my child."

USA Today published a Boys & Girls Clubs of America survey of 565 people under the age of 18:

•34% said it is okay to meet someone they've been "chatting" with online for a long time.

•28% said it's okay to give their real name in a chat room.

•23% said it's okay to put their address and their picture on the Internet. [33]

Experts on children's use of the Internet strongly agree that a computer should never be in a child's bedroom. Locate the computer in a family room or area where you can easily notice and talk about what your child is doing. The best ways to protect your child are to be educated and involved.

5. Sometimes the most effective way of protecting our children is by empowering them to make the right decisions.

When Jennifer was a child, I believed I knew how to protect her. When she was in sixth grade, she went to a party. I knew the parents very well. They were one of the most respected and well-known families in Colorado. When she came home that night, she told me that beer had been available and that many of the children were drinking. I was astonished. Jennifer was eleven! I was suddenly confronted by something I should have previously acknowledged. I could not be everywhere to protect Jennifer nor could I trust the families she was with to not have beer or other substances available to eleven year olds!

I said to Jennifer, "I thought I could protect you from parties where liquor is available. I now realize that I cannot. You are going to have to make a decision right now—tonight—as to whether or not you are going to drink or smoke. It is a decision that will impact your life, at least through middle school and probably through high school and college. It is a serious decision." I have no way of knowing whether or not that very short discussion led Jennifer, now 31, to make what appears to be a lifetime decision to not drink, take drugs or smoke.

Another way to build self-esteem is to allow children to make age appropriate decisions. I've watched my niece and nephew, Debbie and

---

[33] Color and Ward, *USA Today,* August 15, 2002

Mac Griffin, empower their son, Chace. When Chace was eight years old, he told his parents that he wanted to change his name to Matt. When they discussed it with him, they realized Chace was very serious about it. So, on a certain date in August, we were going to start calling him Matt. Debbie didn't say, "Why in the world do you want to change your name?" She honored him as a person. She honored what was important to him. When the day came, Chace decided to keep his name, but Debbie and Mac were empowering him by honoring decisions that he was making as a child.

I called him one day when I was writing this chapter and I said, "I have a simple question for you. "Do you believe you are successful?" He said, "Yes. I do." I said, "And why do you believe that?" He said, "Because I get good grades and I was chosen as a student council representative." I couldn't stop smiling for the rest of the day. Yes, he is successful and one of the reasons he is, is because he has been treated with respect and empowered to make some of his own decisions.

I will never forget a dear friend of mine who asked me to address the Rotary Club of Dallas. It was during a time in my life when I was traveling at a frenetic pace. Sometimes two cities a day. I looked at the flight schedule and realized I could have a night at home with Larry and Jennifer and fly to Dallas on the first flight out the next morning. The only hesitation I had was that if the plane were cancelled, I would miss the luncheon. I called my friend and "ran it by him." This was his response, "I know you will make the right decision." He couldn't have said anything worse. Suddenly, there was *no doubt* what I would do. I called United and booked a flight for the night before.

Sometimes, when we give our children the complete responsibility for making decisions, they are more likely to make better decisions than if we tell them what to do. Of course, young children cannot be expected to make appropriate decisions without help, but the process has to start when they are very young. If we have taught them and been the best role models we can be, then we must stand by while they make their choices and then face the positive or the negative consequences.

6. Build your child's self image by positively acknowledging what he does right, rather than what he does wrong.

At the beginning of the school year, a teacher gave his students a personality test. He was then able to ascertain which students had low self-esteem. Those students became his targets for sexual abuse. Many priests, when searching for their next victims, choose boys who come to them for counseling due to their low self-esteem.

When I addressed teachers about how to motivate students, I always talked about Billy. Every teacher has "a Billy" in his class. Billy is in third grade. His assignments are usually late, his handwriting is atrocious—as is his spelling. For the first time, the teacher asks his students to write a short essay on any subject they choose. Billy can hardly wait to get home to start his essay. He knows exactly what he's going to write about. Dinosaurs. He knows all about tyrannosaurus rex. The next day, he hands in his assignment and cannot wait until his teacher reads it.

Billy is so excited when the teacher returns the assignments, but when he looks at his paper, there are big red marks on it, correcting his spelling, slashing through sentences with comments like "needs a verb—is not a complete sentence, etc." Billy feels ashamed of his paper and hides it. Before the class period is over, the teacher gives the same assignment, "Write an essay on anything that interests you." Billy can't wait to write about cars. He loves cars. Old ones. New ones. When he gets his paper back, there are all those red marks and slashes again.

When Billy is given his third assignment, he doesn't care very much any more. If only the teacher had written this on Billy's first paper, "No one has excited me about dinosaurs more than you did in this essay, Billy. We need to work on your spelling and grammar but you did a great job on the subject matter." (from a talk I heard Leo Buscaglia give.)

Again and again research tells us that pedophiles choose children who have low self-esteem; children who are vulnerable. Focus on what your child *does right* to build self-esteem.

After addressing a sales meeting, the president of an insurance company asked me if I would read a book he had written about his life and then write the foreword. When he was in junior high, he always found D's or F's on returned assignments. He hated writing reports and he hated getting them back. But one day he was given an assignment that really excited him: Trains. He loved trains and he wrote passionately. He said, "When I got my paper back, I couldn't believe

463

it. The teacher didn't give me an A. The teacher didn't give me an A+. The teacher, in large writing, gave me an A ++." He wrote, "That teacher did more for me that day than anyone, outside my family. I'm sure I didn't deserve it but I just kept staring at it and staring at it. For the first time, I began to have a glimmer of belief in myself."

If your child plays 99 notes on the piano right and one wrong, please comment on the 99 notes right and refrain from commenting on the one note that was wrong.

When Jennifer was in 7th grade, we had a surprise birthday party for Larry. It turned out to be a disaster. Larry loathes surprises. He has told me this for decades. That night I was reminded, "When someone tells you how much they dislike surprise parties, believe them." Listening and believing is important. I had made a decision that was not a good one! The next morning, as I was driving carpool, Jennifer said, "Mom, because of the party, I didn't get my Spanish homework done. Would you write an excuse for me?" (Her school was *very* strict about homework being done.)

I said, "No, Jennifer. You knew about the party. You didn't plan ahead."

"Have I *ever* asked you to write an excuse for me?"

"No, Jennifer, you haven't and yes I will, but I won't lie." Jennifer gave me a piece of paper and a pencil. When we arrived at the school, I wrote, "Please excuse Jennifer from her Spanish homework."

Her first class period was Spanish. Around one o'clock that afternoon, I received a phone call from her *math* teacher. "Mrs. Atler, I am concerned about the note Jennifer gave me today excusing her from her math test and her math homework."

I said, "You're not nearly as concerned as I am!" I called Larry at the office and told him about the note. She had obviously erased and added "math test" to the note. She had lied, betrayed—I'm sure we had many more words that day that would have described her unacceptable behavior. We had agreed on her punishment. It was severe. Something about being grounded, no phone, no television—the works!

When Jennifer opened the back door and started up the steps, I was waiting for her. As Jennifer reached the top step, I said, "Jennifer—it's about your math test and your math homework."

She burst into tears. She didn't start crying, she started sobbing. She ran back to her room and threw herself on the bed. I couldn't begin enumerating the *list* of punishments until she could hear me. As I waited for her sobbing to abate, I began to rethink what I was about to say and the message she would hear.

When she was finally able to stop crying enough so she could hear me, I said, "Jennifer you are the most special daughter. I can never remember you lying to me, disappointing me, embarrassing me. We are so proud of who you are. So proud. You've goofed on this one and you will need to talk to your math teacher and make it right with her but you have no problem with your dad or me. You are such a blessing to our lives."

I gave her a huge hug. When I left her room, I felt like jumping up and clicking my heels while crying out, "Yes!" I had come so close to giving her the wrong message, "You are a liar. You embarrassed us. You disappointed us." Her sobbing allowed me time to think about what I was going to say. Although there was no question that what she had done was wrong, I left *her* with the responsibility of talking with her math teacher, and I left her with the message, "You are a good child and we are so proud of you." That was the truth and I realized more than ever, that day, the power every adult has in molding how children think about themselves.

If my son played quarterback on his 5th grade football team and he was having trouble connecting with the running back, I would hope the coach would, during the half time, show a video in which my son had thrown a perfect pass and the running back had caught it and run for major yardage. I would hope the coach would show that ten-second play at least fifteen times until the boys were ready to go back into the second half with a winning pass imprinted on their minds.

For many parents, it is "learned behavior" to tell our children what they are doing wrong because so many of our parents chose that path. Instead, we need to listen to ourselves when we make comments to our children, and point out what they do right, so we can build their self-esteem.

Babe Ruth was asked, "What do you think about after you strike out?" He responded, "My last home run."

7. Never spank your child.

This point should be included in the one above because it also addresses how to build your child's self-esteem (which is key to empowering your youngster) but it is too important to not have its own heading.

I know. Your parents spanked you and look how you turned out. It's a generational thing.

Maya Angelou said, "We did what we knew. When we knew better, we did better."

When Jennifer was born, my mother said, "Don't pick her up every time she cries. You'll spoil her." I said, "That doesn't make any sense to me." She said, "I'm telling you. Don't pick her up. I didn't pick you up and after a while you stopped crying."

Now it made sense. If you don't pick up a baby when she is crying, the baby will learn that no one listens. No one cares. Finally the baby will stop crying. You have taught your baby that no one hears her. My mother's mother taught her that. Now she was teaching me. However, just because it has been handed down through the generations doesn't mean it's right.

When I was working with Mike (chapter 14), one of my goals was to bring his mother back into his life because he wanted this so desperately. During one of our meetings, his mother said, "I know you are angry with Mike for beating up Mark." I said, "Yes. I am." She said, "He grew up being hit. I hit him. His father hit him. His grandmother hit him. It's what he knew." Then in a remarkable show of courage, she turned to Mike and said, "I'm sorry, Mike. So very sorry."

I know the Biblical quote. "Spare the rod, spoil the child." The Bible also tells us that I can sell my daughter into slavery, Exodus 21:7. Exodus 35:2 states that someone who works on the Sabbath should be put to death. Another scripture says a rebellious child can be brought to the city gates and stoned to death.

In the 19th Century, under English law, a woman was property. A husband was allowed to beat his wife as long as the stick he used wasn't thicker than the circumference of his thumb. That's where the saying, "a rule of thumb" comes from. It is now against the law for a husband to hit his wife but it's not against the law to hit a small child.

In the airport recently, I saw a little boy hit a little girl. Their mother then whacked the little boy and said, "How many times do I have to tell you, never hit your sister." Where is the logic? Just be sure you stop hitting when your child turns 18, because hitting an adult is illegal.

A questionnaire was sent to the principals of all of Washington state's 376 private and 1785 public schools, regarding corporal punishment. The second major reason why students were hit by teachers was because the students had hit other students. [34]

The American Academy of Pediatrics has been very clear on this issue. It recommends a ban on spanking in schools. "Children usually feel resentful, humiliated, and helpless after being spanked." [35]

Richard Belzer, a television star, said, "During my childhood, a lot of people hit their kids, some more than others. My mother was quite heavy-handed in that area. Any kid who gets hit thinks he's not loved." (Seligson, *Parade,* p. 8)

Some people still believe it is okay to hit a child. I am stunned by the reason I am most often given—"My parents hit me. I hit my kids." Our children should view us as their safe place, not as people to fear.

Spanking communicates that hitting is an acceptable way to solve problems and that it is all right for a big person to strike a smaller one. [36]

Fifteen years ago, I tutored a precious 8-year-old boy. His father "whooped" him on a regular basis. Three weeks ago, the son was arrested for domestic violence.

When former Congresswoman Pat Schroeder asked me to fly to Washington, D.C. to testify before a Congressional subcommittee on Family Violence, I spoke with a leading congressman just prior to testifying. He said, "We hit our children. How else do you teach a two year old not to cross the street alone?" I was too stunned to stop myself from saying, "And tell me why your two year old is near a street alone?"

There is never a reason to hit a child. Never.

8. At every available opportunity, teach your child

---

[34] Grossman, Rauh and Rivara, *Pediatric Adolescent Medicine* 1995, p. 149.

[35] Samalin & Whitney, 1995, ERIC 2000

[36] Murray Straus, founder of the Family Research Laboratory at the University of New Hampshire, July 2002

about winning and losing.

Many children won't play unless they believe they can win. Many children won't run for office unless they believe they will be elected. Most children decide at an early age whether or not they are "successful." Winning is a part of the fabric of America. Children with low self-esteem are far more likely to be victims than children with confidence. How your child perceives himself can be influenced by the messages and conversations you have about this very important issue.

When I was giving motivational speeches to teenagers, I developed a short quiz for them to take. In one or two sentences, I would tell them about a person and then ask them if they thought that person was a success or a failure. Here are a few examples:

He wanted to write and illustrate children's books. His first book was rejected 54 times by different publishers.

As a child/teen, he drew very differently than other students. At the end of his first high school art class his teacher said, "You'll never learn to draw. Why don't you just skip this class for the rest of the term?" But in his late 20's he decided to write a book. It was turned down 54 times by different publishers. A friend of his at Vanguard Press decided to take a chance and, at age 33, Ted Geisel, better known as Dr. Seuss had his first book *And To Think That I Saw It On Mulberry Street* published. It sold over 300,000 copies. He wrote 43 other books, which have sold more than 400 million copies.

He wanted to be a world renowned movie director. He applied to the University of Southern California Cinema School twice and was turned down both times.

Oscar-winning Steven Spielberg's hit movies include, *Saving Private Ryan*, *E.T.*, *Jurassic Park*, and *Schindler's List*.

He wanted to become famous by sharing his wit and wisdom. In high school he flunked English, Latin, physics and algebra. His grades weren't good enough to go to college. Wanting to be a cartoonist, his drawings were rejected for his high school yearbook.

Charles Schulz once said, "I was a bland, stupid-looking kid who started off badly and failed everything." He learned art through correspondence courses, and worked as an art instructor at the Minneapolis Correspondence School. *Peanuts* became the most widely syndicated comic strip in history. When he died at age 77, Charles

Schulz was earning $30 million *a year* as a cartoonist.

He wanted to be President of the United States. He ran for political office seven times and was defeated each time.

Abraham Lincoln:

1832: Lost job. Defeated for legislature

1833: Failed in business

1834: Elected to legislature

1835: Sweetheart died

1836: Nervous breakdown

During the next 24 years Abraham Lincoln was elected only *once* to Congress and yet he was:

Defeated for Speaker of the House

Defeated for nomination of Congress

Defeated for Senate

Defeated for nomination of Vice President

Again defeated for Senate

Seven political defeats, really *nine* failures out of eleven tries. Was Abraham Lincoln a success or a failure? He was both.

In a recent poll, he was selected as the most outstanding President *ever* in the United States.

She wanted to be the #1 singer in the world. She joined a group which was eliminated on Star Search and then dropped from a record label before they had even released an album. Her father sold their family home to try to keep them going.

Beyoncé Knowles launched her solo career in 2003 with an international chart-topping single and a best selling debut album. In 2004, she won five Grammy awards and sang the national anthem at the Super Bowl.

He wanted to be a great scientist. He never graduated from high school and then failed the entrance exam when he tried to enroll in an Institute of Technology.

As we neared January 1, 2000, television shows spent endless hours debating who would be *the* outstanding person of the 20th Century. *Time* magazine chose Albert Einstein. His high school teacher told him he would never amount to anything. He left high school without graduating and then failed the entrance exam to the Institute of Technology. Later, when he submitted what he considered to be an important research paper to a well-known university, they rejected it as impossible. Einstein said that it was his determination and his constant focus on mathematical problems that brought about his remarkable theories. He read books on math with "breathless attention." He thought, constantly, about the mysteries of the universe. He is considered the greatest scientist of all time.

He wanted to compose music but became deaf at age 28.

Take a man whose whole life is music, make him deaf and you have a defeated man. Take a man who *lives only* for his music, make him deaf and you have Beethoven. Beethoven was only 28 years old when he began going deaf. Did he stop composing? No. He said, "If I can't hear the music in my ears, then I'll hear it in my mind." He composed *The Moonlight Sonata* just *thinking about* what it would sound like.

He wanted to play professional basketball, but was cut from his high school team.

Michael Jordan was cut from his high school basketball team, but went on to be, perhaps, the greatest player in the history of the sport.

They wanted to publish a comic strip. One wrote, the other drew. For six years they made hundreds of strips and for six years they were rejected by publishers.

Finally, a small publishing company ran Jerry Siegel's and Joe Shuster's comic strip. It was the first Superman story, which became the best-selling single comic strip in the world.

She wanted to write children's books. As a single mother, she couldn't afford a baby-sitter. She was on welfare and had to borrow money from friends. Her apartment was so small and cold, she took her baby to a coffee shop to stay warm and wrote while the baby slept.

J.K. Rowling, author of the Harry Potter books is one of the best selling authors in the world. She was only 31 when her first Harry Potter book was published. She rewrote the first chapter ten times. She writes every day. Many times for 11 hours. Always longhand.

Each of the men and women above has been both a success and a failure!

The time I find the concept of success or failure to be the most appalling is during the Olympic Games. Sports reporters go up to young men and women who have just won silver medals and ask, "How disappointed are you that you didn't win the gold?" The athletes have just placed number two *in the entire world,* and the reporters, by their question, are making it clear they weren't winners.

Teach your children *by talking back* to the television reporter. Say, "He just placed number two *in the entire world.* How dare you insinuate that he didn't win. Congratulate him. He just won, big time!"

Find everyday experiences to reinforce this message. Research has shown that people forget 90% of what you say to them in one week. They remember only 5% in two weeks. However, they recall over 60% of a message that has been repeated six times. To have only one conversation with your children is to not drive home the point. (Dave Johnson, The Power of Positive Intimidation in Selling, p. 37)

It's important to help your children understand what the words "success" and "failure" mean to them because how they think of themselves will determine, in great part, how they live their lives and how they are, or are not, empowered to protect themselves or seek help when they need it.

9. Who makes it a bad day?

Children need help learning how to take responsibility for their own happiness and peace of mind. We usually have the opportunity to determine the quality of our day. (I exclude traumatic experiences from this.) When Jennifer came home from school one day, I said, "How was your day?" She did not give her usual response, "It was a great day, Mom. A really fun day." Instead, she said, "It was a bad day, Mom. Pete teased me and teased me, saying things like I am a tall string bean. He really made me mad."

I responded, "I'm so sorry, Jennifer. No one has the right to tease you. I'm sorry that happened, but did Pete make you mad—or did you *allow* Pete to make you mad? No one can make you mad. You had a choice and you allowed him to make you mad. Can you think of one or two ways you could respond differently, if he teased you again?"

She wasn't jumping right in to this concept so I said, "Maybe say, I really am a tall string bean. I like being tall." Or…and I waited for her to think of something. She said, "Well, maybe I could just ignore him." "Exactly. It takes practice to allow someone's teasing to not bother you but I'll bet you can do it and when he sees you aren't reacting, he'll probably stop."

Most days, I must admit, Jennifer really didn't want to hear my, "Who made it a bad day?" philosophy. She just wanted to be heard, not instructed. I was mindful of picking the times when I would bring it up. It is a thin line between helping children to look at things in a different way and just validating their feelings. We have learned, in our family to say, "I'm just sharing…" if we want someone to *just listen* and not try to "fix it."

At first blush, helping children learn how to take responsibility for their own happiness by how they respond to daily experiences, may not seem to fit under ways in which you can help keep your child safe. However, this goes to the core of self-esteem and confidence and is a critically important ingredient in helping to keep children safe.

10. Talk to your children about how to avoid dangerous situations.

When Jennifer was growing up, I shared with her the wonderful experiences I had had as Miss America and when I was living in New York City, but I also talked to her about why (when I was the banquet speaker) I would not attend an after-the-banquet reception or party in someone's home. I had learned from experience after finding myself in too many uncomfortable situations when I was traveling alone. I told her about the night, in Detroit, when the producer of a show I was in, told me that all the cast members were meeting in his room right after the show. (All of us were staying in the same hotel.) When I arrived, he said no one else was able to make it. I had allowed myself to be in a potentially difficult situation.

I also learned I would never attend a party or reception away from the banquet area because I could find myself needing a ride back to my hotel. Experience had taught me to avoid even the possibility of that happening.

When your children are young, start a game that can lead into different situations as children become teens. The game is, "How could you solve this?" You're coming out of the supermarket and you say to your ten-year-old. "Let's play the game. How would you solve this? When we get to the car, I realize I locked the keys inside. What should I do?"

Your child may say, "Call Daddy and ask him to bring another set of keys." Your response could be, "That's a great idea, that's worth 10 points. What if Daddy were out of town?" Your child may say, "Call Aunt Suzie and ask her to go to our house and bring us the other set of keys." Your response, "Super idea, another 10 points for you." "What if Aunt Suzie isn't home?" And the game goes on (the goal is to get 50 points or higher). Let your child give you a challenging question next. Make it fun and take turns. What the game is teaching a child is that there are a number of ways to solve a problem.

When your daughter begins dating, she has been educated to know there are several ways she can approach difficult situations. If her date is making her feel uncomfortable, for any reason, she can call a cab (she should have money with her always), call you…and then ask her what other ways she might come up with.

Boys need the same kind of guidance with safety and problem solving skills. Teaching our children to look ahead and foresee situations can give them an invaluable resource—their own ingenuity.

11. What you do and how you live your life are crucial.

I had been addressing specific things parents could do for almost a year before I realized I was leaving out *the* most important thing a parent can do to protect her or his child. In fact, if every parent did just this one thing, child abuse would plummet.

No message you ever give your child will be louder or clearer than the way you live your life. If you are a parent and you allow your spouse to hit you or slap you or speak to you disrespectfully, you are teaching your children how to be victims and/or victimizers.

"Why wouldn't my son tell me?" Because he saw every day of his life that you could not or would not defend or stand up for *yourself*. Why would it ever occur to him that you would or could stand up for him?

It was, without question, the most damaging thing my mother did to me. She allowed my father to treat her any way he wanted. When he yelled at her to, "Sit down, God damn it, and shut up," she would do just that without one word or gesture of protest. And then she would tell me—and everyone she knew—how happy she was and how perfect her marriage was. Never once did she say, "I will not allow anyone to speak to me that way."

When the 7-year-old son of Warren Moon, a famous football player, called 911 and cried, "My daddy's hitting my mommy," there was still hope for a positive lesson for that child…until his mother refused to press charges. When the state pressed charges, she claimed *she* was the one who hit the large, muscular, menacing quarterback. Although the police had taken pictures of her battered face, she still claimed it was all her fault. The medical examiner said her assault was indicative of "manual strangulation." At the scene, she said, "He beat the shit out of me." There were no visual injuries to the football player. Years earlier, there had been "three assaults on Mrs. Moon…The last of the assaults occurred in front of the children when Mr. Moon struck Mrs. Moon with a closed fist."

I believe her son learned that you can beat your wife and she will take responsibility for it. Neither acted as a responsible parent. Both role modeled for their son that it's okay to beat your wife and the mother of your children. I believe the children also learned how to be victims: you just take it.

That's what my mother taught me and I learned the lesson well. It was just too high a price for any child to have to pay.

"Children don't have to be the direct victims of family abuse to be harmed: repeated exposure to parental fighting can enmesh kids in a cycle of violence that sets them up to be either victims or perpetrators of abuse. Fighting between parents can be very harmful, even if the children are not the victims…*violent behavior is learned.*" (Peterson, *USA Today*)

Many women who are victims of domestic violence believe their children don't know they are being hit or battered. Kim Cini, the director of Denver's Safe House reports, "A woman who is being abused by a boyfriend should be aware that her children likely know about it—even if she's certain that they were asleep or in another room when the incidents occurred. The majority of abused women who come to Safe House Denver say their children didn't see what was going on. Yet when questioned 92% of kids say they did indeed know. And if your kids tell you they're being hit, listen to them. We need to believe our children." [37]

I believe the most important way you can protect your children, is to never allow yourself (man or woman) to be a victim. If someone speaks to you disrespectfully, teach your children how to speak up for themselves by saying, "Maybe you could rephrase that. Could you say 'I would appreciate it if you would…'" Or be blunt. "Please never speak to me disrespectfully."

Using the word "I" when responding to an abusive situation can be very effective. Rather than saying, "Don't *you* ever speak to me that way," try, "I feel hurt and angry when I am spoken to that way and I won't stand for it."

I always had a voice when I was in my role as a professional speaker. I wouldn't think twice about walking into a ballroom and asking that the table setup be changed because a different configuration can directly impact how cohesive an audience feels. But in my personal life, I had no power. I remember being on an airplane in the deep South in August. It was very hot outside. The minute I boarded the plane and sat down, I was frozen. The air conditioning was on high. I was too shy and voiceless to ask the flight attendant for a blanket. So I froze. Empowering myself (in my private life) took many years…and many baby steps.

One day I said to a tennis coach, "I would like to work on my backhand today. I'm feeling comfortable with my forehand—so just backhands today?" We began hitting back and forth. He was hitting me forehand after forehand. He had completely ignored my request. For someone who has never felt powerless, I'm sure it seems like a simple thing to just say, "Backhands only please," but for someone who has no voice and no personal power, it is a huge deal. I finally had the courage to say, "Could we work just on my backhand?" Again, he hit me some backhands but many forehands, as well. As we were picking up balls, I went to the net and said, "I only want to hit backhands. Just backhands. Please." He finally got the message and I went home feeling 12 feet high. I had finally been able to stand up for myself. It was a major baby step.

Another day, I was standing in a very long line at the supermarket. There were only two checkers and at least six people in each line with

---

[37] *The Denver Post,* January 9, 2000

full carts. I decided to take another baby step. I approached one of the checkers and said quietly, "Would it be possible to call another checker?" She said, "Sure." Within a minute, another line was open.

It didn't seem possible that I could be so powerful in my professional life and so powerless in my personal life. When a reputable doctor on 5th Avenue in New York raped me during a medical procedure, I didn't call the police and press charges. When I lost jobs as a result of my refusal to go along with sexual harassment, I didn't start the fight for women's rights in the workplace.

I firmly believe all of this is directly related to my being brought up in a family that taught me I did not have the right to demand personal respect. It took me years of agonizing healing work to find my strength and power. I had to search for loving relationships and then have the courage to let the unhealthy ones go.

Our children watch us and learn from us. I believe what they need to see is that we will work hard to find and maintain respect, dignity, honesty, encouragement and love.

We can even teach children who are not our children. One afternoon, late in my recovery, I was walking through a park. Young boys, seven or eight years old, were playing soccer. As I neared them, I heard one of the coaches screaming angrily, "You are so stupid, Andy. Why can't you get it right just once?" As I walked nearer, the berating of the child continued and was so abusive, I started running toward the coach. When I was within twenty feet of him, I said (yelled would be more accurate), "Don't you ever speak to that boy that way again." The coach looked at me as if he couldn't believe what he was hearing or whom he was hearing it from. He said, "What did you say?" I said, "Don't you *ever* speak to that boy that way again." As I repeated it, every little boy stood in stone silence. He said, "Lady, this is none of your business." I said, "Yes it is my business." Suddenly the other coach (it appeared as if they were both fathers of players) broke in and said, "Okay. We're here to have fun. Now let's get back to the game." The coach and I glared at one another one more time, and then I walked on.

Andy knows that one adult would stand up for him and that the coach was wrong to treat him that way. The first signs I had of finding my voice were when a child was being mistreated. I was incapable of just standing by.

One of the unique conversations I have had about childhood sexual abuse occurred while I was flying to Los Angeles. I was answering survivor letters during the flight. I knew the man sitting next to me was occasionally reading what I was typing on my laptop. As I was closing down my computer for landing, he said, "Forgive me for reading some of your writing. What do you do?" I said, "I'm a child advocate." I knew that didn't really answer him so I said, "I'm an incest survivor and I'm flying to Los Angeles to be a guest on a television talk show—helping people understand how prevalent child sexual abuse is."

I quickly realized that explanation had stopped him cold. It was fascinating to see his mind immediately drift away. I could almost see him turning back the clock to a time in his childhood. He said, "I had an experience once. I was a Boy Scout. One night, my Boy Scout leader crawled into my tent and began touching me. I said, 'Go away.' And he did. He left." I was stunned by his recollection. I had never once had an adult tell me that, as a child, he had been able to say, "Go away." When I asked him how he had the power to do that, he said, "My parents let me make my own decisions so I became empowered at an early age and I knew my dad was in another tent not far away." I said, "Did you tell your dad?" The man hesitated for a moment. "No." "Did you *ever* tell your dad?" "No." Even though he had been unable to tell his father what had happened, he had been able to stand up for himself.

No message we give our children will be louder or clearer than the way we live our lives. If we allow a spouse to hit us or speak to us disrespectfully, we are teaching our children how to be victims and victimizers. When we stand up for ourselves and others, we role model ways our children can empower themselves. A positive self-image is the most potent protection your child can have.

Chapter 29 – You Have Power!

You have the power to create change! Mothers Against Drunk Drivers began with one mother. Laws that forced colleges and universities to disclose crime rates on their campuses began with one couple. Most of us will not make nationwide changes, but each of us can do something. All our voices are important.

What can one person do? Write a letter or an e-mail. When I was in my early 20's, I was the television spokeswoman for AT&T. After the show, I would receive fan mail. Public relations executives told me that one letter represented hundreds of people who had not taken the time to write. I was surprised by how important they considered individual letters to be.

I began to understand the power of one. The result, for me, was to write letters of appreciation, especially to people who likely never received pats on the back. Once my story became public, I began to write letters to educate society about sexual abuse. Almost every day, in every local newspaper, there is an article or editorial that needs to be challenged, corrected or, occasionally, reinforced. One letter can make a difference.

If writing a letter seems daunting, or you aren't sure what to say, use one of the following letters as fodder and then use research in the book to support your comments.

Here are four examples of letters I have sent. They are responses to real situations.

When we were vacationing in Southern California, a local news reporter told about Cameron, a seven-year-old girl who was missing. Police, family members, neighbors literally hundreds of people were helping to search for her. Each night the story was updated and each night the hope of finding her diminished. Finally, on the eighth night, the television reporter said, "We have good news about Cameron. She's been found. She was kidnapped, raped and locked in the trunk of a car. She has been examined by a doctor and we are happy to report she is fine."

This is the letter I wrote to the reporter:

Dear Reporter:

I join you in being grateful that Cameron was found alive but she is not "fine." Unless reporters begin using accurate words to describe the horror she has been through, many people will continue to believe that rape is just "a bad twenty minutes" or a bad experience "but now she's safe and she can move on with her life."

We must educate people that rape isn't just a bad experience. Rape murders the soul; rape destroys trust. Rape is I-have-never-felt-safe-since-that-night trauma. Rape is don't-ever-touch-me-no-matter-who-you-are trauma. Rape is I-must-lock-all-the-seven-locks-on-the-doors-before-I-go-to-bed trauma.

My father incested me as a child and teen. He has been dead for 14 years; I am now 65 years old. Time has not healed the imprinting of not feeling safe—ever—anywhere.

Cameron is not fine. Her terror may last a lifetime. Not fear, terror. Terror so extreme she will be unable to speak or yell or think. It is mind numbing, body paralyzing. It is possible, if not probable, that no one can help her feel safe ever again.

Only when society can begin to comprehend the destruction of a spirit when a child or teenager is terrorized, do we have any hope of putting our resources into prevention and intervention. Words can be healing. Words can be destructive. Words can make horrific events seem like inconsequential experiences.

You have the forum to shine a bright light into the murky, terrorizing world of a child who has been assaulted or raped. If you don't shine the light again, and again, who will? Please, help us educate.

Sincerely,

Marilyn Van Derbur

To Steve Lopez, columnist

Los Angeles Times

As an incest survivor, it took me years to work through repressed rage, but it is nice to know I can still access anger when appropriate.

When I saw the picture of Tamara Brooks, 16, and Jacqueline Marris, 17, on the cover of *People* magazine, I instantly knew that this was a new day for America. Only days after their horrific experience of being kidnapped, terrorized and raped, they were speaking publicly. Finally there were young women who knew immediately that there was no reason to feel shamed, guilty or responsible.

In the midst of their role modeling courage for the one in three young women who will be sexually assaulted before the age of 18, you assaulted them with your accusations and viciousness. You wrote, "I almost wanted to go tell them to get back in the house and slam the door." Right. You wanted them to slam the door behind them and sit alone in the dark and feel shame, degradation, and humiliation. How dare you!

Then you wrote, "What parent would allow a child to talk about it…" Allow? I pity your children. How ignorant you are. Their parents were incredibly wise to honor whatever decisions their daughters made and then to stand beside them as they made it clear, just by their presence, that the shame belonged to the rapist. There is no shame in having been raped. It only took me 53 years to figure that out.

How dare you try to violate these two amazing young women with your words. Fortunately, you were outnumbered by literally hundreds of other writers who understood the unique moment in history we were privileged to experience.

Shame on *you*!

Marilyn Van Derbur

David Kelly, ABC Television Executive Producer, "The Practice."

Dear Mr. Kelly,

You educate millions of viewers every week by shaping their opinions on important issues, but with that power comes responsibility.

A recent story line focused on a 16-year-old girl who had been murdered. Her stepfather's semen was found on her body. We were told that the stepfather had been having "an affair" with his teenage stepdaughter. Wrong! He wasn't having "an affair," he raped her.

Because I taped the show, I could replay it to see how many times you used the word "affair." Six times.

Ten times we are told he "slept with her." He did not sleep with her. He raped her. We are told he "made love to her." He didn't make love

481

to her. He raped her. We are told that he had a "sexual relationship" with her. He did not have a sexual "relationship" with her. He raped her.

Although "statutory rape" was mentioned four times, those accurate words were lost among the 18 times you chose devastating, inaccurate words.

My father pried me open for 13 years. We were not having "an affair." It's called "incest" or "parental rape." It is the ugliest act to have perpetrated upon one's body and soul.

You send the wrong message to us and to our rapists. The word "affair" implies a consensual relationship. Fathers who rape daughters once or hundreds of times must have some twisted belief that their daughters are somehow enjoying a "consensual relationship." You feed those vicious rationalizations by using your unique forum irresponsibly.

When you write another show with a similar theme, please think about a 14- or 16-year-old young girl you care about. Picture her with a stepfather before you begin writing.

Marilyn Van Derbur

Orange County Register

Dear Editor,

In today's paper there was a short article about man who barricaded himself inside an apartment threatening to kill his twin two-year-old daughters. Police broke through the door and murdered the man in front of his daughters. The article ended: "Neither child was hurt."

The two children felt the terror of being barricaded in with their father, heard police screaming, watched the door being bashed in and then saw their father being shot. They then watched him die. "Neither child was hurt?"

We will not put our major resources into *the prevention* of childhood trauma until society understands the long-term impact of even one terrorizing event.

Preverbal infants who are traumatized will never be able to tell anyone what happened to them, but they can and do remember. Dr. Joseph LeDoux, a neuroscientist, is one of many who reports, "…events in early life, particularly those experienced with strong emotion, can and do remain an influence throughout our lives." (Karr-Morse and Wiley, *Ghosts From the Nursery,* p. 40)

When a child psychiatrist studied children under the age of five who had experienced serious trauma from birth to three, "…the children clearly showed that they had retained behavioral memories of their traumas which were reenacted in part or in their entirety in their play." (Karr-Morse and Wiley, *Ghosts From the Nursery,* p. 42)

Dr. Bruce Perry, an expert in trauma and early brain development, reports that even *one intense exposure* to trauma will have long-term consequences.

Rather than ending the article with, "Neither child was hurt," please, in the future, write, "Unfortunately, even small children are impacted by trauma. Without proper treatment and care, they will be adversely impacted into their adult lives." Your brief comments will raise awareness that what we do to babies and children does impact their future lives.

Please join the teaching effort!

Sincerely,

Marilyn Van Derbur

Change usually begins with one but if there is purpose and passion, others want to be involved. Most people want to make a difference.

In an earlier chapter, I wrote about the 1,100 people who came to our first survivor meeting in Denver and, how, after my talk, they lined up for almost three hours to talk with Larry, Jennifer and me. Jennifer had just completed her sophomore year in college. It was close to midnight when the last remaining survivors finally left the church. Jennifer turned to me and said, "I will work for women and children." Although she became a corporate lawyer with the prestigious law firm, Holland & Hart, she hoped that an opportunity would ultimately arise where she could make a significant difference in the lives of women and children.

During her first months as an attorney in Denver, a senior partner asked if she would like to work pro bono (for free) for Invest in Kids. She accepted. Within a year, she was on the board. The following year, they asked her to leave the law firm and become the associate director. Bill Rosser, an extraordinary leader, one of the founders and the then executive director of Invest in Kids, was Jennifer's amazing mentor. Upon his retirement, the board of directors named Jennifer the executive director.

Invest in Kids is a nonprofit child advocacy organization. It was formed by a group of community leaders (most of whom were attorneys) who were greatly concerned by the numbers of young children coming into the juvenile justice system with increasingly severe crimes. They were also seeing high rates of child abuse, low-birth weights, and teen mothers. In order to address these issues, Invest in Kids investigates and selects the best researched programs in America that have proven effectiveness, and then acts as the catalyst to implement the programs in local communities.

The first program Invest in Kids adopted was the Nurse-Family Partnership. Dr. David Olds, a brilliant, compassionate researcher, and his colleagues, developed this program in the late '70s. It is a voluntary nurse home visitation program that works with low-income, first-time mothers and their families. Visits start as early as possible during the pregnancy and continue through the children's second birthdays.

Through a series of randomized, controlled trials over the last 25 years, the program has shown unparalleled outcomes:

- *79% fewer cases of child abuse and neglect*
- 69% fewer arrests among mothers
- *54% fewer arrests and 58% fewer sexual partners among 15 year-olds* validating how important the early years are.

This program began with one person's belief that child abuse could be reduced by supporting and educating first-time, at risk-mothers.

Another example of the power of one: an attorney who passionately believed the state foster care system was not working. Other attorneys quickly joined in and The Colorado Lawyers Committee sued the state. The attorneys gratuitously gave their time and resources in order to bring change. A negotiated settlement was reached after almost two years. Two of the resulting changes were a 39% increase in the number of case workers and improved training. Did this incredible effort rid the foster care system of all flaws? Certainly not, but it did bring about change. It almost always begins with one. One letter. One phone call. One person's passion for change.

I wondered why somebody didn't do something and then I realized, I was somebody!

Chapter 30 – Beware of "Friendly" Places

The purpose of this chapter is to give you a glimpse of the extent of the betrayal children experience while in the care of organizations we trust. This information is stunning and disturbing. It may be the most important chapter concerning keeping your children safe. If it becomes overwhelming to you, scan the pages and read only the **bold type.**

As parents, we want our children to enjoy experiences that will provide intellectual, physical, emotional and/or spiritual enrichment. **We assume, too often, that the organizations that provide these experiences will have, as their top priority, keeping our children safe. Unfortunately, that is not always the case. However, we cannot be alert to the potential dangers until we understand the risks.**

Colleges and Universities

As parents, if we believe the top priority of any college or university is our children's safety and well-being, we couldn't be more wrong.

"Rape is being hidden by colleges and universities to protect their image among prospective students and families because publicizing violence is no way to recruit students." [38]

"In a landmark study, research psychologist Mary Koss reported that approximately one in four college women was the victim of rape or attempted rape."(Freyd, *Betrayal Trauma,* p. 190)

In fact, a recent survey, cited by the U.S. House of Representatives, reported that 38% of college women questioned had either been raped or were victims of felony sexual assaults. [39]

"Sexual assaults often happen to victims in the first week of college." (Bohmer and Parrot, *Sexual Assault on Campus,* p. 26)

When Jennifer was considering Duke as the university she would like to attend, we flew to North Carolina to see the campus. As we walked down one of the most beautiful paths I had ever seen that

---

[38] *NBC News,* February 2002

[39] Clery, *Campus Watch,* November 2001

linked one part of the campus to another, I felt incredible anxiety. It had dense foliage and was very isolated. No one was on the path but us. There were telephones every now and then but who could say to an attacker, "Excuse me, there's a phone about a block from here…" I told Jennifer how unsafe I felt she would be on this path. Only later would I learn that Nancy Hogshead, an Olympic gold medal winner in swimming, had been raped on that path. (Nancy was courageous enough to report the rape. She began speaking openly about it in her 30's.) We were never advised that anyone had ever been attacked on that path.

Furthermore, **we were never advised that students had been raped in the dorm in which Jennifer would be living.** If I had known, I would have spoken to the dorm resident-adviser about ways to keep freshman safe. Since *the* major danger is allowing outside doors to be propped open for pizza deliveries or an expected friend's arrival, I would have looked deep into the adviser's eyes and said, "I'm holding you personally responsible for being sure outside doors are never allowed to be propped open. If that means having consequences for students who do this, then that 'penalty' should be talked about at the next meeting."

If you, as a parent, would feel uncomfortable and squeamish about such a demand, just remember the statistic. One in four. And we're talking about *your* daughter. **We didn't know how dangerous our campuses were or that most administrators were doing everything possible to conceal the facts. "Many administrators resisted publicizing statistics for fear the information would tarnish their images and cause enrollment to drop."**(Kalette, *USA Today,* p. D01)**And we thought colleges and universities were putting our children's safety first.**

Jennifer had been a competitive swimmer in high school and wanted to keep swimming laps while in college. She told me how unsafe she felt in the west women's locker room. Anyone could walk in. When a girl from her dorm was showering, she suddenly saw a man peeking at her through a side of the shower curtain. She was terrorized but she neither reported it, nor did she ever go back to the pool area. I wrote to the Duke administration and asked them to please make the locker room safer. I suggested some sort of procedure, such as using i.d. cards. They didn't respond. I sent another letter return receipt requested, "I am giving you written notice that the west women's locker room is not safe. Anyone can come in or out. I am holding you responsible if any student is violated in any way." Again I received no response, but at least I had put them on notice. If I had it to do over again, I would have sent a letter to a specific person so that an individual would have known I could publicly hold him or her personally responsible and then I would have sent copies to other administrators.

Immediately after your child is enrolled in college, find out the names of the president of the university/college, the chairperson of the board of trustees and the head of campus security. If you have concerns, write letters and be sure to copy all of the key administrators, as each has a different perspective of potential liability.

The Justice Department's Bureau of Justice Statistics estimated that there were **500,000 sexual assaults on women on college campuses, including 170,000 rapes and 140,000 attempted rapes, annually.**(Clery, *Campus Watch,* 1995)

This is what was happening on college campuses when Jennifer was in college:

At Brown University, three students filed sexual assault charges against a professor. They assumed the police would be notified. The university policy, however, was to handle "these matters" internally. No criminal charges were filed.

At St. Mary's College in California, 37 faculty members charged officials with trying to discourage four students from reporting rape to the police. The professors called it "a cover up." [40]

A student at Syracuse University was raped in a park, which she later learned was *notorious* for rapes and violence. If she had known, perhaps she wouldn't have gone into that park alone.

When publicity began to surface about rapes on campus at Carleton College, the college adopted a sexual harassment policy which stated that "victims could not talk about the attacks with other students, nor would victims ever be told the outcome of their complaint." When a student reported being raped, the Dean discouraged the young woman from going to the police. He said she would not be believed and that

---

[40]The Chronicle of Higher Education May 17, 1989

"the matter" would be best handled by the Dean himself. [41]

A student was raped at the University of Missouri. Her mother asked the administrators how many rapes there had been that year, she was told there had been three. When the mother called the rape crisis center, she was told over 100 student/victims had come to the rape crisis center that year. [42]

A freshman at Virginia's William and Mary College was raped. She went to the school officials. They said they would handle the problem. A university hearing found the male student guilty but he was allowed to stay in school and he was never criminally charged. [43]

What finally brought change?

Only 30% of student newspaper editors received direct access to campus crime reports in 1994. When the student newspaper at UCLA tried for 18 months to get information on how many rapes had occurred on its campus, the administrators stonewalled its requests. Students believed they had a right to know so they sued and won. Within two days, UCLA implemented a policy on sexual harassment. They said the timing was purely coincidental.

A student newspaper editor at Miami University, Jennifer Markeiwicz, looked at the University's records that showed there had been five rapes on the campus in five years. Digging deeper, she found there had actually been 119 sexual assaults on or near the campus during that period. She sued the University to force it to release accurate and complete crime records. The case went to the State Supreme Court. She won.

What finally brought major changes was a personal tragedy. During her freshman year, Jeanne Clery was tortured, raped, sodomized and murdered in her dorm at Lehigh University in Ohio. Her murderer entered her dorm through a door that had been propped open with a pizza box. There had been 181 reports of propped-open doors in her dormitory in the four months prior to her death. [44] In the three years

[41] Press release dated March 29, 2001, Minn. Carla Kjellberg, "Suit Filed Against Carleton College for Condoning Campus Rapes"

[42] Connie Clery, cofounder of Safety on Campus, *The Bertrice Berry Show,* September 9, 1994

[43] *NBC Nightly News,* April 13, 1991

[44] Clery, *Campus Watch,* November 2001

before their daughter's murder, Howard and Connie Clery learned there had been 38 violent crimes on the campus, yet administrators had done nothing to make sure students had that knowledge.

The Clerys quickly began to understand that **universities were more interested in their reputations than they were in the safety of their students and that it would take a federal law to force administrators to release crime statistics.** They founded Security on Campus, Inc., a non-profit corporation, which lobbied Congress for campus crime disclosure and prevention laws. The Jeanne Clery Act was passed into law in 1998.

Now, when parents and students are considering colleges, **they can ask for a crime report,** which gives a listing of how many rapes, assaults, or burglaries have occurred during the past year. Certainly everyone expected this federal law would *force* honesty. It didn't.

"The Education Department audited more than 100 colleges' crime reports and found problems with nearly every one." For example, The University of Florida "acknowledged *excluding* 35 rapes." Minnesota State University-Moorhead "reported *one* sexual assault but the local rape crisis center indicated there were 35 alleged sexual assaults." (Leinwand, *USA Today)*

Senator Arlen Specter, R-Pa. said he was "madder than hell" when **he found colleges looking for "technicalities and loopholes to avoid reporting because of bad publicity."** (Leinwand, *USA Today*) It became necessary to amend the reporting requirements. Under the revised federal law, passed in 2000 (due in great part to Howard and Connie Clery), colleges filing false reports now face a $25,000 fine for *each* misrepresented figure.

When a co-ed at Mount St. Clare College was raped during the second week of her freshman year, she reported it. When the college did not report the rape, it was fined $25,000. (Leinwand, *USA Today*)

How can you protect your college-bound daughter or son? Be knowledgeable. The Education Department now has information on the Internet about crime on 6,700 college and university campuses. Every parent and student should go online and check the crime statistics. (www.ope.ed.gov/security)

Security on Campus, Inc. also has an important website for current information: www.campussafety.org. If you choose one college over another because of this information, write the college you have excluded and tell them this is the reason. We must force colleges to confront violence and nothing will get their attention more quickly than *knowing they are losing students and money* because you found they were not doing enough to keep students safe.

Also, sex offenders who enroll or work in a college or university are now required to register with campus police. States who do not have campus sex offender registries risk losing a portion of their federal criminal justice grant funding. The law also requires that students and employees be notified where to find the information about sex offenders. Look at those registries.

Finally, **talk to your college-bound teenagers.** Discuss the crime report you have received. Arm your daughter with the knowledge that, usually *during her freshman year*, one in four girls is sexually assaulted/raped while in college. (Two of my extended family members were raped during their freshman year in college.) Tell your sons, as well, urging them to be alert and protective of young women. And talk to your daughters *and sons* about date rape. Our **colleges and universities are dangerous places;** take every possible precaution to keep your children safe.

Arm your daughters and sons with cell phones. If they feel unsafe, they can have a number already in place so all they have to do is push "send." Other ways they can protect themselves are: mace, pepper spray and not walking alone. Many universities, including Duke, have security escort services.

Only if you, or someone very close to you, has been sexually assaulted, can you have any understanding of the life-time trauma that most often results. Since "…college women are at greater risk for rape…than women in the general population or in a comparable age group…their victimization warrants special attention." [45]

Many people say that college was the best four years of their lives. Let's do all we can to be sure our children have the same wonderful memories.

In The Locker Room

"Every Parent's Nightmare." Those three words were splashed **on the cover of Sports Illustrated magazine** (SI), followed by this

---

[45] Report by Fisher, Cullen, Turner by U.S. Department of Justice, December 2000

sentence, "The child molester has found a home in the world of youth sports, where as a coach, he can gain the trust and loyalty of kids—and then prey on them." [46]

"We used to think 'this is an isolated problem—just a few bad apples.' **Now we know that sexual abuse by coachesis pervasive...and should be viewed as a public health problem.**"(ibid. Dr. Steven Binsbing, clinical psychologist, who studies sexual abuse of children by authority figures)

"The average coach child molester victimizes about 120 children before he is caught." (ibid.) I know that number, 120, is difficult to integrate into anyone's mind. Unfortunately, in too many cases, 120 is conservative.

Norman Watson admitted to molesting "a couple of hundred" children during his 54 years. Most were boys between the ages of 11 and 14. This San Bernardino, California, Little League coach was on probation during much of the time he coached, after having been found guilty of sexually molesting boys in neighboring Riverside, California. How did he endear himself to boys and their parents in a new community? "This glib, engaging soul...generously baby-sat their kids, took them to movies and bought them expensive gifts." (S.I.) He had spent more than five years in two mental hospitals for child molesting before becoming a coach. How could parents have protected their children? By doing a simple background check. The cost and time involved in such a check is minimal.

Clyde Turner's teams won four California state championships in the 1990's in track and field. In 1999, he was found guilty of sexually molesting a boy on his team.

Although in youth sports, **it is usually men who are violating young boys, heterosexuals violate children far more often than homosexuals. "Studies show that most men who have sex with boys are not homosexual with adults...**Dr. Gene Abel, who has studied sex offenders for decades says that of the several hundred molesters he has studied, 21% of the men who molested boys were exclusively homosexual." (Boyle, *Scout's Honor,* p. 183)

Richard Hoffman was raped when he was ten years old. Over a 40-year period, he molested *500 boys,* ages 9 to 12, while he was a trusted

---

[46]September 13, 1999

coach in Allentown, Pennsylvania. He was arrested twice and allowed to plea bargain. When he was arrested the third time, he was considered a first time offender. He was finally sent to prison. [47]

John (Jay) Davidson, 41, was a coach and founder of the highly successful New England Mariners youth baseball club. Four days after being charged with sexually assaulting boys on his team, he sliced his arms open with a knife and bled to death. The boys he assaulted will experience a different kind of death.

Sexual abuse by coaches is not limited to boys. Olga Korbut, four time Olympic champion gymnast, has publicly disclosed that she was sexually violated by her coach.

A Florida skating coach was sentenced to three years in jail after pleading guilty to molesting a female student whom he had coached since she was nine years old. Suffering from anorexia, she dropped to 84 pounds. [48]

Most pedophiles seduce their victims and even their families. Kenneth Lanning, an FBI agent who is an expert on child molesters, writes, "The word pedophile means, literally, 'lover of children.' The seductor sees himself as a kind of Don Juan of deviance...**these men seduce children in exactly the same way that men and women have been seducing each other since the dawn of mankind...they flirt with them, laugh at their jokes and shower them with attention,gifts and affection.** They size up their weaknesses, their vulnerabilities, their needs. They target the kids who are more vulnerable, the kids who are not having their needs met elsewhere...these extended courtships might take weeks or even months... **The only difference between seducing an adolescent boy and seducing a woman is that it's a thousand times easier to seduce a boy, because of the ease of sexual arousal." (SI) "...Add to this equation the fact that almost all boys never tell and you have the perfect setting for a coach who will violate up to 500 boys in his lifetime."** (Roger Young, an expert on crimes against children. S.I., p 45)

One study of ice skaters found that **22% had experienced sexual**

---

[47] *Geraldo,* November 17, 1997

[48] Cox News Service, Talking Figure Skating, by Beverly Smith, McClelland and Steward Inc., 1997

intercourse with authority figures. 20% said this happened when they were under 16 years of age.

The only reason Michael Egelhoff reported his coach—23 years after he had been molested—was because his two children were becoming active in sports and the thought of them being molested motivated him to hire a private investigator to track down the coach who had molested him when he was 11 years old. What did he find? **The coach was still sexually molesting young boys, 23 years later.**(ibid.)

Coaches and other pedophiles use many different strategies to lure their victims. **Pornography is a common tool.** As they watch pornographic videos, perpetrators convince young children that this kind of sexual activity is something everyone does. I was stunned when, the U.S. Supreme Court ruled that computer-generated child pornography or "virtual child pornography" was legal. Although I'm aware of the slippery slope of censorship, I find their decision reprehensible.

Pedophilia is not curable. Most, if not all, continue to molest children until they are caught. When released, they often begin again.

How can you help to keep your child safe? **Never think, "Not this coach."** Be *involved* in your child's sports life and be absolutely positive that every coach has had a background check. Organizations like "Backgrounds USA" perform background checks nationally and internationally. (www.backgroundsusa.com)

Should you consider keeping your children out of sports? Absolutely not. Playing sports should be an important part of every child's life and so should the protective involvement of parents.

In The Sanctuary:Serial Rapists Who Should be Kneeling in Shame

Fourth grade boys are not mini-men. They are precious, vulnerable children who often serve as altar boys in the Catholic Church.

While writing this book, I frequently spent three days a week in solitude in Vail, Colorado. Only once did I have to close my computer, pack up my books, call Larry and say, "I can't read one more word. I am fluctuating between deep, heart breaking sadness and fuming rage. Priests raping little boys and girls. I have to stop. I'm coming home." I had just finished reading two books that focused on priests who had raped or sexually violated children while bishops covered up the scandals. Between 1984 and 1992, 400 priests had been reported. (Berry, *Lead Us Not Into Temptation,* back cover)

The next few pages are difficult to read. From the thirty pages I wrote originally, I have culled the key examples necessary to understand the gravity of the problem.

In January, 2002, *The Boston Globe* broke the story of how the Boston archdiocese coddled pedophile priest, John Geoghan, *triggering the scandal* within the Catholic Church..." (*Boston Globe* Investigative Staff, *Betrayal,* inside cover) How big a scandal was triggered?

Since January of 2002, **Cardinal Law,** the Archbishop of Boston, **"has turned over the names of nearly 100 priests against whom credible allegations of abuse have been made."** [49] **I know it's easy to read a number and then move on but take a minute to register: 100 priests in Boston.**

Cardinal Keeler, head of the Archdiocese of Baltimore, "posted on the Internet the names of 56 priests and other clergy members who have been accused of preying on children along with details of the allegations." **56 in Baltimore.** [50]

In the early months of 2002, as a result of the Boston scandal, more than 170 priests had either resigned or been taken off duty, nationally. In the early *months...***170 priests.** (*Boston Globe* Investigative Staff, *Betrayal,* p. 55)

When the media was flooded with stories of priests being accused of sexual abuse in January 2002, what startled me was why America was so shocked. It was as if this was some new, horrific epidemic we were hearing about for the first time. **There was nothing new about priests raping and sodomizing thousands upon thousands of little boys and girls.**

In 1992, Father Thomas Doyle said, "...3,000 American priests may be fixated on young children." (Berry, *Lead Us Not Into Temptation*, p xx)

---

[49] *The Boston Globe,* April 10, 2002 , p. A22

[50] *USA Today,* November 30, 2002

In 1993, a highly regarded priest, Father Andrew Greeley, reported that a conservative conclusion that one out of ten priests is a pedophile is too high and one out of 20 priests is too low. [51] The news wasn't new in 2002.

In 1997, Indianapolis, Indiana. "The diocese has been rocked by...sexual misconduct by 16 priests..." [52]

In 1997, a church-law expert, who formerly worked in the Vatican Embassy in Washington, D.C., said, "nearly 1,000 pedophile priests have been identified over the last 15 years, through criminal or civil charges..." (Egerton, *Dallas MorningNews*, p. 35A) The news wasn't new in 2002.

In 1998,"...at least 20 priests have been removed from the ministry in the Santa Fe, New Mexico, Archdiocese and more than 165 abuses cases were settled." (Moffett, *The PalmBeach Post*, p. 1A)

"One in eleven Catholics say they have 'personal knowledge' of child sexual abuse by a priest." (Grossman, *USA Today,* p. 1) Has it been common knowledge all along? Or did *The Boston Globe's* shocking stories just force Americans to deal with the truth?

On April 8, 2002, it was reported that six New York priests were asked to resign because of "allegations of sexual misconduct...this came less than a week after the archdiocese said it had given the Manhattan district attorney's office a list of cases involving priests who had been accused of sexual misconduct with minors." [53]

The statistics are startling. The news wasn't new in 2002. And the individual stories are heartbreaking.

As a teenager living in Hartford, Connecticut, Frank Martinelli wanted to become a priest. Father Brett, a newly ordained and charismatic priest seduced the teenager into having oral sex. The priest said, "It's okay. It's another way of receiving Holy Communion." [54]

I relate that story, not to make you physically sick, but to clarify and make more vivid the word "abuse." One of the most horrific

---

[51] *Boston Globe*, March 19, 1993

[52] Linkup, November 12, 1997

[53] *Rocky Mountain News*, April 8, 2002, p. 22

[54] Linkup, Clergy Crimes, April 1, 1998

pictures I have of a television news story is the young boy whose father poured kerosene over him and then set him on fire. His entire body had been severely burned. Even after many operations, his skin was bright red and horribly scarred. No one said his father "abused" him. And yet article after article tells us that 9-, 10-, and 11-year-old boys and girls were sexually "abused."

These children are left with gaping psychic wounds and oozing emotional puss that can't be seen because the pain is inside, but the life-long trauma is there. The next time you hear someone say, "A priest 'abused' him," I hope you will picture the boy whose face was burned beyond recognition. That's what the word "abuse" feels like to so many adults who were sexually assaulted as children. More accurately, we should replace the word "abuse" with "violated," "attacked," "assaulted," "invaded," "traumatized" or some other term that denotes the severity of the injury.

After I addressed our 1,100 survivors in Denver and then Roseanne broke her silence by addressing them, I invited Frank Fitzpatrick to keynote our next meeting. When Frank was 12, Father James Porter invited him to play a game but, instead, Porter insisted Frank eat mincemeat pie. The pie contained some kind of drug. When he awakened, he found Porter on top of him, raping him.

At age 39, when flashbacks threw his entire being into chaos, Frank became obsessed with finding Porter. When he went to the Diocese and told them why he was looking for Porter, the Monsignor said, "Leave it in the hands of the Lord." (Evidence disclosed that the Church hierarchy knew *thirty years earlier*, that Porter had sexually abused 30 boys.)

After a long search, Frank found Porter, living in Minnesota. Frank attached a recorder to his phone and called his former priest. Frank said, "Why would you molest children?" Porter said, "I don't know..." and then he laughed. **When Frank asked him how many children he had molested, Porter said, "Oh, jeez, I don't know—well, anywhere from 50 to 100, I guess." Over a three year period, through Frank's monumental efforts and obsessive persistence, 130 men and women finally came forward to accuse Porter, who had finally left the priesthood, married, had children and was currently sexually violating his children's baby-sitter, among others. What stopped Frank Porter? Frank Fitzpatrick's courageous lawsuit.**

498

Father Porter, at age 63, was finally convicted after having drugged, raped and sexually violated hundreds of young boys and girls for 34 years as the Catholic Church kept transferring him whenever he was accused. Although the names of priests changed, there was nothing new about the headlines that began to dominate the news in 2002.

On *Oprah*, one of the women who had come forward to accuse Porter said, "For every one of us who came forward, there were hundreds behind us who just couldn't—my classmates, my friends—there are hundreds and hundreds of children for each one of us who is able to stand up and at some point come forward with the truth." [55]

When Porter was sentenced to 20 years in prison for sexually molesting children, Cardinal Law was infuriated by the press's obsession with the case. Law "went after The Globe with a holy wrath" and said, 'By all means, we call down God's power on the media, particularly The Globe." (Burkett and Bruni, *Gospel of Shame,* p. 49)

When I was asked to address a luncheon of West Palm Beach's most prominent leaders, my host asked me to not ask survivors to stand. Reluctantly, I agreed. When I arrived home, a fax awaited me. An acquaintance who had attended the luncheon said, **"As I was walking out the door, I heard one man say to another, 'This never happens in West Palm Beach.'"** At that exact time, here is what was happening right near West Palm Beach:

Father O'Connell was sent to Palm Beach, Florida, to replace a Bishop who had been removed when it was disclosed that he had sexually violated children. **The new Bishop O'Connell said, to his congregation, "Sexual abuse can never be condoned in any way. It is criminal and sinful." Only days later, a 34-year-old man filed a lawsuit against Bishop O'Connell, charging eight years of sexual abuse. O'Connell's lawyer called the suit, "a blatant ploy for publicity," until phone messages surfaced where the Bishop was heard pleading with his victim to not file a lawsuit or say anything publicly.** [56]

Days later, the Bishop changed his message from "sexual abuse is criminal and sinful," to, "I want to apologize as sincerely and as

---

[55] *Oprah,* October 23, 1995

[56] *Rocky Mountain News*, March 23, 2002

abjectly as I possibly can." Within days, more men came forward to charge him. O'Connell "has never served a day in jail. He was never defrocked. He is living a quiet retired life with no supervision, no monitoring, and pedophiles are not cured." (*Oprah,* March 28, 2002) **Why isn't this serial rapist in prison?**

ABC News wanted to know if there were priests who had been convicted of sexually assaulting children or who had settled in civil cases who are still working in the Church. ABC News found 30 such priests.

Here is one example from the ABC special, "Bless me father.": Alexandra Neihal was the president of her church youth group in St. Petersburg, Florida, when at age 14, she went to talk to her priest, Father Matthew Berko. He offered her a drink and said, "Don't worry, it's only church wine, like what you take for Holy Communion." And then he sexually assaulted her.

"I kept saying, 'Father, please don't.' To this day I can still hear myself saying, 'Father, please don't,' but he didn't stop. She was so upset, she considered suicide. Criminal charges were brought. Father Berko pled guilty and received a one-year suspended sentence. A year later, he was back at Alexandra's church as a priest, with the bishop telling the local newspaper that the case was, quote, 'a minor thing.'" Father Berko said, "I pled guilty only because of the advice of my attorney...I'm still innocent, as far as I'm concerned."(*Aired on April 3, 2002*) After reading hundreds of children's stories, Alexandra's plea plays in my head like an old record stuck in a groove, "Please don't, Father. Please don't."

And what price do children pay?

Father Rudy Kos, a charismatic priest in Dallas, was charged with sexual abuse and rape. One man after another came forward to testify about how Father Kos had molested them, a total of about 1,350 times. Jay Lemberger found the trauma too overwhelming to deal with. He spent six months in a psychiatric hospital and tried to commit suicide twice before taking a gun and killing himself in a park at age 21—after 10 years of sexual abuse by Father Kos.

The jury awarded the other former altar boys $118 million which was later reduced to $24.4 million. The jurors delivered a one-page letter to the diocese saying, "Stop this now!"

Peter Pollard, sexually traumatized by a priest when he was in his teens, said, "To those who ask that we forgive and forget, please understand that each of us, in his own way, has spent our lives trying to move on, always weighing the options. For some of us, suicide, substance abuse or violence ended the struggle early...the betrayals are inexorably woven into the texture of who we have become." (*Boston Globe* Investigative Staff, *Betrayal,* p. 9)

Lorenzo Najera, raped by his priest from the time he was 12 until he was 17 said, "I was really screwed up. My life was a mess. When you've been abused you don't know who you are. People think it's like a cold. You catch a cold and it goes away. It's not. It's something that stays forever. It affects your life every day. Every day I deal with it." (Kornblum, *USA Today,* p. 6D)

"Survivors tell familiar stories of years of depression, anxiety, self-loathing and fear of others. They organize their lives around their wounds. Many hate their bodies, which betrayed them by attracting the abuse. They eat too much or too little, suffer from bulimia or anorexia. Others can't sleep, besieged by nightmares. Some find sex so dirty they cannot bear to be touched; others fall into promiscuity. Plagued with fears and self-doubts, they shut down emotionally, sometimes with the help of drugs and alcohol. They destroy their marriages. Sometimes, they destroy themselves. A victim of one Florida priest hanged himself in his parents' backyard. Before he died, he asked his brother to contact his abuser/priest and tell him, 'I forgive you.'" (Burkett and Bruni, *A Gospel of Shame,* pp. 138–139)

Did the Church hierarchy respond to victims with compassion and support?

As the statutes of limitation were lengthened in some states, victims began going to court. Rather than acknowledging victims' wounds, Church leaders "responded with a plan to fight legal claims with every means possible including the humiliation of victims and accusations against them of instigating the abuse..." (Shupe, *Wolves Within the Fold,* p. 140)

"...a Midwestern bishop referred to a woman who had been sexually abused by a priest when she was fourteen as a 'little Lolita' who was now trying to milk as much money as possible out of the Church." (Burkett and Bruni, *A Gospel of Shame,* p. 175)

"In Philadelphia, the diocese filed a counter suit against the

parents of one of the victims, alleging that they negligently failed to discover the abuse over eight years." [57]

In Dallas, Texas, **Monsignor** Robert Rehkemper **said,** in a one-hour interview during the Father Kos case, **"No one ever says anything about what the role of the parents was in all this."** He continued, **"Boys who were as young as 9 when the abuse began, knew what was right and what was wrong. Anybody who reaches the age of reason shares responsibility for what he does."**

In Cleveland, Ohio, "Church leaders refused to hand over abusers' personnel records. Bishop Quinn even encouraged diocesan officials to send priests' files to the Vatican Embassy in Washington, D.C., where diplomatic immunity would protect the documents from being subpoenaed. He said this was preferable to destroying files, which would be an obstruction of justice." (Burkett and Bruni, *A Gospel of Shame,* p. 161)

When the Pope came to America and spoke in Denver, Colorado, His Holiness claimed that "In America, the present lack of family values and morality has contributed to, if not created, the opportunity for priests 'to make mistakes.'" A few weeks later, the Vatican released the statement that clergy sexual abuse was an American and Canadian problem." [58]

Is pedophelia an issue for North America only?

"In Ireland, the Church was forced to confront sex abuse among the clergy that generated a controversy *that brought down an Irish government.*" [59] "The Church agreed to pay $110 million. Critics say that with an estimated 3,000 victims, the contribution is insufficient." [60]

"In Spain, a study of the Catholic clergy claims that 60% of priests are sexually active." (Shupe, *Wolves Within the Fold,* p. 140)

Why did some in the Catholic Church hierarchy change?

"Jury hits church wallet over pedophile priest." (Aynesworth,

---

[57] *60 Minutes,* May 15, 1994

[58] Linkup, Tom Economus, 1998.

[59] Associated Press 6/27/1999

[60] *Wall Street Journal,* January 31, 2002, front page

The Archbishop of **Santa Fe** has removed twenty priests and settled **165 clergy sexual abuse cases.** The cost? An estimated $50 million which was raised by selling Church property. Archbishop Sheehan has appealed to each of his 77,684 Catholic households to give more money. It was reported that the Diocese of Santa Fe was driven to the brink of bankruptcy. [61]

The Linkup states, "There are over 800 priests that have been removed as a result of allegations against them. We also know of 1,400 insurance claims on the books and that **the Church has paid out over $1 billion in liability claims with an estimated $500 million pending. One noted expert claims that there are over 5,000 priests with some type of allegation against them."**

My research on priests, bishops, archbishops, cardinals and the Pope has been, in exponential proportion, the most difficult to read in preparing this book. These men who should be held to the *highest possible standard,* perpetrated rape, sodomy, humiliation and shame on trusting, loving, vulnerable young children.

When the U.S. Conference of Bishops released its newly approved policy on sexual abuse, I was hopeful. I really was. It was my hope that the Bishops really did want to protect children. Then I read, "Victims must bring claims by age 28, the statute of limitations under church law…" (Stammer, *LA Times*, p. A22) There isn't a person, not one person, who knows anything about the sexual abuse of children, who doesn't know that we do not come forward in our 20's. It takes decades for most of us to make the connection between our emotional and physical problems and having been sexually traumatized as children. Oprah was 39 when she disclosed. When Frank Fitzpatrick, 39, came forward, 129 more men and women slowly came forward to stand with Frank. I can assure you, most of them were older than 28. The Bishops know. There should be no statutes of limitation when childhood sexual abuse is involved. The Church's new policy makes a deafening statement as to its sincerity.

It can take the Church a long time to admit wrong-doing and then publicly apologize. In 1633, Galileo was summoned to Rome by the Inquisition to stand trial for heresy for saying that the sun, not the

---

[61] Linkup, March 22, 1998

earth, was the center of the universe. He was sentenced to life imprisonment which was commuted to permanent house arrest. The Church crushed his last years. In 1992, 329 years later, a papal commission acknowledged, for the first time, "an error in Galileo's case."

On March 12, 2000, the Pope, "asked God's forgiveness for the sins of Roman Catholics through the ages." This one-sentence sweeping apology was hailed as "unprecedented." I cannot imagine one adult, sexually violated as a child by a priest, who found any healing in his apology. Perhaps a healing process would have begun if the Pope had "wept bitterly" as the apostle Peter did or if the Pope had spoken in language as forceful as Jesus used when he spoke of adults violating children, "Whosoever shall offend one of these little ones that believe in me, it is better that a millstone were hanged around his neck and he were cast into the sea." Mark 9:42

My intent is not to besmirch all priests. There are thousands of dedicated, moral priests who have lovingly ministered to adults and children. **My intent is to express my outrage with the lack of leadership by those persons in authoritative positions within the Church who have committed, permitted and ignored flagrant sexual violations of innocent children.**

In the Bible, it says, "Faith, hope and love and the greatest of these is love." There are some occasions when I believe the greatest of these is *hope*—hope that someday **a Pope** will call to Rome, all adults who were sexually violated, and beg forgiveness for the blatant lack of leadership, discipline and morality that has existed for so many decades, if not centuries. Then He **will vow dire consequences for those who attempt to cover up or perpetuate the ravishing of God's precious children by the serial rapists ordained to love and protect them.** With faith and love destroyed for so many, hope is what's left. Hope.

"Death is not the greatest loss in life. The greatest loss is what dies inside us while we live." —Norman Cousins

Chapter 31 – Do They Ever Stop?

"Oh, my God, I thought I was the only one. I never should have left you. It's my fault." My sister Gwen's words still haunt me. She thought she was the only one. She is the eldest, and I am the youngest. There was never any doubt in my mind—never—that he stopped with me.

We were both wrong. You will recall that I was 47 when I saw him lying in the casket with his hands across his chest. I knew the second I saw the middle fingernail of his left hand had been filed off that he hadn't stopped, but I had to not think about it…until I received the letter nine years later: "About twenty times in 1983." That's what she had written. My father was 75. Even after I confronted him and he had said, "If I had known what it would do to you…" He never stopped.

When I spoke in an affluent suburb of Dallas recently, to educate and raise funds for a Children's Advocacy Center, I was told that the oldest perpetrator in Texas was 94. He had violated a 13-year-old boy. Most never stop.

After giving a speech in Omaha, survivors lined up to share their stories with me. Two women approached me together. "We are sisters. We are two of 19 children. Our father molested each of us. What we didn't even consider, was the fact that he would go on to molest our children. All of our children." Most never stop.

Why is this information important? Because 20 years ago we didn't know that most sex offenders never stop or that most are family members or highly regarded people in positions of trust. They don't look like monsters. No one suspects that the charismatic gymnastics coach, or the gentle priest, or the fun grandfather is a sexual predator.

Why is it important to read the research and learn about other people's experiences? Because once we know the facts, *we can never again say*, "It never occurred to me that he or she would continue to rape and molest children of the next generation." Most never stop. Now we know!

"One study of sex offenders in Connecticut prisons revealed that 74% had one or more prior convictions for a sexual offense against a child." [62] Most sex offenders are never caught. That 74% were caught

---

[62] Jack Levin, a sociologist at Northeastern University in Boston. *Chicago Sun-Times*, August

again is only an indication of how many hundreds of victims had been assaulted. An offender who has a compulsion to sexually molest children, will almost never stop with just one child or just one time. With each violation, each child is given a life sentence of trying to cope with the long-term impact of the sexual abuse.

It's important to note that there are different kinds of sex offenders. A man like my father, who chose girls, generally victimizes relatively few while a man who preys on non-related boys, "will victimize as many as 280 male victims." (Baker, *Protecting Your Child From Sexual Predators,* p. 27)

"Men who violate non-related boys have more victims and abuse them more often than any other type of sex abuser." (Boyle, *Scout's Honor,* p. 32) Boy Scout leader, Franklin Mathias was named "Scouter of the Year" in Eastern Oregon. The following year, with a stunned community wondering how this could have happened, he was arrested. He estimates that "over 30 years, his victim total was around 242 boys." (Boyle, *Scout's Honor,* p. 32)

Research on priests concludes that "each pedophile tends to abuse an average of 265 victims." (Mission Statement, www.thelinkup.com)

In studying 411 sex offenders, Gene Abel et al found that on average, over a 12-year period, each offender had 336 victims. That averages out to be two+ victims per month. (Retraining Adult Sex Offenders, Safer Society Press, Fay Honey Knopp—Greig Veeder)

Dr. Wayne Hunt, who ran the sex offender treatment program for the Maryland Department of Corrections, was asked, "What is the right sentence for sex offenders?" He replied, "If you want to guarantee they'll never offend again, *lock them up forever.*"

"Research on incarcerated sex offenders who were polygraphed revealed that, on average, perpetrators had committed sex offenses for 16 years prior to being identified as a sex offender." (Ahlmeyer et al, *Sexual Abuse,* p. 123–138) And, "Sex offenders, after being discharged from the Massachusetts Treatment Center, continued to re-offend over a 25 year period." (Prentky et al, *Law and Human Behavior,* pp. 635–659)

Research concludes that adults who violate their own children are reconvicted at a lesser rate than adults who violate others' children.

16, 1995, p. 14

That may be true *but* it is also true that it is *highly unlikely* for an incest victim to report a first time. Reporting a second time is almost unheard of because the child will have learned that he or she has devastated the family. Almost always, the child learns—either due to shame, guilt or fear—to never speak of it.

Recently, when I was scheduled to talk in Atlanta, my host, Sharon, met me at the airport. We clicked immediately. I felt as if I had known her for years. She disclosed to me that she had been incested by her father when she was seven. Her parents were divorced. Her maternal grandfather suspected abuse because she fought so hard to never spend time with her father. She finally told. A trial followed during which she testified against her father.

When Sharon drove me back to the airport after my presentation the next day, she said, "I have something I need to tell you. I didn't tell you the truth last night. At the trial, I didn't testify against my father. I couldn't. I just couldn't. I said that he didn't do it. There is no way to tell you how much shame I feel about that. I don't know why I couldn't tell the truth. With him in the courtroom looking at me, I had to deny what I had said. I recanted."

Most daughters want to protect their fathers from going to prison. If you ever wondered why Sharon did not testify against her father, go to an elementary school playground and look at a seven-year-old. She is a *little* girl. Who could possibly believe she could stand up to her father? Of course adults who violate their own children are reconvicted at a lesser rate. It is astonishing a child would ever speak against a parent. Inconceivable that the same child would do it twice.

"When children who had reported molestation by a relative were asked if they would report again, almost 100% said, "No." [63] It is not an issue of recidivism within families because it is clear that the abuse continues. The difference is that it is reported far less often.

Do offenders want to stop?

The Ohio Department of Rehabilitation and Corrections is proud of its sex offender rehabilitation program in its Lebanon facility; however, an article on the program disclosed that an inmate must ask to be a part of the program. Of the 16 sex offenders who started in the voluntary program, 13 dropped out. "They dropped out because they

---

[63] Personal communication with William Marshall, MD, February 19, 2003

were unwilling or unable to face up to their crimes, figure out why they committed them, and try to develop ways to keep from reverting to similar behavior in the future." (Marino, Cleveland Scene)

Research with polygraph tests, involving 128 sex offenders who were *under supervision* and participating in offense-specific *treatment,* concluded that *"86%* were engaging in 2.5 different high risk behaviors and/or new crimes. This would indicate that many offenders *continue* their patterns of perpetration *while* participating in sex offender *treatment. "*(Tanner, *High Risk Behaviors)*If 86% continue to perpetrate while in treatment, knowing they will be taking a polygraph test, one can only imagine how many perpetrators keep violating when they are out on their own.

It is startling to review how many offenders are compelled to initiate high-risk violations. Research showed that 113 child molesters each committed an average 88.6 offenses, and:

• 54% admitted to molesting a child while another child was present.
• 23.9% when another adult was present.
• 44.3% when they knew the other person was awake.
The child molesters listed the following reasons for molesting a child while a non-offending child or person was present:
• 77% sense of excitement
• 77% sense of mastery
• 75.2% compulsion

This research confirms that sexual acts on a child can occur in the visiting room of the prison even though the visitation is supervised by the Department of Corrections. In fact, it would *add to the sense of excitement…* [64]

What drives this need for dangerous sexual excitement? When a child is terrorized, "The early brain can become hard-wired to deal with high fear states. When these children become adults, they'll feel empty or bored if they aren't on the edge," says Dr. Jay Giedd of the National Institutes of Health. [65]

I know this explanation was true for me. I chose a life that put me,

---

[64] Do Sexual Offenders Molest When Other Persons are Present? 1999, Underwood, Patch, Cappelletty, and Wolfe—Greig Veeder

[65] *Frontline* PBS, "Inside the Teenage Brain, January 31, 2002

on an almost daily basis, in a constant state of terror, whether it was racing on my college ski team or addressing 15,000 people without a note or an outline to support me. The reason I chose this life was because terror had been a normal state for me as a child and I was subconsciously driven to stay in this state. Only when I made the connection between my need to live in terror and the childhood cause, could I stop choosing terror. And I did stop...at age 53.

Similarly, I believe the reason many perpetrators sexually violate children while there are other people in the room is because they are driven to achieve that heightened sense of excitement that accompanies extreme risk. No child, under any circumstances, is safe with a perpetrator. Ever.

Even knowing that most perpetrators don't stop, many judges give sex offenders probation, suspended sentences or community service, instead of jail time. In fact, research shows that, "65% go directly on probation and of those who are incarcerated, 95% are paroled." [66] They are then free to go back to their compulsion. How could there be so little regard for our children's safety?

Experts in the field write, "When you recognize the effect and scope of the trauma caused by nonviolent sexual manipulation, the amount of consideration given by the criminal justice system to such offenders because they are nonviolent is baffling. Physically batter a child and you are locked up, but psychologically batter ten children and you are left on the street because you are nonviolent." (Boyle, *Scout's Honor*, p. 144)

As private citizens, we must express our outrage at judges who do not send perpetrators to prison. Probation for a sex offender should never be an option without mandatory treatment and should only be an option when the offenders have confessed, taken responsibility for their sexual behavioral problems and met every criteria for admission to a comprehensive, effective treatment program...if one can be found.

I'm sure there are some who do not re-offend, but would you risk your child's future (and that is what you are risking, in most cases) that the perpetrator you know is one of the rare exceptions?

Perhaps my greatest concern is that many pedophiles truly believe they cause no harm. Thomas Hacker, convicted twice of sexually

---

[66] Editorial, *The Denver Post*, October 27, 2002

molesting boys while a Boy Scout leader, said it was right because he was loving people. And that love leads to sex. He couldn't understand why anyone was upset because he wasn't "hurting boys." (Boyle, *Scout's Honor,* p 147) When one of his victims tried to commit suicide, he said, "I feel guilty about not feeling guilty." (Boyle, *Scout's Honor,* p. 282)

Holly Wakefield, a member of the advisory board of the False Memory Syndrome Foundation (FMSF), an organization which claims that some therapists implant false memories of sexual abuse into their patients' minds, said, "It would be nice if someone could get some kind of big research grant to do a longitudinal study of, let's say, a hundred 12-year-old boys in relationships with loving pedophiles." [67]

Ralph Underwager, one of the founders of the FMSF also proclaimed that there is nothing wrong with pedophilia i.e. having sex with children. In an interview he said, "Pedophilia is a responsible choice...Pedophiles can boldly and courageously affirm what they choose. They can say that what they want is to find the best way to love. I am also a theologian and...I believe it is God's will that there be a closeness and an intimacy, unity of the flesh, between people." [68]

Never leave your child with an adult who has sexually violated a child. Not for sixty seconds. Not even if he is 93 years old...because most never stop. Some even believe it's God's will.

Should we keep trying to find ways to help those who do want to stop?

I believe there are thousands of adults obsessed with sexually violating children who want to stop. An organization called "STOP IT NOW!" offers helpful publications as well as referral agencies who answer questions and provide support for offenders who want to stop. (www.stopitnow.com)

After I spoke in Medford, Oregon, a woman stood during a question and answer period to say that she was devoting her time to helping perpetrators stop. I said, "I am so grateful to you for what you are doing. It is not my focus but I am thankful that this is your mission. There is such a need. Thank you." Later, several people told me they

---

[67] Paidika: vol 3, no. 1, issue 9, 1993

[68] Paidika vol 3, no. 1, issue 9, 1993

were surprised at my response. Some were even offended that I would be interested in violators. I believe there are some offenders who live in agony over their compulsion with, or attraction to, children.

Offender treatment is a complex issue. There are some child molesters who do not believe they are doing anything wrong, some who don't care, and some who are intent on doing harm. We have to find ways to keep them in prison or away from children forever. There are many types of offenders with many different types of sexual behavior problems (exhibitionism, "peeping toms," lewd phone calls, as well as molesters and rapists). On the other hand, there are some who desperately want help and our current system makes it almost impossible for them to find it because to come forward for help results, in most cases, in immediate prosecution.

A story of hope

I addressed over 600 survivors in Kansas City. During the question and answer period, an athletic-looking man in his mid-20's, standing far in the back, stood to speak. Instead, he began weeping. Not crying. Not sobbing. Weeping. The tears poured down his face as he tried to relate how *he* had been violated. His words came one at a time, with agonizing slowness, "And…then…I…violated…my…little…sister. I have to die. I have to die. How could I have violated my little sister? How could she ever forgive me?" He just kept repeating those words; he was so overcome with grief and shame. I left the podium, walked down the very long aisle and inched my way past the people sitting in his row, and I just held him. He put his arms around me and wept uncontrollably. I believe the first step to stopping the sexual violations of children is to have the offender get in touch with his or her pain. For an adult to stop needing to dominate, terrorize and humiliate a child, he or she must make the excruciatingly painful connection as to what drives this behavior. It is, I believe, the most important way he can begin the process of changing behavior.

I have known several adult survivors who, like the young man in Kansas City, were molested as children and then, as young teenagers, violated other children. Ultimately, each made the painful connection, did the work of healing and never offended again.

When I spoke in Grand Junction, Colorado, it was to a small group—perhaps eighty people. While I was speaking, I noticed twelve men seated in the last row. After my presentation and a question and answer period, people came forward to speak with me. Before leaving the podium, I said, "Would the men in the back please stay? I would like to talk with you." I knew they were perpetrators. I did not know they were there with an armed guard. After the last person in line left, I went to the back of the room and asked if we could put the chairs in a circle so we could talk.

I didn't need to say, "I know who you are." They knew I knew. I began by telling them I wanted to understand...I wanted to learn...what had caused them to sexually violate children? Was it an addiction like heroin or cocaine? A compulsion that you just cannot stop? Heads nodded. They knew I was coming to them, not as an accuser, but as one who had questions. We talked for almost thirty minutes. For those who responded to me, "compulsive behavior" was an accurate, descriptive term for what they felt. (I'm sure it isn't as easily categorized as that.) Several of the men spoke of wanting to find ways to stop their compulsive urges.

Why weren't they in a 12-step program, comparable to that of Alcoholics Anonymous? Not instead of prison, but in addition to prison. We will never successfully prosecute all child molesters. Most will be back in our neighborhoods. I am grateful to others who are searching for ways to help those who are released from prison and who want to stop.

I believe organizations such as STOP IT NOW!, Safer Society Foundation, and The Association for the Treatment of Sexual Abusers are making important inroads into how to help those perpetrators who desperately want to be helped. Nevertheless, I urge you to never leave your child with someone who has sexually violated a child. While I support those who are working to help offenders stop, I know that the groups devoting themselves to this are few and far between. I also believe it is way too early for us to know whether or not certain therapies or experiences work. An alcoholic who relapses may pass out or lose his job. A sex offender will devastate a life and the lives of those who love the victim.

What can be done?

There are 97,077 known sex offenders in California. (Hofman, Los Angeles Times, p. K1) If there are 97,077 known offenders, can you imagine how many more there are who have not been discovered? In my experience with thousands of survivors, most perpetrators are never charged, much less convicted. What is additionally disturbing is that the Associated Press reported that, "California has lost track of

512

more than 33,000 convicted sex offenders...and many overworked police departments are not following up...nationally, 52% of rapists are arrested for repeat crimes within three years of leaving prison." [69]

More than 3,000 registered sex offenders are on probation or parole, living anonymously in the Denver metro area, with inadequate supervision or treatment to keep them from re-offending. Knowing that most will strike again, what can be done to protect the thousands of children and adults from the life sentence they will receive when assaulted by these registered sex offenders who are living in their community?

An editorial in *The Denver Post* [70] states that Greig Veeder has come up with "a concept worth studying." Veeder has focused his attention on housing sex offenders in a restrictive campus-like setting where they would have intensive treatment. Dr. Stephen Brake believes that the one to three hours of treatment a week most offenders receive is insufficient. (ibid) Veeder believes offenders need to live in a contained area while working in nearby communities. "It would be a place where they could be constantly monitored, evaluated and treated." (ibid) *The Post* editorial concluded, "The campus concept may not be a perfect solution, but we think...it's certainly preferable to 3,000 human time bombs ticking away in anonymity."

This chapter is not written to instill *paranoia*. It is written to validate why it is important to be vigilant and aware about where your children are, what they are doing and with whom. You (usually painstakingly) teach your child to drive at the appropriate age and talk, again and again, about drinking and driving because you understand the dangers of drunk drivers and the long-term impact of how a collision can paralyze or even kill your child or others. Likewise, it is important to understand the lifetime devastation sexual abuse can have on your child. We need to talk about it, write letters of protest to judges who do not incarcerate child molesters, support comprehensive rehabilitation programs for offenders and be vigilant—because these actions may be our only hope for protecting our children once an offender is released from prison.

---

[69] *The Denver Post*, January 9, 2003

[70] *The Denver Post*, October 27, 2002, p. 6E

Chapter 32 – The Good News Is: Trauma Doesn't Have to Last a Lifetime

When letters from survivors began arriving in mailbags, I was astonished that the preponderance of letters were from men and women in their late 30's and 40's. It seemed as if, out of nowhere, childhood memories and feelings were intruding into, and often shutting down, their adult lives. Why?

One reason is that as children, we were unable to talk about, rage about, cry years of tears about what happened. Because of our isolation and our secrets, we were never able to work through the emotional and physical tortures we experienced.

Until we can connect those childhood feelings to our adult actions, many of us will continue to act in inexplicable ways and bring our childhood dysfunction into our adult lives. Richard Berendzen's entire life crashed into smithereens as he learned this lesson. Berendzen graduated from M.I.T. and received his masters and doctorate degrees from Harvard. He reached the pinnacle of success when he was named president of American University in Washington, D.C.

One day the University went on alert when indecent, lewd phone calls were causing women to be traumatized. Women who offered child-care were asked very disturbing questions that hinted at incest and sex with children. As the calls became more frequent, the police were brought in. Instead of hanging up or trying to end the conversation, one woman asked the man to call back. A series of conversations became more grotesque and graphic. Within a short time, the calls were traced to the president's office. Berendzen was 49 years old. He resigned immediately and was taken to the Sexual Disorders Clinic at Johns Hopkins University.

It was there that his history of childhood sexual abuse emerged. He had never told anyone. For many years, not even himself. While in group therapy, he cried, vomited, and cried again. He was given "truth serum," the sodium amytal interview that I had wanted so desperately when I was in recovery. When he was awakened from the medication and they played back what he had said, he was stunned. He gave intimate details of when his mother would say, "Come here." Sexual relations with his mother began when he was in 3rd grade, just eight years old. They stopped when he was 13. He had managed to repress the trauma until his father died and he was forced to return to the house and the room where it had all happened. It was immediately after being in his mother's bedroom that he began making lewd phone calls.

When I met with his wife Gail, she said, "I sat outside the room when he was being interviewed and I heard him sobbing, 'What does this have to do with what happened to me when I was eight?' He couldn't make the connection."

During his stay in the hospital, Dr. Fred Berlin, a world-renowned psychiatrist, explained to him that the calls were, "an attempt to find a surrogate for his mother to elicit an explanation for her behavior. In his own troubled way, he had re-created his trauma to try to resolve the questions around it."(Berendzen and Palmer, *Come Here*, p. 32)

Berendzen said, "The trauma is always there, carved like a fault line through your being. I appeared normal until one day there was a trigger. For me, it was my father's funeral that unleashed an earthquake inside of me which reduced the world of everything I had ever known to rubble." (ibid p. 38)

He learned that he suffered from post-traumatic stress disorder (PTSD) as so many of us do. PTSD is a real illness, which too few people understand. Flashbacks, rage, denial, intrusive thoughts, numbing, nightmares, acute anxiety and depression are all symptoms of PTSD that a survivor of childhood sexual abuse is likely to experience at some point in his or her life. (ibid p. 44)

Berendzen lost his job and his home but not his family or close friends. In time, the University re-hired him as a professor. He slowly began to rebuild his life as he made the connection between his behavior and the cause.

We repeat the same situations we grew up in, unless and until we make the connection as to *why* we are doing what we do. Most people vow that they will never hit their children if they were hit, or divorce if their parents were divorced. But too many repeat the same pattern.

Years ago, I read Jesse Jackson's biography. It was heart wrenching to learn that his daddy was the man next door and how young Jesse grieved when his daddy would take his kids on vacation and leave him home. He knew the pain of being born an "illegitimate child" and he knew he would never do that to a child of his.

When President Clinton needed religious counseling after his sexual entanglement with Monica Lewinsky, Reverend Jackson was his spiritual leader. What the public didn't know was that as the Reverend was counseling Clinton, he was having an affair with a member of his staff, Karin Stanford. During this same time period, Stanford gave birth to a child, fathered by Jackson. Now he has a child who may grow up with the same feelings of illegitimacy. Stanford and their child live thousands of miles from Jackson. He is repeating the same pattern.

"We are unconsciously automatically drawn to situations that will repeat the unresolved experiences of our past. If you want the freedom to create the life you want, then you have to heal the unresolved pain of the past." [71] That cannot be done until we make the connection between how what happened in the past is now driving our present— and will, unless we confront the demons, drive our future.

I received a letter from a medical doctor in New Jersey. He was in despair because his wife was going to divorce him because he was a sex addict. He had recently gone into therapy and had finally made the connection between being sexually violated by an older woman when he was nine years old and being an adult sex addict. Now that he was beginning to understand his obsessive drive, he believed he could start to change his behavior. Could I meet with him?

Three weeks later, he drove to a presentation I was giving about sixty miles from his community. We talked for two hours. He was filled with remorse and shame. Would I write his wife a letter, explaining what he was going through? Explain the "recovery process?" I told him I would write the letter immediately. Unfortunately, his marriage did not survive, but he is on the road to changing his behavior by making a connection with what has caused his obsessive drive.

A young woman I know grew up in a stable, loving environment. She married a man who grew up in complete chaos and dysfunction. It has been sad to watch him create chaos in his new family unit. It is my very strong belief that he has no idea that he is replicating the craziness of his childhood.

But it doesn't have to be that way. Tom Hanks' parents divorced

[71] John Gray, *Oprah*, September 23, 1998

when he was five. He attended 10 different schools before he was 10 years old. His father divorced and remarried three times. He knew he would never subject his children to what he had been through, but he did. He married, had a child and divorced. After his divorce, he went into "intense psychotherapy." He then married Rita Wilson and has been in a stable relationship for many years. We break the chain of dysfunction when we walk right into the pain of our childhoods, when we confront our past through *intense* psychotherapy.

I had chosen a career that kept me in the eye of a tornado of terror. Unfortunately, I was in my late 40's before I made that connection.

Dr. Judith Herman writes that when our bodies are over stimulated, we experience a flood of adrenalin, all systems go on "red alert," and we become immediately ready for "fight or flight." If there is no way to express and release the supercharged emotion, the energy "tends to persist in an *altered* and exaggerated state *long after* the actual danger is over." (Herman, *Trauma and Recovery,* p. 34)

Before researching trauma, I had never connected what Dr. Herman refers to as an "altered state" with how I coped with incest. If we can't "fight or flee," we go into an altered state. One such state is "freezing." We don't decide to freeze. It's involuntary. "If the terror continues, the child may move from freezing to complete dissociation appearing to 'go away' or to disengage mentally and emotionally from the immediate environment." (Dr. Bruce Perry in Karr-Morse and Wiley, *Ghosts From the Nursery,* p. 167)

What happens to people during an altered state varies. Some of the descriptions include: "My mind went blank;" "I froze and everything slowed down; I couldn't think of anything;" "It was like I was standing outside my body watching what was happening. I couldn't feel anything." I have always said, "I split my mind." For me, those words fit the experience I had…splitting into a day child and a night child.

Traumatic energy must be released.

Dr. Peter Levine, who has worked with trauma survivors for twenty-five years, says the single most important factor he has learned in uncovering the mystery of human trauma is what happens during and after the freezing response. He describes an impala being chased by a cheetah. The second the cheetah pounces on the young impala, the animal goes limp. The impala isn't playing dead, she has "instinctively entered an altered state of consciousness, shared by all mammals when death appears imminent." (Levine and Frederick, *Waking the Tiger,* p. 16) The impala becomes instantly immobile. However, if the impala escapes, what she does immediately thereafter is vitally important. She shakes and quivers every part of her body, clearing the traumatic energy she has accumulated.

When I was nine, my father gave me a black and white pinto horse. I called her "Beauty." I rode her bareback. Many mornings, I would walk the long distance to the meadow and just watch her grazing in the early morning sun. Suddenly, there would be a sound that would cause all of the horses to instantly lift their heads, perk their ears straight up and not move a muscle, listening. When they felt safe again, they would go back to grazing but not before they shuddered, as if they were shaking something off their bodies. I now know they were releasing the energy that was stimulated in their bodies from the moment they sensed danger.

I couldn't find a way to release the energy. Only after I began reading about trauma did I begin to understand that just as animals released energy after they had "frozen," humans also needed ways to recover from highly stressful encounters. I was unable to release the heightened sexual and fearful energy and so I was forced to store it in my body. That produced long-term consequences that did not dissipate over time.

Dr. Levine writes, "Words can't accurately convey the anguish that a traumatized person experiences. It has an intensity that defies description." (Levine and Frederick, *Waking the Tiger,* p. 47)

Un-discharged toxic energy does not go away. It persists in the body and often forces the formation of a wide variety of symptoms such as anxiety, depression, unexplained anger, and physical symptoms from heart trouble to asthma. (Levine and Frederick, *Waking the Tiger,* p. 20) Feelings that can find no means of expression are jammed into our bodies and left to scream inside and torment us in ways we do not understand until we find a way to examine, understand, and finally release the psychic pressure. This process begins by understanding the connection between the original trauma and the resulting long-term effects.

"All emotions, even those that are suppressed and unexpressed, have physical effects. Unexpressed emotions tend to stay in the body like small ticking time bombs—they are illnesses in incubation." (Northrup, *Women's Bodies, Women's Wisdom,* p. 19)

519

A vivid experience of how incest erupted into physical pain occurred in my late 40's. I began to have severe chest pain. So severe that, many times, I would double over in anguish. Finally, I went to see a cardiologist who did every conceivable test—including a stress test, which required my walking/running on a treadmill while my vital signs were monitored. After all the test results came in, he said, "There is nothing wrong with your heart; you're in great shape."

At my next therapy session, I burst into heaving sobs and said these words, "He broke my heart." It was one of the first times that I instantly knew the connection between my physical and emotional pain. The chest pains stopped—never to return. Making the connection, naming it and then feeling the deep emotional pain of the truth had freed me.

When I related that example during a question and answer period in Chattanooga, Tennessee, a woman came up to me after the meeting and said, "When you talked about your chest pain, I suddenly knew why I had gone from doctor to doctor trying to find answers for the heavy, crushing feeling I have in my chest. The weight is so heavy and no doctor could help me. Tonight, I know exactly what it is—it's my father's heavy weight on my child body." She had made the connection and articulated it. She could now begin to release those feelings.

When, in recent years, I began working out with weights, I couldn't stop doing the bench press. Instead of twelve reps, I would do thirty. Lifting a heavy weight up and off of my body was a feeling I had wanted to experience all my life. I found it incredibly empowering. I still do twice as many reps on the bench press as I do with any other weights.

"Once an experience is emotionally articulated and physically expressed, it can no longer influence us unconsciously...Many times healing cannot begin until we allow ourselves to feel how bad things are. Doing this frees emotional and physical energy that has been stuffed, stuck, denied, or ignored for many years." (Northrup, *Women's Bodies, Women's Wisdom*, p.16)

More than 25 years ago, a psychiatrist did one of the first studies of children who had been traumatized. A bus driver and 26 children between the ages of five and 15 were kidnapped while on a school bus, taken to an unknown destination and then ordered to go into a dark underground enclosure. They would learn later that it was an old trailer truck that had been buried. It was lit by flashlight. The children and the bus driver believed they were doomed. When the roof began to collapse, a 14-year-old boy began to focus his energies on escaping. He began digging. Soon others joined him but he had been the one to lead the charge. When the children were finally found and examined by a physician, everyone was ecstatic that the children were "fine." Months later, a psychiatrist, Dr. Lenore Terr, began to wonder if they were, indeed, fine. What she learned through personal interviews with the children was that every single child was experiencing post traumatic stress symptoms from the frightening experience. However, Bob Barklay, the teenager who had been the leader in digging them out of the hole, was the least traumatized. The reason? It is speculated that he didn't "freeze" as the other children did. He went into the "fight or flight" mode, using the terror energy this experience had evoked by digging—and, by doing so, he discharged some of the energy other children had not been able to discharge because they had frozen.

Like Barklay, who was able to release his traumatic energy, if I had hit my father with my fists, kicked my legs, screamed bloody murder, or run a mile for help, I could have dissipated some of the feelings. Similarly, if I had had a support system to help me through my healing process immediately after the trauma, the pain would not have had to last a lifetime.

When research was done with children under the age of 12 who had been sexually abused, it was found that 92% were *severely* traumatized. "The research suggested that it was not the sexual abuse alone that caused the long-term trauma to be so severe; it was what happened to the children *in the years following the abuse…*The most significant factor was the fact that the children proceeded through childhood *without assistance or rescue.*"(Hindman, *Just Before Dawn*, p. 83)

In his books, Dr. Alexander Lowen put into words the anguish I could not describe. He explained how a repressed experience was converted into a physical symptom. Intense sexual energy that had not been resolved or discharged would be forced into muscles, causing chronic muscular tensions. Finally, someone understood my pain…at least that one. Chronic muscular tension may not sound like a big deal but I have lived in a body primed for lifting a car. The muscles never let go. Even when I awaken, they are flexed to the max. It's called "muscular armoring." When I read those words, I called Larry to tell him that someone knew what I was feeling. I wasn't crazy; what I had was real.

"Don't touch me." Those were the words I would cry out, much the same as someone with Tourette's Syndrome will involuntarily blurt out words. The words were not only unexpectedly expressed, they were screamed with rage, "Don't touch me!" I began to stop these verbal explosions once I made the connection that my father started the night by lightly massaging my skin. My skin has its own memories and it didn't want to be touched.

Dr. Christine Northrup, in her amazing book, *Women's Bodies, Women's Wisdom*, writes that, "the uterus has memories, the heart has memories, skin has memories. The mind can no longer be thought of as being confined to the brain or to the intellect; it exists in every cell of our bodies. Every thought we think has a biological equivalent. Every emotion we feel has a biochemical equivalent..." So, she continues, "...*when a part of your body talks to you*, through pain or other manifestation, are you prepared to listen to it?" (p. 30)

I obviously was not prepared to listen. I unconsciously tried, in every way, to avoid the process by ignoring my night child, who embodied all of my unresolved emotions. She would continue to torment me until I was forced to turn to her and empathize with her.

What helped me be able to listen? Finding ways to communicate with my night child. To those of you who have never had to regress to deal with horrific childhood experiences that you unconsciously, successfully buried, I know this sounds like hokey voodoo. "So you talked to yourself? That's how you dealt with chronic insomnia?" Actually, that's true. "Our illnesses often exist to get our attention...if you don't heed the message the first time, you get hit with a bigger hammer the next time." (Northrup, *Women's Bodies, Women's Wisdom*, pp. 44–54)

Dr. Northrup writes about a woman who came to her because of continual menstrual spotting. She said, "I don't want to think about anything below my waist. I hate that part of my body. I wish that part of me would just go away." Dr. Northrup wrote, "This was an important understanding for her; it indicated where she needed to take a step toward her healing. Her menstrual spotting continually drew her attention back to a disowned part of her body that needed healing." (p. 29)

It was also interesting to read Dr. Northrup's belief about what causes a breech birth. "It's clear that in some cases the baby is breech because of the tension that the mother holds in the lower area of her body." (p. 451) Looking back over Jennifer's breech birth, there's no doubt in my mind that that was true for me.

When I addressed the Denver Medical Society, a physician said, "I cannot think of one woman who has come to me with chronic pelvic pain, who was not sexually abused as a child." Our bodies, many times through illness, force us to pay attention to profound emotional issues we avoid.

We tend to place our pain where our trauma occurred. I suffered severe menstrual pain every month. Endometriosis was excruciating. One thing I have never told anyone but my very close family, is that if I see a story on television of a child being badly hurt or if someone tells me, in detail, about a gross operation someone witnessed, I register pain in my vagina. I have a strong, painful, almost violent contraction. My sisters knew this as we grew up and teased me about it. Their teasing never offended me. In fact, I joked along with them. But in reality, how sad is it that to this day I continue to experience that pain. Some long-term effects are entrenched for life.

We can change our physical health when we do the work of healing. "People who perceive their stress as inescapable actually release opioid like substances that literally numb the cells of their bodies rendering them incapable of destroying cancer cells and bacteria if this goes on chronically. It is not *stress itself* that creates immune system problems, it's the perception that the stress is inescapable—that there is nothing a person can do to prevent it...if we don't work through our emotional distress, we set ourselves up for physical distress...diseases such as rheumatoid arthritis, multiple sclerosis, certain thyroid diseases and lupus erythematosus are all called autoimmune diseases, meaning the immune system attacks the body." (Northrup, *Women's Bodies, Women's Wisdom,* p. 35)

I could never change what happened to me as a child but I could change my perception, gain an understanding and that would change my life. I had to find a way to integrate the night child into the day child, rather than ignoring her, as I had tried to do my entire life. Until the night child had been fully heard, honored and integrated, I, the adult, would continue to fear the night and clutch at my clenched body. The only way she could get my attention was by tormenting me.

"No matter what has happened in her life, a woman has the power to change what that experience means to her and thus change her experience, both emotionally and physically, and [therein] lies her healing." (Northrup, *Women's Bodies, Women's Wisdom,* p. 41)

When I read the words, "a woman has the power to…change her experience," I knew overcoming my fear that my father would come into my room, even after he was dead, would be one of my biggest challenges. Because he had come in so many hundreds of times, I had been indelibly conditioned. I guess that's why I call it the "work" of healing. It is grueling, nose-to-the-grindstone-work to change long held beliefs and accompanying emotions…but it can be done.

If your body is screaming in pain, whether the pain is muscular contractions, anxiety, depression, asthma or arthritis, a first step in releasing the pain may be making the connection between your body pain and the cause. "Beliefs are physical. A thought held long enough and repeated enough becomes a belief. The belief then becomes biology." (Northrup, *Women's Bodies, Women's Wisdom,* p. 34)

If we do not work through and resolve emotional issues, the suppressed emotions will impact our physical health, specifically our immune systems, and that can lead to serious illness. Finally, after five decades, I slowly acquired an appreciation, love and respect for how the child within me endured. As my psychic war began to find peace, my physical pain began to subside. The pain of sexual abuse does not have to hurt for a lifetime. Finding and coming to terms with the truth can set you—and your body—free. I was 61 the day I realized I was truly free. It was Jennifer's wedding day...

Jennifer and her flower girl, Kimmie Horwitz.

Jennifer and Joel on their wedding day.
I finally had the son I longed for.

Chapter 33 – A New Beginning

Larry, Jennifer and I had one concern about her finding the right man to marry. When she dated in college and law school, she would always tell her dates she was going to live in Denver where her family lived. Many times when her date would join us for a walk in the park or a weekend in Vail, Jennifer would somehow end up walking and talking with Larry or me. We are such a tight threesome, we knew finding a fourth would be a challenge. Her wedding would make it very clear how all of this was going to turn out.

We had often talked about her wedding day. Every time I asked her what she wanted for that day, her response was always the same, "I just want Nan there." Nan, Larry's mother, our quintessential matriarch. Jennifer's and Nan's lives had been inextricably woven together since the day of her birth. They were a Norman Rockwell painting. They deeply loved one another. Each fall, when Jennifer would leave for college and then for law school, I would see the look in her eyes; a deep sadness, knowing that Nan was 86, 88 or 91, knowing she might never see her again.

I began to ponder how I could make Nan a part of Jennifer's wedding if she weren't physically with us. Since Jennifer was not deeply in love with anyone, a wedding was not imminent. One day, knowing how smart and savvy Nan was and fearing she would figure out what I was doing, I very reluctantly said, "Nan, I've been thinking about Jennifer all day, what her life will be like, whom she will marry…her wedding…what I will be feeling. What would you want to say to Jennifer on her wedding day?" I just didn't know how to do it better than that. Nan didn't miss a beat. She began talking about her wishes for Jennifer and when she finished, I said, "I'd love to put those thoughts on a cassette. Would you do it?" (I just happened to have a cassette player ready to go.) I turned it on and again, Nan shared her dreams for Jennifer. I could have wrung my heart out like a sponge. Her words were so loving and wise.

When Nan was 93, Jennifer became engaged to Joel Rosenstein. Joel was the son I had longed for. I would never have cried every month because I couldn't get pregnant again if God had said to me, "I'll give you a son in 27 years, a son so perfect, you couldn't even dream him." And that would have been an accurate statement: I couldn't have dreamed him.

Now, their wedding was a year away. I asked Nan if she would record her message again; this time, including Joel, whom she adored...as did everyone else in the family. The cassette was redone. At least Jennifer and Joel would have Nan's blessing, her spoken blessing, on their wedding day.

Suddenly, the wedding was only a few weeks away. Nan would soon be 94; Jennifer's wish had come true. When I envisioned Congregation Emanuel's sanctuary, filled with 400 guests, and Nan walking down the very long aisle, with Larry and Janey supporting her, I could hear Nan's recorded words over the sound system. Nan's loving words would distract our guests from her very slow walk and give them a reason to pull out their hankies and wipe a tear or two away as they heard Nan say, "In a...few days...I will be...94 years...old..." Everyone who knew us, even slightly, knew Nan. She was almost always with one of her children or grandchildren.

As I visualized Nan walking down the aisle, I suddenly envisioned Jennifer walking half way down the aisle and then stopping. As our guests turned to see the bride, she was standing very still as we heard *her* voice over the sound system, saying to Joel, who was awaiting her at the altar, "Joel, I fell in love with you when I saw a toddler wander over and curl up in your lap. I fell in love with you when you campaigned day and night for a political candidate because you fervently believe one person can make a difference...I fell in love with you when..."

I called Jennifer at work. "What would you think about this? You talk to Joel over the sound system, then he responds to you, 'I fell in love with you when...' as you both stand looking at one another. After he completes his thoughts, you would then proceed down the aisle." She said, "I love it, Mom." I said, "So...what if each of your eight bridesmaids recorded a message to be played as she walks down the aisle, such as, 'I'm Kim Fuller. Jenn and I became friends when...' That way our guests would know who these young women are as they watch them walking down."

We ended up with two grandmothers, eight bridesmaids, eight groomsmen, and the bride and groom all talking about their relationships as they walked down the aisle. It worked like a dream. Our guests laughed as most told a funny story about their relationships with Jennifer and Joel.

Immediately after Jennifer and Joel spoke to one another, Jennifer

528

was to wait until Larry and I joined her at the halfway mark. The three of us would then walk the rest of the way together. Originally, I had wanted Larry to walk her down the aisle. I knew I would be crying and I wanted to be watching from the front row, but Jennifer insisted, "It's always been the three of us, Mom. The three of us will walk down together." The plan was set. So, just as Joel completed his message to Jennifer, Larry and I prepared to walk down to Jennifer, as she waited for us. The problem was, she didn't wait for us. The second Joel's words were finished, she made a beeline for him. Her total focus was joining hands with him as they were going to be married. As Jennifer reached Joel, he whispered to her, "You forgot your parents." Jennifer broke into laughter, snuggling into Joel as she realized what had happened.

I said to Larry, "Well, let's go!" As we walked down, I said to the people on the aisles, laughing all the way, "She forgot us." What a perfect way to begin their marriage. It was very clear that Jennifer had found her soul mate, and we had found our fourth.

When it was my time to speak at the reception, I heard myself say, "Today is the happiest day of my life." Only minutes before, I had watched Joel, his parents and two brothers lovingly interacting and I realized I had broken the chain forever. I knew it by whom Jennifer had chosen to marry. Joel is funny, kind, warm, loving, caring, thoughtful, so smart and—although I know it's not supposed to matter—drop dead gorgeous! When we come from abusive homes, too many of us choose abusive marriages because that's what we grew up with. And then our children do the same because that's what *they* grew up with. By fighting, kicking and crying my way through an agonizing recovery, I had come through the pain into a joy I had never dreamed possible. Yes, it was the happiest day of my life.

Two years later, our precious Nan, our beacon of unconditional love, passed away at age 96. Now, we have just welcomed our first grandchild, Max. Jennifer and Joel live five minutes away (four minutes and ten seconds if you make the light). With this book published, I put a bright blue ribbon on the trauma that so dramatically and adversely impacted my life, and prepare to move on. I'm "nesting" big time…as "Nanny Lynn."

It is my hope that this book has caused you to think about your life because that was my purpose. Thank you for walking this journey with me. With Larry, Jennifer, Joel, my family members and the thousands of survivors who have shared their lives with me, I can say from the depths of my being, my life has been blessed, truly blessed.

"All I know about love is that love is all there is."

—Emily Dickinson

Larry, Nan, and Jennifer at Jennifer's bridal shower. Nan was ninety-four years old.

Jennifer and Joel on their wedding day.

Acknowledgments

My Van Derbur and Atler families have played the major role in my life. I can only imagine how difficult it was for members of my birth family to have my story front-page news for many days. It is my fervent hope that the important issues I address in this book will justify bringing my story, in even greater detail, into the light one more time. It is extremely challenging to hold a family together when incest blackens the waters. The road has not always been smooth. When a hurricane of emotion ripped a most cherished sister from my life for many years, I mourned. Deeply. Until the recent restoration of our relationship, it oppressed my life. Another sister has always lived in Minnesota or California, but distance never diminished her steady and continuing friendship and support. Although I omitted these two middle sisters from this book, at their request, their love has been critically important to me. My eldest sister, Gwen, played a major role in my recovery.

The members of my Atler family, most of whom live within a few miles of Larry and me, have always been an island of unconditional love. Larry's parents became my parents. Larry's two sisters, my sisters. His older sister, Greta Horwitz passed away in 1997; I will miss her always. In addition to being a decorator and photographer extraordinaire, my sister, Janey Lozow, has devoted her life to taking care of people. Janey has always "been there" for me and I cherish our friendship. Although some brothers-in-law in both of my families have been more involved than others, all have been supportive.

My many nieces and nephews in both families have always been an integral part of Larry's and my life. We have climbed mountains, galloped horses, ridden the waves, played games and talked for hours. They are dear and treasured friends.

Many people supported me during the writing of this book: Laura Palmer was a loving mentor; Scott Hansen was a tireless computer coach; Carole Harrison, is a cherished friend, meticulous reader and informal editor of every page; Susan Zimmerman and Cindy Tew were valued readers; Marilyn Ross from About Books, Inc., patiently guided me through publishing; Sharon Lions played the most important role. She and I spent many weeks in Vail discussing, rewriting and editing—especially the last third of the book. I have turned to Sharon many times for wisdom and counsel. My love and respect for her know no bounds.

LuAnn Glatzmaier's counsel was wise and cherished; Jim Terrien, my highly skilled and compassionate Rolfer, helped transform my muscles from feeling like piano wire to "Play-Doh." Jim's role in my physical comfort cannot be overstated; Pauline Warren's bedrock work ethic, integrity and friendship have meant so much to me; Catherine Joy's smile and laughter are infectious. She is a cherished friend.

My niece, Debbie Griffin, is an indomitable spirit and a true wonder woman. She gives of herself completely to anyone and everyone, asking nothing in return.

Others who have been important in my life are my childhood friend, Robin McDougal and my cherished college roommates: Georgie Palmer Swanson, Judy Retz and Lendy Firestone Brown. Lynda Meade Shea and Celeste Seymour Judell were devoted friends during the two difficult years I lived in New York. Carol and Howard Torgove have been an integral, loving part of my life. They have taught me so much about unconditional love and friendship. Cheryl de Priest came into my life, as a blessing, when she was only 15. It has been a joy to watch her grow into a successful woman. Leo Goto has been a constant support to me since high school. Sandy Tenenbaum ("Occasions by Sandy") patiently guided me through Jennifer's wedding and continues to be a dear friend. No one has more fun or does weddings better or more lovingly than Sandy and Barry, her husband and partner.

Barbara Engel and Judy Fruland are loving, gentle friends. Rex John makes me laugh the second we say "hello." He is a close confidante. Sandy Cummins, Ann McAdams, Joan M. Smith, Gayle Williams, Ardis Young, Jena Lei Deere, Annie Johnson, Kathy Hallinan, Kelly Gallo, Nancy Silla, Elissa Paparone are dedicated friends. Tanny Lewis passed away leaving a void no one will ever fill. Arlene Hirschfeld, John Eichenour, Fran Denmon, Nancy Livingston, Saul Rosenthal, and Peter Boyles had unique roles in my life. Julie and Art Seiden continue to role model enduring optimism and dedicated love.

I remain in awe of my dear friend, Karen Harvey, who has come through the most agonizing recovery I have witnessed, with grace, spirit and incredible courage.

Many of Jennifer's friends in elementary and middle school were, and are, an integral part of my life: Kaia Borgen, Megan Bee, Katherine Rickenbaugh Rich, Valerie Lewis McCarthy, Liz Romer, Marnie Engel Hayutin, Allison Engel, Carey Talmage Davis, Lindsey Schwartz Gutterman, Kim Fuller Jacoby, Rebecca Rich and Stephanie Ellis Sabga.

Wise and skilled therapists who were central to my healing: Dr. Kim Nagel, Phyllis Rubalcaba, Dr. Jane O'Carolyn, and Bobbi Furer. Doctors who have played key roles in my life are Marvin Schwarz, Rick Abrams, Harold Hepner, Fred Abrams, Joe and Gary Friedland and Mike Horwitz.

Andrew Vachss is a personal hero of mine and an indefatigable advocate and fighter for children's rights.

Kudos to the librarians at Ross Cherry Creek and the downtown Denver Public Libraries who were endlessly patient in helping me track down books, articles and arcane research.

A special thank you to the men and women, buried in isolated laboratories, who finally found a way to stop night terrors by mixing miraculous ingredients into a little yellow pill. Bless you.

To the media: Oprah shared her story and she continues to address the long-term impact of sexual abuse. Maria Shriver did my first network interview and her questions and insights helped society better understand the issues. Montel Williams has been a powerful force in educating society by shows he continues to do; Geraldo Rivera has been a dogged champion of children and abuse issues as were Maury Povich and Sally Jessy Raphael. "Hats off" to Sandy Gleysteen and Liz Frillici, the best producers I know; Vickie Bane, an intelligent and compassionate reporter for *People* magazine; Carol Kreck; Dawn Denzer, society reporter extraordinaire and Mike Keefe, an insightful political cartoonist.

My profound appreciation to the Denver reporters, editors and photographers for *The Denver Post* and the *Rocky Mountain News* and the television news reporters, directors and producers who first brought my story forward and facilitated the creation of a movement in Colorado that spread nationwide. They portrayed me as a woman of courage and integrity. With the exception of one columnist, the truth of what I was saying was never questioned. The words, "she alleges," were never used. The result of days of saturating the media with my story changed my life dramatically and survivors began pouring out of their isolation with the hope that they, too, might be believed and accepted. I am forever grateful to the men and women who literally took my life in their hands and gently shared my story. They were the ones who finally carried me across the valley of the shadow of shame into a new world of acceptance.

And, finally, a personal message to our son-in-law, Joel Rosenstein: I waited 27 years for you. Thank you for being the son I ached for, for so many years.

Resources

DVDs:

A Story of Hope: $13.95 A DVD recording of Marilyn's first public presentation of her story of childhood incest and her victorious road to healing and recovery. She spoke to an audience of 1,100 survivors and supporters. 55 minutes.

The Journey of Recovery:$13.95 A DVD of Marilyn's most recent presentation. For survivors, it is amazing to see the difference in her presence and message from her first talk "A Story of Hope" (listed above) and this most recent talk. 58 minutes.

Once Can Hurt a Lifetime: $13.95 This DVD addresses sexually inappropriate behavior between children and teens and encourages those who have experienced sexual abuse to seek help and support.

Change your Life, 2 DVDs: $29.00 Eight 30 minute presentations Marilyn gave which resulted in her being named "The Outstanding woman Speaker in America." If you have a goal you think is unattainable or if you are feeling helpless or hopeless, these ideas (which sustained Marilyn during her recovery) can be life-changing.

To place an order, please visit our website at:

www.MissAmericaByDay.com

Artists: Ariel Orr Jordan: arielorr@aol.com; Keane Eyes Gallery P.O. 15098, Santa Rosa, California 95402

Web sites:

www.ChildTrauma.org Dr. Bruce Perry is internationally known for his knowledge of how trauma alters the developing brain. He is skilled in translating medical jargon into understandable language. His research has had a profound impact on my thinking.

www.jfcadvocacy.org Justice for Children'smission is to raise the consciousness ofsociety about the failure of our governmental agencies to protect victims of child abuseandprovide legal advocacy for abused children.

www.backgroundsusa.com An international records/information source for all public records, including criminal records, arrest records, registered sex offender information. Verifies employment histories, tenant checks and personal references.

www.enough.org Dedicated to addressing the sexual exploitation of children, women, and men by illegal pornography.

www.stopitnow.com Their mission is to call on all abusers and potential abusers to stop and seek help and to educate adults about the ways to stop sexual abuse.

www.survivorconnections.net Information for survivors and how to become an activist. Survivor Connections was founded by Frank and Sara Fitzpatrick.

Bibliography

Ahlmeyer, S. P. Heil, B., McKee, and K. English. "The Impact of Polygraphy on Admissions of Victims and Offenses in Adult Sex Offenders." *Sexual Abuse: A Journal of Research and Treatment* 12, No. 2: 123–138.

Angelou, Maya. *I Know Why the Caged Bird Sings.* New York: Random House, Inc., 1970.

Arnold, Johann C. *Seeking Peace.* Plough Publishing Company, 1998.

Aynesworth, Hugh. "Jury Hits Church Wallet Over Pedophile." *The Washington Times,* July 25, 1997, p. A9.

Baker, Leigh. *Protecting Your Children From Sexual Predators.* New York: St. Martin's Press, 2002.

Bass, Ellen, and Laura Davis. *The Courage to Heal.* New York: Harper and Row, 1988.

Berendzen, Richard, and Laura Palmer. *Come Here.* Villard Books, 1993.

Berry, Jason. *Lead Us Not Into Temptation: Catholic Priests and the Sexual Abuse of Children.* New York: Bantam Doubleday Dell Publishing Group, Inc., 1992.

Bohmer, Carol, and Andrea Parrot. *Sexual Assault on Campus.* New York: Lexington Books.

Boston Globe. "Betrayal: The Crisis in the Catholic Church." *Boston Globe,* 2002.

Boyle, Patrick. *Scout's Honor: Sexual Abuse in America's Most Trusted Institution.* California: Prima Publishing, 1994.

Bradlee, Ben. *A Good Life: Newspapering and Other Adventures.* New York: Simon & Schuster, 1995.

Burkett, Elinor, and Frank Bruni. *A Gospel of Shame: Children, Sexual Abuse, and the Catholic Church.* New York: Penguin Books USA, 1993.

Cannon, Angie. "Is There Any End in Sight?" *U.S. News & World Report,* April 22, 2002, p. 49.

Color, Jori, and Sam Ward. "Your Views of Online Safety." *USA Today,* August 15, 2002, p. A01.

Chu, James A., M.D. *Rebuilding Shattered Lives: The Responsible Treatment of Complex Post-Traumatic and Dissociative Disorders.* New York: John Wiley & Sons, 1998.

Davis, Laura. *I Thought We'd Never Speak Again: The Road from Estrangement to Reconciliation.* New York: HarperCollins Publishers, 2002.

Della Cava, Marco. "Abuse 'Just Became a Part of My Life.'" *USA Today,* July 24, 2002, p. 7D.

Douglas, Kirk. *The Ragman's Son.* New York: Simon and Schuster, 1988.

Ducharme, Elaine, M.D. *Must I Turn the Other Cheek?* Denlan Productions, 2000.

Dziech, B., and Judge Charles Schudson. *On Trial.* Boston: Beacon Press, 1991.

Egerton, Roger. "Documents Show Bishops Transferred Known Abuser." *The Dallas Morning News*, August 31, 1997, p. 35A.

Farrow, Mia. *What Falls Away: A Memoir.* New York: Bantam Doubleday Dell Publishing Group, 1997.

Finkelhor, David. *Sexually Victimized Children.* New York: Free Press, 1979.

Fonda, Peter. *Don't Tell Dad.* New York: Hyperion, 1998.

Freyd, Jennifer. *Betrayal Trauma.* Cambridge: Harvard University Press, 1996.

Goodall, Jane, and Phillip Berman. *Reason for Hope: A Spiritual Journey.* New York: Soko Publications Ltd., 1999.

Grossman, Cathy. *USA Today,* March 21, 2002, p. 1.

The Healing Woman newsletter. PO Box 3038, Moss Beach, CA 94038.

Hellmich, Nancy. "A Family in One Fell Swoop." *USA Today,* August 25, 1999, p. 1D.

Herman, Judith Lewis, M.D. *Trauma and Recovery: The Aftermath of*

Violence From Domestic Abuse to Political Terror. New York: HarperCollins Publishers, 1992.

Herman, Judith, M.D., and Emily Schatzow. "Recovery and Verification of Memories of Childhood Sexual Trauma." *Psychoanalytic Psychology* 4, No. 1 (1987): 1–14.

Hindman, Jan. *Just Before Dawn: From the Shadows of Tradition to New Reflections in Trauma Assessment and Treatment of Sexual Victimization.* Oregon: AlexAndria Associates, 1989.

Hofman, Michelle. "Megan's Law." *Los Angeles Times,* November 17, 2002, p. K1.

Holmes, William, M.D., and Gail Slap. "Sexual Abuse of Boys." *Journal of the American Medical Association* 21, Vol. 280 (December 1998): 1859.

Horovitz, Bruce. "Anheuser-Busch: King of Super Bowl Comedy." *USA Today,* January 27, 2003, p. B5.

Imse, Ann. "Orphanages Are an Option." *Rocky Mountain News,* May 7, 2001, p. 5A.

Kalette, Denise. "Campus Crime Fighters: New Law Ends Parents' Tragic Battle." *USA Today,* November 12, 1990, p. D01.

Karr-Morse, Robin, and Meredith S. Wiley. *Ghosts From the Nursery: Tracing the Roots of Violence.* New York: Grove/Atlantic, 1997.

Kornblum, Janet. "Love of Family Brings Measure of Acceptance." *USA Today,* July 24, 2002, p. 6D.

Leinwand, Donna. "Campus Crime Underreported." *USA Today,* October 4, 2000.

Levine, Peter A., and Ann Frederick. *Waking The Tiger: Healing Trauma.* California: North Atlantic Books, 1997.

Lowen, Alexander, M.D. *The Betrayal of the Body.* New York: Macmillan Publishing Company, 1967.

Maas, James B., Dr., Megan L. Wherry, David J. Axelrod, Barbara R. Hogan and Jennifer A. Blumin. *Power Sleep: The Revolutionary Program That Prepares Your Mind for Peak Performance.* New York: HarperCollins Publishers, 1998.

Maltz, Wendy. *The Sexual Healing Journey: A Guide for Survivors of Sexual Abuse.* New York: HarperCollins Publishers, 1991.

Moffett, Dan. "Ground Zero Molestation in the Catholic Church." *The Palm Beach Post,* June 28, 1998, p. 1A.

Moore, Mary Tyler. *After All.* New York: G. P. Putnam's Sons, 1995.

Northrup, Christiane, M.D. *Women's Bodies, Women's Wisdom: Creating Physical and Emotional Health and Healing.* New York: Bantam Doubleday Dell Publishing Group, 1994.

Prentky, R., A. Lee, R. Knight, and D. Cerce. "Recidivism Rates Among Child Molesters and Rapists." *Law and Human Behavior* 21 (1997): 635–659.

Peterson, Karen. "Harm of Domestic Strife Lingers." *USA Today,* February 21, 1996.

Rader, Dotson. "Nothing Could Stop Me But Me." *Parade,* August 19, 2001, pp. 4–5.

Roesler, Thomas, M.D., and Tiffany Wind. *Telling the Secret.* Denver: C. Henry Kempe National Center, 1992.

Ronai, Carol. "Multiple Reflections of Child Sex Abuse." *Journal of Contemporary Ethnography* (January 1995): 406.

Rothschild, Babette. *The Body Remembers: The Psychophysiology of Trauma and Trauma Treatment.* New York: W. W. Norton & Company, 2000.

Seligson, Tom. "Just Say What I Believe." *Parade,* April 15, 2001, p. 8.

Shapiro, Marc. *Carlos Santana: Back on Top.* New York: St. Martin's Press, 2000.

Shupe, Anson. *Wolves Within The Fold: Religious Leadership and Abuses of Power.* New Jersey: Rutgers University Press, 1998.

Smith, Holly A. *Fire of the Five Hearts, Memoir of Treating Incest.* Brunner Routledge, 2002

Smith , Holly A. and Edie Israel. *Sibling Incest.* Reprints: 3400 Broadway, Boulder, CO 80302.

Snyderman, Nancy, M. D., and Peg Streep. *Necessary Journeys: Letting Ourselves Learn From Life.* New York: By the Bay Productions, 2000.

Sorenson, Teena, and Barbara Snow. "How Children Tell: The Process of Disclosure I Child Sexual Abuse." *Child Welfare* LXX, No. 1: pp. 3–15.

Stammer, Larry. "Bishops Ratify Policy on Abuse." *Los Angeles Times,* November 14, 2002, p. A22.

Summit, R. C. "The Child Sexual Abuse Accommodation Syndrome." *Child Abuse and Neglect* 7: 177–193.

Tanner, James, PhD. *High Risk Behaviors and Relapse Among Sex Offenders in Outpatient Treatment.* Project Final Report for Teaching Humane Existence, Inc, Denver, Colorado, February 4, 1999.

U.S. Department of Health and Human Services. *Third National Incidence Study of Child Abuse and Neglect.*

Williams, Linda Meyer. "Recovered Memories of Abuse in Women with Documented Sexual Victimization Histories." *Journal of Traumatic Stress* 8, No. 4 (1995): 649–673.

van der Kolk, Bessel A., M.D. *Psychological Trauma.* American Psychiatric Press, 1987.

van der Kolk, Bessel A., M.D., Alexander C. McFarland, and Lars Weisaeth. *Traumatic Stress: The Effects of Overwhelming Experience on Mind, Body, and Society.* New York: The Guilford Press, 1996.

Whitfield, Charles L., M.D. *Memory and Abuse: Remembering and Healing the Effects of Trauma.* Florida: Health Communications, 1995.

Wiehe, Vernon R. *Sibling Abuse: Hidden Physical, Emotional, and Sexual Trauma.* California: Sage Publications, 1997.

Williams, Esther, and Digby Diehl. *The Million Dollar Mermaid.* New York: Simon & Schuster, 1999.